Houston Bound

AMERICAN CROSSROADS

Edited by Earl Lewis, George Lipsitz, George Sánchez, Dana Takagi, Laura Briggs, and Nikhil Pal Singh

Houston Bound

CULTURE AND COLOR
IN A JIM CROW CITY

Tyina L. Steptoe

UNIVERSITY OF CALIFORNIA PRESS

University of California Press, one of the most distinguished university presses in the United States, enriches lives around the world by advancing scholarship in the humanities, social sciences, and natural sciences. Its activities are supported by the UC Press Foundation and by philanthropic contributions from individuals and institutions. For more information, visit www.ucpress.edu.

University of California Press
Oakland, California

Published in association with the William B. Clements Center for Southwest Studies at Southern Methodist University.

Library of Congress Cataloging-in-Publication Data

Steptoe, Tyina L., 1975- author.
  Houston bound : culture and color in a Jim Crow city / Tyina L. Steptoe.
    pages   cm.— (American crossroads ; 41)
  Includes bibliographical references and index.
  ISBN 978-0-520-28257-5 (cloth : alk. paper)
  ISBN 978-0-520-28258-2 (pbk. : alk. paper)
  ISBN 978-0-520-95853-1 (ebook)
    1. Minorities—Texas—Houston—Social conditions—20th century.
2. Houston (Tex.)—Emigration and immigration—History—20th
century.   3. Houston (Tex.)—Ethnic relations—History—20th
century.   4. Music—Social aspects—Texas—Houston—History—20th
century.   5. Houston (Tex.)—History—20th century.   I. Title.   II. Series:
American crossroads ; 41.
  F394.H89A27   2016
  305.8009764′2350904—dc23   2015019103

Manufactured in the United States of America
25 24 23 22 21 20 19 18 17 16
10 9 8 7 6 5 4 3 2 1

For Jerome

CONTENTS

ILLUSTRATIONS

FIGURES

MAPS

Introduction

WHEN WORLDS COLLIDE

ON AUGUST 15, 1929, a seventeen-year-old migrant from Louisiana named Elizabeth gave birth to a baby girl on Live Oak Street in Houston's Third Ward. Originally from the Lafayette area, the unmarried woman of color probably had not lived in the city for long, and her early experiences in Houston were less than ideal. Sometime after arriving to the city, Elizabeth met a married man who had also moved from Louisiana. The two began an affair that resulted in a pregnancy. Elizabeth tried moving back to Louisiana, but her family refused to allow her to stay with them. Young and alone, she decided not to keep the child she carried. After returning to Houston and giving birth, she paid her midwife five dollars to strangle the newborn baby. The midwife refused, though. Elizabeth then asked her to call Arthur Berry, a black railroad worker from Shreveport who lived across the city with his wife, Leanna, a migrant from rural East Texas. The couple discussed Elizabeth's predicament and quickly made the decision to adopt the child. One day later, Arthur and Leanna arrived to take the infant girl, named Mary Rose, from Third Ward to their home in Fifth Ward. There, they raised the daughter they affectionately called "Mae" for the next eighteen years.

The Berry family did not tell their relatives or neighbors that the baby they informally adopted was the product of an illicit relationship between a teenage girl and a married man. And twenty-nine-year-old Arthur Berry would hide from everyone, including his wife, the fact that he was the man who fathered that child after carrying on an affair with Elizabeth.[1]

The story of the two women named Elizabeth and Leanna became an essential part of Berry family folklore, a tale Mary Rose passed down to her children and grandchildren after she learned the truth in 1960. The story traces how her family got to Houston, but also emphasizes the meeting of two groups who were central to the development of black Houston since the 1920s—migrants from Louisiana, and migrants from eastern Texas. Promises of higher wages in a rapidly industrializing city appealed to the people living in the rural areas of those states. During World War I, economic mobilization led to the expansion of the ship channel at the Port of Houston and a local population boom. Economic growth spurred migration that would continue for decades as people poured into the city for work. Like the majority of black people who moved to Houston after World War I, Leanna Edwards Berry had roots in East Texas. She came of age on a cotton farm in Wharton County, where her family worked as sharecroppers. Meanwhile, Arthur and Elizabeth joined the wave of Louisiana migrants who also came to Houston in search of work and to find respite from natural disaster. The number of people from the Pelican State living in Houston swelled in the aftermath of the devastating Mississippi Flood of 1927, which sent more migrants across the Sabine River into Texas.[2] Mary Rose's family—biological and adopted—represented migrations that altered the shape and sound of black Houston.

But beneath those statistics lies a more complicated story of race and migration. Elizabeth and the Berry family were Negroes by law, but they were two different groups of African-descended people. Arthur Berry hailed from northwestern Louisiana, where the English language and Protestant faith dominated, and he and Leanna shared those cultural traits. Elizabeth and the majority of Louisiana migrants, on the other hand, migrated from the francophone southwestern part of the state, a region shaped by a history of contact between Africans, Indians, and French and Spanish settlers. A group from this region known as "Creoles of color" began to settle in Houston in the 1920s. The law categorized black Texans and Creoles of color as Negro; however, Creoles of color identified as a distinct group—a racial combination of black and white. When they made contact, the groups did not always agree on the definition of racial blackness, which complicated their relationships in segregated spaces. Black Texans and Creoles of color also noted cultural distinctions when they made contact in Houston. Their different racial identities, religious practices, languages, and even musical styles bore the imprint of an Afro-Anglo heritage versus an Afro-French/Afro-Spanish heritage of southwestern Louisiana. Transnational histories of colonization and slavery gave the southern portion of Louisiana a distinct racial legacy that distinguished that region from northern Louisiana and eastern Texas. Although most studies of Creoles of color focus on Louisiana, the migration of Creoles of color allowed them to further disseminate their cultural practices and notions of race into new places.[3] The meeting of people from francophone Louisiana and anglophone African Americans is one legacy of the rural-to-urban migration experience.

Mary Rose Berry came of age in a society where these worlds converged. The Berry family settled into a section of Houston known as Fifth Ward, the part of the city most influenced by French-speaking migrants. To outsiders, Mary Rose's community was one of Houston's many black neighborhoods. Yet the sights and sounds of Fifth Ward indicated the diversity among Houston's "colored" population. At her school, French words mingled with English on the playgrounds. When Mary Rose walked to school, she may have passed itinerant blues singers from East Texas plucking guitars on street corners or Louisiana-born musicians playing a music with accordions. Mary Rose's churchgoing neighbors from Texas mostly worshipped at Protestant churches, but Creoles of color attended mass at Catholic churches. And while children from Texas laughed at the antics of Br'er Rabbit, Creoles of color told stories of "Compair Lapin." In Fifth Ward, two parts of the African diaspora connected, and their cultural practices indicated the multiplicity of the community's residents.[4]

Creoles of color and black Texans influenced the racial politics and culture of Mary Rose Berry's neighborhood. The two groups lived near one another and shared social space. Children from both groups attended the same schools, and their parents made contact at work. Differences in skin color and language could cause friction between the groups. At the same time, proximity led to some cultural ties. By the time she was eighteen, Berry had converted to Catholicism, and she attended the same parochial school as the children of Louisiana migrants. Her notions of culture and race were shaped by contact between people from either side of the Sabine River.

If the convergence of black East Texas and Creole Louisiana influenced Mary Rose's childhood and young adulthood, contact with a different group would especially characterize her later years. At the same time that Creoles of color settled in Houston, a growing numbers of ethnic Mexicans also entered the city. In the first one hundred years of Houston's history, ethnic Mexicans made up only a tiny fraction of the local population, but new labor opportunities drew them to the city in the early twentieth century. A small number of immigrants from Mexico began moving north into Houston in

1910 with the outbreak of the Mexican Revolution. Tejanos—Texans of Mexican descent—also came to the city from southern and central Texas. Comprising people from Mexico and rural Texas, Houston's ethnic Mexican population grew from around six thousand in 1920 to twenty thousand in 1940.[5]

Ethnic Mexicans and Creoles of color shared some similarities. Religious, linguistic, and racial distinctions marked ethnic Mexicans and Creoles of color as newcomers. Both tended to practice Catholicism in a Protestant-majority city, and the appearance of Catholic churches was an early sign of Mexican and Creole population growth. These religious spaces also served as meeting places and sites of entertainment for migrants. Since Creoles of color spoke French and the majority of ethnic Mexicans spoke Spanish (especially those who were born in Mexico), linguistic differences could distinguish both groups from Houston's English-speaking majority. And like Creoles, Mexicans and Tejanos acknowledged histories of racial mixture, but also grappled with a black/white racial binary in a Jim Crow city where most people were Anglo and African American.

During Mary Rose Berry's early childhood in Fifth Ward, she made little contact with ethnic Mexicans. They occupied two different sides of the color line, which meant that they did not attend the same schools or occupy the same segregated spaces. More ethnic Mexicans moved into black neighborhoods after the 1960s, though, when new waves of immigrants entered the city. Latinos outnumbered African Americans in some of those neighborhoods by the turn of the twenty-first century. When Mary Rose approached her eighth decade of life in Houston, the two groups made up two-thirds of Houston's population, and Latinos were the largest ethnic group in the city. The community in northeastern Houston to which she'd recently moved was a place largely populated by African Americans and people with roots in Latin America. Black and Latino children attended the same schools and lived in the same neighborhoods, which transformed the local relationship between the groups. By the late twentieth century, these groups shared social space. This communal engagement is reflected in the city's sonic landscape. From rhythm and blues to hip-hop, music from the city bears the indelible imprint of ethnic Mexican and black spatial contact.

Between 1920 and the end of the twentieth century, Houston transformed from a town with the forty-fifth-largest population in the United States into the nation's fourth-largest city.[6] In the process, Houston transitioned from a society with an Anglo and African American racial dynamic into a multiethnic/multiracial metropolis. These dramatic shifts, spurred by over-lapping migrations, illustrate how the movement of diverse groups into urban America affected race and culture. U.S. cities expanded demographically as different groups arrived and established communities. The influx of migrants from other countries in the late nineteenth and early twentieth centuries coincided with the Great Migration. As people of African descent from different parts of the United States made contact in migration cities after World War I, they also encountered recent arrivals from Latin America, the Caribbean, and Europe. The meeting of these groups profoundly affected the different ways race and culture have been articulated in this country. In Houston, black and Anglo Texans with ancestral roots in the Southeast encountered an increasing number of migrants from rural southwestern Louisiana and people of Mexican descent, both of which altered the local cultural and racial terrain. Migrants negotiated the meanings of blackness and whiteness, struggled over space and power, and created cultural forms that allowed them to forge coalitions and express their own notions of race.

This book uses the experiences of the English-, Spanish-, and French-speaking people who moved to Houston to illustrate the dynamic, polycultural nature of race at the very moment that Jim Crow laws attempted to fix black and white into monolithic categories.[7] *Houston Bound* focuses on diverse migrants who brought different definitions of blackness and whiteness, and multiple understandings of racial categories, to the city. The arrival of new groups did not lead to the creation of new segregation laws; rather, in the racialized spaces created by segregation, Houstonians were either Negro or white by law. Yet a more diverse reality lurked just beneath the city's black/white political veneer. From rural eastern Texas came black migrants whose grandparents had been enslaved at the time of the Civil War, and whose notions of race had been shaped by their acknowledgment of slave ancestry and their postbellum experiences with segregation. Creoles of color from rural southwestern Louisiana embodied a history of racial mixing that legal segregation attempted to deny and repress. Ethnic Mexicans likewise represented a history of mixing (*mestizaje*) that challenged dominant notions of whiteness and racial purity.[8] *Houston Bound* shows that, although these groups relocated to a Jim Crow city that legally defined their place in the racial hierarchy, migrants were also rooted in other local, regional, and national racial imaginaries that defined categories like white, black, Creole, and ethnic Mexican in different ways at different times. Out of these multiple divisions and contradictions emerged what scholar Robin D. G. Kelley calls our "polycultural world," a world where countless social, cultural, and political transformations influence the development of racial categories that are constantly in motion.[9]

Whereas much of the historiography on race and migration following World War I has focused on cities in the Northeast and Midwest and on the West Coast, *Houston Bound* examines how multiple groups shaped a city located in the former Confederacy.[10] Houston's geographic location makes the city a revealing laboratory for showing how overlapping migrations affected race formations. The Gulf Coast city is located near lands claimed by Spain, France, Mexico, the United States, and the Confederate States of America at various points. In the nineteenth and early twentieth centuries, Houston's proximity to a nearby plantation belt with a black majority influenced its economy, politics, and demographics. But Houston is also equidistant from San Antonio, the Tejano-majority city located 200 miles to the west, and Lafayette, the center of Creole/Cajun culture located just 216 miles to the east. Within this expanse of land, diverse heritages produced a variety of racial constructions. Migrants from these societies brought notions of race to Houston that were shaped by their histories in those places. This book refers to Houston as part of the "western South," a designation that emphasizes a racial legacy of chattel slavery, Reconstruction, and Jim Crow that linked the city to the U.S. South, while also acknowledging that the creation of Houston and its surrounding plantation belt was part of a process of western expansion in the nineteenth century.[11] The city's location in the western South has made it a junction for the convergence of English-, Spanish-, and French-speaking groups and their multiple understandings of race.[12]

Houston Bound builds on the scholarship on race formation in the United States while pushing beyond the themes that have dominated this area of study, such as a concentration on whiteness and an emphasis on legal and political constructions of race.[13] Histories of race formation often depict the changing nature of whiteness through explorations of European immigrants, ethnic Mexicans, and people of Asian descent.[14] But if the notable achievement of scholars working in this vein has been to insist that we understand whiteness as a complex and constructed racial category, *Houston Bound* gives due attention to the similarly volatile nature of racial blackness. This book explores how people in different societies have defined blackness in dissimilar ways. Furthermore, in this former slave society, a newcomer's status and rank often depended upon her or his proximity to racial blackness, which in turn determined the day-to-day experience of racialization in the Jim Crow era.

For ethnic Mexicans and Creoles of color, as well as the smaller population of European immigrants, that could be based on their ancestry or their spatial proximity to descendants of slaves. Constructions of blackness and whiteness thus played a role in shaping how Houstonians, old and new, negotiated race.

Understanding how migration affected race formation also requires us to foreground sociocultural interpretations of race instead of relying primarily on legal/political interpretations. This study distinguishes between the color line, which refers to the broad categories of "black" and "white" enforced by segregation laws, and the multitude of practices that affected racialization at the local level. In his groundbreaking work *Working toward Whiteness,* David R. Roediger calls for historians to consider racial formation "as a process in social history in which countless quotidian activities informed popular and expert understandings of race" instead of foregrounding political and legal activities that can limit our understandings of the complexities of race.[15] This book responds to that call, but emphasizes a cultural, as well as social, history of migration and urban community building that treats the law as only one aspect of racialization. An array of sociocultural factors affected how urban migrants experienced and conceptualized race. In local practice, then, race was far more complex than state-sanctioned categories indicated.

Houston Bound especially focuses on how racial subjectivity, spatial negotiations, and cultural practices factored into race formations in twentieth-century migration cities. A person's racial subjectivity did not always correspond to her or his legal racial status in the Jim Crow era. Subjectivity, as defined by historian Nan Enstad, refers to "the particular way that an individual becomes a social person, part and product of the corner of the world she or he inhabits." Furthermore, subjectivity "is based on the premise that *who one is* is neither essential nor fixed, but is continually shaped and reshaped in human social exchange."[16] Racial subjectivity is thus a product of a group's history in a particular society, and could hinge on how that society attached meaning and assigned social status based on issues like ancestry, skin color, cultural practice, and access to space. Jim Crow laws forced Creoles into the category of Negro, for example, but Creoles claimed a racial subjectivity that was neither black nor white, based on their shared group experiences in southern Louisiana, the formation of a Creole neighborhood in Houston, and the maintenance of cultural practices once they arrived in the city. A person's racial subjectivity may or may not, therefore, conform to the understandings of race enforced by the color line.

Negotiations over use of space can also affect racial subjectivity and a person's place in a racial hierarchy. The ways that migrants grappled with urban space, therefore, form a major part of this study. Geographers and urban historians have pointed out that people in cities experience and conceptualize space in various ways. First, the notion of space refers to the physical environments that are "concrete and mappable," to borrow geographer Edward Soja's description. Neighborhoods, buildings, parks, and other physical structures shape our awareness of space.[17] The mappable version of early-twentieth-century Houston was a product of civic maneuvers from 1839, when officials divided the city into four wards. They incorporated Fifth and Sixth wards later in the nineteenth century. (See map 1.) Individual wards elected one representative, who served on the city council. The creation of the wards affected how neighborhoods developed, and how racial communities emerged. Each ward was home to its own business districts and schools, which further established the wards as distinct parts of the larger city. Black enclaves had taken root within each ward by the end of the nineteenth century. Houston did not have one black belt, then, since people of African descent settled across the city. The local government stopped officially recognizing the five wards as geopolitical units in 1905, but these districts still shaped how Houstonians made sense of the city after World War I.[18]

The constellation of murky bayous that snake through the city gave Houston its first nickname and also marked the parameters of the wards. The Bayou City is home to approximately twenty-five hundred miles of waterways. As one Houstonian attested, "[I]f straightened out and laid end to end . . . they'd stretch from here to Boulder and back, with enough left over for a round trip to Austin."[19] Augustus and John Allen arrived in southeastern Texas via Buffalo Bayou in 1836, and they founded the city on the banks of that waterway at a site still known as "Allen's Landing." These clay-bottomed bayous (pronounced "buy-yos" by some Houstonians) formed natural borders between most of the wards. Fifth Ward lies north of Buffalo Bayou, which flowed horizontally, while Second Ward is on the southern side of that waterway. West of downtown, Buffalo Bayou also separated Sixth Ward from Fourth Ward. Meanwhile, the White Oak and Little White Oak bayous, located north of downtown, delineated Fifth Ward from First and Sixth wards. Often separated by geographic borders, the wards made Houston feel like a series of small towns, a place that historically lacked a center.

People attach social meaning to geopolitical environments like Houston's six wards, which adds a second dimension to how we experience space.[20]

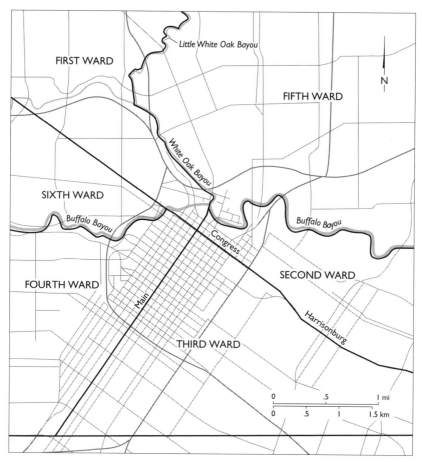

MAP I. Houston's wards. Map by Bill Nelson.

Social interpretations of space have historically shaped the racial hierarchies produced by slavery and Jim Crow. Historian Stephanie Camp asserts, "At the heart of the process of enslavement was a spatial impulse: to locate in plantation space and to control, indeed to determine, their movements and activities." Slaveholders crafted a "theory of mastery" based on the restrictions they placed on slaves' access to space.[21] Slaves' physical captivity on plantations of the antebellum South reflected their status as subjugated property and reinforced white supremacy. The spatial aspects of the Jim Crow racial regime grew out of new circumstances, including the establishment of spaces that had not existed in the antebellum era—like the expansion of public transportation in towns and cities, and the proliferation of spaces for commercial leisure. During the Jim Crow era, the legal division of space reinforced white social power. More than a means of maintaining racial separation, segregation enforced white supremacy by relegating nonwhites to substandard spaces. Daily performances, such as when African Americans stepped aside on sidewalks to allow whites to pass or sat at the back of streetcars, mirrored black people's place in society.[22] Segregation in public spaces, according to historian Joel Williamson, "facilitated the subordination of the inferior race by constantly reminding the Negro that he lived in a world in which the white man was dominant. . . . Further, the impression of Negro inferiority would be constantly re-enforced by relegating the baser element, whenever possible, to the use of inferior facilities."[23] The partitioning of public spaces provided a physical foundation for the social order of white over black.

Access to space continued to shape racialized notions of power and rank in urban societies in the twentieth century. "The lived experience of race has a spatial dimension, and the lived experience of space has a racial dimension," argues George Lipsitz. "People of different races in the United States are relegated to different physical locations by housing and lending discrimination, by school district boundaries, by policing practices, by zoning regulations, and by the design of transit systems."[24] These spatial divisions confer power and privilege on certain groups, while limiting marginalized groups' access to opportunity. Space, then, fundamentally contributes to the production of racial disparities in the United States. "The arrangement of space," writes historian Gaye Theresa Johnson, "has been one of the most important ways to distribute and hinder opportunity along racial lines."[25] Terms like *ghetto* and *barrio* point to the continued association of physical spaces with sociopolitical understandings of race, confinement, and power. The notion that a neighborhood is a ghetto or barrio is based on a person's cognitive interpretation of a racialized space. As historian Thomas Sugrue contends, "The ghetto was not simply a physical construct; it was also an ideological construct. Urban space became a metaphor for perceived racial difference."[26] The history of race in the United States is, therefore, intertwined with the meanings that people have historically assigned to space.

Social meanings attached to physical space can create hierarchies, but they can also influence how a person identifies as a member of a racialized group. A third aspect of space that *Houston Bound* adds to this conversation involves the production of racial subjectivity. When they arrived in Houston, marginalized people of African and Mexican descent often faced exclusion from certain spaces, but they also forged social spaces that allowed them to solidify their racial subjectivity in a new place. These neighborhoods did not appear on maps, but the communities—and the names assigned to them—indicate how migrants perceived of themselves as members of distinct groups. Migrants created neighborhoods with names like "Freedman's Town," "Frenchtown," and "Segundo Barrio" in the wards, and in the process, they attached their understandings of race and group membership to those urban spaces.[27] The appearance of cultural institutions with French and Spanish names further marked those spaces as "Creole" or "Mexican." Long after the city government stopped referring to wards, these districts still shaped people of color's subjectivity. The 1990s rap group called the Fifth Ward Boys, or the entertainer Beyoncé's description of herself as "Miss Third Ward" on her 2013 album, *Beyoncé,* shows the enduring significance of the wards in the local imagination, and the ways that those spatial understandings shape local subjectivities.

The myriad meanings and uses of space emphasize the malleability of race in local practice. Negotiations over shared space between different groups produced new subjectivities and new understandings of community among people from different states, regions, and nations. "When people share a culture, resources, and the use of physical spaces in a single geographical location," writes scholar Michael Innis-Jiménez, "they form community not only through interacting with one another but also by considering themselves part of the group."[28] Over time, interactions between migrants in churches, schools, nightclubs, and dance halls also became the foundation for a host of social and cultural expressions of racial subjectivity. Notions of race and group membership would be shaped and reshaped by the experience of moving to a new place, and the spatial relationships that developed in an adopted hometown.

Houston Bound borrows its title from a blues song performed by Sam "Lightnin'" Hopkins—a native of Centerville, Texas, who moved to Houston in the late 1930s—and this study uses music and other forms of culture to chart the urban transformations at the heart of this story. As Lipsitz argues, forms of popular culture like music can help us uncover "hidden histories" that go untold in official narratives. The "historical changes that are only remotely registered in history books, newspapers, or the pronouncements of politicians can appear in vivid relief and full complexity within products of the popular music industry—if we learn how to read them correctly."[29] Music provides a record of how migrants adapted to their new environs, conceptualized race, and forged social space. Whether they played music professionally or paid to hear professional musicians, migrants like Hopkins made claims to urban space by using sound. "Music making," writes geographer Susan J. Smith, "was also a vehicle sealing people's identification with particular localities."[30] For people whose lives were typically circumscribed by segregation, parades, church bazaars, and street performances allowed them to articulate a sense of place in a new environment. These musical practices demonstrate how migrants negotiated their racial status and subjectivity in the Jim Crow city.

The focus on culture in this book also reveals the complexities of race that can be obscured when we focus only on law and politics.[31] Although Houston was a black and white city on paper, the diverse cultural practices found in the city reflect the heterogeneity of the people defined as white or Negro. The racial diversity that existed in Houston can be seen in the proliferation of churches, musical styles, languages, and other cultural expressions that arose from new neighborhoods and institutions. The sounds of accordion-based music with French lyrics emanating from Catholic church bazaars by the late 1920s spoke to the diversity that existed within the expanding category of "Negro." And while people of Mexican descent were legally categorized as white, cultural practices set them apart from the Anglo majority, which affected their ability to claim the benefits of whiteness. Cultural distinctions between Tejanos and Mexican immigrants also indicated the groups' different experiences on opposite sides of the Rio Grande. Jim Crow laws flattened race, but the diversity of cultural practices spoke to Houston's growing racial complexity.

In diversifying migration cities, ideas about race and status frequently centered on cultural practices like language and religion. Cultural racism, "the veiling of racial thinking in cultural terms," was part of the process of racialization for migrants. Anglos crafted a language of difference that focused on culture in order to distinguish themselves from newcomers like ethnic Mexicans. Furthermore, policing culture was a fundamental part of enforcing racial difference.[32] Cultural institutions like churches, and amusement establishments like saloons, were part of a racial terrain "as hotly contested as wage labor or electoral politics" in the Jim Crow era.[33] Debates over these establishments in popular discourse reveal how changes in demographics affected the ways people discussed race and, within cultural spaces, how different sets of racial hierarchies developed when diverse people made contact.

Sound has traditionally played a crucial role in race formation in the United States, so racial history is also sonic history. Perceptions of racial difference rely on aural and visual cues. Americans have historically thought they could *hear*, as well as see, race. Music scholar Ronald Radano points out, for example, that sonic practices influenced the formation of what became known as racial blackness. "Slave sounding practices," Radano argues, "supplied a kind of musical foundation for the emergence of American commonalities repeatedly cast off as black."[34] Sonic demarcations of race also played an integral role in shaping white supremacy during the era of Jim Crow. Segregationists used music to enforce hierarchy and establish difference, thereby denying the polycultural reality of race in the United States.[35] Musical practices can also reveal how groups have understood and expressed their own racial subjectivity. The music that migrants carried with them— from East Texas blues to the *corridos* of South Texas to the "la-la" of southwestern Louisiana—reveals how the political economies of the western South shaped the racial subjectivities of the people living there. The emergence of the new forms of music produced in Houston also illuminates how urban transformations altered those subjectivities.[36] More than a source of entertainment, genres like the blues, jazz, *orquesta,* zydeco, and soul informed the production of race and formations of community.

These musical expressions do not just reflect social process; they frequently provide the foundation from which those social processes emerge. Sonic practices have long provided the basis for the emergence of new communities and societies in the Americas. Although it was not simply a "universal language," music was an easier mode of communication than verbal languages that relied on specific grammatical structures.[37] This was crucial in a city where people who shared institutions spoke different languages. The development of new musical cultures formed the basis for new coalitions and articulations of community that developed in a place where multiple understandings of race circulated. Music was an integral part of the process by which Creoles of color immersed themselves in the same social institutions and economic structure as black Houstonians, and the roots of the first spatial and cultural engagements between Mexican Americans and African Americans in the city lay in their explorations of music. The emergence of shared musical practices did not collapse racial boundaries, but it did allow people from diverse backgrounds to forge complex social and economic relations in their neighborhoods and institutions.

Houston Bound is divided into three sections that illuminate how migration affected the city's racial landscape and soundscape in the twentieth century. Part 1 chronicles the creation of migrant enclaves across Houston's varied "wards" in the 1920s and 1930s as each of the arriving groups put the stamp of language, music, and culture on the clusters of city streets they claimed as their own. The opening chapter begins with the often-violent struggles for power that occurred when the city was home to an Anglo and African American majority, and shows how black migrants from Texas articulated a particular definition of racial blackness rooted in their history as descendants of enslaved southerners living in a Jim Crow society. The Houstonians who called themselves "New Negroes" expressed a particular construction of blackness through their sociopolitical and cultural activities, which would inform their response to new groups of migrants who entered the city after World War I. Histories of the postwar New Negro often root the movement in the Great Migration to the urban North, but New Negroes in the Bayou City demonstrate how this generation approached de jure seg-regation and used racialized notions of gender to fight white supremacy.[38] Furthermore, black Houstonians' cultural expressions buttressed a consumer economy that fueled their project of using spatial autonomy to subvert Jim Crow.[39] Additionally, the cultural practices and consumer economy that developed around those practices in black communities would become the basis for a host of interracial and interethnic relationships as new groups moved into Houston.

While New Negroes pushed for autonomy, and Anglos shored up white supremacy through violence and Jim Crow laws, blackness and whiteness were in flux. Ethnic Mexicans and Creoles of color brought their own under-standings of race to Houston. Their experiences in Mexico, the Rio Grande Valley, central Texas, and southwestern Louisiana influenced the way they defined themselves. Houston's segregation laws dictated which institutions they could access, but migrants expressed their racial subjectivity through cultural practice and the creation of distinctive communities. The emergence of new neighborhoods signaled the city's demographic transformation as Creoles of color and ethnic Mexicans altered the cultural landscape of the city. As the second chapter shows, the legally defined black/white color line did not change, but migrants' cultural and spatial practices demonstrate how, at the local level, race was becoming increasingly unstable as newcomers altered how blackness and whiteness looked and sounded.

Part 2 investigates how Houstonians created hierarchies based on one another's varied languages, rituals of Christian worship, musical rhythms, and physical characteristics. Discussions of race among the Anglo and African American majority increasingly revealed their concerns about the influx of migrants who did not speak English or practice Protestant Christianity. Chapter 3 reveals how their estimation of these migrants' cultural attributes influenced how black and white Houstonians in the 1920s and 1930s articulated ideas about status and power in a diversifying city. Additionally, new forms of segregation developed at the local level, especially in neighborhood institutions like schools and churches, and these practices sometimes operated outside of the black/white binary enforced by law. The cultural rhetoric used to articulate difference, and the spatial divisions that developed, further demonstrate that race was not just a matter of the state-sanctioned color line in the Jim Crow era.

The diversity of skin tones and languages that could be seen and heard on city streets by 1930 also complicated how Houstonians experienced and conceptualized racial hierarchy. As the fourth chapter of *Houston Bound* demonstrates, some migrants could avoid the repressions of Jim Crow by making claims to whiteness and avoiding the stigma associated with dark skin. For ethnic Mexicans, this meant protecting their legal status as white by seizing on narratives that made racial categorization a matter of the Castilian blood in their veins more than the brown hues that might color their skin. Other people of Mexican descent opted to "pass" for Anglo. Some Creoles adopted a similar strategy; the very light color of one's skin allowed some racially ambiguous Creoles of color to pass for white when they ventured outside of their community.[40] Black and ethnic Mexican activists voiced concerns over passing, arguing that the practice impeded group progress. These conversations also emerged in the broader literature, music, and film of the Jim Crow era. Both cultural and political commentators tended to focus on women, so commentary on skin color and passing consisted of racialized and gendered discussions. Conversations about passing and skin color highlight tensions surrounding the color line, racial subjectivity, and group membership during this era of migration. Key to this dynamic was the simple fact that the fiction of "whiteness" was ever more difficult to sustain in interwar Houston, where people from different parts of the world converged. The meanings assigned to ancestry, cultural practice, and physical characteristics affected the ways migrants experienced race and articulated hierarchy.

Part 3 of *Houston Bound* uses the development of jazz, orquesta, zydeco, rhythm and blues, and soul music to show how sound also shaped the contours of Houston neighborhoods, fostered social ties between different groups, and led to the development of the new articulations of race over time. Musical interactions highlight the community-building efforts of people who initially considered themselves members of different groups. Chapter 5 argues that, beginning in the mid- to late 1930s and continuing into the 1940s, musical innovations helped forge a shared culture in the spaces where black Texans and Creoles of color made contact. At the same time, ethnic Mexican music showed Spanish-speaking communities' sonic engagement with music produced by people of African descent, and illustrates the development of an urban Mexican American subjectivity in the decade before World War II.

Chapter 6 examines hybrid forms, like zydeco, that emerged in the 1950s and the diverse iterations of soul music that reveal the development of new racial subjectivities in the postwar United States. Musical exchanges between black people with roots in East Texas, Creoles of color, and Mexican Americans arose during the civil rights era, when their interactions influenced the rhythm and blues scene.[41] Numerous historians have pointed out that, at the political level, ethnic Mexicans and black Houstonians showed little unity during their struggles for civil rights in Texas. After World War II, they staged two different movements to overcome what Brian Behnken describes as the "double Jim Crow system" of Texas.[42] But while political leaders found little common ground, musical expressions show a cultural relationship hidden beneath a political history of fractured civil rights struggles. At the city's Gold Star studios, a diverse cadre of artists recorded versions of rhythm and blues and soul music in French, Spanish, and English that mirror Houston's transformation into a multiethnic, multiracial city. Their use of soul—a racialized concept—illuminates transformations in Creole and ethnic Mexican racial subjectivities that were influenced by radical political movements of the 1960s, and changing attitudes toward these groups' relationship to blackness and whiteness.

The experiences of migrants like Mary Rose Berry and the diverse people who became Houstonians frame the discussion of race, migration, and culture found in these pages. The same characters often reappear, especially musicians like Lightnin' Hopkins, Lydia Mendoza, Sammy Price, Clifton Chenier, Frank and Ventura Alonzo, Sippie Wallace, Milton Larkin, Rocky Gil, and Illinois Jacquet; activists from the National Association for the Advancement of Colored People (NAACP), El Club Femenino Chapultepec, and the League of United Latin American Citizens (LULAC); and families such as the Berry clan, the Prejeans from southwestern Louisiana, and the Tijerinas of central Texas and Mexico. These characters give voice to the experience of migration, community building, and cultural production. The languages they spoke, the music they created, and the neighborhoods and institutions they forged demonstrate how regional, national, and international mobility informed a wide variety of racial experiences in a Jim Crow society. At its core, *Houston Bound* is about the multiplicitous, ever-evolving nature of this thing we call race.

PART ONE

ONE

————

The Bayou City in Black and White

HUDDIE LEDBETTER SPENT VERY LITTLE TIME in Houston during his years in Texas, but when he began his stint at Central State Prison Farm in Sugar Land in 1920, he quickly learned about the culture and politics of the Bayou City. The road between Sugar Land and Houston was not a long one. Many of Ledbetter's fellow inmates had made the twenty-mile trek from the city to the rural prison farm to serve their sentences. When prisoners chanted in call-and-response patterns as they toiled in the relentless heat of the Brazos River bottoms, or when they shared folk songs and stories at the end of an arduous day in the fields, the men swapped vernacular expressions and local knowledge from the places they called home. Ledbetter brought performance styles he had cultivated in the clubs along Fannin Street in Shreveport, in the Deep Ellum entertainment district in Dallas, and at country dances in the small towns and rural hamlets that dotted East Texas and western Louisiana. Meanwhile, references to nearby Houston populated the songs and stories shared by other inmates at Sugar Land.

It was through these Houstonians that the man who came to be known as "Leadbelly" heard firsthand accounts of the city located east of the prison, cautionary tales about the run-ins with police officers that had landed so many of them behind bars in the first place. When Ledbetter began singing his own version of the song "Midnight Special," he likely was alluding to the people and places his fellow inmates mentioned in their tales:

> If you ever go to Houston
> Boy, you better walk right
> And you better not squabble

And you better not fight
Bason and Brock will just arrest you
Payton and Boone will carry you down
And you can bet your bottom dollar
Oh Lord, you're Sugar Land bound.[1]

Ledbetter's take on "Midnight Special" points to a relationship between urban law enforcement in Houston and rural punishment in the surrounding countryside. He and the men he encountered in Sugar Land drew on a folk tradition that enabled them to impart knowledge about a region and its power structure through their cultural expressions. "Midnight Special" maps the nexus of power that flowed between country and city, revealing a history of place and displacement in eastern Texas.[2] Known ominously as the "Hell-Hole of the Brazos," the prison in Fort Bend County was a site of forced labor that had entrapped African Americans before and after the Civil War. Slaves once cultivated the sugarcane fields that gave the town and prison in Sugar Land their names. Following the war, local plantations leased convicts to work the land. The state of Texas later purchased land in the area and built the penitentiary there in 1908.[3] By the time Ledbetter arrived at the onset of the '20s, the prison was an established part of the white power structure that relied on subjugated black labor. "Midnight Special" may even refer to some of the people who helped maintain that system—specifically, white police officers in the Bayou City. Superintendent Clarence Brock served as Houston's chief of police during World War I, while George Payton and Johnnie Boone worked as detectives in the city's black neighborhoods. Men who ran afoul of these police officers could easily land in the fields of Sugar Land. The violent confrontations that led to the Houston Riot of 1917, the vicious tactics of a reborn Ku Klux Klan that had police support, and continued brutality in the 1920s confirmed that urban law enforcement and rural prisons physically embodied white supremacy in the region.

Before twentieth-century migrations altered local demographics, Houston was a town where Anglos and African Americans made up the majority of the population. Notions of race and power were rooted in the creation of a slave society in Houston and the surrounding countryside in the antebellum era and the establishment of a black/white binary. Black migrants further established a group subjectivity when they flooded into Houston from places like Fort Bend County following the Civil War and established a network of free black communities decades before the Great Migration. In the face of black cultural and economic growth, white supremacists in the early twentieth century worked to maintain their dominance through legal maneuvers and the steady perpetuation of the type of violence Leadbelly describes in "Midnight Special."

The black migrants who poured into Houston over the years worked to build an alternate geography over this landscape of violent white supremacy. Black Houstonians strove to create autonomous neighborhoods in order to forge a spatial—and psychological—distance between themselves and the white power structure. This project began when the first freed people arrived in Houston after the Civil War from places like Sugar Land, but it especially gained momentum during the New Negro era: a nationwide commitment to militant struggle against Jim Crow and racial violence during and after World War I. Writer Alain Locke described New Negroes as black people with "renewed self-respect and self-dependence."⁴ Militant Houstonians articulated this identity through their willingness to use armed self-reliance in response to white-led violence, their use of older vernacular traditions to critique authority, and their emphasis on creating black neighborhoods that lay outside of white control. These assertions were often motivated by concerns about race and gender. A history of violence between white men and women of color especially influenced black Houstonians' push to claim space and power.

Cultural expressions buttressed New Negroes' efforts to achieve those goals. The food they ate, the stories they told, the music that inspired them to dance, and the beauty products they sold became the basis for a consumer economy that supported the sociopolitical project of black autonomy. Musicians like Huddie Ledbetter, along with writers and urban entrepreneurs, did not just offer cultural responses to that agenda. Culture products often provided the foundation for their claims to space. In the process, black migrants articulated a racialized subjectivity that was informed not only by their legal status in a segregated society, but also by cultural practices that served as the building blocks for the establishment of black communities.

FROM THE SUGAR BOWL TO THE
SAN FELIPE DISTRICT: RACE, POWER,
AND THE ORIGINS OF HOUSTON

When newcomers moved to Houston in the late 1910s and 1920s, they entered a place shaped by nearly a century of black history and settlement. That history shaped the meanings of blackness and whiteness that later groups of migrants would encounter and negotiate.

The connection between Houston and the nearby plantation belt developed in the nineteenth century, and the continued movement of black bodies between those places reinforced that link. Before moving to Houston and marrying Arthur Berry, the woman once called Leanna Edwards came of age in Wharton County, which was adjacent to Fort Bend County, where Huddie Ledbetter served his prison sentence. The Edwards family worked as sharecroppers on a cotton plantation in Wharton, and their enslaved ancestors had likely toiled in that area as well. Wharton and Fort Bend were part of a sugar- and cotton-producing region, dubbed the "Texas Sugar Bowl," that also included Brazoria and Matagorda counties. (See map 2.) Located along the lower Brazos and Colorado rivers southwest of Houston, the region historically boasted a substantial black population. English-speaking white settlers realized they could grow cotton and sugarcane in the fertile river bottoms, and they rushed to amass land and slaves. The Sugar Bowl had a dense concentration of large-scale slave plantations between the 1830s and the Civil War, and in 1850, each Sugar Bowl county had a slave majority. By 1860, slaves made up 72 percent of Brazoria County's population, and over 80 percent of Wharton County.[5] Although confined to the eastern part of the state, the slaveholding area of Texas was as large as Alabama and Mississippi combined at the onset of the Civil War.[6]

Houston's proximity to some of the most profitable plantations in Texas made the city the connective tissue that linked the countryside to the port on Galveston Island. City founders Augustus and John Allen saw the potential of a city located "in the heart of a very rich country" of pine and swamp. In 1836, they used black slaves and Mexican prisoners of war from the Battle of San Jacinto to clear the "marshy, mosquito-infested" bayou land that originally formed Houston, named for the commanding general who led the attack on the Mexican army that year. Human chattel and crops traveled between the city and the farms and plantations of the Sugar Bowl via the San Felipe Trail, a path that allowed the city to prosper on the productivity of the slave-filled countryside.[7] Houston subsequently became central to Anglo economic interests in southeastern Texas. When he visited the city that locals called "Hewston" in the 1850s, Frederick Law Olmsted found a city full of churches, saloons, magnolia blossoms, and a thriving slave market. "There is a prominent slave-mart in town, which held a large lot of likely-looking negroes, waiting purchasers. In the windows of shops, and on the doors and

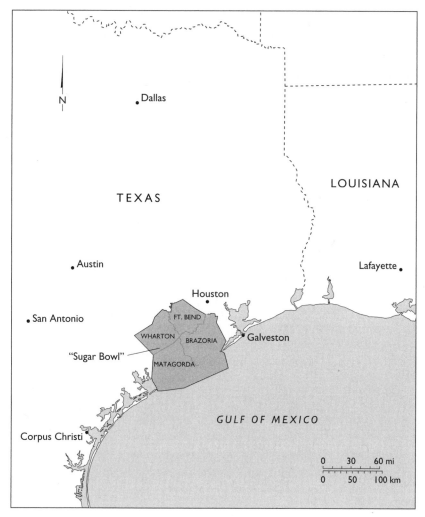

MAP 2. Houston and the western South. Map by Bill Nelson.

columns of the hotel, were many written advertisements headed, 'A likely negro girl for sale.' 'Two negroes for sale.' 'Twenty negro boys for sale,' etc."[8] Most of those slaves wound up in the fields of places like the Sugar Bowl.

The notions of blackness and whiteness in this area were an outgrowth of the social-spatial construction of eastern Texas as a slave society with a plantation-based power structure in the antebellum era. When they moved west to Texas, slaveholders and slaves brought notions of race and power shaped by two centuries of plantation ideology forged in the Southeast.[9] The white and black people found in antebellum eastern Texas were typically English-speaking southerners who hailed from other slave states. Forty-three percent of the Anglos living in Texas in 1860 migrated there from one of the other ten states that would form the Confederate States of America one year later. The number of Anglos there who were born in Tennessee, Alabama, Georgia, and Mississippi nearly equaled the number of people born in the Lone Star State.[10] The elite slaveholding class used their economic power in an agricultural, plantation-based society to impose their values and shore up power. The creation of this slave society in eastern Texas demanded the imposition of the white-over-black racial hierarchy and the implementation of a plantation regime.

Black East Texans' conception of racial blackness developed from the shared circumstances of enslavement and the act of rebuilding a society and culture in a new place. In slave cabins, cotton fields, plantation kitchens, and brush harbors—secluded arbors where slaves practiced Christianity—they formed a group subjectivity. African Americans forced west strove to re-create the cultural practices that had sustained slave communities for centuries.[11] Ripped from family and the land they had once called home, slaves brought cultural practices cultivated in the Southeast to the counties of eastern Texas. The work songs heard for nearly two hundred years in Virginia's tobacco fields slaves now used to keep time while chopping cotton along the Brazos River. In places like Brazoria County, slaves built conjurers' cabins with bakongo cosmograms inside to help ward off evil spirits, and praised Jesus in their ring shouts at the end of the day.[12] They emerged from the Civil War with a sense of racial community based on their shared experiences in eastern Texas and the necessity of re-forming social networks and cultural practices in a new place.

Former slaves from the Sugar Bowl and other parts of East Texas were some of the first free black people to settle in Houston after the Civil War. The first influx of freedpeople arrived soon after June 19, 1865, the day remembered as "Juneteenth," when word of Robert E. Lee's surrender at Appomattox in April finally reached enslaved Texans.[13] Labor motivated some freedpeople to make the transition from rural to urban. Using labor contracts, Anglo landowners compelled former slaves in the county to pick cotton, chop sugarcane, or conduct other forms of agricultural labor that reminded them of the years they had spent in bondage. Freedpeople frequently signed labor contracts that bound them to white-owned land for a set amount of time. These sharecroppers earned a percentage of the crop they grew, but white landowners typically found ways to pay them little to nothing for their labor.[14] Thousands of freedpeople decided to abandon the country in favor of cities. Freedpeople from the Sugar Bowl trekked to Houston using the San Felipe Trail, which connected the city to the countryside. Only around one thousand African Americans were living in Houston in 1860, but that number tripled over the next decade. After the Civil War, generations of African Americans from the Sugar Bowl continued moving to Houston.[15]

When they first arrived in Houston from the country in the summer of 1865, the penniless former slaves moved into Fourth Ward, near downtown. Homeless migrants found shelter at a dilapidated warehouse that locals dubbed "Hotel d'Afrique."[16] The sight of newly freed people searching for labor and housing became common in those years following the war. Some Anglo Houstonians lamented the "crowds of idle negroes" in the downtown area: "We cannot help but pity the poor freedmen and women that have left comfortable and happy homes in the country and come to this city in search of what they call freedom," wrote one Houstonian in the local *Tri-Weekly Telegraph*.[17] But black Houston quickly took root. By 1870 the city was just under 40 percent black. Former slaves created a neighborhood called Freedman's Town in 1865 at the place where the San Felipe Trail ended in Fourth Ward. A concentration of families, businesses, and institutions made the area south of the Buffalo Bayou and west of downtown a noticeable black neighborhood by 1870. Freedpeople handcrafted bricks to line the community's streets, and they used cypress trees that grew nearby to construct houses in the fledgling neighborhood.[18]

Freedman's Town emerged as an early center of black political and cultural life. With the support of former abolitionists, a black school called the Gregory Institute opened in 1870 on San Felipe Street. That thoroughfare became the hub of Freedman's Town. The neighborhood was home to politicians, pastors, draymen, domestic workers, and a diverse range of former slaves—and some white families—seeking to rebuild after the war. In 1870, a white Radical Republican named William H. Parsons—who supported the Fifteenth Amendment, which gave black men the right to vote—lived in an area where most of his neighbors were former slaves.[19] Antioch Baptist Church, which opened in 1872, aided freedpeople who wished to buy land and purchase homes, and served as the site of the city's first black college. Antioch, under the leadership of a freedman named Jack Yates, also served as the meeting place for the biracial Harris County Republican Club, which solidified the church as a political and religious space.[20]

The name "Freedman's Town" spoke to the emergence of a racialized group subjectivity developed by diverse people from different states who forged social space. Because of the history of slavery and forced black migration to eastern Texas, Freedman's Town looked like a map of the antebellum South, since residents hailed from every state of the former Confederacy. The majority of residents were most likely survivors of the "Second Middle Passage," people sold to Texas via the interstate slave trade that had thrived before the Civil War.[21] In 1870, 58 percent of black Houstonians had been born outside of Texas. For most families, only children under the age of eighteen were born in Texas. The Yates family offers a typical story. The Yateses had been born into bondage in Gloucester County, Virginia. The enslaved married couple lived on different farms, but when Harriet's owner decided to move to Matagorda County, in the Texas Sugar Bowl, in 1863, Jack convinced his owner to sell him so that he could move west with his wife and children. The Civil War ended when Jack was thirty-seven years old and Harriet was around twenty. Rather than remain in the Texas countryside, the Yates family relocated to Houston that year.[22] In their Fourth Ward community, 12 percent of their black neighbors also hailed from Virginia. Most of the other adults in Freedman's Town were born in Louisiana, the Carolinas, Georgia, Alabama, or Mississippi. The Yates family lived next door to the Smith family from Mississippi, while another neighbor, Abram Chambers, was born in North Carolina. These demographics distinguished Houston from cities in the Southeast. While 90 percent of black Atlanta was born in Georgia, only around 40 percent of black Houstonians were Texas natives during Reconstruction.[23] The majority of adults in Freedman's Town likely shared a history of forced migration to Texas as enslaved people and the more recent experience of relocating from the country to the city. Those commonalities gave the black community a collective sense of a shared history. They further acknowledged those ties by making claims to urban space. Their cultural institutions such as churches, and the communal land they purchased for parks, marked the neighborhood as their own.

In the years following the Civil War, former slaves also spread beyond Freedman's Town to establish communities in other wards. Black Houston existed in several different places at once. The geographically dispersed population meant that people of African descent were not historically confined to one part of town like their peers in some northern industrializing cities. As in southern cities like Atlanta and Richmond, black Houstonians lived in communities scattered across the city.[24] By necessity, black Houstonians had to create and maintain businesses and institutions across the city. White people made up the majority of the city as a whole, but each ward had a black section. Black Third Ward first developed around Emancipation Park, a ten-acre area located at the corner of Dowling and Elgin streets. The congregations of Antioch Baptist Church and Trinity Methodist Episcopal raised eight hundred dollars to purchase the park in 1871. Black neighborhoods developed in other wards during Reconstruction, most notably in Fifth Ward, on the north side of the city, where the commercial and cultural hub of the black community was Lyons Avenue. More black residents lived in Fifth Ward than Anglos in 1870: 578 residents were black, while 561 were white.[25] Businesses and institutions in Third Ward, Fourth Ward, and Fifth Ward made those areas the major centers of African American life in the Bayou City.

The wards made Houston feel like a collection of small towns rather than one city. Thelma (Scott) Bryant, who was born in Third Ward in 1905, commented that her neighborhood felt "very much like the country" in the early twentieth century. Likewise, musician Arnett Cobb, who came of age in Fifth Ward, described the community of his youth as a "country town." Indeed, many of the people who moved to his neighborhood from the country continued the same customs and agricultural practices they had brought with them from the countryside. Most families raised chickens and grew okra, greens, corn, and other subsistence crops in their backyards. The style of architecture reflected the style of black residences found across the post-emancipation South. Working-class families typically lived in white, one-room shotgun houses—structures so named because a person could shoot a gun through the front door and watch the lead travel straight through the house and exit the back door.[26]

While free black neighborhoods developed, white supremacists adopted measures to disfranchise descendants of slaves and relegate them to inferior status in society. A series of laws targeted black Texans by segregating them from white people in public spaces, and by stripping black men of the right to vote. The state constitution segregated public schools in 1876. Texas Democrats enacted the state's first Jim Crow law in 1891 by passing a bill that segregated state railroad travel, making Texas one of nine states to do so since 1887. To ensure their continued dominance in state politics, legislators established a poll tax in 1902. They further excluded black Texans from voting in primaries in 1923.[27]

White lawmakers completed the Jim Crow–ing of Houston in the first two decades of the twentieth century through a series of city ordinances. The Democrat-ruled local government prohibited integration in every space where black and white people made contact. A 1903 ordinance segregated streetcars. Four years later, the city council segregated theaters, hotels, restaurants, and public facilities. A different law segregated local parks that year. Legal segregation in public facilities—from streetcars to theaters to saloons—reminded African Americans of their place in society by forcing them into inferior spaces. They were either barred from entering certain establishments or relegated to specific areas. Black customers, when permitted to patronize white-owned restaurants, received their food from a back window or ate in the basement. Some laws targeted interracial sex. In 1908 a justice of the peace Jim Crow-ed houses of prostitution by issuing an order that made it illegal for white and black prostitutes to conduct business under the same roof. Another ordinance, in 1922, prohibited interracial cohabitation.[28] These laws marked racial difference and enforced a hierarchy of white over black.

While the number of segregation laws increasingly limited black mobility in Houston, the descendants of slaves who lived in the wards strove to create and nurture their own institutions within their neighborhoods. Their businesses, community celebrations, and athletic organizations allowed African Americans the opportunity to promote their own leaders and maintain their own cultural practices without feeling inferior to the white majority, especially as racial restrictions tightened in the age of Jim Crow. Banned from attending most city-sponsored Fourth of July festivities, black Houstonians celebrated Juneteenth at Emancipation Park, where they barbecued and danced to the sounds of local bands.[29] When white Houstonians barred black people from an autumn festival, created in 1899, called the No-Tsu-Oh (*Houston* spelled backward), black Houstonians established the De-Ro-Loc (*colored* spelled backward) for themselves. And since the white baseball team, the Houston Buffaloes, excluded black athletes, African Americans played for the Houston Black Buffaloes. A group that had included the Alabama-born educator Edward Ollington Smith also petitioned for a black library, and after six years of activism, the Colored Carnegie Library opened in 1913—complete with a black librarian.[30]

The most dramatic example of local autonomy in the area occurred just outside the city. Black Houstonians took advantage of the availability of land on the far north side when they formed a township called Independence Heights. On January 16, 1915, with a population of about four hundred, residents voted twenty-two to two to officially break away from Houston. Local newspapers covered the vote, and the *Houston Chronicle* noted that Independence Heights was the first "all Negro city" in Texas. At the time, the town covered about three square miles. During the first election, residents chose a Houston attorney, G. O. Burgess, as the mayor, and also elected a black sheriff to enforce the law. Land ownership was a point of pride for Independence Heights residents. Of the 183 households listed in the 1920 census, 145 families lived in homes they owned.[31]

In the World War I era, Independence Heights must have seemed especially appealing as black neighborhoods in the wards became sites of violent battles over space and power. Black Houstonians learned that their neighborhoods in the wards were contested terrain. Racial violence especially erupted in Fourth Ward. By the 1910s, the area once known as Freedman's Town had grown from its origins as a small settlement of former slaves into a thriving black community. As the memory of slavery grew more distant, the black residents of Fourth Ward changed the name of their first neighborhood from Freedman's Town to the San Felipe district, named for the major thoroughfare in the community. The district faced a constant white presence in the form of law-enforcement officials. Police officers buttressed the white power structure in Houston by enforcing Jim Crow authority and demanding submission from an expanding black population.

One of the most notorious white officers who patrolled the San Felipe district had roots in the Sugar Bowl. Named Lee Sparks, the police officer embodied the connection between rural and urban white supremacy. He had moved to Houston in the early 1900s, so by the summer of 1917, Sparks had lived in Houston "off and on" for over a decade and had served on the city's police force for four years.[32] The area where he spent much of his workday was a hub of black life in Houston in the early twentieth century. White law-enforcement officials in the San Felipe district routinely clashed with black people who strove to govern their own affairs in their community. Sparks and his partner, Rufus Daniels, rode through the neighborhood on Clydesdale horses that allowed them to tower over residents. The officers expected a type of deference from San Felipe residents that defied their sense of freedom. Furthermore, Sparks and Daniels wielded the authority—and weapons—to use force when black Houstonians did not comply. They regularly used both physical violence and verbal degradation to dominate local people. San Felipe residents nicknamed Daniels "Daniel Boone" because of his large stature, and they considered Sparks a "brutal bully." The duo was not typically a welcome sight in the neighborhood.[33]

Sparks and Boone were central figures in a bloody contest over race, gender, space, and power that erupted in the San Felipe district in August 1917, shortly after the United States entered World War I. Racial tensions flared that summer when the military stationed the Third Battalion of the Twenty-fourth Infantry in Houston to guard Camp Logan, a training center being built near Fourth Ward. As one of the units once known as "Buffalo Soldiers," the Twenty-fourth Infantry enjoyed hero status in Houston that summer.[34] The soldiers spent considerable time in the San Felipe, where residents appreciated the sight of black uniformed men during the early days of World War I. One soldier wrote in a letter to the *Crisis,* the official journal of the NAACP, about his experiences in Houston at the time: "[T]he people of color of Houston are proud of their brother soldiers and opened wide their homes and churches, and have welcomed us with a generous hospitality."[35] White Houstonians were less impressed. Soon after the soldiers arrived, accounts of public confrontations between them and white civilians on streetcars and city streets filled local newspapers.[36]

On the morning of August 23, Lee Sparks publicly beat a black woman named Sara Travers in the San Felipe district, and when a black soldier attempted to intervene, the situation escalated. Sparks had entered Travers's house while chasing a crapshooter, but when the woman questioned his actions, he slapped her. He then called Travers and another black woman who witnessed the scene "God damn nigger bitches" and placed Travers under arrest. Private Alonzo Edwards of the Third Battalion approached Sparks and Daniels and asked them to release Travers, an act that Sparks considered impudent. The officer raised his six-shooter and whipped the soldier. Sparks later confessed that he hit Private Edwards four times. "I beat that nigger until his heart got right," he boasted. "He was a good nigger when I got through with him." An eyewitness claimed Sparks also said, "That's the way we do things in the South. We're running things not the d——— niggers." Sparks and Daniels arrested both Travers and Edwards and sent them to jail.[37]

Lee Sparks embodied the connection between rural and urban white supremacy. He reasserted his authority over the San Felipe district through violence and a reminder of his roots in the Sugar Bowl. As Sparks had retorted on the morning of the riot, "I'm from Fort Ben(d) and we don't allow niggers to talk back to us. We generally whip them down there."[38] He intended to continue practicing that type of violence against black migrants in the city. Sparks stressed that Private Edwards was "as drunk as he could be" when he confronted him, though the soldier's alleged inebriation was probably less of a concern than his audacious assumption of public authority toward a white man in front of a black audience. Later that afternoon, another soldier, Corporal Charles Baltimore of the Third Battalion, confronted Sparks and Boone to inquire about the arrests. Sparks retorted, "I don't report to no niggers." Sparks then beat Corporal Baltimore to the ground. To avoid further blows, Baltimore escaped and ran into an empty house nearby, with Sparks chasing and firing his six-shooter. The soldier hid underneath a bed, but Daniels and Sparks dragged him out, the latter striking him twice more with the barrel of his gun. A patrol wagon then carted Baltimore to jail. When asked why he felt the need to pistol-whip the unarmed Baltimore, Sparks later explained, "Why, I wasn't going to wrestle with a big nigger like that." The policeman was also cognizant of the crowd of spectators watching the exchange, many of them standing behind the soldier. Sparks would later note that "there was niggers all around there."[39] Any sign of compliance with a black man would have been an open acknowledgment of equal status in front of the very people he needed to dominate on a daily basis. Furthermore, Sparks may have also held some fears about the soldiers' influence on these black Houstonians. He purportedly told Travers, "Since these sons of bitches soldiers come here you are trying to take the town."[40] When Private Edwards questioned Sparks, the black soldier was asserting his authority in a black-majority community that the white officers tried to dominate on a daily basis.

For the black infantrymen stationed at the city's Camp Logan, the war to secure democracy began in Houston instead of on European soil. News of the events in the San Felipe district reached Camp Logan as early as 10:30 that morning, the approximate time of the Edwards beating. News of the assaults, along with rumors that a white mob would attack Camp Logan, circulated and motivated at least two groups of infantrymen to rebel. As the drizzly afternoon transformed into a night that one soldier described as "dark as a stack of black cats," the men collected rifles and ammunition and prepared for retribution. "Forget France," one soldier declared. "Let's go clean up the God damned city. Let's get to work!" That night, approximately one hundred armed black soldiers left camp and marched through the streets in military formation in search of white police officers.[41] The soldiers' revolt began in the neighborhood surrounding Camp Logan, but the columns of men were bound for the San Felipe district, the scene of that morning's violence. As they marched in step down the main drag of the community, West Dallas Street, black Houstonians offered encouragement from open windows. According to one witness, the spectators "were just cheering them up and hollering, 'This is what we call a man!'"[42] Some of the black witnesses undoubtedly found the soldiers' act of retaliation heartening. The soldiers' actions reclaimed the historic area as black-controlled space, if only for a few hours. In total, twenty people died that night: fifteen Anglo Houstonians (including five police officers), one ethnic Mexican man killed by stray gunfire, and four black soldiers. Rufus Daniels died that night in the streets of San Felipe, struck by soldiers' bullets while Sparks sat at home. Chief Clarence Brock, the superintendent of police, had suspended Sparks for twenty-four hours due to his activities that morning.[43]

In the Jim Crow era, the hierarchy of white over black was not marked just by disfranchisement laws or the exclusion of African Americans from certain spaces; the daily presence of white police officers in black neighborhoods, and the steady perpetuation of violence, shored up the privileged status of whiteness. By pistol-whipping and shooting the residents of neighborhoods like the San Felipe district, these policemen reminded black Houstonians of their inferior status in the Jim Crow society. Sparks and other officers continued to be a problem for black Houstonians that summer. Sparks killed a black man named Wallace "Snow" Williams just one week after the riot. According to a witness, Williams had fled from the scene of a craps game while Sparks fired shots after him. The blasts hit him in the neck and between his shoulders.[44] After he fell to the ground, Sparks kicked him in the head. An eyewitness to the scene later questioned whether the United States was actually "the Land of the Brave and the home of the Free" or if the law was only "for just one race . . . Lee Sparks and his kind of murderers." Just days later, Detective Norfleet Hill shot a black man named Andrew Hewitt, claiming that he had rushed him with a pitchfork. Hewitt actually was carrying a table fork.[45]

Huddie Ledbetter's ominous warning about Houston rang true for the black migrants who entered the city during and after the war. Since Reconstruction, Houston had attracted migrants from the rural countryside who wanted to escape agricultural labor and live in urban communities with black institutions; however, Lee Sparks and other police officers reminded black Houstonians of their inferior status in the Jim Crow society. Ledbetter arrived at the prison farm just three years after the riot of 1917 and the shootings of Wallace Williams and Andrew Hewitt, so these stories likely influenced his depiction of Houston. As "Midnight Special" cautioned, people of African descent could certainly face death or imprisonment in Sugar Land if they did not "walk right" in the eyes of white-dominated law enforcement.

Despite the negative national attention caused by the riot and subsequent acts of racial violence, the Bayou City grew even blacker over the next decade. A new wave of migrants took part in a larger history of movement between the country and the city that had shaped Houston since Reconstruction. Thousands of people of African descent relocated to the city in the Jazz Age as black Houston grew at a faster rate than most other cities in the former Confederacy. The African American population surged from just under twenty-four thousand in 1920 to over sixty-three thousand in 1930.[46] Beginning in 1919, a Republican-backed organization called the Lincoln League of Texas placed full-length advertisements in black newspapers to promote migration to what they called "Heavenly Houston" (a boast that must have seemed ironic to anyone who remembered the summer of 1917). The headline described the city as "The Workshop of Texas, Where Seventeen Railroads Meet the Sea." According to the ad, "Heavenly Houston" not only boasted "the finest drinking water in the South," but was also home to sixteen black elementary schools, two black hospitals, and three black newspapers. The Lincoln League especially noted the availability of labor by assuring readers that the city "offers unexcelled industrial opportunities to the colored man," a claim bolstered by economic growth during World War I. The people who flocked to the expanding city would transform black Houston. They tried to break from patterns of white domination and black subjugation by abandoning field labor, through political organizing, by promoting armed self-reliance against racial violence, and through the use of cultural traditions from the country that they adapted to an urban context.

The city's wartime economy appealed to rural migrants in search of industrial employment. Both economic boom and labor scarcity created an especially appealing situation for migrants. Buffalo Bayou, which connects Houston's ship channel to Galveston Bay and the Gulf of Mexico, was key to the city's economic growth. Before the war, the ship channel was primarily used to ship goods to Galveston Island, where they would then be sent to international ports; however, the island city on the Texas coast never fully recovered from the devastating storm of 1900. When workers dredged the Houston ship channel to make it wide enough to accommodate oceangoing vessels in 1914, Houston replaced Galveston as the export center of Texas. The high demand for cotton during the First World War allowed the city's cotton firms to expand locally and internationally, and they used the ship channel to export their goods. Allied forces in Europe used Texas-grown cotton for smokeless powder, military uniforms, and multiple other uses, and their demand for the product accelerated the local economy. By 1930, Houston was the "largest cotton market and export center in the world." The war era also marked Houston's transition into an oil town. The number of petroleum shipments from the Port of Houston jumped from 31,584 short tons in 1915 to 293,400 one year later.[47]

Urban labor at places like the ship channel allowed for a break from agricultural contract labor, and enabled black Texans to earn higher wages without leaving the state. Sharecroppers acquired everything from farm tools to food and personal items through credit; thus, they rarely purchased goods with cash. As credit tightened, the crop lien system became even more inescapable for tenant farmers and sharecroppers.[48] Furthermore, natural disasters like flooding, combined with the ravaging effects of the boll weevil, made agricultural work in the country increasingly undesirable. Rather than picking the cotton that would then be moved to the inland port city, thousands of rural migrants flocked to Houston to load cotton and other products onto vessels at the ship channel. By trading agricultural labor in the country for industrial or domestic labor in the city, many African Americans who had once worked on "quarters" or "thirds" as sharecroppers became wage laborers for the first time. The possibility of work at the ship channel attracted a steady stream of workers, and black men historically held the majority of the jobs. They were also the first to organize a chapter of the International Longshoremen's Association (ILA) at the Port of Houston in 1914.[49] The sounds of black longshoremen singing and chanting in time as they heaved products onto ships became part of the sonic landscape of the city as they adapted the work-song tradition they had brought from the fields of the rural South to the urban docks of the Port of Houston.[50]

Black women were excluded from the industrial labor opportunities afforded men, so most took jobs as domestic workers in white homes. Between 1920 and 1940, about 40 percent of all black workers in Houston were women, and they made up the overwhelming majority of female cooks, maids, and other domestic workers employed in the city.[51] In the early twentieth century, white southerners expected black women to prepare their food, scrub their floors, and even nurse their babies. Classified advertisements in white-owned newspapers like the *Houston Chronicle* and *Post* described jobs specifically for "colored" nurses, cooks, and laundresses. The labor of black women was so important to white Houston that when Juneteenth landed on a Friday in 1917, the swank Rice Hotel held a "rescue party" for families left without their black cooks.[52] Some women came to Houston from the farms of East Texas because they could support themselves with their domestic jobs. Leanna Edwards cleaned homes in white neighborhoods when she moved to Houston as a single mother, and she continued long after she married her husband, Arthur Berry.[53] Similarly, a woman named Ella Larkin moved to Houston after her husband, Milton, died in around 1912, leaving her with four small children and no source of income in Grimes County. Since Ella had kept house in the country, she transferred those skills to domestic labor in the city. "My mother came along in an era when she was doing housework or the laundry or the cooking," remembers her son, Milton, Jr., born in 1910. Young Milton supplemented his mother's household income by cutting lawns and doing odd jobs, but she remained the primary provider.[54] Women's wages were a necessary and crucial part of black Houston. Whether earned from lifting cargo onto ships or from scrubbing floors in white homes, migrants' wages helped fortify expanding black communities.

Rural-to-urban migration spurred sociopolitical as well as economic change as some black residents adopted a decidedly more confrontational tone in their efforts to fight white supremacy. Some of the city's most influential black Houstonians—from postal employees to newspaper editors to educators—responded to the climate of racial terror by forming a new group, the Civic Betterment League (CBL), to focus on political and social issues in Houston and surrounding areas. In 1918, its membership having grown to about 230, the CBL decided to convert the local organization into a branch of the NAACP.[55]

The leaders of the fledgling NAACP branch were among the most militant activists in the city. Some members, like E. O. Smith, thought cooperating with municipal and county authorities would ensure cordial relations between white political leaders and black activists. Another faction, however, vowed to make the Houston NAACP an "aggressive, progressive, fighting organization."[56] Clifton Frederick Richardson, a journalist who had worked as the CBL's civil and social director, emerged as a one of the leaders of this second, more militant faction. Richardson was born in 1891 in the town of Marshall. A journalist by trade, he graduated from Bishop College in his hometown. After finishing his studies in 1909, he moved to Houston and eventually made a home in the San Felipe district with his wife, Ruby Leola, and their three sons. Richardson began writing for and managing a black-owned newspaper called the *Houston Observer* in 1916. Three years later, Richardson and two partners formed the Informer Publishing Company, and he began editing the newspaper that would make him notorious, both locally and nationally. He was twenty-eight years old when the *Houston Informer* debuted in 1919.[57] A renaissance man who sang and played bass guitar, he frequently promoted black arts as an example of his race's postwar ascendance. Richardson eventually served as president of the Houston NAACP and at least four other organizations: the Texas Association of Branches of the NAACP, the Real Building and Loan Association, the Coleridge-Taylor Choral Club, and the Houston Negro Business League. He cofounded the Houston Citizens Chamber of Commerce and served as director of the Texas Association of Negro Musicians for the South Texas District. Richardson was also a churchgoer who attended Bethel Baptist Church (and served as chairman of its board of trustees). Additionally, he participated in fraternal organizations such as the Ancient Order of Pilgrims, the United Brothers of Friendship, the Knights of Pythias, and the Odd Fellows, and he served on the governing bodies of many of those organizations.[58] From his arrival in Houston in the 1910s until his untimely death in 1939, he was one of the most visible black men in the city. (See figure 1.)

Richardson, along with fellow journalist Henry L. Mims, was financially independent. This allowed both men to make politically volatile remarks without fear of economic reprisal from white bosses. Like Richardson, Mims published a newspaper. When they lobbied for an NAACP chapter, Richardson argued that his group was in a better position to aggressively push for civil rights because they had greater financial independence and better means to reach the black public than E. O. Smith, who worked as an educator within a public school system governed by a white board. "The Negro down here to whom you must tie is the Negro who is willing to fight for his rights," Mims wrote to John Shillady, secretary of the NAACP. "I mean fight in the courts, in the Press, in the pulpit, in vigorous protest and in every conceivable way to bring about results." Mims's group eventually won the battle. Mims became first president for the Houston and Harris County Branch of the NAACP, and Richardson served as its secretary.[59]

Seeing police brutality as one of the most pressing issues for African Americans in the post-riot city, the new NAACP decided to take a legal approach and challenge the city head-on, a strategy that the more conservative Smith found "unduly hasty." In 1918, they sued the city of Houston after a white police officer beat a black man with a six-shooter. They also hired a

FIGURE 1. Clifton F. Richardson in 1923. C. F. Richardson Papers,
Houston Metropolitan Research Center, Houston Public Library.

black lawyer to prosecute a white deputy and constable who killed another
black man they had arrested. The officers shot the man as he retreated and
then took him to a police station in Harrisburg, a town near Houston. He
died from gunshot wounds within three hours. "We are going to endeavor to
convict these murderers," Richardson promised the national office.[60]

In their letters to the national headquarters in New York, Richardson and
Mims used language popular among "race men" of the war era. By describing
themselves as "aggressive" men who would "fight" for citizenship rights, they
rhetorically linked their activism to the New Negro movement, which the
Informer frequently referenced in the years following the war. New Negroes
saw themselves as part of a nationwide commitment to militant struggle

against Jim Crow and racial violence. Richardson's work with the *Informer* personified what one contemporary called the "growing consciousness of the race" after World War I.[61] A story from the Associated Negro Press (ANP) in the summer of 1919, for example, heralded the arrival of "a new awakening for justice in behalf of the people of our racial group," because so much had been written about race relations in the black press that year.[62] As the *Informer* asserted in 1920, "The 'new Negro' is demanding a 'new deck and a new deal.'"[63]

Although he was a churchgoing man, Richardson raised hell in Houston. His motto was "Getting 'Em Told," and he used the *Informer* as a platform to tackle local race problems and people who impeded racial progress. He called the segregationists "Hellish Huns" and "Lynchocrats" for allowing lynching to run rampant, and he publicly chastised black Houstonians who they felt bowed to white supremacy. When a local black preacher refused to join his militant protest, Richardson called the minister a "pussy-footing pulpit pimp." He was not a man who minced words.

Richardson urged black Houstonians to rethink their relationship to white people who held political power in society. In 1927, for example, Richardson accused a local black high school principal of having "cold feet" when it came to race issues. Richardson felt that the man, William Leonard Davis, was cowed by the white school board. According to Richardson, the school administrator had "joined the ranks of the pusillanimous, pussyfooting principals who betray and sell their race for a position of honor and preferment, and endeavor to stick their fingers in the white people's eyes in order to land certain 'plums' and be known and rated as 'good niggers' who know their place and 'stay in their place.'"[64] Davis sued. A judge found Richardson guilty of libel that year.

The insults hurled at W. L. Davis constituted more than a public spat; Richardson's choice of words indicated his vision of New Negro activism. He was one of many black urban dwellers who wished to create a separation between themselves and the old vestiges of plantation authority. *Informer* contributors reserved the epithets "darky" and "nigger" for African Americans who (in their estimation) behaved in a subservient manner around white people.[65] Their transforming relationship to white people was a key aspect of New Negro identity espoused by Houstonians in the 1920s. They lived at a time and place in which Anglos often used degrading images of black people to construct whiteness and negate black political, economic, and social aspirations.[66] For them, the image of the plantation Negro contrasted sharply with modern

Negroes who demanded the right to vote, built urban communities, and organized labor unions. Identifying as a New Negro meant creating a spatial separation from East Texas plantation society through migration and changing their relationship to white people once they arrived in the city.

New Negroes were often convinced that they took a more aggressive position on racial injustice, and they attributed the change to differences between the World War I generation and older African Americans. When a black Houstonian named Johnny Walls began a job as a postal worker in 1918, he immediately encountered problems with older employees. The "old-time Negroes," he said, "were hat in hand." According to Walls, the older men took abuse from white people and removed their hats before entering buildings, which the younger men interpreted as a sign of subservience. Walls organized the Postal Employees' Alliance of Houston to counter the older generation, who were "merely holding their jobs through their obsequiousness and loss of manhood."[67] Richardson was younger than thirty when he launched the *Houston Informer,* and he also saw generational differences between younger and older African Americans. In an address to the Houston Business Men's Luncheon Club, he pointed out that younger men were taking part in business, whereas that had previously been the domain of older men. This change, he argued, was a result of World War I and the apparent "new vision on the part of younger men."[68] These views may have fueled Richardson's quest to wrest control of the local NAACP chapter from older activists like E. O. Smith.

The visions of aggression and militance influenced black Houstonians' response to racial violence in the 1920s. The establishment of the Houston NAACP in 1919 occurred in the same year as the city's Ku Klux Klan revival, and black Houstonians had to defend themselves from white men in robes and hoods as well as officers in police uniforms. The twentieth-century Klan marched into Houston on October 9, 1920, during a Confederate Veterans parade. They carried banners that read, "We were here yesterday, 1866," "We are here today, 1920," and "We will be here forever." After picking the name Sam Houston Klan no. 1, a moniker that linked them to a hero of the Texas revolution, this chapter became the first in Texas and the first located west of the Mississippi River. Texas eventually sent the first twentieth-century Klan senator to Washington, D.C., in 1923 after Democrats voted Earle B. Mayfield into office. Whereas the KKK that had first emerged during Reconstruction was most active during elections, the post–World War I Klan portrayed itself as a fraternal association that protected "American interests." Klansmen initially had the full support of white city leaders in Houston. For the Klan's first night parade, the city blacked out the lights, and the police force protected the marchers.[69]

Black Houstonians targeted by the Houston Klan were typically middle-class professionals and business owners. The most widely known Klan attack on a black Houstonian occurred in 1925 when Klansmen kidnapped a dentist named Dr. R. H. Ward and tarred and feathered him before tying him to a post. Hearing rumors that African Americans would retaliate for Ward's treatment, the Klan came out, "armed and badged," to patrol the city streets.[70] C. F. Richardson's son, Cliff, recalled that the KKK also "emasculated" a black doctor, claiming that he had been having a sexual relationship with a white woman. Incendiary critiques of white supremacy in the *Informer* led the Klan and its supporters to vandalize the newspaper's office several times. According to Richardson family lore, the Klan created several plots to kill the outspoken editor. On one occasion Richardson's enemies allegedly planned to have a police officer arrest him, and when they walked him across the courtyard square a sniper would shoot him. A black waiter spoiled another alleged plan when he overheard his employers discussing their intention to lure Richardson into a building on Main Street and kill and dismember him, with each murderer taking a piece of his body away to hide the evidence and to have a souvenir. Because of his editorials on police brutality, Richardson had to defend himself from police officers and the Ku Klux Klan. After he wrote an exposé on the Klan for the *Informer* in the 1920s, police officers stopped the newspaper editor for a defective headlight and then whipped him. Richardson survived the attack, but according to his son, he eventually "went to his grave" with scars from the beating that left him needing thirty-five stitches.[71]

In the decade following the war, newspaper reports and family recollections suggest that black Houstonians practiced armed self-defense when they encountered violence from white police officers or Klansmen. Other cases of gun violence between black men and white police officers made front-page news in the 1920s. Pete Chester, a fifty-three-year-old African American man, killed a white police officer in Fourth Ward in 1927. A lawyer hired by the NAACP successfully argued that Chester killed the officer in self-defense, and Chester was acquitted a year later. Some white Houstonians seethed over Chester's acquittal, and anger may have fueled a subsequent attack.[72] Months after the not-guilty verdict, a black man named Robert Powell fatally wounded a white police officer during a shootout in Fourth

Ward. A white mob then abducted Powell from Jefferson Davis Hospital, where he was being treated for gunshot wounds, and lynched him over a bridge. The murder of Powell attracted national attention since it occurred just days before the Democratic National Convention, which would be held in Houston.[73] Both the Chester and Powell cases featured black armed self-defense in Fourth Ward, which showed that black Houstonians would use weapons to protect themselves from violence.

Armed self-reliance could inspire community support in 1920s Houston. After writing a particularly scathing critique of the Klan, Richardson received a note bearing a drawing of a dagger and the words "Nigger, leave town. Don't let the sun go down on you." Rather than flee the city, the editor and a group of friends armed themselves and guarded his home overnight. The Klan never appeared. In this era of racial violence, their neighborhoods were perhaps their best defense against terror.[74] Richardson began carrying a pistol after repeated threats on his life. Hearing rumors that the editor had armed himself in response to these attacks, the chief of police reportedly visited him and said, "Richardson, I understand you carry at all times." When Richardson confirmed that the rumor was true, the chief reportedly replied, "Well, I don't blame you. As long as I'm chief, you don't have to worry about it."[75] The character of racial violence in Jazz Age Houston suggests that local New Negroes had exchanged "Passive Resistance" for the "terrible weapon of Self-Defense," as W. E. B. Du Bois articulated in a 1919 issue of the *Crisis*.[76] Signs carried by Marcus Garvey's supporters in Harlem at a Universal Negro Improvement Association parade in 1920 bore the words "The New Negro Has No Fear," and the visible use of armed self-reliance from African Americans across the nation supported that claim.[77]

Gender politics also fueled male New Negroes' rhetoric on violence and activism in the Bayou City. Black women were quite visible in Houston's public spaces; they traversed the city for work and school, and to find amusement. Male New Negroes often based their definition of manhood on their ability to shield the women in their families and communities from violence. "This age demands REAL HE-MEN," asserted an Independence Heights resident in 1927, "men who love their families and guard with their lives the sanctity of home."[78] Dr. Benjamin Covington, an affluent physician who lived in Third Ward with his wife and daughter, avoided riding public transportation because he could not "be a man" and protect the women from insults hurled at them by white people.[79] Some male New Negroes after World War I even referred to their activism as the "Manhood Movement."[80] Editorials in the *Informer* rooted the Houston Riot of 1917 in a black soldier's defense of a black woman from white policemen. A 1923 editorial reminded readers, "Two local police officers were taking advantage of a defenseless and helpless colored woman and were placing her under arrest attired only in her house garments—she was virtually nude and even not properly dressed to come out on her front porch." While the *Informer* staff did not condone the murders that occurred on August 23, 1917, they reminded readers, "Every truthful person knows that the beating up and shooting at one of the colored sergeants, who remonstrated with a local police officer for the brutal and barbaric manner in which he (the white officer) was treating a colored woman, was really the last straw that broke the camel's back."[81] Examples of violence against black women in Houston, and the legacy of sexual exploitation of slaves and free black women in the South, left African Americans wary about potential assaults from white men. Rape, argues historian Danielle McGuire, "served as a tool of psychological and physical intimidation that expressed white male domination and buttressed white supremacy."[82] Concerns for black women in the growing city fueled New Negro activism.

Even when black women used the *Informer* to expose indignities they faced in a Jim Crow society, male writers used their complaints to appeal to black manhood. In 1919, Libbie Boutte, principal of an elementary school, received a letter in the mail from the Union National Bank of Houston with the suffix "nig" after her name. Boutte sent the letter to the *Informer* offices, and it appeared on the front page. The newspaper showed indignation over the insult to Boutte and posited a solution: "We possess the remedy, the potential strength, within our race, if we will only get up sufficient manhood, backbone and business stamina and launch such businesses among our race."[83] To the *Informer,* black business would shelter the women of their community from indignity. Although Boutte was a community leader, the newspaper's emphasis on "manhood" positioned men as the saviors of the race, and women as figures who needed their protection.

Black women, however, asserted an image that countered the notion that they needed male protection. While domestic labor in white homes was quite common among African American women, the development of black institutions and neighborhoods gave them the opportunity to find white-collar employment and launch their own businesses that catered to members of their race and gender. In the dozens of black public schools, women worked as administrators and teachers. Women like Libbie Boutte assumed leadership positions in their community institutions. Boutte began her professional career as a teacher, and by 1918 the Third Ward resident worked as principal of Eighth Avenue School.[84] Female black migrants also became vocal within the local chapter of the NAACP. Lula B. White and Christia Adair moved to Houston in the early 1920s, and both emerged as leaders within the organization. White eventually worked as the NAACP's executive secretary, with White serving as her administrative assistant. These women actively pushed for black rights, proving that the New Negro movement was not solely a man's game.[85]

Some of the most powerful New Negro articulations of the right to space and the rejection of white supremacy came from black vernacular traditions imported from the countryside. Houstonians who opened fresh issues of the *Informer* on Fridays may have been especially delighted to read about the exploits of a fellow named Cimbee, the protagonist of the weekly column "Cimbee's Ramblings." Cimbee hailed from the piney woods and red dirt roads of East Texas, but by the end of World War I he lived in Houston. An observer of humankind, he spent much of his time wandering through the city and meeting new people. He was especially interested in race relations, and he devoted a significant amount of space in the column to criticizing how race and power functioned in Texas and the South. In 1919, for example, Cimbee embarked on a quest to understand the ways of white folks. He met a white doctor who explained the meaning of the phrase "the white man's burden." Cimbee was interested to learn that, according to the doctor, "the white folks were over here in America tending to their own business, and our fore parents stole some Dutchman's ship and brought ourselves over here and made the white man feed us and clothe us for 200 years. That's where the saying arose, 'The White Man's Burden.'"[86] The use of humor to subvert white supremacy and address interracial concerns became a hallmark of "Cimbee's Ramblings."

Although his *Informer* column depicted real people and places that readers would have recognized, Cimbee was not an actual person. A local writer and educator named Simeon B. Williams created the character, and Cimbee functioned as his alter ego. The name "Cimbee" played on Williams's first name and middle initial—Simeon B. The men also shared a common hometown and migration experience. Like Williams, Cimbee had arrived in Houston from Marshall. He roamed the streets of his new city, and then wrote letters to his friends "Gus" and "Lee" back home that described his adventures. At least twenty years before Langston Hughes's "Jesse B. Semple" character appeared in the *Chicago Defender,* Cimbee strolled through Houston, issuing humorous but biting observations on the people living in the Bayou City.

"Cimbee's Ramblings" served as a community-building tool in a migration city, but also indicates how *Informer* writers conceptualized racial blackness. The column frequently reminded readers of a shared ancestry as descendants of slaves and a common struggle against black degradation. When Cimbee referred to a Dutchman's ship that brought his ancestors into contact with white people, he reminded readers of their history as descendants of Africans who had arrived in Virginia two centuries earlier, in 1619. Williams used humor to remind readers that they had common roots and a longer history of combating white supremacy. Weekly columns mocked the social customs that reinforced the racial hierarchy of Jim Crow society. In one of his first issues in 1919, a white Houstonian refers to Cimbee as "Uncle"—a derisive term for adult black men. Cimbee retorts, "I ain't got no nephews that I remembers that belongs to that particular race . . . but I must have been his uncle cause he said so, and I don't like to argue with kin-folks."[87] By feigning ignorance, Cimbee poked fun at white paternalism while simultaneously protesting social norms that marked black inferiority in the Jim Crow era. White southerners had the power to verbally degrade African Americans by calling them names like "Auntie" and "Uncle." Meanwhile, they expected black people to address them as "ma'am" and "sir." When an adult African American had to call a white child "sir" but could only expect to be called "boy" in return, it left no question as to who was the dominant race.[88]

The column further addressed a shared racial heritage by drawing on older forms of black American folk culture to voice the concerns of a community transitioning to urban life. Williams paid close attention to working-class, rural expression. Cimbee obviously strove to evoke laughs from his readers; the illustration above the column even featured a clownish-looking figure bopping happily along, snapping his fingers. But Cimbee was no simple fool. His column contained humor, but the comedy took the form of a "laughing to keep from crying" sensibility that drew on a rich folkloric tradition of using trickster figures to critique power and subvert authority. Like the popular African American tricksters derived from African forebears, Cimbee celebrated the cunning wisdom of black folk culture while exposing the ignorance of the powerful. In African American folklore, tricksters are not typically the strongest, fastest, or wealthiest characters in the tales, yet they outwit stronger opponents who have access to more resources. The popular Br'er Rabbit routinely dupes quicker foxes that would like to eat him for dinner. He defeats adversaries with his cleverness. Cimbee perhaps most closely resembles the human trickster named John, a fictional slave living in the antebellum South. In countless tales that survived into the twentieth century, John outmatched his master and proved that he was not intellectually weak.[89] African Americans had used these cultural and intellectual traditions for generations to combat notions of black inferiority. Williams reinterpreted these trickster figures in the twentieth century during an era of migration, while highlighting the subversive nature of black working-class expression.[90]

The community-building aspect of "Cimbee's Ramblings" extended to the style of the prose. After the first few issues, Williams wrote "Cimbee's Ramblings" in a dialect that reflected the cadences and rhythms of rural, southern black speech. The character's dialect was a source of humor in the column, but it also served as a sonic indicator of group membership and history. At a time when some educated African Americans would have cringed at the idea of placing rural black dialect on the front page of a "race paper," Williams celebrated that aspect of rural heritage while also using the column to discuss racial problems. Cimbee issued a satire on race relations in 1923, for example, by remarking, "I luvs my w'ite fokes, an' has bin wurkin' hard ever since 1619 ter try ter maik civilized nashun outen 'em." The *Informer* staff heralded his work as a prime example of the vibrancy of African American culture. Editor C. F. Richardson praised Williams as "a delineator of Negro dialect" and "the best writer of his type in American journalism."[91]

When Cimbee reported on Houston in his letters to East Texas, Williams used cultural expression to transmit knowledge about this specific place and its power structure to the droves of migrants entering the city. For example, he discussed black migrants' relationship to the white-dominated legal system in Houston.[92] After W. L. Davis sued Richardson for libel in 1927, Cimbee supported his editor by calling the whole affair "Nigger Mess." Cimbee opined that Davis's insistence upon taking the issue to a city courthouse to be decided upon by a white judge impeded racial progress. Cimbee reminded readers of their roots in rural areas like the Brazos River valley to further ridicule Davis's decision to sue. For Cimbee, the case illustrated that "whut we lurnt down in Brazzus bottom er sum uther bottom 'bout tuckin' awl our lil sturbmints ter de w'ite fokes fer settlement ain't got outen us."[93] By specifically naming the Brazos River valley—an area within the eastern Texas plantation belt—Cimbee used a spatial indicator of group membership. Readers had moved to Houston from similar places, and they had a similar history with white supremacy. The old pattern of dominance and subjugation that had existed in the country, he opined, should not order race relations in the city. Like Huddie Ledbetter, Cimbee used this folk tradition to transmit information and impart wisdom about the realities of Houston in the decade after World War I.

NAACP campaigns and Richardson's editorials in the *Informer* were not, then, the only ways that African Americans voiced their concerns about life in the city or made claims to space. Folk traditions made up what scholar Clyde Woods calls the "blues bloc," an epistemology developed in rural working-class black communities that spread as a result of rural-to-urban migration. As an art form, the blues had allowed rural black southerners to articulate a "collective sensibility in the face of constant attacks by the planta-tion bloc and its allies."[94] "Cimbee's Ramblings" adapted the blues impulse that permeated black artistic expression. As writer Ralph Ellison noted, the blues impulse is a three-step process found in diverse art forms that involves identifying the source of pain, expressing that painful experience in a "near-tragic, near-comic" voice, and finding affirmation of one's existence in the process. The blues often sounded mournful, but embedded in the often-melancholy lyrics was a message of self-affirmation. By singing about travails, blues singers express their humanity.[95]

Thematically, the blues offered an individual's response to a specific or general condition. Just as Cimbee commented on white authority through satire, musicians often conveyed their ideas about status and rank in their songs. In songs by Alger "Texas" Alexander, the singer describes an unjust white power structure that threatens his personal freedom. An itinerant musician, Alexander traveled in and out of Houston in the 1920s and 1930s. He laments in "Levee Camp Moan Blues":

> They accused me of murder
> And I haven't harmed a man . . .
> They have accused me of forgery
> And I can't write my name.[96]

The unnamed "they" of Alexander's song is a criminal justice system that often targeted black men in eastern Texas. Being black increased one's odds of facing a life sentence at a prison farm or even the death penalty. Eighty-four percent of the Texans sentenced to the electric chair between 1924 and 1928 were African American. Of the forty-five Texans who died in the elec-tric chair, seven were white, four were of Mexican descent, and thirty-four were African American. As one black Houstonian noted, the death penalty "was nothing more than legalized lynch law . . . instead of legal prosecution it was racial persecution."[97] Songs like "Levee Camp Moan Blues" and "Midnight Special" provided a cultural response to the hardening of Jim Crow and continued violence against African Americans.

Cimbee did not sing or play guitar, but his antics were steeped in a blues tradition. As Simeon Williams understood, blues-impulse art could also make people laugh. "Sad as the blues may be," writes Langston Hughes, "there's almost always something humorous about them—even if it's the kind of humor that laughs to keep from crying."[98] Cimbee embodied blues-impulse humor. Like generations of singers, poets, novelists, and playwrights, Cimbee acknowledged black struggle, but he articulated this pain in a humorous voice that gave audiences a collective sense of shared struggle and resilience.

Houston's New Negro era was shaped by migrants who drew on their shared history in the rural plantation belt as they established an urban black community. Perplexed by violence, but also emboldened by community-building efforts, wage labor, militant activism, and shared cultural expressions, they strove to redefine themselves in a new place. The *Houston Informer*, led by Richardson and his fiery editorials, became a place where migrants negotiated the transition from rural to urban. Through "Cimbee's Ramblings," Simeon Williams adapted older traditions for a people who were reestablishing a collective racial sensibility in a new place. The character allowed *Informer* readers to feel more urban through the act of reminiscing about a shared past. That collective nostalgia helped them form an identity as urban people.[99] Cimbee reminded readers that they were a community, people who came from the same region and who rebuilt homes in a new place. This idea of a shared past—and a shared racial future—affected how black Houstonians responded collectively to the segregation and racial violence they encountered in the city.

BLACK CULTURE AND BLACK SPACE

The vernacular traditions that singers and writers brought into the city did not just provide commentary on the racial politics of Houston; these cultural expressions became the foundation for sociopolitical and economic projects for black autonomy.[100] This vision for independent black space within the city was made possible by the economic shift that accompanied rural-to-urban migration and the surge in black political activism, but it was largely sustained by the proliferation of cultural forms that bolstered the consumer economy that flourished during the Jazz Age. An urbanizing form of blues music, as well as numerous businesses that catered to women, especially provided the backbone for the consumer economy that aided efforts for black autonomy.

As a growing city with a substantial black population, Houston attracted blues musicians looking for paying audiences. The first generations of blues artists in Houston likely found audiences in vice quarters. When Sammy Price visited Houston for the first time, in the late twenties, the piano player from rural northeastern Texas came in search of the "bordellos and good-time houses" that he heard populated the Houston–Galveston area. Born in the small town of Honey Grove, he had long rejected his family's strict Protestant values by the time he came to the Bayou City. Aside from earning money as a pianist, Price was also a hustler who enjoyed "fast women and nightclubs and gamblers and confidence men." He found his element in Houston. Dubbed "Vinegar Hill" by locals, the oldest entertainment district in Houston originated soon after the Civil War. One Houstonian declared that "Tin Can Alley," the street that led to Vinegar Hill, was "the toughest place in the South." Notoriously short-tempered and quick on the draw, Vinegar Hill habitués acquired a reputation for lawlessness among Houstonians. Down on Tin Can Alley, a three-hundred-pound woman called "Auntie" reportedly dealt cocaine, and "brawls were as common as mongrel cats."[101] In 1908 the city council established a ten-block red-light district called the Reservation in Fourth Ward, and the area reportedly housed over four hundred prostitutes before the local government closed the district after World War I.[102] Both Vinegar Hill and the Reservation served as entertainment districts where earlier generations of musicians could find work.

Urban wages helped build a viable music scene for aspiring artists after the war. More recreational sites emerged within black communities and outside of vice quarters in the 1920s. A growing professional class of musicians could earn a living in one place instead of relying on an itinerant, nomadic existence. Houston had an infrastructure for black entertainment by the end of the 1920s. The city appealed to black migrants who did not necessarily want to make money working at the ship channel or cleaning white homes. Musicians from small towns and farms in East Texas made their way to the Bayou City in search of audiences eager to dance after putting in long hours at work.

Often played by migrants acclimating to the Bayou City, the sounds of the blues filled Houston's swampy air. East Texas blues emphasized guitar licks and moans, a method of vocalization that did not use words. Described by Cornel West as a "guttural cry," the moan illustrates how African Americans tackled "black sadness and sorrow, black agony and anguish, black heartache and heartbreak without fully succumbing to the numbing effects of such misery—to never allow such misery to have the last word."[103] Musicians like Sam "Lightnin'" Hopkins brought these sounds into Houston from the countryside. Hopkins, "a cocky, loping figure with a guitar slung across his back," first wandered into Houston as an itinerant musician in the late 1920s, before permanently settling in the 1930s. Since they could be made by hand, guitars tended to be popular in rural working-class communities in the twentieth century. Country blues musicians often roamed the countryside, stopping in various burgs to play for weekend parties and picnics, so guitars also suited the itinerant lifestyle. Hopkins spent years as a young man traveling the red dirt roads of East Texas in search of his next gig, but the lure of paying audiences convinced him to settle permanently in Houston, where he helped shape the city's blues sound. As music historian Alan Govenar asserts, he "embodied the music's transition from rural East Texas to Houston." He became a fixture at the intersection of Dowling and Holman streets in Third Ward, a place that locals came to known as "Lightnin's Corner."[104]

Musicians' incorporation of new instruments into their repertoire offered sonic representations of the material changes that resulted from migration and wage labor. While Hopkins and other blues artists often came to city with guitars, the popularity of new instruments offered one a sign of black urbanization. Ella Larkin's sixteen-year-old son, Milton, bought himself a trumpet that he called a "pea shooter" for forty-nine dollars with savings from working odd jobs that helped supplement his widowed mother's earnings. From then on, he used the instrument to make more money, earning between fifty cents and a dollar a day by blowing the blues at bus stops.[105] Poor families rarely had the means to purchase pianos. "Pianos were not accessible to black musicians," explained Sammy Price. "If you don't have a piano, how the hell you gonna be a piano player?"[106] But urban churches gave some musicians access to pianos. Sippie Wallace first stroked the black and white keys of a piano in church. Wallace was born Beulah Thomas in Houston in 1898. (She acquired the nickname "Sippie" because of a childhood lisp, and later married a man named Matt Wallace.) She began singing at Shiloh Baptist Church in Fifth Ward, where her father served as deacon, when she was still a young girl. After church elders caught her skipping Sunday school to tinker on the organ, the congregation decided to give her music lessons. Similarly, I. H. "Ike" Smalley learned to master several different instruments while playing in the church orchestra at Antioch Baptist, which eventually led to paying gigs in secular spaces.[107] These instruments allowed musicians to experiment with new ways of playing the blues. By adding new instruments to a genre associated with guitars in the country, these musicians created a style of blues increasingly associated with urban life.

Piano blues especially flourished in Houston due to the Thomas family and a Fourth Ward–based collective of piano players called the Santa Fe Group, named for the railroad line that ran through the neighborhood. Musicians like Robert Shaw, Black Boy Shine, Buster Pickens, Rob Cooper, and Pinetop Burks played in roadhouses near the Santa Fe Railroad. There, they developed a style that combined blues and ragtime. Ragtime pianists improvised melodies with their right hand, while their left hand played repeating bass patterns. Meanwhile, both Sippie and her brother Hersal Thomas played piano in a style that emphasized rich bass patterns, and both wrote blues lyrics to accompany the music they composed. The blues-tinged ragtime of the Santa Fe Group, as well as the Thomas family's piano blues, were some of the first popular styles produced by African Americans in Jazz Age Houston. As these musicians adapted to the city, life in an urban environment affected which instruments they played and the way they played them. Some artists incorporated the sound of the city into their songs. The Santa Fe Group became known for pounding piano melodies that mimicked the sound of the nearby trains.[108]

Some race leaders responded enthusiastically to the emergence of the music scene. C. F. Richardson praised the musical accomplishment of black artists, perhaps because he was also a performer. When he was not editing the *Informer,* Richardson sang with the Coleridge-Taylor Choral Club, played bass guitar, and served as director of the Texas Association of Negro Musicians for the South Texas District. He cited music as proof of the race's achievement: "A music renaissance or revival is taking place in America, and the so-called Negro music is rapidly coming into its rightful place as the music of the classes and masses."[109]

Other prominent black Houstonians did not celebrate the popularity of music emerging from the wards, though. The principal of the city's Booker T. Washington High School, for example, despised the popular music that flourished during the Jazz Age. "My school principal didn't like music," remembered Milton Larkin, who entered Washington High in the 1920s. "He said it was going to hell."[110] The spaces where musicians of color performed in the early days linked the music to lowbrow culture. When he first began blowing his trumpet around the city in the 1920s, Larkin entertained audiences at bus stops: "That was the life of the band—to play at bus stops," he recalled.[111] When these musicians did move indoors, they often played in places associated with the copious consumption of liquor and/or prostitution, like Vinegar Hill and the Reservation. Some critics considered blues, as well as early jazz, to be lowbrow forms, then, since the music did not originate in the physical structures that people of European descent typically associated with high art. Europeans and elite white Americans deemed a form of music respectable only when it was performed in concert halls. These concert halls, in turn, mimicked the structure of churches in Western society. Listeners celebrated music produced in these venues because it reminded them of the experience of religious worship. Indoor music performed in a concert hall was prestigious; music played in the streets or in saloons was not.[112]

Nevertheless, the proliferation of blues helped bolster a black consumer economy in Houston. Musicians and business owners profited from the growing number of wage-earning music lovers who would pay for entertainment. Music also provided alternatives for black women in a city where so many worked in domestic service. Sippie Wallace and Victoria Spivey parlayed their talent into national acclaim with recordings in the 1920s.[113] Wallace eventually worked with New Orleans–born musicians Louis Armstrong and King Oliver after she left Houston. By 1923 "The Texas Nightingale" was in Chicago recording lyrics like "When I get full of my moonshine, I'ma take your man for mine" and other songs written by her or with her brother Hersal.[114] I. H. Smalley's musical prowess attracted attention from other musicians, which enabled Smalley to book gigs before he finished high school. "I'd have to leave the church orchestra on Sunday nights to go make the little gig," he said.[115]

By the late 1920s, more venues emerged that offered opportunities for performers to play for wage-earning audiences. These establishments joined other businesses that sold culture products to African Americans and formed the backbone of the consumer economy. West Dallas Street emerged as the center of the black commercial world of Jazz Age Houston. (See figure 2.) That thoroughfare housed 95 percent of the city's black-owned businesses as early as 1920.[116] The most popular music venue in the decade following World War I was a dance hall in the Pilgrim Building, where the owners of a music club booked local acts and touring bands. The black-owned Pilgrim Building boasted gold-colored bricks, marble and granite walls, elevators, and a garden roof. The four-story structure at 221 West Dallas Street,

FIGURE 2. Black business district on West Dallas Street in the San Felipe district (Fourth Ward). Houston Metropolitan Research Center, Houston Public Library.

in the heart of the San Felipe district, was the first major shopping and entertainment area to offer services black people could not obtain in white-owned stores. Other black-owned businesses made the San Felipe district a center of black culture and enterprise. Just a few blocks away from the Pilgrim Building, fraternal societies and other local groups and businesses could meet at the Odd Fellows Hall on Louisiana Street.[117] "Old Freedman's [T]own was such a wonderful place to grow up in because we were so sheltered," remembered Houstonian Paulette Williams Grant. "We had everything right in the neighborhood, you know, there were stores, your beautician, your school, your music teacher—everybody was right there and it was like just a big, happy family."[118]

Visitors paid particular attention to black economic growth in Houston. By the 1930s, observers noted the products of previous decades of community-building efforts. "More businesses are owned and operated by Negroes here than in any other Southern city," commented a writer with the Work Projects Administration.[119] When Howard University–educated scholar Lorenzo Greene visited Houston in 1930 to sell black history books, he was impressed by the "young and democratic" character of the African American population and its successful businesses. Greene worked for black historian Carter G. Woodson, founder of the Association for the Study of Negro Life and History and the *Journal of Negro History*. Woodson paid for

Greene to travel to black communities across the South and Southwest to sell history books, and the traveling salesman kept a journal detailing his exploits. While in Houston, Greene spent a day selling books in the San Felipe district. In the pages of his journal, he marveled at the Odd Fellows Hall, the Franklin Beauty School, the Houston Negro Chamber of Commerce, the Harris County Young Negro Civic Club, and the Pilgrim Life Insurance Company building on West Dallas, which he described as "the most beautiful [building] owned by Negroes I have seen." During his time in the city, Greene noted that local African Americans had "about eight colored gasoline filling stations, one finance company, several chain drug stores and independent drug stores, several insurance companies, beauty shops, two hat shops, one dry goods store, ten or more groceries, one soda water manufacturer, several ice men, several fruit dealers, and a theater." He added that about eighty black physicians and fifteen black dentists worked in the city, and that Houston's three black high schools made it unique among southern cities. After his journey through the city, Greene concluded that African Americans in Houston were "the most enterprising and most appreciative group of race people in the South."[120]

Black Houstonians found more opportunities to open businesses in the 1920s, which provided an alternative to working for white employers. Enough wage-earning African Americans lived in Houston neighborhoods to support enterprises launched by members of their race. A study produced by Fisk University in 1930 estimated that 890,000 African Americans living in seventeen of the largest southern cities, Houston included, had $308 million in purchasing power.[121] Some African American business owners used their race as a selling point. The James Green Grocery and Meat Market placed ads that urged readers to "[g]ive your race man a trial, and be convinced that he will treat you right." A dentist named W. J. Howard placed a picture of himself alongside an advertisement for his office, alerting readers that he was a black man.[122]

The high number of businesses and institutions was an outgrowth of the city's size. Houston's boundaries grew alongside its population. "The city occupies an incredibly large area," commented Greene during his visit in 1930. "It seemed as if we would never be able to get out of Houston."[123] A decade later, when the city was the twenty-first largest in the nation, Houston occupied approximately seventy-three square miles. Boston's population, by contrast, was nearly twice as large Houston's at the time, but at forty-six square miles, Beantown was nearly half the physical size of the Bayou City.[124]

The spatial dynamics of Houston influenced black community-building efforts. Since they lived in several different neighborhoods, by necessity black migrants had to create and maintain businesses and institutions across the sprawling city. The wards had their own black business and entertainment centers, most notably West Dallas Street in the San Felipe district, Lyons Avenue in Fifth Ward, and Dowling Street in Third Ward. The geographically dispersed population meant that black Houstonians were not historically confined to one part of town like their peers in some northern industrializing cities.

The existence of these venues also allowed black entertainers to take part in an economy that was not completely dominated by white people. In this era of Jim Crow laws, police violence, and threats from the Klan, black Houstonians strove to distinguish their neighborhoods from a larger Jim Crow city. In fact, they called the act of leaving the wards and visiting downtown Houston "going into town." Houston proper was physically and psychologically distant from their neighborhoods. When black Houstonians went into town, though, they sat at the back of a streetcar. They could not try on hats in the stores that lined Main Street. If they could gain access to these shops at all, they entered through a back door and waited until all white customers had been helped. But in their neighborhoods, which dotted each of the wards, black Houstonians felt some sense of control of their own space.

As black communities swelled and violence continued, activists campaigned for more businesses in an effort to establish autonomous spaces where African Americans could conduct their daily business without coming into contact with white people, and protect themselves if a white mob tried to attack. When black women complained that white salesclerks and retail workers insulted them while they shopped downtown, the *Informer* pushed readers to create and support black businesses: "Our women have been assaulted, cursed, insulted and generally maltreated in several local stores owned and operated by other races for their own benefit, and yet they are compelled to continue to patronize these stores and thereby make it possible for additional impositions and cruelties to be heaped upon them with impunity." By the 1920s mass-produced and mass-marketed goods had created a culture of mass consumption in which women were central actors. The responsibility of purchasing household goods and clothing for the family largely fell to women, especially in cities where fewer food goods could be grown or raised at home.[125] This meant that black women faced segregated stores on a regular basis. The *Informer*'s solution to this problem was to create and support black-owned businesses. Writers campaigned for a black department store in the downtown shopping district. Not only would women be shielded from disrespect from white store workers; the store would also economically benefit black communities because young African Americans could work there. Throughout the year 1921 editorials stressed the need for a black-run department store, arguing that people who did not support the efforts were "content to forever serve in the 'Sambo,' 'Uncle Ned,' 'Aunt Dinah' and 'Sally Ann' role from both a political, commercial and civic viewpoint."[126]

Black activists recognized that economic autonomy and self-government undermined white supremacy. Cliff Richardson, Jr., always asserted that his father's struggles with the Ku Klux Klan and city police officers were due to their anger over his economic autonomy. If white Houstonians met an African American who was self-employed, Richardson recalled, "the stuff was in the fan."[127] After all, what did white supremacy mean if black people were running their own affairs and did not submit to white authority? Billie Mayfield, editor of Houston's Ku Klux Klan newspaper in the 1920s, once asserted, "[T]he negro must realize, and does realize that this is a white man's country. [It is] to be owned by the white race, to be run by the white race, and that to divide its control between two races will only in the end bring on bloody conflicts and fiery prejudices that will finally result in a war of extermination."[128] Through the construction and management of businesses and institutions in Houston's black neighborhoods, African Americans strove for autonomy, and they understood that this independence was tantamount to their ability to live outside of white supremacy. Houstonian Dr. "Teddy" Bryant made this message clear when he wrote to the white Americans who felt the need to dominate his economic, political, and personal affairs: "Simply loose me and let me go."[129]

Black business aided this effort for autonomy. The black sections of the wards were, as Houstonian Thelma Scott Bryant described, "self-contained." Bryant came of age on Live Oak Street in Third Ward in a house her parents purchased for fifteen hundred dollars. When she rode the streetcar to school in Fourth Ward, she passed through a neighborhood where black business flourished: "Well, there were many thriving businesses around the high school. I remember we had an ice cream factory right next door where we liked to go and buy ice cream cones. There was a dry goods store, restaurants, barbecue stands, funeral parlor—every kind of business that the Negro had, it was more or less contained in that area." Black enclaves in the wards offered a sense of place that former slaves could not find in Houston proper. The wards had schools, churches, shops, and restaurants, so African Americans left only for economic reasons. "We had everything we needed for our entertainment," asserted Bryant.[130]

Businesses that sold culture products to black women especially thrived in the 1920s. Some local women profited from an emerging beauty and fashion industry. Since African Americans were not allowed to try on hats in the white-owned stores on Main Street, O'Neta "Pink" Cavitt opened a hat shop of her own in the Pilgrim Building.[131] When assessing the state of the race for the year 1927, the *Informer* cited these businesses as examples of how black women contributed to the race's achievements: "In the land of progress, colored women of America, in organization and economic attainment, are setting a marvelous pace."[132] When Cimbee made his way through Houston, he noted businesses owned by black women. In 1924, for example, the rambler stopped into Madame Nobia Franklin's beauty parlor in the Pilgrim Building. Franklin created an empire around beauty culture, capitalizing upon wage-earning African Americans, who by World War I had more "expendable income and access" to mass-produced consumer goods.[133] Born in the small town of Cuero, Texas, Nobia A. Franklin began selling and creating products when she moved to San Antonio as a young woman. She operated a business in Fort Worth before settling in Houston, where she established a school and salon sometime between 1915 and 1917. By 1919 Franklin was a local celebrity. The *Informer* entertained readers with stories of her lavish parties, even announcing the menu and guest list of a dinner party she threw in 1921. They printed her travel plans when she took an extended out-of-state trip, and when Franklin renovated her downtown Houston parlor in 1924, the paper provided a detailed description of the new décor.[134] Because the black literacy rate passed 50 percent in the first decades of the twentieth century, print ads could reach more people, and local businesses acknowledged the importance of that market by advertising in newspapers. Women like Franklin used black newspapers to further their enterprise.[135] Few issues of the *Informer* reached black Houston without an advertisement from Franklin's company. Although she also opened a school and business in Chicago, Franklin retained her iconic status in Houston.[136]

The most lucrative black enterprises in the country were part of the beauty business geared toward women. Historian Tiffany Gill argues that beauty culturists "were among the most economically autonomous members of the black community in the twentieth century."[137] Nationally, Franklin's business ranked third behind Annie M. Turnbo-Malone's company, Poro, and Madame C. J. Walker's beauty empire. And, judging from the number of advertisements in the *Informer,* several other women in Houston alone gave Madame Franklin competition. Madame Janie C. Smith's Hair Preparations advertised a six-week hair treatment for $1.10, while Mrs. J. D. Collins sold the Collins Hair Grower from O'Neil Street.[138] In 1925, the Madame Rose C. Wiley-Williams School of Beauty Culture opened at 1301 Meador Street in Houston, and Wiley-Williams used the location as a salon, school for beauticians, and store that sold her pressing oils (products that aided the hair-straightening process), shampoo, and "Hair Grower."[139] Obviously, these products were popular. Every young woman in the 1928 yearbook for Houston's Booker T. Washington High School, for example, wore her hair in a straightened style.[140]

Built around an emerging black urban culture, these businesses contributed to a consumer economy that fueled anti–Jim Crow activism and provided a strategy for subverting white authority. Black-owned businesses meant that blacks could receive services from members of their own race without bowing to the spatial notions of race and hierarchy they encountered "in town." Furthermore, the existence of a consumer economy allowed black Houstonians to distance themselves economically and psychologically from the plantation power they sought to escape via migration. Black Houstonians used these to articulate an alternate sense of place in a Jim Crow city. Activism centered on the establishment of autonomous neighborhoods that gave African Americans a sense of ownership and authority over black-majority spaces. Their popular culture also contributed to African Americans' efforts to establish an alternate geography in a Jim Crow society. Urban wages allowed for the establishment of physical structures for the dissemination of musical styles, and the new sounds that emanated from those spaces provided aural evidence of urbanization. In the process, activists, writers, musicians, and other actors of the New Negro era established a black urban subjectivity. And when people from diverse backgrounds began to settle in the wards, the history of black community building and activism in these neighborhoods informed black residents' reactions to newcomers.

TWO

Old Wards, New Neighbors

ON THE MORNING OF THE FLOOD, the Prejean girls rose early to begin their household chores, just as they did every day. The familiar routine came to a halt on that particular July morning, however, when twelve-year-old Mable, the eldest, noticed floodwater creeping steadily toward the family's farm near Scott, Louisiana, a rural area west of Lafayette. Alarmed, Mable called her father. Victorien Prejean ventured outside and placed a stick in the ground to mark how rapidly the water was rising. After re-marking the water line several times, Prejean decided that it was no longer safe to remain at home. The family packed as many personal items as they could fit into a buggy wagon and evacuated to higher ground. When the Prejeans returned home days later, they found their farm in ruins: floodwater had destroyed the crops, drowned the livestock, and risen over three feet inside the house. The only animal that remained was the horse that had pulled their wagon to safety. Rebuilding would have taken more time and money than the large Prejean clan had at its disposal, so, hearing rumors about economic opportunities in Texas, they decided to leave Louisiana and move west of the Sabine River. The French-speaking Catholic family eventually settled in Houston's Fifth Ward, near the black neighborhood in that area.[1] (See figure 3.)

During that same summer of 1927, a young woman named Janie Gonzales hitchhiked her way to Houston with only an apple and twelve cents to her name. Gonzales was born in Sandyfork, Texas, in 1908, and during her childhood her Mexican-born parents worked on various cotton farms in the south-central part of the state. The eighteen-year-old woman decided to leave rural life behind in 1926. She lived in Austin for a year before she and a friend decided to try their luck in Houston. After hitchhiking all day, they arrived in the Bayou City at around 6:30 in the evening. "[W]e thought we had never seen anything

FIGURE 3. Agnes (Sonnier) and Victorien Prejean with their first child, Julius, in 1903. Photo courtesy of Denise Labrie and the Prejean family.

so big in our lives," Gonzales remembered. Since she had worked in cotton fields most of life, she got a job at a cotton compress company in Houston. (See figure 4.) "I had been raising cotton all those years," she said, "so I knew how to sell my cotton, buy my cotton, sample as to whether it was first-grade or third-grade." Gonzales moved to Fifth Ward, where her sister resided on Wayne Street. She immediately noticed evidence of black community building. When Gonzales walked to her job in downtown Houston, she passed through what she called "a complete black city" in Fifth Ward.[2]

The city that Gonzales and the Prejean family encountered was in the throes of transformation. Once a sleepy town on the banks of Buffalo Bayou,

FIGURE 4. Felix and Janie (Gonzales) Tijerina. Felix Tijerina, Sr.,
Family Papers, Houston Metropolitan Research Center, Houston
Public Library.

interwar Houston was a bustling city with little memory of its former status
as a frontier community on the western edge of Dixie. The railroad yards
and ship channel docks held the promise of wage labor for farmers and
sharecroppers, and thousands responded. They headed southwest to Houston
using the red dirt roads of East Texas; they trekked westward from the flood-

ravaged swamps of lower Louisiana; they trudged eastward from central Texas farm country; and they crossed the Rio Grande from south of the border in order to escape a Mexican nation torn apart by revolution. As new groups settled into the city, Texans with English surnames like Berry, Sparks, Richardson, Mayfield, and Price encountered people with Spanish and French names like Gonzales, Tijerina, Chevalier, Prejean, and Metoyer. Around twelve thousand Afro-Louisianians and fifteen thousand ethnic Mexicans lived in Houston by 1930. Of the 63,337 Houstonians marked as "Negro" in the 1930 census, around 19 percent were born in Louisiana. In total, one-quarter of the people who migrated to the city between World Wars I and II hailed from Louisiana. At the same time, the ethnic Mexican population grew from less than 1 percent in the early twentieth century to over 5 percent in 1940.[3] Interwar Houston was beginning to look and sound like a different city.

The community-building experiences of Spanish- and French-speaking migrants reveal the multiple ways that race operated in a segregated migration city. Migrants moved into a society where Jim Crow defined their status at the state level. But at the local level, a wide range of racial subjectivities, cultural practices, and new neighborhoods reveal the diversity that segregation laws denied. As migrants moved into Houston, the ways that they defined themselves as racial subjects could differ from legal definitions of race. The law counted Creoles of color as black, and ethnic Mexicans as white; however, their experiences in southwestern Louisiana, the Rio Grande Valley, central Texas, and Mexico created notions of race and hierarchy that were not rooted in a black/white binary. Sex across the color line in the Americas produced multiple identities that Jim Crow laws ignored, but even in the presence of segregation, some migrants cultivated racial subjectivities that acknowledged histories of mixing between Indians, Africans, and Europeans. Their distinct racial subjectivities influenced the ways that migrants related to one another and built community.

The emergence of new social spaces and the diversity of sounds that escaped from those spaces also indicated the demographic shift happening in Houston. Migrants reshaped Houston's wards into ethnic enclaves where they could live around people with similar racial subjectivities. Physical changes in Second Ward and Fifth Ward provided the earliest signs of Houston's gradual shift from a town with a largely Anglo/African American racial dynamic to a multiethnic metropolis. Migrants marked these spaces with French and Spanish place-names that distinguished them from the rest of English-language-dominated Houston. The diversity of sonic practices emanating from these neighborhoods further revealed the local diversity that legal categories obscured.

In some cases, migrants' distinct racial subjectivities were constituted through culture. Different sonic practices, including language and musical culture, marked the difference between Creoles of color and black Texans. Music was a core aspect of black social life in Houston, a cultural practice that strengthened a consumer economy used to combat the most debasing aspects of segregation. Yet Creoles of color nurtured a different set of cultural practices that did not conform to mainstream understandings of racial blackness. People of Mexican descent were also quite a diverse group. They were Tejano and Mexican, so people from opposite sides of the Rio Grande noted their differences in music and speech when they made contact. Both groups of ethnic Mexicans brought cultural practices into Houston that marked them as different from Anglos, even if they legally stood on the same side of the color line.

The spaces, sounds, and racial subjectivities cultivated by people like Janie Gonzales and the Prejean family signaled that a more complex racial landscape was taking shape beneath Houston's black/white veneer. Their community-building efforts reveal the myriad understandings of race that circulated in the United States during this age of migration and urbanization.

FRENCHTOWN AND BLACK FIFTH WARD

The growing Afro-Creole presence in Houston could largely be linked to two factors—labor opportunities in the Bayou City, and dire economic conditions exacerbated by natural disaster in southwestern Louisiana. Devastating effects of the Great Mississippi Flood of 1927 encouraged people like the Prejeans to leave Louisiana and move to Texas. On the morning of Good Friday, April 15, record-setting amounts of rain in the states of Missouri, Illinois, Arkansas, Mississippi, and Louisiana caused the Mississippi River to overflow. Floodwaters damaged a swath of land from the Midwest to the Gulf Coast. After only one week, the *New York Times* reported that seventy-five hundred square miles of the Mississippi Valley were underwater and sixty thousand people had lost their homes. By early May, thirteen parishes of northern Louisiana were flooded; the water reached the bayou land to the south a week later. Growing numbers of "shivering and hungry" evacuees crowded the riverbanks. As reports of the flood filled national newspapers, journalists wrote about the effects on black southerners. The *Times* noted that the "Negro tenant farmers" that made up the majority of levee towns on the river had lost nearly all of their possessions. Meanwhile, the *Houston Informer* reminded readers that "[s]ince so many of our people reside in the lowlands around most of the Southern rivers," black Americans should aid in relief efforts. C. F. Richardson announced that the Coleridge-Taylor Choral Club would stage a benefit concert on May 1.[4] While Houstonians read about the flood and attended these benefits, Louisianians poured into the city that spring and summer.

By the 1930s, the trek from southwestern Louisiana to Texas was so popular that it became part of regional folklore. Song lyrics spoke of men leaving family behind in order to make a new life in the Lone Star State. When a Cajun singer called Mr. Bornu performed a song called "Belle" that described taking the train home from Texas to visit his ailing sweetheart in Louisiana, he echoed the sentiments of thousands of workers who left family in the country while they chased jobs in places like Houston. Songs like Bornu's "Belle," and "When I Left Home for Texas," by Joe Falcon and Leona Breaux, circulated east and west of the Sabine. By the time Alan Lomax made his way through Louisiana during the Great Depression to record examples of regional folk music, he noted that the theme of migrating to Texas was "ubiquitous" in local songs.[5]

The increased migration of Louisianians to the Bayou City occurred in the decade after boosters promoted it as "Heavenly Houston" and stories of urban wealth inspired countless people to migrate from the countryside. When Anderson Moss moved to the city in 1928 after the price of rice fell in his hometown of Maurice, Louisiana, he heard stories of Houstonians who flaunted legendary riches. A man called "Silver Dollar Jim West" was said to have built a tunnel lined with silver dollars that connected his house with his mother's home a block and a half away. He allegedly hired a crew of men just to keep the coins shiny. "Sometimes he'd go to where you were working," Moss recalled, "he'd line you up, and he'd throw a bunch of silver dollars in the air. He'd say, 'Come on fellows, I'm going to see how many y'all can catch.' It was just like feeding a bunch of chickens."[6] Stories of affluent Houstonians like Silver Dollar West contributed to the city's economic appeal.

Just as labor had lured East Texans to the city after World War I, the availability of industrial wage labor also attracted the largely rural population of southwestern Louisiana. French-speaking Gilbert Jacquet of

Broussard, Louisiana, for example, moved to Fifth Ward after being hired by the Southern Pacific Railroad to build train engines. He eventually sent for his wife, Marquette, and their three sons. Moving away from Louisiana meant they had to leave family members behind; in Broussard, other Jacquets had lived near their farm. But in Houston, industrial labor improved their economic standing. In Louisiana, the Jacquets had rented land on a farm; by 1930, after working and living in Houston for a few years, they owned a home worth twenty-seven hundred dollars on Welton Street.[7] Other employers hired Pelican State migrants readily, and Louisianians eagerly accepted the economic opportunities. "Louisiana people took over this town," Anderson Moss boasted. "All you had to do was say you was from Louisiana, and they would hire you right there." Ernest Henry, another migrant, asserted that he quickly found employment in Houston because Louisianians had a reputation for being hard workers: "Myself, that's how I got hired. The man wouldn't hire nobody if he wasn't from Louisiana."[8]

A growing cluster of Louisianians settled on the northern edge of Fifth Ward, and this choice of location was perhaps due to the area's proximity to labor. Approximately five hundred French-speaking Louisiana families recruited to work for the Southern Pacific Railroad began moving there in 1922. (See figure 5.) The Southern Pacific and Missouri Pacific lines ran through Fifth Ward, so workers could live near their jobs.[9] Because the Southern Pacific recruited laborers from Louisiana, railroad employment was common in Fifth Ward. In 1930, 23 percent of the residences in the area most densely populated with Louisianians housed men who worked in railroad shops. Other men commonly found work at the ship channel, at the cotton and oil mills, and as steamship stevedores. Over a quarter of the women in the area worked for wages, and 96 percent of those female laborers cleaned, cooked, or laundered clothing.[10]

When Louisianians began making homes in Fifth Ward in the 1920s, they settled near a black community that had existed since Reconstruction. Black Fifth Ward had continued to expand since World War I. The "complete black city" that Janie Gonzales described mostly lay between Jensen Drive and Chew Street. By 1925, over forty African American–owned businesses lined Lyons Avenue, the main artery of the black neighborhood on the north side. Phillis Wheatley High School, built in 1927, accommodated the growing community. Routinely ranked as "one of the largest black high schools in America" in the Jim Crow era, the school housed sixty teachers and over twenty-six hundred students.[11] When Lorenzo J. Greene visited Houston in

FIGURE 5. Southern Pacific Railroad workers, 1931. Burns Family Collection, The African American Library at the Gregory School, Houston Public Library.

1930, he praised the school: "Wheatley High School, which for sheer artistic beauty, surpasses any colored school that I have yet seen."[12] African Americans in Houston championed the maintenance and protection of black communities as an issue of race pride, and they used neighborhoods like Fifth Ward as buffers against white supremacy. Increasingly, though, the area filled with French-speaking people from Louisiana.

Louisianians tended to move near one another as they settled into the northern section of Fifth Ward. On the fringes of a black community, the Prejeans and their neighborhoods helped build the place locals dubbed "Frenchtown." Bordered by Jensen Drive on its west end and Waco Street to the east, Frenchtown was already taking shape by 1930. Families from the Pelican State especially clustered in the ten-block area north of Liberty Road. Over 80 percent of residents of Delia, Josephine, and Lelia streets hailed from Louisiana, for example. The Prejean family settled on Delia, where they lived next to other Louisianians with French names like Landry, Bareis, Hollier, Bronarard, Darron, Bibaunt, and Broussard. Less than eight years after the establishment of Frenchtown, and only three years after the Mississippi flood, nearly half of the people living in that section of Fifth Ward were native Louisianians.[13]

Black Houstonians noted the presence of Louisianians in the *Informer*, and references to that group increased over time as their numbers grew. The weekly newspaper began to appeal to the Louisiana-born population in the 1920s with a new section called "New Orleans News." (The majority of migrants who moved to Houston from the Pelican State hailed from rural southwestern Louisiana, not New Orleans; however, the *Informer* staff likely had an easier time finding news from the city than from rural areas.) Using the headline "Spicy! Racy! Newsy!" for that section, the newspaper perhaps tried to expand its circulation by including content about Louisiana. "New Orleans News" contained information on Southern Pacific fares between Houston and Louisiana towns, as well as news items about activism among New Orleans's black population. As the population of Louisianians grew, so did the section of the *Informer* dedicated to their home state. The section began as a few columns, but by 1929 it had expanded to several pages.

In the pages of the *Informer*, writers often referred to the year 1619 in discussions of race, using the arrival of sub-Saharan Africans to the Chesapeake colonies three centuries earlier to remind readers of a shared racial history; however, the Louisianians moving into Frenchtown did not acknowledge a racial heritage originating in the slave society that British settlers established in colonial Virginia. They linked their history to French and Spanish rule over colonial Louisiana and the distinctive racial order that developed there. Black East Texans and people of color from Louisiana thus came from societies with different racial histories. Consequently, these groups did not share the same constructions of racial blackness.

Migrants from southwestern Louisiana who created Frenchtown recognized three racial groups: white, black, and Creole of color. The notion that Creoles of color represented a separate racial group was shaped by their history in Louisiana, especially the fact that their ancestors had not been enslaved in 1861 when the Civil War began. Social divisions among people with varying amounts of African ancestry were, therefore, based on their ancestors' antebellum legal status. Creoles of color who moved to Houston were descendants of a free, mixed-race population that emerged from colonial Louisiana in the eighteenth century. Coerced sexual relationships, complex negotiations, and outright rape led to the appearance of a sizable mixed-race population in the colony. The French (and later, Spanish) men who engaged in sexual liaisons with African woman often emancipated the black slave women who bore their children. Most of the slaves in colonial Louisiana who gained their freedom were either the concubines or children of slave-holding white men.[14] Mixed-race people with white fathers and black mothers became the progenitors of a group known as the *gens de couleur libre* (free people of color). Released from the yoke of bondage, the *gens de couleur libre* made up a separate racial group in French Louisiana, with members that considered themselves to be neither white nor black, but a combination of both races.[15] Their freedom, and the fact that many owned land granted to them by their white fathers, gave them legal and economic status that distinguished them from the enslaved population. A proverb shared by people of African descent in colonial Louisiana depicts a triracial society made up of black, white, and "mulatto" people, and suggests economic competition between the groups:

> *Nègue pas capab marché sans mais dans poche,*
> *Ce pou volé poule,*
> *Milâtre pas capab marché sans la corde dans poche,*
> *Ce pou volé choual,*
> *Blanc pas capab marché sans l'arzan dans poche,*
> *Ce pou volé filles.*

> Negro cannot walk without corn in his pocket,
> It is to steal chickens,
> Mulatto cannot walk without rope in his pocket,
> It is to steal horses,
> White cannot walk without money in his pocket,
> It is to steal girls.[16]

The song used economic status to articulate racial hierarchy between different groups. Enslaved Africans lacked food, so they stole chickens. While mulattoes had enough to eat; they did not own horses. The white men at the top of the hierarchy possessed chickens, horses, and money, which enabled them to marry or entice women using financial negotiations. Class reinforced the divisions found in the triracial society.

Many of the migrants living in Frenchtown were the descendants of land-owning families who had been free before the Civil War. Before moving to Houston, Clay Chevalier came of age surrounded by family members who owned land in Saint Martin Parish. His paternal grandparents, Sylvestre and Marie, both born free in around 1840, oversaw a plantation. Mulatto planters named Placide and Arsene Chevalier also lived in the vicinity. Likewise, members of the Prejean family considered themselves to be both African and French, with roots in France and Canada. Their first French ancestor to leave Europe, Jean Prejean, moved to Acadia (modern-day Nova Scotia) from Brittany in 1671. One of his descendants later set sail for Louisiana in the mid-1700s, eventually settling in Opelousas. (The term *Cajun,* which refers to descendants of the French-Canadians who settled in southwest Louisiana, is derived from the word *Acadian.*) In addition to farming and raising cattle and horses in the French colony, the Prejean family purchased slaves. The mixed-race side of the family began with Louis Gustave Prejean, born in Louisiana in 1812. By the late 1850s, he was a widower raising three young children. At some point, he entered into a sexual relationship with an enslaved black woman. That union produced a child named Victor Prejean, whom Louis Gustave freed. Generations of white and mixed-race descendants of Louis Gustave Prejean lived in the same parish until the twentieth century, when the Afro-French branch of the family tree stretched across the Sabine River to Houston.[17]

In some cases, the relationships they cultivated with white family members also shaped Creole of color racial subjectivity. The "relations of affection" that existed between some white men and their Afro-French children led these fathers to consider their offspring "not as Negroes but as persons of their blood."[18] Some Cajuns even acknowledged kinship ties with Creoles of color. The white physician Louis Agree Prejean, also a descendant of Louis Gustave, made house calls to his first cousin Victor when family members needed medical attention. Victor also received formal education, financed by his white father. He was able to pass land to his son, Victorien, who moved to Texas with his family in 1927.[19] With links to white society, land, and freedom, Creoles of color considered themselves to be a distinct racial group. They saw few similarities between themselves and the descendants of people whose ancestors were enslaved at the onset of the Civil War. As historian Blair L. M. Kelley writes, "Creoles of color had an exclusive identity; their sense of self was fixed in the past, drawn from their French ancestors and their forebears' free status in the age of slavery."[20]

In the postbellum South, though, Jim Crow laws targeted both the descendants of free people of color (who became known as Creoles of color in post-emancipation Louisiana) and the former slaves who asserted economic and political rights. Granted the right to vote with the Fifteenth Amendment, freedmen and Creoles of color entered political office, served on juries, and posed a significant threat to white supremacy. Republican lawmakers also legalized interracial marriage in Louisiana from 1870 until 1894.[21] During that time, white men like Eriole Sonnier could marry black women, as he did when he wed his wife, Marie, sometime in the 1870s. By 1880 Eriole and Marie Sonnier were married and raising a family together in Lafayette.[22] White Democrats, eager to seize power from black and Creole Republicans, drafted legal measures to segregate Creoles of color alongside black descendants of slaves. In 1890, they passed the Louisiana Separate Car Law, which stated that black people were restricted to the smoking car of trains during travel. Creoles of color were alarmed to learn that the designation of "negro" applied to them as well as to the formerly enslaved people who had been emancipated by the Civil War. The descendants of *gens de couleur libre* balked at the idea that they should submit to segregation laws.[23]

Creoles of color and black descendants of slaves in urban Louisiana organized to protest segregation. Homer A. Plessy, a so-called octoroon from New Orleans who was seven-eighths white, challenged the Separate Car Law in 1892 by purchasing a first-class ticket and demanding to be seated. A group of Creoles called the Comité des Citoyens ("Committee of Citizens") chose Plessy as a test case, likely since he bore the physical characteristics of a white man. The Criminal Court of New Orleans found him guilty of violating the segregation ordinance, but with white northern attorney Albion Tourgée acting as his lawyer, he appealed the decision and the case went to the U.S. Supreme Court.[24] In his brief for the Plessy case in 1895, Tourgée challenged the very concept of race to prove that racial separation could not be legally sanctioned in Louisiana or elsewhere: "Is not the question of race, scientifically considered, very often impossible of determination?" he inquired. "Is not the question of race, legally considered, one impossible to be determined, in the absence of statutory definition?" Furthermore, noted Tourgée, it was infeasible for the law to determine the racial status of people of mixed ancestry.[25] The Supreme Court decided against Plessy in 1896, however, and declared that "separate but equal" facilities for blacks and whites were constitutional, and that Plessy had indeed violated the law. The Supreme Court's sanctioning of the Anglo-enforced racial binary with the 1896 *Plessy v. Ferguson* decision has roots in the racial hybridity of the western South.

Plessy not only became the legal blueprint for racial segregation in the South; the decision established a legal precedent for defining blackness for the twentieth century. By ruling that the state of Louisiana could demand that a man who was seven-eighths European sit in the "colored" section of a train car, the Supreme Court also created a legal basis for counting people of mixed ancestry as Negro. *Plessy v. Ferguson* legitimized the Anglo-enforced black/white binary that denied mixed-race people any privileges of whiteness.

Post-*Plessy,* the state's definition of race differed from how Creoles of color defined themselves as racial subjects. Creoles of color maintained their identity as a distinct group, regardless of how the law classified them. The population living in rural Louisiana could perhaps avoid the binary imposed by Jim Crow laws a bit more easily than those living in New Orleans. In towns and cities, segregation laws ordered urban space. But rural Creoles of color living on farms did not encounter segregated seating on streetcars or colored water fountains on a daily basis. Those spatial signs of racial hierarchy were not as visible in the country hamlets of the southwestern part of the state. "I never heard anybody say that we were black or white or whatever," recalled rural-born Inez Prejean about her life in Louisiana before moving to Texas. "We were just mixed and we were a big family, and we didn't make any difference."[26]

Furthermore, they preserved their culture and property by marrying other Creoles of color. Frank Sonnier, the product of the interracial marriage between Eriole Sonnier and the former slave Marie, eventually wed Alzina Breaux, the daughter of a free woman of color who owned a cotton farm in Jennings. That union produced Agnes Sonnier, who later married Victorien Prejean, the grandson of a former slave and slave owner.[27] With ancestors who had been free before the Civil War and land inherited from white fathers, the Sonnier-Prejean offspring did not think of themselves as the same race as black descendants of slaves, and they carried that subjectivity into Houston.

Socially, some Creoles of color maintained a distinction between themselves and descendants of slaves. A folkloric tale reveals how divisions between Creoles of color and other Afro-Louisianians remained part of southwestern Louisiana society in the twentieth century. According to legend, a black accordion player once received an invitation to perform at a country dance party. When the excited musician arrived at the fete, however, he discovered that he was the only dark-skinned person in a room full of Creoles of color. The light-skinned hosts demanded that the darker musician don a pair of white gloves, leave the house, and stand outside a window. That way, he could stretch his arms through the window to play his accordion and the dancers would not be troubled by the appearance of black skin.[28] The social practices of Creoles and black Louisianians maintained a line between the two groups, even if both were Negroes in the eyes of the law.

The existence of people called "mulatto" was not, of course, unique to the former French and Spanish colony of Louisiana. People across the nation bore the physical signs of sex across the color line. Census takers often marked light-skinned people of African descent as mulattoes between 1870 and 1920, the last time the government used that designation. In Houston in 1920, before the major influx of Creoles of color, around 25 percent of the black population was mulatto, according to the federal census.[29] For Creoles of color, however, the mulatto designation referred to more than skin color or the presence of European ancestry. For them, their history in Louisiana became the basis for a racial subjectivity that endured into the twentieth century. When they made contact in Fifth Ward in the 1920s, then, some Louisiana migrants did not share feelings of racial kinship with English-speaking black Texans like Leanna Berry, a descendant of enslaved plantation laborers from the Texas Sugar Bowl. Her granddaughter, Barbara Jean Berry, who came of age in Fifth Ward, noted that the Creoles of color she met identified as French. "[T]hey were so proud to be French. . . . They were proud of their heritage. Oh, they were proud."[30] In a time and place where blackness meant state oppression and violent suppression from the police force, Creoles of color had little incentive to identify as Negroes.

The specific recruitment of Creoles of color by the Southern Pacific, which led to the establishment of Frenchtown, may have been based on racialized ideas about Creoles of color as well as geography. The railroad line began in New Orleans and ran westward through Houston. Men living in southwestern Louisiana, the region that lay between the two cities, were a logical choice for labor. But race possibly informed the decision to recruit Creoles of color to work in Houston. Some white supervisors thought the black Texans moving to Houston from plantations, farms, and small towns of East Texas were less effective as industrial workers because of a history of enslavement and racial subordination. "The Negro has not lost his slave complex yet," asserted one white labor union member.[31] Another white man who worked at the ship channel blamed black men's attitudes for racial problems on Gulf Coast docks when he stated that the "trouble along the water front in the Gulf is the Negro. He is used to a master."[32] But Creoles of color had a more distant relationship to slavery than most black Texans, which may have interested labor agents who stereotyped black men as "slavish." Indeed, their lack of identification with black Texans could have improved their ability to earn jobs in Houston.

Some black Houstonians found Creoles' assertions of racial distinctiveness irritating. One of the first discussions of Creoles of color and racial subjectivity in the *Informer* appeared in the "Cimbee's Ramblings" column in 1925. That year Cimbee encountered a person who claimed that he was "Creole" and not, therefore, a Negro. Cimbee took issue with the notion that Creoles of color were a different racial group from other black Americans. He further opined that white people would not know, or care, that Creoles did not identify as black. "Now whut do de w'ite folks keer 'bout black Creoles inny mo' den dey does 'bout black Afferkins, whare dey keers 'bout culler a tawl."[33] In other words, to white people, Creoles of color were Negroes.

Cimbee did have a point. In an urban segregated society with a black/white binary enforced by Anglos, Creoles of color frequently entered black spaces. When men took jobs at Southern Pacific, they typically joined black coworkers like Arthur Berry. When they sent their children to public schools, those youth attended segregated schools for colored children. Barbara Berry saw them in her classrooms at Crawford Elementary and Wheatley High in Fifth Ward. The Creoles of color who moved to Houston could not avoid segregated public spaces, nor could they ignore the fact that they frequently shared space with black Texans when they left Frenchtown.

A work of fiction reprinted in the *Informer* in 1928 suggested that the groups could find common ground, even as the author acknowledged the unique racial history shared by Creoles of color. *Mississippi Love,* written by Caroline Stanwix, describes their society in southern Louisiana, but also depicts the economic struggles they faced. Published just one year after the 1927 flood, *Mississippi Love* focuses on Rose Arceneaux, the daughter of a business-owning family in Plaquemine, Louisiana. The Arceneaux clan was similar to the Creoles of color who came to Houston in that they "had been free long before the Civil War." And, like a number of the Louisianians in Houston, the main character was light-skinned. Rose, described as "the color of rich cream," is supposedly the most "beautiful girl in the whole state of Louisiana." The narrative also alludes to the steady number of people migrating out of the state. The Arceneaux family owns a store that has lost business because "a large number of their colored friends and customers had left the surrounding country to go to New Orleans, Houston, Dallas, Birmingham, St. Louis, and Chicago." The family thinks that if their daughter, Rose, marries the wealthy man she has met in Baton Rouge, they can save the store. But instead of accepting the hand of her rich suitor, Rose falls in love with a black gambler named Henry Manning from across the river in Natchez, Mississippi. When Manning uses his gambling earnings to buy a barbershop in Baton

Rouge, Arceneaux decides to marry him. His successful business enables Rose to save her family's business in Plaquemine.[34]

The romance at the center of *Mississippi Love* symbolizes a union between the English-speaking black South and the Afro-French South. The story links Creoles of color to descendants of slaves through matrimony and economics. Rose Arceneaux finds happiness with a dark-skinned man from Mississippi despite their differences. Furthermore, the Creole woman and her black husband join forces to save the family store, which also aids a community on the brink of economic disaster. The story suggested that Creoles could benefit from ties with darker neighbors. Alliances between the two groups could uplift their communities. This message perhaps resonated with Houston readers living near Creoles of color in Fifth Ward. The story made it clear that, even if the Louisianians did not share their racial history, the groups could join together to form one community.

Community building between the residents of black Fifth Ward and Frenchtown was a difficult project, though. When they first made contact, the noticeable distinctions between black Texans and Creoles of color were aural as much as they were visual. For one thing, they spoke different languages. The Prejean family, when they first arrived, talked to one another in a dialect they described as "Creole French." "When I moved [to Houston] I didn't know how to say 'yes' or 'no' in English," said Inez Prejean, who felt humiliated when she tried to speak in class at Crawford Elementary. "If I would get up and say a word I think was right, and it was wrong, the teacher and the kids would laugh at me.... The teacher would be laughing with them." Gilbert and Marquette Jacquet's children also felt out of place at Crawford because of linguistic differences between them and their English-speaking black classmates. Jean-Baptiste Illinois Jacquet, the future tenor saxophone player, spoke French when his father, Gilbert, moved them from the small town of Broussard to Houston for his new job. His speech marked him and his brothers as outcasts when they arrived in the 1920s. "Everybody was running from us," he recalled.[35] Language was yet another way that people with roots in southwestern Louisiana felt separate from black Texans.

Second, the groups cultivated different musical practices. While black Texans produced a more citified version of the blues in Houston, Creoles of color danced to a form of music they called "la-la," which had roots in rural southwestern Louisiana. The term *la-la* referred to the country parties where the music was performed, as well as to the music itself. A la-la musician usually played with an accordion and a washboard as accompaniment, while wailing lyrics in French patois. In addition to the linguistic difference, this instrumentation also distanced la-la from Texas blues as well as mainstream ideas about sonic blackness. Scholar Barry Shank notes that "the sounds of a banjo evoked blackness" in the nineteenth century, but Afro-Creoles in southwestern Louisiana had been playing accordions instead of banjos since before the Civil War.[36] Invented in Vienna in 1829, accordions appeared in Louisiana twenty years later. A daguerreotype from the region from 1850, called "Accordion Player," shows a well-dressed man of African descent carrying the instrument. Accordions appeared in popular representations of southwestern Louisiana by the end of the nineteenth century. A short story called "A Night in Acadie" describes a white party in around 1897 where a black trio consisting of an accordionist and two fiddlers provide entertainment. Forty years later, musicians could purchase accordions that cost anywhere from twenty-eight to two hundred dollars from the Sears catalog. In the 1930s, most people played lighter, less expensive single-row accordions (which had one row of buttons), but double- and triple-row versions developed by World War II.[37] Since the French language and accordions were not widely associated with black people in the rest of the United States, Afro-Creole music had sonic qualities that distinguished it from most Americans' conception of "Negro music."

The structure of la-la tunes also differed from the blues found in English-language traditions. Amédé Ardoin, born in 1898, emerged as one of the most popular accordion players in the 1930s through his mastery of two-steps and waltzes—styles typically associated with European traditions brought to Louisiana by Acadians.[38] One of the first Creoles of color to record, Ardoin established a repertoire of songs with titles like "Amadie Two Step" and "Valse de Opelousas." The 3/4 time signature especially distanced his waltzes from the 4/4 time of African American blues. Some of Ardoin's tunes are labeled as "blues," but songs like "Les Blues de Crowley" would not have been recognized as blues by audiences in places like East Texas and the Mississippi Delta. Although the song employs some repetition, this and other examples of "les blues" veered from the AAB format and other stylistic trends commonly found in black American blues.

La-la helped shape the cultural idioms and vernacular used by Creoles of color. The people who moved to Houston from southwestern Louisiana came from the country, and their music revealed their relationship to rural life. La-la often accompanied agricultural labor. Louisianians harvested and canned snap beans in June, and during this labor-intensive process, accordion players provided music for the workers. Because of their importance to local diet and labor, beans became part of la-la lyrics and local vernacular. French-speaking Louisianans used the expression "*les haricots sont pas salés*" (the beans aren't salty) to describe periods of economic depression. Creole cooks traditionally added salted meats to their bean dishes, but during hard times, meat was hard to come by. A song called "Les haricots sont pas salés" became the most popular la-la tune in the southwestern Louisiana and Houston, especially during the lean years of the Great Depression.[39]

Cultural practices transplanted from southwestern Louisiana to Houston functioned as community-building events in Houston. House dances were part of the social and cultural fabric of rural Louisiana. Boozoo Chavis, born in Lake Charles in 1930, stressed the importance of the house-party tradition of his youth: "It was all house dances. We ain't had no electricity, but man, that's where that music was." Neighbors communicated news of an evening dance to everyone they saw, and "the next thing that house would be full." Canray Fontenot, born in L'Anse aux Vaches, described a typical scene: "So they take out all the furniture in the front room, and they put some bench all around the wall, and they take some sheets and put on the bench so everybody will sit down nice and clean and look good." One musician, who once witnessed twenty to thirty people jammed into a single small house, claimed that because house parties were popular, he could find work as a fiddler by just wandering the roads: "In them times, I used to take the fiddle and hit the road. Whenever they see the fiddle, I get a ride."[40]

By the Great Depression, house parties had become part of the culture and economy of Frenchtown. The tradition shifted from rural to urban as Afro-Creoles adapted to city life. Residents described weekend house parties as one of the most important community-building efforts in that neighborhood. Inez Prejean remembered attending house parties nearly every weekend after her family moved to Houston. "Mama used to give a little house dance," Prejean recalled. "If Mama didn't give it someone else would. So, we would go house to house on weekends and dance."[41] Creole migrants found that they could earn money in the city by playing at Frenchtown house parties. Anderson Moss, who listened to la-la and Creole waltzes as a child in Maurice, Louisiana, "played everywhere there were French people to hire him," when he got to Houston in 1928. Moss remembered a party where the house got so full of people that the ceiling caved in.[42] La-la served a social and economic purpose for Louisiana migrants, whose cultural practices distanced them from the majority of Houstonians.

The music emanating from Frenchtown was one of the characteristics that made visitors to Fifth Ward recognize it as a distinct community. As part of Franklin D. Roosevelt's New Deal, writers for the Work Projects Administration produced monographs about local populations during the Great Depression. When participants in the Texas Writers' Project visited Houston for a book on the city's history, the authors observed the Creole of color population when describing black Houston neighborhoods: "'Frenchtown,' on Liberty Road near the northern city limits, is inhabited almost exclusively by descendants of Louisiana Negroes who have preserved their patois." By calling residents "Louisiana Negroes," the visitors clearly saw the people of Frenchtown as racially black, as most outsiders probably did. They observed, however, that residents were "for the most part independent," which may have referred to their relationship to the rest of Fifth Ward. From the perspective of outsiders, Frenchtown appeared to operate as a separate community. They especially noted the distinctive language, food, and music found in the neighborhood. The authors noted, for example, that the community published a newsletter in their native language. They also commented that women in Frenchtown "are known for their creole cookery, but usually will not accept employment as cooks." The music also stood out to the writers, who mentioned the "elaborate rituals" performed by residents, who showed a "passion for music and dancing." Musical practices were clearly a community-defining aspect of Frenchtown. As WPA observers wrote, "Nearly every person in the Frenchtown community can play a musical instrument."[43] For the visitors representing the WPA, the most distinctive characteristics of Frenchtown related to culture.

The cluster of Afro-Creole residents in Frenchtown, and their distinctive cultural practices, made the neighborhood on the northern edge of Fifth Ward an identifiable place. The name "Frenchtown" further acknowledges that this was a different part of the city, something distinct from black Fifth Ward. The finished WPA book, *Houston: A History and Guide,* appeared in print in 1942, which means that Frenchtown was already a noticeable enclave, even to outsiders, by World War II. Frenchtown had emerged within the fifteen years following the Mississippi Flood. By bringing their cultural practices to Houston and maintaining a subjectivity that separated them from descendants of slaves, the people in the neighborhood illustrated the growing diversity and changing sociocultural landscape of the Bayou City.

While black Texans and Creoles of color noted their differences in Fifth Ward, a community made up of both Tejanos and Mexicans took root across the bayou in Second Ward and other parts of the city. These converging migrations gave Houston a noticeable ethnic Mexican presence for the first time in the city's history. Houston attracted few people of Mexican descent between 1836 and 1920. German-born Houstonians actually outnumbered Mexicans in the years following the Civil War. "While Mexicans during that period were sought after in the farmlands of South Texas, the ranchlands of West Texas and the urban economy of San Antonio," writes historian Arnoldo De León, "no equivalent calls were initiated from East Texas."[44] The railroads, cotton gins, warehouses, and banks that emerged in the city in the mid–nineteenth century existed primarily to serve the surrounding agrarian counties, which relied on African Americans to produce lumber, grain, sugar, and cotton well into the twentieth century.

The growth of ethnic Mexican communities in Houston was part of an overall surge in the ethnic Mexican population of the United States in the early twentieth century. Largely in search of labor, over one million Mexicans migrated to the United States between 1900 and 1930. Most settled in the southwestern states that had once made up the northern section of Mexico: California, Arizona, New Mexico, and Texas. The majority of the Mexican immigrants became agricultural workers, toiling in the fruit, vegetable, and cotton fields seasonally.[45] Urban enclaves did appear in the interwar era, though, and not all were confined to the Southwest. The ethnic Mexican population of Chicago, for example, grew considerably between the two World Wars as migrants moved to the midwestern city for industrial labor.[46] Although the number of ethnic Mexicans in Houston remained comparably smaller than the rural Texas population until the late twentieth century, several Spanish-speaking communities dotted the urban landscape by the 1930s.

Ethnic Mexicans spread across Houston, establishing neighborhoods in different parts of the city. The first group of migrants settled in Second Ward, which lay south of Fifth Ward, on the other side of Buffalo Bayou.[47] Another cluster of families lived in a suburb east of Houston called Magnolia Park, which attracted workers because of its close proximity to the ship channel. A different neighborhood developed in an area called Denver Harbor, near the Southern Pacific Railroad yards. (See map 3.) Known as "El Crisol," the

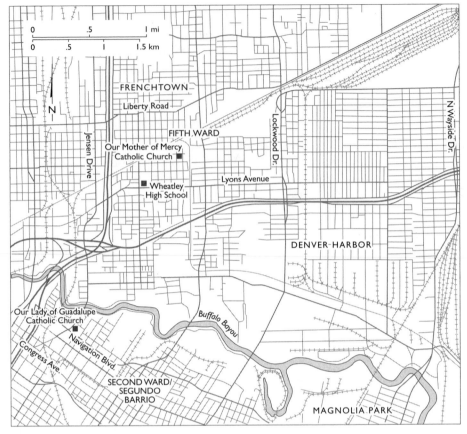

MAP 3. North side and east side of Houston. Map by Bill Nelson.

Denver Harbor community's name was derived from the word *creosote*, which describes a brownish oily liquid used to preserve railroad ties.[48] Finally, a small settlement also emerged on the west side of the city in Sixth Ward near the railroad yards, a cotton-oil company, and other industries.[49] By 1930, ethnic Mexicans lived in pockets across the city.

When they entered Houston, people of Mexican descent encountered a place that bore the spatial and linguistic signs of a society dominated by English-speaking people with roots that extended east of the Mississippi River. In Texas cities like San Antonio and El Paso, the very names attached to public spaces reflected a Spanish and Mexican past. But in the Bayou City, most street names were in English rather than Spanish. Houston also lacked the presidios and missions found in the Southwest. Instead, wealthy Anglos turned eastward for architectural inspiration, building white-columned houses with magnolia trees in the front yards. The ratio of Mexican Americans to African Americans also distinguished Houston from other parts of the Southwest. In 1920 the black population of Houston was five times larger than the ethnic Mexican population.[50] But Houston's economic ascension in the early twentieth century made the city an attractive destination, and ethnic Mexicans flocked to the city in unprecedented numbers. Soon, they would alter the way the city looked and sounded.

The ethnic Mexicans who moved to Houston came from both sides of the Rio Grande, so Tejanos and Mexicans brought an array of distinctive linguistic practices, cultural expressions, and ideas about race and hierarchy. Like Creoles of color, Spanish-speaking migrants often had racial subjectivities that did not conform to the legally enforced black/white racial binary. People who migrated from Mexico in the twentieth century typically acknowledged three racial groups. Ten percent of Mexicans saw themselves as *raza blanca,* or white, at the turn of the century. Although they made up only a fraction of the overall population, people in Mexico who claimed membership in the group *raza blanca* exerted the most political and economic influence. As a result, some members of *raza blanca* considered darker Mexicans with visible Indian and African ancestry to be their "social inferiors." Elite Mexicans maintained that they were of Spanish descent in order to retain higher status. Meanwhile, around 30 percent of Mexico's population identified as *raza indígena,* or Indian. The majority of Mexico, or 60 percent of the nation's fourteen million residents, considered themselves *raza mezclada,* or mixed race, in the early twentieth century. Mexicans who identified as mestizo, the term used for mixed-race people, often were of Indian and European ancestry.[51]

The category of "mestizo" also included people with African ancestors. Colonial Mexico was home to one of the largest African populations in the Americas at one point in its history, with around two hundred thousand Africans living there in the sixteenth and seventeenth centuries.[52] By 1810, around 10 percent of Mexico identified as Afro-Mexican. After the Mexican Revolution, however, the government removed "mulatto" from its list of racial classifications. From that time onward, anyone with mixed ancestry— regardless of whether that ancestry involved Indians or Africans—became known as "mestizo."[53] As historian Ruben Flores points out, the post-revolution government attempted to integrate the nation's diverse cultures and racial groups into one democratic body in the twentieth century. Through art, as well as educational programs, the Republic of Mexico promoted an image of itself as a "melting pot" in the early twentieth century, a place comprising people of different hues who all contributed to the character of the nation.[54] This state project in Mexico stood in stark contrast to Jim Crow Houston, where segregation laws ignored a history of mixing and enforced a binary that guaranteed Anglo supremacy. When they moved to Houston, the Mexicans who proudly acknowledged a mixed heritage had to carefully exclude any mention of African ancestry from their assertions of racial subjectivity, since referring to blackness could leave them open to being categorized as a Negro.

Given the historical diversity of Mexico, some people of Mexican descent living in Houston likely had Africans in their family tree. In 1920, the census described 23 of the 4,126 Mexican-born people living in Houston as mulatto. That racial designation may have been an Anglo census taker's attempt to account for darker-skinned Mexicans who bore the physical signs of African ancestry.[55] Anglo Texans had long noticed physical characteristics associated with racial blackness in the state's ethnic Mexican population, though. Frederick Law Olmsted was struck by the "many Mexicans of mixed negro blood" he encountered in Texas during his visit in the 1850s. The northern traveler eventually reached the conclusion that, "[i]n their tastes and social instincts, they approximate the African. The difference between them and the negro is smaller, and is less felt, I believe, than that between the northern and southern European races."[56] Racial hybridity had worked as an impediment to ethnic Mexicans in antebellum Texas. Being viewed as partly African threatened their social and economic mobility in a developing slave society. As historian Neil Foley notes, "Only by insisting on their Spanish blood and the absence of any African blood were some Mexicans . . . able to claim whiteness in order to purchase land."[57] Since some white settlers believed that Texas Mexicans had "the reputation of naturally consorting with negroes, and falling into an intercourse with them," they considered people of Mexican descent to be unworthy of the privileges of whiteness. Ethnic Mexicans were not "acknowledged as 'white folks'" by the thousands of settlers from the Southeast who swept into the state between the 1820s and the Civil War.[58] Anglos used the centuries of interracial contact between indigenous groups, Spanish colonizers, and Africans as evidence that people of Mexican descent could not truly claim whiteness, especially in the Rio Grande Valley.

Most Texas Mexicans who moved to Houston hailed from the southern and central parts of the state, where a recent history of segregation informed their notions of race and power. In the Rio Grande Valley, Anglo settlers imposed a capitalist system that expanded their economic influence in the region at the turn of the twentieth century. Elite ethnic Mexicans, especially those with light skin, often found ways to hold on to their economic privilege. Some also intermarried with Anglos. Working-class Tejanos, on the other hand, faced increasing amounts of discrimination. As more Anglos claimed political power, some counties enforced a system of Jim Crow that used spatial divisions to reinforce a racial hierarchy over the ethnic Mexican majority. Signs that read, "No Mexicans or dogs allowed" littered "the Valley," as locals called the region.[59] School boards in central Texas and the Valley also created segregated schools for ethnic Mexican children. The first separate schools designated for Spanish-speaking pupils appeared in 1902 in the town of Seguin. By 1930, 90 percent of all schools in South Texas had followed suit. Segregated schools for Anglos and people of Mexican descent existed in at least 122 school districts in fifty-nine counties by the early 1940s.[60]

Violence enforced the emerging social order. In 1915, the tense atmosphere of the Rio Grande Valley flared into a bloody rebellion. In the "Plan de San Diego," a group of ethnic Mexican insurgents intended to attack the Anglo power structure and free Texas and the Southwest from its grip. They drew inspiration from the revolutionaries in Mexico, where war had erupted in 1910. The plan, which originated with a manifesto written in the South Texas town of San Diego in January of that year, called for a "liberating army" that would include black Americans and Indians. The insurgents in Texas began by raiding ranches and railroads—two symbols of Anglo economic domination. Texas Rangers and Anglo mobs immediately organized to quash the rebellion, and the aftermath of the Plan de San Diego proved to be more violent than the original uprising. Over the next few years, hundreds of ethnic Mexicans died by execution.[61]

Even as lynchings and mass executions targeted ethnic Mexicans, Spanish-speaking people in the Valley critiqued Anglo supremacy through cultural expression. The music of Tejanos protested their social conditions. They detailed their plight through a style of music known as the *corrido*. The corrido tradition developed at the exact moment that Anglos worked to install a new social, political, and economic structure over South Texas in the late nineteenth century. By the early 1900s, these songs incorporated the theme of conflict between ethnic Mexicans and Anglos. Structured as a narrative ballad, the corrido "functions historically as an expression of stark cultural contrasts in the conflict surrounding Anglo-Mexican relations in Texas," according to scholar Manuel Peña.[62] Like much of the blues played by black Americans, corridos portrayed the bitter realities of life in a Jim Crow society.

Songs like "El corrido de Gregorio Cortez" described actual events. The protagonist is an ethnic Mexican man apprehended by an Anglo official, Sheriff Brack Morris, who was searching for a reported horse thief in 1901. Cortez protested his arrest, and a fight ensued. During the struggle, the sheriff shot Cortez's brother, Rumoldo. Cortez then shot the sheriff, who died after crawling into the brush. Fearing that he would be lynched, Cortez eluded law enforcement for ten days. Songs like "El corrido de Gregorio Cortez" portrayed Anglos as weak men who cowered in the presence of powerful Tejanos:

Venían los americanos
más blancos que una paloma,
de miedo que le tenían
a Cortez y a su pistol

Decían los americanos,
decían con timidez:
—Vamos a seguir la huella
que el malhechor es Cortez.

Le echaron los perros jaunes
pa' que siguieran la huella,
pero alcanzar a Cortez
era seguir a una estrella.

Tiró con rumbo a Gonzales
sin ninguna timidez:
—Síganme, rinches cobardes,
yo soy Gregorio Cortez.

. . .

Decía Gregorio Cortez
con su pistola en la mano:
—No corran, rinches cobardes,
con un solo mexicano.

The Americans were coming
they were whiter than a dove,
from the fear that they had
of Cortez and of his pistol.

Then the Americans said,
they said fearfully:
"Let us follow the trail;
the wrongdoer is Cortez."

They set bloodhounds on him
so they could follow his trail,
but trying to overtake Cortez
was like following a star.

He struck out for Gonzales
without showing any fear:
"Follow me, cowardly Rangers,
I am Gregorio Cortez."

Then said Gregorio Cortez,
with his pistol in his hand;
"Don't run, you cowardly Rangers,
from just one Mexican."[63]

Called "hero corridos," the tradition allowed disfranchised Texas Mexicans to assert a heroic folk tradition at a point when Anglos asserted political and economic dominance.[64] The corrido tradition described the creation of an Anglo/Mexican racial system in South Texas. These songs offered a cultural response to racial violence and segregation in the Valley.

The struggles for economic and political power that had led Anglos to segregate the large Mexican American populations of South and Central Texas did not occur in Houston, where Anglo lawmakers legalized Jim Crow at a time when that population was still very small. The nativist, anti-immigrant sentiments held by some Americans after World War I certainly affected people of Mexican descent in Houston, but legal segregation did not target them as it did the African Americans who made up over 30 percent of the population. Houston developed a black/white binary; therefore, since the few ethnic Mexicans living in Houston were not considered black at the time that Anglos wrote Jim Crow into law, in the first decade of the twentieth century, they became legally marked as white. Legally, then, they had access to white space.

Ethnic Mexicans and African Americans were on different sides of the color line in Jim Crow Houston. Rather than joining the Black Buffaloes, a Negro-league baseball team, ethnic Mexican players donned the uniform of the Houston Buffaloes, the white team. Women of Mexican descent joined the white branch of the Young Women's Christian Association, while black women organized through a separate "colored" branch. When entering a streetcar, an ethnic Mexican passenger sat in the "white only" section; meanwhile, black Houstonians paid their fare and made their way to the rear. The first wave of ethnic Mexican migrants sent their children to Rusk

Elementary in Second Ward, a school designated for white students. This meant that black Houstonians had little direct contact with ethnic Mexicans, since they did not share space in legally segregated institutions.

Some Texas Mexican families moved to Houston to improve their social and economic standing. Houston had, as historian Thomas Kreneck notes, an "urban, ultra-capitalist ethos" that "fostered, at least marginally, more openness to Mexicans than existed in most other parts of South and Southeast Texas." This attitude "offered Mexicans the hope of a better niche for themselves."[65] When the Cortés family realized that Houston's school district had "black schools and other schools for everybody," they left the town of Sabine and headed to the Bayou City.[66] As their numbers grew by the late 1920s, ethnic Mexicans saw increasing discrimination from Anglos, but in the early years of settlement, the black/white color line motivated some Tejanos to move to the city.

Texas-born Mexicans like Janie Gonzales found themselves living near people from south of the Rio Grande like Mary Villagomez, Feliberto Tijerina, and Melesio Gómez, who left after the Mexican Revolution erupted in 1910. The people who moved to Houston from Mexico versus rural Texas had different reasons for relocating to the city. Both were pulled to Houston because of economic opportunities, but while Tejanos were also motivated for racial reasons, Mexicans made the trek because of warfare. When the Mexican Revolution erupted in 1910, some Mexican families fled the war in stages, gradually inching northward, sometimes leaving family members behind. By the time Ralph Villagomez was fourteen and his sister Mary was six, his family had moved several times in attempts to escape the devastation wrought by warfare. The Villagomez family originally hailed from Guanajuato, but they had relocated to a safer location when the war began. Constant raids by the Zapatistas and Villistas, who scoured the countryside for food, forced the Villagomezes north to Nuevo Laredo. Finally the pater-familias announced, "We're going to the other side." Carrying eight hundred dollars' worth of pesos, they paid a man to transport them by boat to an island in the middle of the Rio Grande. From there, they waded to Texas.[67] Other families could not risk or afford to bring the entire family to Texas at once. Soldiers abducted Melesio Gómez near his home in San Luis Potosí during the war, but he escaped and hid in the mountains for six months. When he heard that the Southern Pacific was "hiring a lot of Mexican people," he left for Houston in 1919. A year later, he brought his wife and daughters to the city, where they settled near downtown.[68]

At the same time that black Texans and Creoles of color encountered a cultural and linguistic divide in Fifth Ward, some Mexicans had trouble making connections with the Tejanos they encountered. The Villagomez family noted that spatial divisions marked the difference between Mexicans and Tejanos. Ralph and his sister Mary described Second Ward as a Tejano neighborhood, while they considered Magnolia Park, near the ship channel, to be an enclave for Mexican-born Houstonians. As teenagers they avoided Second Ward because they saw the groups as "different type(s) of people." The Villagomez siblings did not feel comfortable among the Tejanos who lived in the other neighborhood.[69]

Language could also divide Mexicans and Tejanos, who spoke different versions of Spanish. "The Tejanos have a lot of corruption in the language," said Mary Villagomez. She and her brother noticed that Tejanos used words like *el traque* for track and *la boyla* for boiler, neither of which exists in the Spanish language as spoken in Mexico.[70] Even people from the same country ate different foods and spoke different dialects of Spanish. On his Sixth Ward street, Felix Tijerina of Monterrey uttered a "very correct, but rapid Spanish" that even his neighbors from other parts of Mexico had difficulty understanding.[71] Meanwhile, many Tejanos hailed from multicultural environs, and their language and culture indicated their contact with Anglos, Germans, and other ethnic groups. Some were multilingual, with names that reflected a diverse heritage, like Mexican German Félix Hesselbrook Morales, who moved to Houston from New Braunfels, in central Texas.[72] Linguistic differences pointed to the diversity that existed among people of Mexican descent.

Mexicans and Tejanos were sometimes antagonistic toward one another's cultural practices. The musical styles they cultivated further reflected the differences of the two groups. Frank Alonzo, whose family hailed from San Antonio, disliked the proliferation of styles from Mexico. Alonzo commented that there were "too many musicians from Mexico right here in Houston." He asserted that, as a Mexican American from Texas, "[y]ou wanted *música tejana* from here—not from Mexico."[73] Both groups played accordions, which had appeared in Mexico in around 1860, but their styles differed. In addition to the corrido tradition, a music called *conjunto* began to take shape in the Valley in the early twentieth century. Conjunto emerged from working-class Texas Mexican communities, where people toiled in the fields during the day and gathered in dance halls at night. Early conjunto ensembles included an accordion and a twelve-string, bass-like instrument called a *bajo sexto*. As the style evolved, musicians sometimes added more instruments, like guitar and the *tambora de rancho,* a drumlike apparatus that musicians fastened to their waists. Rural musicians did not make enough money to support themselves by performing. Narciso Martínez, the most popular musician to emerge from the conjunto scene in the 1930s, worked the fields during the week and played music on weekends.[74]

Mexican music lovers, on the other hand, may have preferred *bolero,* a guitar-based style that blended Spanish and indigenous traditions, as well as the rural-based *canción ranchera.* Ranchera developed in Mexico around the turn of the twentieth century. In some ways, ranchera was similar to country-and-western music. The styles had some similarities, including a rural setting on ranches in the countryside. Rancheras often told romanticized stories of cowboys and ranch hands that contrasted idyllic country life with modern industrialization—which may have especially appealed to rural transplants living in the city.[75] Although born in Houston, when singer Lydia Mendoza began performing rancheras in the 1930s, she appealed to Mexicans because she incorporated songs and fashions from south of the border. Mendoza had spent about four years living in Monterrey as a child after her family briefly returned to Mexico. That experience undoubtedly influenced her music and her decision to wear Mexican-styles dresses when she performed. She also sang tunes learned from her Mexican mother. As a result, the Mendoza family's repertoire contained songs so old that "almost nobody knew them" in Texas.[76] Their cultural practices highlighted the distinctiveness of people born on different sides of the Rio Grande.

By the 1930s, social and cultural practices provided evidence that Tejanos and Mexicans did engage with one another in Houston. Frank Alonzo may have wished for fewer Mexican musicians in the city, but he had to acknowledge others' desire for styles from Mexico. He had to satisfy that audience. In fact, Alonzo married a woman born in Mexico named Ventura, who also played music. When the two began performing in Houston in the '30s, they worked to master a range of styles that would satisfy a diverse Spanish-speaking audience. Tejanos and Mexicans mutually created social space in their fledgling communities. As the Frank and Ventura Alonzo example indicates, they also married one another. Janie Gonzales eventually married a man born in Mexico, Feliberto Tijerina, whom she met in the city. Institutions and businesses in Second Ward, Sixth Ward, and other neighborhoods were owned and supported by people from both groups. Several businesses and institutions indicated that Second Ward had become a center for the city's growing ethnic Mexican community. Residents soon rechristened the area with a Spanish name: El Segundo Barrio.

The area around Congress, Preston, Franklin, and Louisiana streets became the hub of an ethnic Mexican commercial district in El Segundo Barrio. A growing number of businesses marked the area as a new part of Houston in old Second Ward. Two business partners from opposite sides of the Rio Grande—Dr. Angel Leyva of Puebla, Mexico, and Alejandro Caneles, a pharmacist from San Antonio, Texas—opened the first ethnic Mexican drug store in Houston, Botica Guadalupana, on the 1800 block of Congress Avenue. The Mexican-born Sarabia family of Guanajuato also established several businesses in the area. José Sarabia and a partner opened the Azteca Theater in 1927, where they showed silent Mexican films and staged vaudeville shows. In 1929 his brother Felipe launched his own store at 711 Preston, where he sold groceries, magazines, and records to a Mexican American clientele. The three Sarabia brothers—José, Socorro, and Felipe—opened the first Spanish-language bookstore in the area, the Librería Mejicana, and later published a monthly magazine called *La Gaceta* and a weekly newspaper, *El Tecolote*. In 1928 Felipe established the first Mexican American–owned business in downtown Houston when he opened a store, on Preston Avenue near Main Street, that sold phonograph records, books, and products from Mexico. Three years later, Felix and Angie Morales of San Antonio opened the first funeral home for Mexican Americans on Navigation Street in Segundo Barrio.[77] For the first time in the city's history, a significant number of Spanish place-names marked social spaces in Houston.

In some ways, ethnic Mexicans and Creoles of color faced similar circumstances when they moved to Houston. They made homes in a city where, initially, they were small fractions of the population. Furthermore, both groups were newcomers in a place where the linguistic and physical markers of space linked the society to an English-speaking heritage. Anglos and African Americans with roots in eastern Texas did not experience the same issues over language that French- and Spanish-speaking migrants encountered. Creoles of color and ethnic Mexicans left societies where their families had lived for generations and carved new communities out of a city where few people looked or sounded like them.

Their efforts to construct communities in Houston demonstrate how legal and local definitions of race could exist at the same time in one society. Legal segregation, and the black/white binary that those laws enforced, ordered migrants' access to space. Jim Crow laws assigned Creoles of color and ethnic

Mexicans to different racial categories, so although they were both new groups moving into Houston at the same time, the color line pushed them into separate spaces. Creoles of color sent their children to the "colored" Crawford Elementary in Fifth Ward because Jim Crow marked them as black. Yet they clung to a distinct racial subjectivity based on their history in Louisiana and their ancestors' status as free people of color in the antebellum South. The development of Frenchtown shows that the first generation of Creoles of color did not intend to merely blend into black Houston. Spatial and cultural practices marked them as different groups at the local level.

Ethnic Mexican racial subjectivities were based on laws and customs in Mexico and Texas. Migrants from Mexico recognized three racial groups, the largest of which was actually a mixed group that acknowledged a diverse heritage. Texas Mexicans, who had been the target of segregation in central Texas and the Rio Grande Valley, hailed from a society where discriminatory laws produced an Anglo/Mexican color line. Yet these diverse ethnic Mexicans from different nations became "white" by the legal definitions that shaped Houston's version of racial categorization in the early twentieth century. At the same time, though, their spatial and cultural practices distinguished them from the Anglo majority, and they would increasingly face discrimination based on those differences.

As the number of French- and Spanish-speaking people in Houston continued to grow, Anglos and black Texans would try to make sense of the city's evolving diversity. Creoles of color and ethnic Mexicans would quickly realize that their status at the local level often depended upon how dominant Anglos assigned meaning to their religion, language, and ancestry.

PART TWO

THREE

Jim Crow-ing Culture

MARY AND RALPH VILLAGOMEZ MOVED to Houston with their family from Guanajuato during the Mexican Revolution. They settled in the growing ethnic Mexican enclave in Magnolia Park, which enabled them to live among people with similar racial subjectivities; however, they had to venture into the larger Jim Crow city for school, work, and other activities. As ethnic Mexicans and other newcomers encountered segregated space, the color line did not change; Jim Crow laws still ordered public spaces along a black/white binary. What changed is that an increasingly wide range of migrants, people with different understandings of racial categories, grappled with that color line. When the Villagomez siblings arrived in the city, one of the first lessons the brother and sister learned about urban life was where to sit on a streetcar. "You go to the streetcar," said Ralph, "the colored people had to sit in the back." But, as Mary recalled, "[w]e didn't have to go and sit in any particular place."[1] The Villagomezes' position on the bus indicated their legal racial status in the Jim Crow city. In a society with a legal racial binary, everyone not marked as Negro or colored was white by law. Since they could legally claim whiteness, people of Mexican descent like Mary and Ralph Villagomez sat at the front of the bus. At the same time, though, ethnic Mexicans realized that their white legal status did not bar them from other forms of discrimination. Slurs like "greaser" often greeted the newcomers when they entered spaces designated for white people. They also faced discrimination based on language, and they had to negotiate a virulent form of anti-Catholicism that informed their position in a Protestant-majority city.

As migrants like the Villagomez family learned, the color line established in public spaces via Jim Crow laws was only one form of segregation that affected racial status in the diversifying migration city. The influx of diverse groups—including ethnic Mexicans, Creoles of color, Italian Americans, and Jewish Americans—affected racial discourse and led to the rise of racial practices that operated outside of the legal color line. While laws dictated which public spaces Houstonians could occupy, a host of other interactions and ideologies also created divisions in society. Notions of rank and status often centered on cultural practices like language and religion. Cultural differences between English-speaking Texans and other groups shaped the ways the Anglo majority enforced hierarchy, and how black Houstonians lobbied for equality. Catholicism especially became part of how Anglos conceptualized difference as Catholics entered into older debates about race, space, and hierarchy. And while Anglos debated religion, forms of segregation took shape within Catholic churches that also revealed how diverse groups conceptualized race and status. Inside specific communities, groups of migrants enacted their own pecking order in the spaces they dominated. The culture of Jim Crow extended to include language and religion.

Ideologies based on cultural distinctions, and different versions of segregation that developed in Houston institutions, illustrate how race and racial exclusion worked on multiple levels. The various versions of segregation that emerged in local spaces did not always conform to the black/white binary. In some cases, hierarchies developed among people who were all white by law. A person's perceived proximity to blackness (and, therefore, distance from whiteness) could also determine his or her place in the local hierarchy regardless of legal categorization. Some groups learned that their relationship to black people could affect the ways Anglos regarded them. Racial hierarchy in a migration city was, therefore, determined by numerous factors that were constantly shifting in local practice.

LANGUAGE AND HIERARCHY

Anglos and African Americans formed the majority of the population in Jazz Age Houston, but over the course of the 1920s, both black- and white-owned newspapers noted the influx of non-English-speaking migrants in their midst. Writers in Anglo and African American newspapers pondered how these migrants fit into older struggles for power between Anglos and African Americans in eastern Texas.

When Anglo newspapers discussed immigrants in the 1920s, they tended to focus on cultural distinctions between themselves and the other groups, distinctions that firmly established a hierarchy between the different people legally marked as white. To their Anglo detractors, ethnic Mexicans' perceived inferiority was heavily linked to cultural practices. They frequently argued, for example, that ethnic Mexicans' cultural differences made them inferior to English-speaking, white Protestants. In a speech delivered to a room full of Anglo Methodists in 1922, P. W. Horn, the former superintendent of Houston schools, stated that U.S. residents were intellectually and morally superior to Mexicans, and he claimed that atheism was on the rise in Mexico: "The Rio Grande marks the line between enlightenment and ignorance, between Christian belief and atheism."[2]

People like Horn helped formulate a hierarchy between Anglo and Mexican by discussing language and religion, but they carefully excluded mention of legal racial categories. Since ethnic Mexicans in Texas were white by law, Anglos "learned over the course of the mid–twentieth century to explain their exclusion of Mexican Americans on the basis of language and culture rather than race," as legal scholar Ariela Gross asserts.[3] This cultural discrimination defined ethnic Mexicans as distinct from—and inferior to—Anglo Texans. In Houston they argued that ethnic Mexicans could not be proper citizens if they insisted upon speaking Spanish. "Without the ability to speak English," wrote one Houstonian in the *Post,* "they can not become efficient citizens." The author linked his concerns about English proficiency to his anxieties about ethnic Mexicans who voted: "[M]any of them who are able to make out their ballots are so meagerly acquainted with the English language as to fall short of the standards of efficient citizenship."[4] Ethnic Mexicans, according to this writer, could become legitimate citizens only by separating themselves from a sonic marker of cultural difference: the Spanish language.

Linguistic differences became the basis for discriminatory practices in local public schools for "white" children. The first wave of ethnic Mexican youth attended Rusk Elementary, near El Segundo Barrio, which was still predominantly Anglo when Spanish-speaking children began to arrive. Admission to these white schools did not mean, however, that Anglos viewed the ethnic Mexican newcomers as their equals. In some cases, school officials created separate rooms for Spanish-speaking students, creating a pattern of isolation between the groups. To justify placing children of Mexican descent in different classrooms, administrators at Rusk labeled them "subnormal." At Hawthorne Elementary, another Anglo-majority institution, a similar pattern developed. Administrators at Hawthorne in the 1930s worked with the Settlement Association of Houston—an organization that helped establish classes in English, citizenship, and the arts—to create programs for ethnic Mexican students. At Hawthorne, the students who participated in these programs had to meet separately from Anglos, in order to discourage the groups from intermingling.[5] Since administrators worked to keep students apart, ethnic Mexican youth felt ostracized from the Anglo majority in white schools.

The first waves of ethnic Mexicans recounted tales of loneliness and school-yard fights in Anglo-majority schools. Spanish-speaking youth were surrounded by people from different cultural and ethnic backgrounds. Catalina Gómez Sandoval, who came from Aguascalientes to Texas in 1927, was one of four ethnic Mexican students at her school in Houston: "At that time there was a lot of discrimination. They used to beat us up and chase us. Every day they used to chase us. We would get home crying."[6] Carmen Cortés and her sister had been the only Mexican Americans in their school. Her sister never adjusted to her minority status and dropped out.[7] Estela Gómez felt like an outcast at school from first grade until high school graduation. She never made friends at Sam Houston High, which was home to four other Mexican American students. "I was never invited to their social affairs," Gómez recalled.[8]

No high schools in Houston developed an ethnic Mexican–majority student body in the Jim Crow era, but a few elementary schools did. The first ethnic Mexican–majority school appeared in the 1920s when Lorenzo de Zavala Elementary opened in Magnolia Park. The school was not legally segregated; however, it existed because Anglo parents grew concerned about the high number of Spanish-speaking students attending the two white schools in the area. Named for a Mexican man who served as the ad interim vice president of the Texas Republic, the school soon had an ethnic Mexican majority. By 1927, 576 children attended de Zavala.[9]

Policies designed by administrators still stigmatized Spanish-speaking youth at de Zavala, even though ethnic Mexicans formed the majority of the school. Language was part of the nationalist atmosphere of the post–World War I era. The Texas legislature passed a law in 1918 declaring that no languages other than English could be used for curriculum and instruction in public schools. Anglo administrators at de Zavala Elementary implemented "no-Spanish-speaking rules" in the classroom and on the playground.[10] These restrictions enforced Anglo supremacy by stigmatizing cultural traditions associated with Mexico.

The case of Houston schools demonstrates how racial divisions could unfold in complicated ways in the Jim Crow era. The Bayou City was home to two types of schools—those built for white students, and others established for Negroes. These were legally segregated institutions, where the state determined people's place. As Houston diversified, ethnic Mexican youth attended white schools, while Creoles of color enrolled at black public schools. On the surface, that division seems to indicate some semblance of equality between Anglo and ethnic Mexican. But within white schools, Anglos enforced a form of spatial separation that created a hierarchy between them and the Spanish-speaking student body. Within "white" space in Houston, then, hierarchies developed that informed migrants' status outside of their legal standing. These practices illustrate how two versions of segregation—one enforced by law, and another determined by local practice— operated simultaneously. At the state (macro) level, Jim Crow established a racial binary codified by laws. At the local (micro) level, the culture of Jim Crow fostered a racial logic that promoted hierarchies and social divisions based on differences in language and religious custom.

Some ethnic Mexicans did manage to find success within Anglo-dominated institutions in the 1920s. Two men, P. L. Niño and Francisco Chairez, attended Rice Institute, a private college in Houston. Both graduated with degrees in engineering in 1928.[11] Ethnic Mexicans were not entirely excluded, then, from the spaces that Anglos dominated. Those who spoke English and assumed the cultural trappings of the majority population had an easier time navigating the racial terrain of Jim Crow Houston. "Texas Mexicans thus occupied a transitional position in the racial hierarchy," writes historian Elliot Young. "If they adopted the 'correct' cultural norms, had enough money, and married Anglos, they could become 'American.'" At the same time that Niño and Chairez attended Rice, though, the school barred all black people from attending. Ethnic Mexicans' ability to matriculate into white schools was not open to people labeled Negro. As Young points out, black Texans "would always be 'niggers' in the eyes of the Anglos."[12]

Black activists paid particular attention to ethnic Mexicans' legal racial status as the number of Spanish-speaking migrants increased. While ethnic Mexicans certainly faced discrimination, black Houstonians resented that Spanish-speaking people, as well as other nonblack groups, could access some of the institutions reserved for white people. Ethnic Mexican children experienced discrimination in schools like Rusk and Hawthorne, but in black Houstonians' view, the fact that they could even attend schools designated for white students indicated that they ranked above people of African descent in the local hierarchy. NAACP activist Christia Adair expressed bitterness over the fact that Anglos and ethnic Mexicans like the Villagomez family could sit anywhere on public transportation when they could not. Furthermore, as Adair recalled, black passengers had to stand if a member of either group needed their seat: "I don't care where a Negro was sitting, if there was not a vacant seat ahead of him . . . then a white person or a Mexican would get on the bus, you had to get up and stand and let that person sit down."[13] Adair's reference to "a white person or a Mexican" indicated that she saw ethnic Mexicans as nonwhite. Nevertheless, her experiences on the bus suggested that ethnic Mexicans had some privileges of whiteness that black people could not claim.

Adair's complaints about streetcars reflect how the racialized public spaces created by segregation were sites of heated discord in towns and cities during the era of Jim Crow. Black resentment toward segregated seating in public transportation was nothing new. Segregation on streetcars triggered some of the first organized black protests against Jim Crow in the South.[14] Houston's city council passed a law in 1903 that required black passengers to sit behind a screen in the rear of streetcars, and after a series of confrontations between white conductors and black passengers over segregated seating, African Americans instigated a boycott. The protesters demanded separate streetcars with black conductors for neighborhoods like the San Felipe district.[15] Streetcars remained a source of racial tension after the unsuccessful boycott. Disturbances on streetcars were an early sign of the animosity between white civilians and the black soldiers stationed at Camp Logan that led to the Houston Riot of 1917. Some soldiers showed their resentment toward Jim Crow by destroying or taking with them the screens that divided the races aboard streetcars. George Patton, a white police officer, confiscated several screens from two black soldiers headed toward the San Felipe area at one point that summer. Patton also heard reports that black soldiers wore the screens to dances, pinning them onto their clothing like badges. A night motorman on the San Felipe line claimed that black soldiers called him a "son of a bitch" and "white trash" when he yelled at them for moving the Jim Crow screens or sitting in the front of the car. In August, a sheriff entered a streetcar and beat Private Richard Griggs of the Third Battalion because he sat next to a white boy in the front. "He was a pretty good nigger when I got him to jail," boasted Sheriff Ed Stoermer.[16] As the recollections of the Villagomez siblings and Christia Adair indicate, though, animosity over race and rank transformed from struggles between Anglos and African Americans into one that also involved migrants from other regions and nations.

Like Christia Adair, other black Americans typically regarded people of Mexican descent as nonwhite people of color. Cyril Briggs of the *Crusader,* a New Negro journal launched in New York in the 1920s, referred to Mexico as "the colored republic to the South" in his writing.[17] African Americans credited Mexico with having superior race relations. They pointed to the nation's multiracial makeup as well as a history that showed some people with African ancestry ascending to positions of political leadership. Vicente Guerrero, who became the second president of Mexico in 1829, had a mixed racial heritage that included a black mother. As a political leader, Guerrero had advocated for the abolition of slavery. Black people living in the Jim Crow era contrasted that history in Mexico with the stringent racial segregation of the United States. A writer for the *Crisis* complimented race relations in Mexico when he wrote, "There is, as you know, no prejudice." Some black Americans moved to Mexico to seek respite from racism. After being convicted of violating the Mann Act in 1912, Jack Johnson spent time in Mexico City during his exile from the United States. He started a land company, bought a mansion, and planned to star in Mexican movies. Cyril Briggs used Johnson as an example while advancing the idea that a more favorable racial climate existed south of the Rio Grande. According to Briggs, Mexico "does not Jim Crow Negroes nor lynch them." Furthermore, he declared that Mexico did not "declare pogroms against Negroes but only welcomes them as it has welcomed Jack Johnson and many other Negroes seeking freedom from persecution."[18] For countless black Americans, Mexico surpassed the United States in the matter of race relations.

In Houston, though, segregation affected black people's relationship with the ethnic Mexicans living in the Bayou City. Black Houstonians wondered why people of Mexican descent accessed opportunities that white Texans did not extend to black people, and some based their protest on linguistic skills. In the 1920s, C. F. Richardson noted in the *Informer* that "[t]here are numerous foreigners in this city, who can barely speak our common tongue; yet these outlandish hordes get far more consideration from the 'powers-that-be' than the colored race with its years of residence in this city, its loyalty to the municipal and county government and its steadfastness to and support of the American ideals and institutions."[19] When they noted that migrants who legally claimed whiteness could vote and access spaces that excluded black people, they often described the people who had recently arrived in the United States in disparaging terms. Using insults, *Informer* contributors argued that foreign newcomers had less experience or knowledge of U.S. politics than the descendants of slaves. These articles indicated a low opinion of immigrants: "It is strange how the Southern white man is willing to regard the Mexican and scum of Europe, Asia and Fiji Islands as worthy partakers of all the rights, privileges and opportunities America affords and then deny the same things to his best friend and most trusted ally—the colored man."[20] Their history of settlement in the city, they argued, should give them an advantage over the Spanish-speaking migrants. These appeals called for a hierarchy based on culture that would privilege native black Texans over migrants from other countries.

Black activists in Houston lobbied for voting rights by asserting that they could speak English, they had knowledge of the political process, and their ancestors had contributed to U.S. politics in the past—factors they thought distinguished them from non-English-speaking immigrants. The more conservative black leadership based their appeals for political equality on a shared cultural history with white southerners and a legacy of African American loyalty to their nation, especially in the years following World War I, when U.S. nationalism intensified. Some used the history of slavery in their assertions for equality. W. L. Davis and E. O. Smith, two men who had criticized C. F. Richardson's militance during the formation of the local NAACP branch, wrote an appeal for black voting rights that argued that slavery had given black and white southerners a tie that Anglos should recognize. Davis and Smith reminded white people of the services provided by generations of people of African descent: "Let us, your true and tried friends, who followed some of your fathers to the battle front away back in the sixties, and when they were wounded climbed over the breastwork of the opposing forces, took up in our strong black arms the shattered forms of our loved ones, nursed them back to life and restored them to their firesides, help to elect good men to fill the official positions in this State."[21] Their appeal illustrates their particular approach to attaining racial advancement. Smith did not believe in agitation. Instead, as he argued in a letter to NAACP headquarters in New York, "[i]n the South, a great deal depends on 'pulling the right string.'"[22] In this case, that entailed pointing out a shared past with Anglos, one that some of the migrants moving into Houston did not share. When black Houstonians pointed out that immigrants could not "speak our common tongue," then, they highlighted cultural attributes that linked African Americans and Anglo Texans, and contrasted them with the other migrant groups moving into the wards. They posited that black Texans' knowledge of English, and what Smith viewed as an interwoven history in the South, should translate into political rights.

Writer and educator Simeon Williams protested the difference in legal rights between black Houstonians and other migrant groups through Cimbee, who was especially interested in the city's ethnic Mexican, Italian, and Jewish inhabitants. The growing number of ethnic Mexicans, and a smaller group of European immigrants, made the wards places where a wide range of languages could be heard at any given time. Houston's Italian and Jewish population had roots in the wave of immigration to the United States that occurred between 1880 and the end of World War I. A small population of Italians made homes in the Bayou City in the early twentieth century. While fewer than one hundred Italians lived in Houston in 1880, 1,315 resided there in 1920.[23] At the same time, Jewish people from southern and eastern Europe also immigrated to the United States in increasing numbers. While the 150,000 to 200,000 Jewish Americans living in the United States at the time of the Civil War had made up less than 1 percent of the total population, over two million settled in the United States after 1880.[24] Most Jewish immigrants in Texas settled on nearby Galveston Island as part of the "Galveston Plan" in the late 1800s and early 1900s. Seeing the growing poverty of overcrowded slums in New York City, Jewish activists urged immigrants to settle in less-populated areas of the country, like the Gulf Coast. Galveston became the primary port of entry in Texas as a result of the plan, but immigrants looking for a larger city often moved inland to Houston, especially after the devastating Galveston flood of 1900.[25]

The flow of Jewish and Italian immigrants slowed dramatically with the passage of the Immigration Act of 1924, which restricted the number of immigrants from southern and eastern Europe. The postwar era was, therefore, a period of rampant ethnic bias. Matthew Frye Jacobson refers to 1924 as the "high-water mark of the regime of Anglo-Saxon or Nordic supremacy," marked by the Johnson-Reed Act and its exclusion of "undesirable" immigrants from southern and eastern Europe.[26] So, while the Mexican population continued to climb in the '20s, Houston's Jewish and Italian populations stagnated.

In one edition of "Cimbee's Ramblings," the character illuminates linguistic differences between black and Italian people, while further pointing out that Italian Americans could claim more political rights in the Jim Crow city. Cimbee converses with an Italian man named "Tony" about the upcoming mayoral election in 1926, and the men's dialects reveal their nationalities. When Tony informs Cimbee that he recently voted for the city's next mayor, the Italian man is shocked to learn that the black man cannot vote.

"W'y Missa Cimbee," Tony says, "yu donna meen ter tella me dat yu binna born in dissa kuntry an' no kinna voat fer de mare uv dissa town?"

"No Missa Tony," responded Cimbee. "I kaint vote fer de mare ner nuthin elce twel munts atter he's bin awlready leckted."

"I bin in dissa kuntry jis erbout er tree yeer, an' I voata fer innyboddy I wanta voat fer."

Cimbee leaves the conversation depressed, noting that "er man whut dident hardly no how minny states made up did yunion, ner whare kongriss meets, ner whut dey meets fer" could vote, when racial restrictions barred black Americans from the polls.[27] Like other *Informer* writers, Simeon Williams claimed that foreign-born migrants had little knowledge of U.S. government, which became the basis for Cimbee's frustration over his own lack of voting rights. Although Italians were relative newcomers to Texas compared with black descendants of slaves, they attained higher legal status, which allowed them to access political rights like voting.[28] If Houston Italians could avoid being labeled colored, they could continue claiming these rights.

By distinguishing between the two men's ways of speaking, the column also highlighted the dissimilar sounds coming from the mouths of people who encountered one another in a diversifying metropolitan area. Sonic change was a prime indicator of Houston's growth after World War I. New sounds emanating from downtown construction sites, car horns, or oceangoing vessels at the ship channel attested to the city's economic expansion and continued urbanization. Language also marked these transformations. When Houstonians created the wards during Reconstruction, the sounds of English words primarily filled the air. But as migration altered the demographics of interwar Houston, native Texans noted the rise of these languages in the city. Spanish and a cacophony of languages and different accents and dialects emanated from Houston neighborhoods by the end of the 1920s. Even the names of new communities like Frenchtown and El Segundo Barrio spoke to the linguistic, spatial, and demographic changes taking place in Houston. Those languages became markers of difference that fueled the development of hierarchies between Anglos and immigrants, while also fueling black political appeals.

But while the sounds of French, Spanish, and even a bit of Italian could be now heard in the wards, black Houstonians could read about Cimbee's exploits in language that gently poked fun at linguistic patterns found in the rural anglophone South. By writing "fokes" instead of "folks" and substituting "cullud" for "colored," Williams used dialect to mark blackness. His writing may have been inaccessible to people with last names like Prejean, Alisi, and Villagomez. In the *Informer*, then, language was a marker of group belonging that excluded many other migrants. And it was probably for the best if other groups of migrants did not understand Cimbee. The character frequently used ethnic slurs to describe the Houstonians he encountered. In a single column from 1927, Cimbee refers to "Mexikin greezers," "Chinks," and "Japs." Slurs were part of the racial soundscape of Jim Crow Houston, where white supremacists often noted black inferiority through the use of degrading racial epithets. Police officer Lee Sparks routinely called the black people in the San Felipe district "niggers." Many of the white Houstonians who took the stand to testify in the wake of the Houston Riot of 1917 referred to the "nigger soldiers" who had shot at them on August 23 of that year. And when Ku Klux Klan supporter Billie Mayfield went on white supremacist tirades in his newspaper, *Colonel Mayfield's Weekly,* he typically called black people "darkies." As newcomers entered the city, Anglos and African Americans used ethnic and racial slurs to further distance themselves from these groups. Barbara Jean Berry remembered that African Americans called the Italians in Fifth Ward "dagos." After Inez Prejean moved to the city, Houstonians called her "coonass," a pejorative term for Cajun.[29] For Billie Mayfield, Italians were "wops" and Jews were "kikes." Williams also incorporated the racialized language heard on Houston streets into "Cimbee's Ramblings." Diverse Texans responded to rapid demographic change by using xenophobic language to assert superiority over other groups.

But language was also a sign of how some of the newcomers who were legally white did not share Anglos' views toward Houston's black population. During Cimbee's exchange with Tony in 1926, the Italian American migrant uses noticeably respectful language when speaking to the black man. Their dialogue implies that the two have an affable relationship devoid of the hierarchical language used between black and white people in the Jim Crow South. Tony refers to Cimbee as "Missa Cimbee," and the East Texas migrant refers to his Italian acquaintance as "my frin." Black people referred to one another as Mr. and Mrs. in their neighborhoods and institutions, but Anglo Texans would not have used these titles to address black people. Cimbee frequently described Anglos who called him disparaging terms like "uncle" and "boy," but Tony does not follow that custom. The column thus portrays the Italian-born man as someone who does not follow the social mores of a Jim Crow society. For *Informer* readers, Tony's linguistic choice distanced him from Anglo Texans. The Italian character benefitted from some of the privileges of whiteness, like voting, but his treatment of Cimbee suggested a difference between him and Anglo Houstonians, who had a longer (and more violent) history with African Americans.

Various Houstonians used language to enforce hierarchy, make claims for citizenship rights, and mark cultural difference. For Anglos, the Spanish language marked ethnic Mexicans as culturally inferior, and they used that linguistic prejudice to justify separating the groups in schools. Through culture, they asserted an Anglo/Mexican division that ordered the "white" spaces where the groups made contact. Ethnic Mexicans learned, in the process, that legal claims to whiteness did not lead to equality with Anglos in local institutions. Black Houstonians also called attention to linguistic differences between themselves and other groups of migrants, especially those legally marked as white, like ethnic Mexicans and Italians. *Informer* writers employed the anti-immigrant sentiment of the postwar era in order to advance black political rights. Yet they also used language to suggest that legally white ethnic groups might not behave in the same way toward them as the Anglo majority. In this era of anti-immigrant nationalism, some Anglos would use European immigrants' relationship with black Houstonians to suggest that these groups were not committed to white supremacy.

IMMIGRANTS, BLACKNESS, AND WHITE SUPREMACY

Jews and Italians counted for only a small fraction of the Bayou City's population, but they were particularly visible to black Houstonians and ethnic Mexicans because of the groups' spatial proximity. European immigrants often lived in the wards, adding to the already diverse blend of cultures and ethnicities found in those districts. When ethnic Mexicans first began moving to Segundo Barrio in the 1910s, the neighborhood was not only one-third black, but also half Jewish.[30] Some Italian and Jewish Houstonians made homes on the outskirts of areas where black people made up the majority. People from Italy tended to live in each ward rather than develop one "Little Italy." Italian families could be found throughout Fifth Ward, for example. In 1920, seven Italian families lived on Gregg Street, which lay between Lyons Avenue and Liberty Road, in the heart of the growing black community in Fifth Ward.[31] Arthur and Leanna Berry's family on Whitty Street paid rent to Italians on Sunday mornings, and they purchased groceries on credit from Italian-owned stores, as did many of their neighbors.

On the periphery of older, more established neighborhoods, foreign-born migrants sometimes lived next door to black families. Farther down Whitty from the Berry family on the edge of black Fifth Ward, Italian-born Joe Alisi and his family resided next door to the Butchers, a black family with roots in Alabama and Texas. And just a few doors away, the Mexican-born Aguire family lived next to the "colored" Bourgeois family from Louisiana.[32] European immigrants also lived in Independence Heights, the black town located on the outskirts of Houston. Sam and Bertha Goldberg, who listed Russia and Poland as their places of birth; the Blazeck family from Germany; and Sterle and Mary Jette from Italy all resided in a town with a black mayor and sheriff.[33]

Jim Crow laws delineated black from white by maintaining a spatial separation; however, the Jews and Italians who lived near African Americans or resided in Independence Heights transgressed the racial order. By the standards of the postwar United States, the Goldberg, Blazeck, and Jette families would have been considered at least somewhat marginal in that they chose to live in a black-majority space. Living in a place where African Americans occupied positions of leadership was a departure from norms established by Anglo Texans. The nonblack residents of Independence Heights thus shared a commonality in that they quite literally lived on the fringes of mainstream white society.

In the pages of *Colonel Mayfield's Weekly*, Mayfield noted African Americans' cultural relationship with non-Anglo migrants. The Klansman unleashed weekly tirades that condemned the social ills he saw plaguing the city in the 1920s, and he and his allies especially worked to derail coalitions formed between black Texans and other groups. Articles in the journal paid particular attention to the relationship between blacks, Catholics, and Jews. Mayfield asserted that the cultural relationship between black, Catholic, and Jewish Houstonians in the decade following the Great War was inspiring black people to push for racial equality. He argued, for example, that the fledgling motion-picture industry threatened white supremacy. One particular film that drew his ire starred a New Orleans–born actor named Ben Turpin, who was also a devout Catholic. According to *Colonel Mayfield's Weekly*, the movie's Jewish producers cast Turpin alongside "negro vamps" in an effort to promote "mixed love affairs" on the silver screen.[34] For Mayfield, Turpin's movie was symptomatic of a racial problem he also saw in postwar Houston: Jews and Catholics making inroads with black people, who were supposed to occupy the lowest position in the segregated society. While anti-immigrant sentiment was characteristic of the Klan in every part of the United States following World War I, tension over the relationship between Catholics, Jews, and African Americans in Houston illustrates how anti-Semitic and anti-Catholic sentiment in that section of the country was also rooted in concerns over how immigration and urbanization would affect the black/white color line in a Jim Crow society. This was another sign that new groups were becoming part of an older racial discourse in eastern Texas that historically concerned the hierarchy of white over black.

Mayfield especially targeted signs of multiethnic coalition building. Any hint of interracial cooperation could lead to violence, as when Klansmen physically attacked a white attorney who had won lawsuits for black clients.[35] One issue of the newspaper claimed that a Jewish man named Julius Rosenfield had started an organization, called the Patriots of America, that included members from diverse backgrounds. The group, according to *Colonel Mayfield's Weekly,* comprised "Jew peddlers, negro truck drivers, Mexicans who have been taking jobs away from good old American boys, [and] negro wash women."[36] The author opined that the organization was actually a front for an economic scheme designed by Rosenfield to make money, and urged his Klan-sympathizing readers to take action against the coalition. Two of the groups mentioned in the article—Jews and ethnic Mexicans—had legal claims to whiteness. But by describing them alongside black people, Mayfield constructs a multiethnic hierarchy that places all of these groups beneath the Anglo majority: Jewish and Mexican Texans may be white according to the law, but they are not equal to Anglos. Along with Anglos' use of language to enforce local hierarchy, *Colonel's Mayfield Weekly* offers another example of how white legal status alone did not define a person's standing in interwar Houston.

Mayfield's views on race certainly countered those of "Cimbee's Ramblings" author Simeon Williams, but both writers depicted recent European immigrants and their descendants as people who didn't always share Anglo Texans' attitudes toward black people. The Klan supporter's editorials made this distinction in order to question whether immigrants would maintain his brand of white supremacy. Articles focused on the ways that non-Anglo groups did not behave like proper white folks, especially when it came to their engagement with people of African descent. The Klan boycotted Jewish merchants who advertised in the *Informer* because of their economic ties to black Houstonians. Sakowitz, a department store owned by two Ukrainian-born brothers who settled in Galveston, appealed to *Informer* readers throughout the 1920s for business. The popular store Zindler's and Sons used the black newspaper to promote everything from "jazz suits"— "the Suit of the hour for young men," for $39.50—to silk dresses for women.[37] According to C. F. Richardson's family, intimidation kept some Jewish advertisers from advertising in the weekly, but the Zindler family never bowed to Klan pressure.[38] As a result, *Colonel Mayfield's Weekly* targeted Ben Zindler, alleging that his sales had dipped because of the Klan. The newspaper openly taunted Zindler by publishing anti-Semitic jokes directed toward the business owner.[39] Their open animosity toward Jewish merchants who supported a black-owned enterprise is emblematic of the Klan's concerns that interethnic ties could form and thereby destabilize Anglo supremacy. The Houston Klan's assertions of superiority over Jewish residents was, therefore, based on how the latter group engaged with black people in the segregated society.

Their economic relationship to merchants like Zindler perhaps influenced the *Informer* staff to depict Jewish Americans in a positive light. When *Informer* writers objected to immigrants' economic position and citizenship rights, they tended to focus on ethnic Mexicans, Italians, and occasionally people of Asian descent. Jewish people, however, were conspicuously absent from these protests. Instead, the *Informer* praised Jewish Americans as an example of a group that triumphed over oppression. In an editorial titled "A Lesson from the Jewish Race," Richardson argued that the accomplishments of "this great race" should "serve as milestones to the colored race." Zindler's and the Sakowitzes' financial relationship to the newspaper likely influenced the editor's stance. The *Informer's* financial success depended, in part, on advertising dollars, and prominent Jewish-owned stores placed ads in the paper. The financial support from these popular retailers likely dissuaded Richardson and Williams from printing negative portrayals of Jewish Houstonians, or protesting the fact that they could vote and sit at the front of streetcars. Instead, Richardson listed the positive qualities he observed among the group: "They are thrifty, progressive, shrewd, sagacious, attending to their own business and letting others alone; being given less to racial prejudice than other groups of the Aryan race."[40]

By referring to Jewish Americans as members of the "Aryan race," Richardson acknowledged the diversity within the category of white. Anglo-Saxon Protestants made up the majority and dominated the city's political and economic institutions; in fact, they used holidays like "San Jacinto Day" (the annual celebration of General Santa Anna's surrender after the Battle of San

Jacinto in 1836) to commemorate how "the Anglo-Saxon people won their way to supremacy in the Southwest," as the *Houston Post* declared.[41] But Anglo-Saxon was not the only version of whiteness in Houston, and the *Informer* showed an acute awareness of this diversity. In their portrayals of their relationships with European immigrants like Jews and Italians, *Informer* contributors often depicted them as white, but a different type of white.

Black Houstonians and ethnic Mexicans contrasted the actions of European ethnic groups living in the wards with the behavior of the Anglo majority. Both noted that the recent immigrants did not share the same racial sentiments as Anglo Texans. Barbara Berry commented that Italians were "friendlier" and "more tolerant of black people" than Anglos in the city, perhaps because they sometimes lived near their black customers and tenants. Like the fictional Cimbee, Berry based these distinctions in social mores that marked racial hierarchy. She commented that, while Anglos expected black people to always say "yes ma'am" and "no ma'am" while avoiding eye contact during conversations, Italians in Fifth Ward did not expect those signs of deference.[42] An ethnic Mexican man living in Sixth Ward also observed that European immigrants did not share Anglo Texans' views of Mexican inferiority. Whereas Anglos often derided people of Mexican descent because of the legacy of the war in 1836, he remarked that "the Battle of San Jacinto didn't mean a damn thing" to the Jewish, Lebanese, Italian, German, and Greek Houstonians in the area.[43] Such statements from ethnic Mexicans and African Americans would have confirmed Billie Mayfield's suspicion that some newcomers neither respected the racial order established by the color line nor shared Anglos' notions of Mexican inferiority.

But *Informer* contributors complained about the Italian migrants living in or near their neighborhoods, even if these newcomers treated them differently. In places like Fourth Ward, where New Negroes stressed autonomy to fight white supremacy, immigrant-owned homes and businesses seemed to threaten their struggle. The *Informer* portrayed this spatial proximity in a decidedly negative light. One editorial argued that the relationship between Italian immigrants and black Houstonians was economically exploitative. "Aside from a few members of the race these foreigners employ (and this is only done for business reasons), not one red cent of this money ever comes back to the race; they aid no worthy and laudable racial causes, support no colored institutions, advertise in no colored publications, and their only interest in our people is devising ways and means to separate the colored race from its hard earned money."[44] Cimbee was one of the first observers to note the diversification of the city's neighborhoods. The wandering trick-ster noted with agitation that Italians (or "Eyetalyuns" as he called them) owned property in Freedman's Town. Cimbee's "San Fillipy nayberhood," or the San Felipe district in Fourth Ward, was also home to his creator, Simeon Williams, who taught in the neighborhood's Gregory School. In Cimbee's opinion, immigrants had too much economic clout in this community. He complained in 1925, "We's set rite cheer in Houston an' let ever furriner on God's green urth cum in heer an' by up ever bit uv vakunt propity rite under our nozes."[45] Two years later, he voiced concerns about the growth of the Italian population in a letter to his friend Gus. "Us black fokes bin livin in dat nayberhood, Gus, for de las 50 or 60 yeers . . . an now yu'll fine awimos es minny Eyetalyuns out dere es cullud fokes."[46]

Cimbee's statements emphasized a half century of African American community-building efforts, which made it a significant black space in the Jim Crow city. Black Houstonians' history of activism and the push for autonomy affected how they perceived migrants from other nations. Residents of communities like the San Felipe district considered these neigh-borhoods to be "theirs." The *Informer*'s discussions of immigrants reveal some of the ways that the New Negro generation responded to the new peo-ple they encountered during this era of migration. And as Billie Mayfield's writing indicated, that history of black/white struggle also influenced the ways white supremacists regarded immigrants.

Billie Mayfield's rants, as well as the ongoing prejudice against the Spanish language, suggest that Anglos considered whiteness more than a legal category. Since Anglos made up the majority of the population, they worked to impose their cultural and social customs on newcomers. As Mayfield's newspaper showed, those mores included maintaining white supremacy through a con-stant acknowledgment of black inferiority in words and actions. Refusing to conform to Anglos' sociocultural notions of racial order made certain groups threats to white supremacy, which meant that Anglos might target them with contempt. As different groups of migrants discovered, then, their relationship to blackness influenced how they ranked within the broad category of white.

CATHOLICS AND "SOCIAL EQUALITY"

Suspicion about newcomers and their commitment to the color line also involved Catholics, whose racial practices became a special cause for concern among segregationists, who worked diligently to maintain white supremacy. As ethnic Mexicans, Italians, and Creoles of color migrated to Houston, the number of Catholic churches in the city increased. These groups forged Catholic religious space in a Protestant-majority city. Black and Anglo Christians in eastern Texas leaned toward Protestant faiths. Built in 1887, St. Nicholas in Third Ward was the only Catholic parish that existed in a black neighborhood prior to World War I. The spread of Catholicism indicated demographic change in Houston.

Anti-Catholicism greeted the Creoles of color, ethnic Mexicans, and Italians who practiced their faith in Houston. As the number of parishes increased in Houston, Anglos frequently discussed distinctions between Catholics and themselves. For Anglo Protestants, ethnic Mexicans' Catholicism was yet another cultural difference that marked them as an inferior group. Some Anglo Houstonians worked to convert ethnic Mexicans to Protestantism. An organization called the Christian Endeavor took missionary trips to the Mexican city of Toluca in the 1920s. When members of the group spoke to Oak Lawn Presbyterian Church about their efforts, they stressed that their work was anti-Catholic, designed to stop the spread of that religious practice. One Anglo woman contended that she focused on educating Mexican youth, since "most of the teachers are Catholic and there is yet danger of the Mexican children falling under their influence."[47] Anti-Catholicism became another way that Anglos portrayed themselves as superior to ethnic Mexicans.

The Catholic churches established by migrants anchored their communities and evolved into significant spaces of contact between different groups. Ethnic Mexicans had erected a church in Second Ward called Our Lady of Guadalupe in 1912, just two years after the revolution began in Mexico, and this parish became a Mexican/Tejano social space. By 1922, church members included people from over a dozen states in Mexico and numerous Texas towns.[48] Janie Gonzales from central Texas; her future husband, Felix Tijerina, of Monterrey; the Gómez family from San Luis Potosí; and Ralph and Mary Villagomez of Guanajuato all attended mass at the parish when they arrived in Houston. Since Tejanos and Mexicans used the church, it served a community-building function for two groups of Mexican-descended people. By sharing space, Tejanos and Mexicans began to articulate a notion of community that included people from different nations.

Regardless of other cultural differences between Tejanos and Mexicans, Catholicism was central to both groups' culture and subjectivity. According to historian Roberto R. Treviño, "Ethno-Catholicism was a part of their very being, of how they understood themselves, related to others, and found meaning in life, as well as the means to deal with life and all it offered—the welcomed, the feared, and everything in-between."[49] The name "Our Lady of Guadalupe" refers to ethnic Mexicans' distinctive version of Catholicism, which had roots in the sixteenth century. According to tradition, in 1531 an Indian man named Juan Diego saw an apparition of the Virgin Mary outside Mexico City. She instructed Diego—in his native language, Nahuatl—to go to the Catholic bishop with a request that the community build a shrine in her honor. The Virgin visited Diego again on December 12, when her imprint appeared on his mantle. He brought this to the attention of the local bishop, who built a shrine on Tepeyac Hill to mark the place where Juan Diego had the original sighting. The Virgin's appearance to an Indian, and her use of an indigenous language, facilitated the conversion of other Indians to the Christian faith. Mexicans and Tejanos alike refer to her as "*la Virgen Morena*" (the brown Virgin) and "*la Morenita*" in addition to "*la Guadalupana*," which also links her to people with Indian ancestry.[50] By naming their first church after a central figure in Mexican religion, they marked that part of Navigation Street in Second Ward as their own. The appearance of the church was the first sign of the area's conversion from Second Ward to Segundo Barrio.

With its priests and nuns, veneration of the Virgin Mary, and practices like weekly Communion and confession, Catholicism certainly differed from Protestantism in terms of structure and theology; however, cultural practices also distinguished ethnic Mexican and Afro-Creole Catholics from the Protestant population. Unlike Baptist and Methodist churches, Catholics sponsored dances and bazaars that featured popular bands playing secular music. For many, even playing blues or jazz meant breaching both religious and family mores. "You couldn't sing a blues like 'I kissed my baby last night and what a thrill,'" Sammy Price says of his childhood among staunch Protestants. "They'd banish you from the house."[51] His churchgoing family considered secular music sinful, no matter if the foot-tapping grooves he heard in church bore some sonic similarity to the blues music he longed to play.

But Catholics rarely had such concerns about secular music on church grounds. They did not draw the same strict dichotomies between the sacred and the secular that their Protestant peers often did. Although churches like St. Nicholas and Our Lady of Guadalupe certainly would not have played the latest Sippie Wallace records during mass, these congregations often held dances on church premises where attendees danced to secular music. Dance was so important to Afro-Catholics in Louisiana that Creoles of color and descendants of slaves had even developed a specific genre—an a cappella style they called *juré*—for church events. *Juré*, which means literally "to testify," is also called *bazar*, most likely because it developed during church bazaars. *Bazar* marches were especially popular during Lent, when couples also incorporated ring games into the celebration.[52]

Catholic churches in Houston sponsored fund-raising dances and concerts during church bazaars, and these events offered ethnic Mexican and Creole artists the space to perform as their communities developed. Some artists played their first gig at their local Catholic church. Because the church could charge for admission, "everybody would profit from that dance," said Illinois Jacquet, who attended St. Nicholas when his family first moved to Houston. Jacquet and his male siblings performed at Catholic church functions as members of the Four Jacquet Dancing Brothers. Through church performances, these entertainers could make money. Our Lady of Guadalupe also held church bazaars, where Spanish-speaking musicians performed waltzes and songs popular in Mexico. Parishioners remembered hearing Spanish-language songs about the Mexican Revolution like "La voluntina" on church grounds. During festivities, parishioners danced to the songs played by brass bands and ate treats like tamales. Lydia Mendoza sang at the church for the first time in 1936, at the beginning of her professional singing career.[53] Church bazaars helped shape a new cultural economy born from the acts of migration and establishing communities in a new city.

Catholics also brought racial and spatial practices into Houston that, on the surface, contrasted with Anglo and African American custom. Black and white Protestants had attended separate churches since Reconstruction, so interracial Baptist or Methodist churches would not have been the norm for most English-speaking Houstonians. Meanwhile, Catholics from assorted backgrounds worshipped at the same church. In the Catholic parishes of southwestern Louisiana, white, black, and mixed-race worshippers often attended mass together in the same church, and their children studied at the church school. This trend startled Texans, like Mary Rose Berry, who converted to Catholicism while her family lived in Fifth Ward. The Berry family of Shreveport had been Protestant, as had her mother Leanna's family in Wharton, Texas. But Arthur and Leanna Berry sent Mary Rose two hundred miles east to Lafayette, Louisiana, to study at Holy Rosary Catholic Church's school for girls. (Since Arthur Berry worked for the Southern Pacific Railroad, his daughter could ride the train from Houston to Lafayette for free.) In Texas, Berry had taken classes only with people who were black by law, but Louisianians from different backgrounds attended her Catholic school in Lafayette. "It was an integrated school," Berry recalled. "There were white, French [Creole], and black students." Born in Houston and raised Baptist, Berry eventually adjusted to the idea of white students sitting next to her in class: "We were all in school together and we all went to classes together. We ate together and [the white girls] were friendly."[54] Unlike her former, segregated school in Fifth Ward, Holy Rosary offered classes to a diverse student body in the Jim Crow era.

Catholics from different racial backgrounds in Louisiana had used the same church by necessity; men of African descent were not frequently ordained as priests, and when they were, they did not practice in the South. One priest, Louisiana-born John Plantevigne, left his university in New Orleans to join the Josephites in Baltimore, where he was ordained in 1907. He soon learned, though, that he was not welcome as a priest in his hometown. Archbishop James Blenk denied Plantevigne the right to preach in New Orleans. As Father Plantevigne remarked two years after the racial slight, "The blood of the Negro boils in resentment of a 'Jim Crow' system in the Catholic Church."[55] Since few priests of African descent worked in the South, most Catholics of color went to churches where white priests presided over mass. In rural parishes, this meant that people of different races attended the same church, and they sent their children to its school, since it was likely the only one in the area.

The practice of diverse Catholics sharing the same religious space continued in Houston. Migrants who were new to the city attended mass wherever they could, even if the first church they found had been created by a different racial or ethnic group. Since ethnic Mexican migrants lived in different parts of a vast city, some decided not to attend mass at Our Lady of Guadalupe. Magnolia Park residents walked to Immaculate Conception on Harrisburg Boulevard, where they attended church alongside Italian Catholics. Similarly, Our Lady of Guadalupe developed into a site of contact between ethnic Mexicans and Creoles of color when the latter began moving to the north side of Houston in the 1920s. Since Frenchtown and El Segundo Barrio were less than one mile apart, some Creoles chose to attend mass at Guadalupe instead of St. Nicholas in Third Ward, which was farther away. The trek from Frenchtown to El Segundo Barrio became a Sunday morning ritual for the Prejeans and other families from Louisiana in their first years in Houston.[56] It was not uncommon to find Italians, ethnic Mexicans, and/or Creoles of color in the same church.

The spread of Catholicism in Houston contributed to the Ku Klux Klan's fear that cross-cultural coalition building would threaten white supremacy. Anti-Catholicism was not unique to Houston's Klan, but the Bayou City version was informed by the possibility of racial exchange between diverse Catholics of color in a segregated city. For Houston Klansmen in the 1920s, this brand of anti-Catholicism was rooted in antiblack racism. Billie Mayfield watched the growth of multiethnic Catholicism with alarm. The diverse Catholics who attended mass at the same time seemed to upset the color line. Klansmen worried that Catholicism would upset the racial hierarchy of Jim Crow by promoting black civil rights, and by allowing interracial contact in Catholic churches. Mayfield and his supporters argued that Catholics condoned interracial sex between black men and white women. Accusations of Catholic-sponsored miscegenation filled the pages of the newspaper on a weekly basis, such as stories of white nuns bathing black male patients in Catholic hospitals. The newspaper informed readers that in San Antonio, a Catholic stronghold due to the large Texas Mexican population, a black Catholic priest described as "a big, burly, black bestial brute" gave Communion to white girls. The writer also pointed to a Catholic convent in Liberty County "where whites and blacks mingle freely."[57] Liberty County, located in East Texas between Houston and the Louisiana border, also had a growing Creole population. Articles in *Colonel Mayfield's Weekly* regularly condemned Catholics by arguing that they were integrationists who wished to subvert Jim Crow. Writers referred to the pope as the "Wop of the Vatican" and insisted that he intended to integrate the United States: "To him, social equality is a fundamental law. To him there can be no distinction between the black man and the white man."

Mayfield frequently used the threat of interracial contact between black men and white women to warn his readers of the dangers of Catholicism:

> Catholicise [*sic*] the negroes and you will have white and black people mingling in the same church, else violate a canon direct from Rome. You will have white priests calling in colored families, you will have colored priests calling in white homes. . . . Catholicise the coons and Father Jackson will be taking confessions from white girls. Black priests will be in control in white convents. Catholicise the coon and you will have social equality.[58]

Klan supporters who read the weekly rag knew that when writers discussed social equality, they were suggesting a sexual threat. "'Social equality,'" asserts historian Timothy B. Tyson, "was the euphemism of choice for the ancient taboo of sex between black men and white women. Virtually any self-assertion on the part of African Americans conjured images of 'amalgamation' in the minds of white Southerners."[59]

For black Texans, the charge of promoting social equality could be deadly. In 1916, a white mob lynched seventeen-year-old Jesse Washington, a black farmhand accused of raping and murdering a local white woman. A jury found Washington guilty and a judge sentenced him to death, but white spectators immediately took Washington from the courtroom and hanged him. As a crowd of thousands gathered to watch, the mob set fire to Washington's remains and took photographs of his mutilated corpse.[60] Mayfield condoned this type of violence: "The South has never been safe from the negro rape fiend. We have hung them by their necks, we have burned them at the stake, and still no woman is safe beyond the range of her husband's rifle."[61] In 1922 a white woman in Houston accused a black man named Luther Collins of raping her in a wood yard near Fourth Ward. According to the woman, a black man forced her and a male companion to the abandoned area at gunpoint. The attacker allegedly placed his gun to the man's head while he assaulted the woman. Although the complainant's male escort later said that he doubted Collins was the attacker, a judge found him guilty and sentenced him to hang in January of 1923.[62] Collins spent much of the next three years in various "death houses" while the Houston branch of the NAACP worked to raise money for his defense. The branch raised two thousand dollars from the public toward Collins's bond of twenty-five hundred dollars and refused to accept assistance from the national office. Because of the efforts of the NAACP, the Texas Court of Criminal Appeals reversed the original decision on the Collins case, and the young man stood trial several times before the district attorney recommended that the case be dismissed due to lack of evidence in 1926. Luther Collins became a free man again in September and soon returned to his former job. The case made national headlines and garnered acclaim for the Houston NAACP, since the local chapter helped a black man beat a rape charge in a state where accusations of "social equality" could result in death.[63]

Of course, interracial sex wasn't entirely the issue. White men considered only sex between white women and black men to be a problem. The *Informer* alleged that white Houstonians knew about black women living with white men in the city. "This paper has been persistent and consistent in its editorial contention for the elimination of these notorious practices of vice, and especially as it concerns white men cohabitating with colored 'mud-hens' and 'fan-feet,'" argued a writer.[64] At the same time that rape accusations against black men led to lynchings across the nation, Richardson asserted that the growing number of mixed-race people in the United States told a different story—sex between white men and black women. "Fully 6,000,000 mulattoes out of 14,000,000 colored Americans speak louder than words that somebody is more anxious for 'social intermingling' than the colored race," argued the *Informer*.[65] In the 1920 census, one-quarter of the African Americans in Houston were described as "mulatto."[66] The history of white male access to black women's bodies certainly left its mark on the people of the western South.

The growth of multiethnic Catholicism exacerbated the Klan's fears about sex between black men and white women. Catholics of different races went inside the same buildings, and social practices like church dances may have also included mixed crowds. Illinois Jacquet claimed that when he was a child in the 1920s and 1930s, St. Nicholas dances were open to anyone willing to pay at the door—regardless of race. "If white people wanted to come, [if] they wanted to hear the music, there was no one gonna stop them," Jacquet recalled.[67] Such practices by the Afro-Catholic parish threatened white supremacy by defying the conventions of a Jim Crow society, especially the taboo against black men sharing social space with white women. People of different races attending mass or church dances in the same place at the same time seemed to undo Anglo-enforced Jim Crow, which demanded spatial separation in order to maintain the racial order. For Anglo Texans like Mayfield, the spaces a person occupied defined her or his racial status. So if a white person and black person used the same church, what marked the two groups as distinct?

But some Catholics of European descent did follow the racial order established by Anglos, which, in turn, legitimated their own claims to whiteness. Ethnic Mexicans and Creoles of color encountered segregationist practices in Catholic churches. At Immaculate Conception, ethnic Mexicans and people of African descent had to sit in the last four pews during mass. St. Joseph's, an Italian American Catholic church in Sixth Ward, banned ethnic Mexicans and people of African descent from attending mass. Church members told ethnic Mexicans that "their church" was across town in Segundo Barrio.[68] Even when diverse groups attended mass at the same church, spatial divisions inside the religious space indicated that Italians did not consider the other groups to be their racial equals.

Creoles of color also claimed that ethnic Mexicans segregated them inside Our Lady of Guadalupe. According to one of the founding Frenchtown families, the ethnic Mexican congregation relegated Creoles to the back pews. Also, Creoles of color could take Communion and confess only after everyone else had finished. Catholics with Spanish and French names could attend mass at the same time, but a spatial separation enforced a racial hierarchy inside the church. Regardless of phenotype or racial identity, Louisiana Creoles like the Prejeans learned that they were considered beneath people like Janie Gonzales and Ralph and Mary Villagomez. These acts of segregation within Italian and ethnic Mexican parishes highlight the ways religious cultures could enforce racial hierarchies.

In the face of segregation, newcomers built new parishes. Ethnic Mexicans formed another parish, Immaculate Heart of Mary, in 1926.[69] Creoles of color also worked to establish a parish in Fifth Ward. They completed the church called Our Mother of Mercy in 1929, and created a school there a few years later.[70] The church was the first physical marker of Frenchtown, and the first institution in a black Houston neighborhood that was not created by English-speaking people. In their book on Houston, WPA writers noted the centrality of the church to the people of Frenchtown: "The lives of these people center in Our Mother of Mercy Roman Catholic church and the adjoining convent school." In 1937, a third Catholic church for people of African descent, St. Anne de Beaupre, began as an offshoot of Our Mother of Mercy in Houston Heights. The presence of Creoles of color helped imbue Catholicism in the Bayou City with a French influence. Their association with French culture may have inspired Creoles of color to name St. Anne de Beaupré after the church and pilgrimage site in Québec.[71]

Churches in Segundo Barrio and Frenchtown could provide a buffer against segregation and stigmatization for people in the local communities. Catholic church schools at these sites allowed Creole and ethnic Mexican students to attend class with people who spoke their language and practiced the same religion—all of which eased the transition to Houston life. Their Catholic schools offered an autonomous space for newcomers with different cultural backgrounds. Witnessing the conflicts and school-yard antagonisms that made the streets and institutions of Fifth Ward spaces of conflict, some Creoles preferred to send their children to Catholic schools. Classroom teasing between Inez Prejean and a black female student led to a physical altercation in their Fifth Ward school. "To tell you the truth, I got scared of them. I'd see them black folks—I would run and get away from them," Prejean later stated.[72] After the constant conflict at Crawford, the Prejeans sent their children to school at St. Nicholas Catholic Church, the first black Catholic church in Houston. Gilbert and Marquette Jacquet also enrolled their sons in the elementary school at St. Nicholas, as did many other Louisianan families before the construction of Our Mother of Mercy in the late 1920s. Sending their children to Catholic school was one way for Creole parents to preserve religious customs while shielding them from people who did not understand their culture. John Castillo, who was born in Fifth Ward in 1919 but moved to Segundo Barrio as a child, attended school at Guadalupe: "At Guadalupe school, it was a predominantly Mexican-American school . . . so, we didn't have no problems."[73] Segregationist practices within some churches subsequently led to the establishment of new congregations where migrants could feel safe from discrimination. Their churches were not just sites of Catholic worship, then; these were racialized spaces created to oppose segregation.

Billie Mayfield feared that Catholics would not maintain the color line; however, the segregation of different groups in parishes across the city shows that hierarchies did develop within local churches. People with Italian and Mexican roots tended to maintain racial divisions in the institutions they dominated. These groups did not necessarily expect the same types of verbal deference that Anglos required in their day-to-day contact, but they upheld racial segregation within the institutions they established. In doing so, they acknowledged the relationship between space and the racial order. Church segregation expanded the reach of Jim Crow into cultural spaces.

In a growing migration city, segregation and race operated on multiple levels. While segregation laws legally divided "black" from "white" in public spaces like streetcars, local racial hierarchies emerged that could both conform to the color line and ignore legal categories. These laws did not require segregation in Catholic churches, but ethnic Mexicans and Creoles of color still faced exclusion and discrimination. Proximity to blackness affected one's place in these local institutions. People with the best claims to whiteness segregated the people they considered closer to black. Creoles of color did not see themselves as black, but other groups did, and they segregated them accordingly. People of Mexican descent were legally counted among the city's white population; nevertheless, their legal classification did not bar them from discrimination by other groups—especially since the history of mixing in Mexico, and the possible presence of Indian and African ancestry, could make ethnic Mexicans "less white" in comparison to European migrants. Regardless of the racial subjectivities they brought with them to Houston, or their legal racial classification, migrants' racial status at the local level could depend on which space they occupied at any given time.

Culture played a significant role in determining rank and status for some migrants. Anglos especially policed the parameters of whiteness by stigmatizing certain cultural practices. School administrators strove to alter ethnic Mexican cultural practices by denouncing the Spanish language and segregating Spanish speakers from Anglos in the spaces where they made contact. They defined Catholicism as a lesser religion and regarded the denomination as a threat to white supremacy. Black Houstonians, meanwhile, used their knowledge of English to argue that they should have equal rights, and felt resentful of the people from different nations who did not share those cultural norms but could nevertheless access more citizenship rights. The ways that Anglos and African Americans used culture shows how the influx of new groups affected racial discourse and racial practice. As the city diversified, myriad racial practices and understandings of racial hierarchy emerged at the local level.

FOUR

"We Were Too White to Be Black and Too Black to Be White"

AS A YOUNG GIRL COMING of age in Fifth Ward in the 1930s and 1940s, Mary Rose Berry had a circle of friends that included people who identified as Negro and "French." Berry lived near Frenchtown, and even attended school at Our Mother of Mercy after converting to Catholicism as a child in around 1939. Her day-to-day life included people with roots in southwestern Louisiana. But one aspect of her relationship with her friends in Frenchtown troubled her. Racially ambiguous Creoles of color could access spaces that excluded brown-skinned Mary Rose. Her lighter-skinned friends transgressed the racial boundaries enforced by legal segregation by "passing" for white temporarily. This was especially noticeable when she and her classmates used public transportation to travel downtown. Berry laughed and talked with her Creole friends while waiting for the bus in Fifth Ward. Once on board, however, the lighter Creoles headed for seats at the front, while she had to sit in the colored section in the rear. "They'd sit up there with the white people," Berry recalled, noting that her friends pretended not to know her once they sat in the white section. "And by the time I'd pay my little money and go back, they'd turn their head to keep from speaking. . . . I mean they really did that a lot."[1] Berry felt resentful toward Creoles of color who "wanted to pass for white" outside of Frenchtown.

As racially ambiguous people, Berry's Creole friends employed different racial practices in different spaces. Creoles of color were legally black, and many families sent their children to segregated schools in Fifth Ward. On city buses and in other public spaces, though, some Creoles of color engaged in "discontinuous passing." They temporarily slipped into spaces designated for white people in order to access privileges associated with white racial status.[2] Yet they returned home to Frenchtown and asserted a Creole subjectivity that rejected racial binaries. Their public activities point to numerous layers of racial identification and racial practice that occurred at the local level. These identifications were a product of multiple heritages and experiences: a racial subjectivity brought from rural southwestern Louisiana, their ongoing community-building efforts in Frenchtown, their legal position as Negroes in Jim Crow society—and their light skin, which gave them racial ambiguity within the black/white binary.

Skin color influenced the countless understandings of race and status that circulated within a diversifying migration city between World Wars I and II. Black Houstonians noted that differences in skin color produced hierarchical notions of status and beauty within local communities. For ethnic Mexicans and Creoles of color, a lighter complexion could allow one to avoid the stigma associated with dark skin in a city that employed a black/white binary. This was especially significant to people of Mexican descent in the 1930s as some government agencies attempted to recategorize them as "colored." Racial ambiguity allowed some Creoles of color to move betwixt and between black and white worlds, escaping the indignity of sitting in the back of the bus, or securing the higher wages of jobs denied to "black" workers. Others used passing to reject the racial dichotomies enforced by Jim Crow laws. Both Creoles and ethnic Mexicans learned that successful navigation of the black/white binary required careful and crafty manipulation of the logics of racial recognition and representation.

The influx of multihued groups who spoke an array of languages complicated one of the central features of a Jim Crow society—namely, the production of racial hierarchy through access to space. The wide range of physical characteristics and the variety of languages seen and heard across Houston by 1930 made a person's race increasingly difficult to ascertain. As scholar Ian Haney-López has shown, "The construction of race thus occurs in part by the definition of certain features as White other features as Black, some as Yellow, and so on."[3] But the features of racially ambiguous people often did not match their legal racial assignment. Black Texans, Creoles of color, and ethnic Mexicans had a variety of different complexions that reflected the hybridity of their ancestries. Their physical characteristics could hinder or enable their ability to access spaces designated for white people, regardless of whether they legally had the right to enter those spaces. Furthermore, the variety of languages migrants brought to Houston meant that people with legal claims to whiteness, like ethnic Mexicans and Italians, did not always speak English like the Anglo majority. A multiethnic public operated within the white/black public face of Jim Crow, and the diverse groups who appeared in segregated spaces made whiteness and blackness increasingly unstable visual and sonic categories.

The issue of passing and the stain of colorism figured prominently in conversations among diverse Houstonians who worried that these practices could potentially distort efforts to build group solidarity in a new place. During the 1930s, people of Mexican descent from Mexico and Texas forged community and asserted a Mexican ethnic identity through labor organizing, and through the creation of social clubs. New Negroes continued pushing for racial solidarity among all people of African descent worldwide. Activists from these communities argued that racial passing and skin-color hierarchies threatened these community-building efforts. If access to space symbolized power in a Jim Crow society, then a person with light skin who passed attained higher status than other members of his or her racial or ethnic group. Racially ambiguous Houstonians could, then, affirm or disavow racial membership (temporarily or permanently) by choosing to inhabit a particular space. Conversations on passing often centered on women, suggesting, perhaps, that women who passed would fail to pass down identity to the children they raised, leading to a loss of culture in the next generation. Skin color, therefore, influenced a person's access to segregated public spaces, but it also figured in intraracial/intraethnic discourse on hierarchy and group membership. The controversies surrounding skin color and passing highlight the complexities of racial subjectivity and racial hierarchy in an interwar migration city.

SKIN COLOR AND CASTE

Within black communities, discussions of skin color were a common part of racial discourse. Black Americans used words like *yellow* and *red* to describe some of the assorted hues found among people of African descent. In the folklore of Texas, perhaps no other woman is as popular as the one remembered as the Yellow Rose. Popularized nationwide by country-and-western singers like Michael Martin Murphy, the song is part of a romanticized origin story for the Lone Star State. According to legend, Mexican general Antonio López de Santa Anna was so enraptured by the beauty of a woman named Emily, the so-called Yellow Rose, that he failed to notice the opposing army's descent upon his camp. Sam Houston's troops won the battle, Emily escaped, and "Tejas" became the Republic of Texas.

But fewer people know the racial story embedded within the song. Some researchers maintain that Emily West was a free woman of color. The word *yellow* has been used to describe light-skinned people of African descent since the earliest days of North American slavery in Virginia, and African Americans continued using the term well after the Civil War. (A black cowboy in West Texas named Lightnin' Washington would sing a spirited song for Alan Lomax called "My Pretty Little Yellow Gal" a century later.)[4] Emily was likely the product of sex across the color line, like so many of the slaves and free people of color described as "yellow." She was born in New York but moved to Mexican Texas, perhaps in hopes of finding less social restraint in an emerging frontier society.[5] Once in Texas, she worked for a white man named Colonel James Morgan on his plantation in New Washington (later renamed Morgan's Point) as an indentured servant. When Mexican troops entered the area, General Santa Anna—whose own wife lived in Mexico City—chose Emily as his new mistress. Some scholars argue that a black man penned the original words to "The Yellow Rose of Texas" to express his affection for Emily:

> There's a yellow rose in Texas
> That I am a going to see
> No other darky knows her
> No one only me
> She cryed [*sic*] so when I left her
> It like to broke my heart
> And if I ever find her
> We nevermore will part.[6]

Lighter skin was one of the primary markers of mixed racial ancestry. When interviewers from the Federal Writers' Project talked with a former Texas slave named Lucy Lewis during the Great Depression, they learned that her husband, Cinto, called her "Red Heifer." As Cinto Lewis recalled, "[H]er pap's name was Juan and he was a Mexican," which gave Lucy a distinct complexion.[7] In Frenchtown, many Creoles of color had just as much European as African ancestry, if not more, and black Texans noted the light complexions of the Louisianians. "Some of them was so light," remarked Barbara Berry about her Creole classmates.[8]

Skin color could also be a divisive issue among the diverse-looking Americans counted as black. People with light and dark complexions noted instances of ostracism by other members of their race. Donaville Broussard, a former slave from Louisiana who lived in eastern Texas, argued that his darker-skinned stepfather disliked him because of his light skin. Broussard had a white father and a white maternal grandfather, and because of his racial heritage, he and his stepfather "couldn't get along." Likewise, Christia Adair claimed that "[t]here was a time when Negro children who were of a mulatto color or very fair, were not looked upon and loved like children of darker skin." Her mother, who had a white father, endured teasing and public ridicule from other African Americans. "They pulled her hair and made fun of her and used vulgar language to her," said Adair.[9]

The sexual exploitation of women of African descent further influenced the ways that former slave societies in the Americas depicted light-skinned people, especially women. Music and films from the era often portray light-skinned women of African descent as duplicitous, hypersexual man stealers with loose morals. The stereotype is rooted in the "Jezebel" myth, which circulated before the Civil War. "Jezebel" was an enslaved black woman who was "governed almost entirely by her libido." The "fancy trade" further tied notions of black promiscuity to a particular phenotype. In the slave market, especially in New Orleans, fancy girls were light-skinned slaves sold to affluent white men.[10] The stereotypical link between women's skin color and sexual availability could be found across the Americas. In Brazil, for instance, a popular phrase asserts that a Brazilian man should have "a white woman to marry, a mulata to fornicate, a black woman to cook."[11] The Jezebel stereotype still informed portrayals of women of color in the twentieth century. In the 1929 film *St. Louis Blues,* a light-skinned woman seduces Bessie Smith's paramour. When discussing the temptress, one character says there was "no telling what a yellow woman will do," implying a lack of morality in women with that skin tone. Later in the film, Bessie Smith calls her romantic rival a "little red slut." *Cabin in the Sky,* released in 1943, uses similar tropes to distinguish between two black women. Church-going Petunia Jackson, portrayed by Ethel Waters, is the exact opposite of Lena Horne's sensual Georgia Brown, who tries to seduce Petunia's husband. The visual contrast between the chocolate-skinned Waters and the lighter Horne visually coded these sexualized racial stereotypes for the audience.[12]

The most widespread tension surrounding skin in communities of people of African descent, however, involved accusations of skin-color hierarchy that placed lighter-skinned black people at the apex of society. Barbara Berry remembered that skin color dictated privilege in her Fifth Ward community, where Creoles of color increasingly entered black institutions in the interwar era: "For school plays and church plays, they always got the cute, light-skinned girl with the curly hair. It always has been like that."[13] Even without the presence of white people, Texans with varying amounts of African and European ancestry acknowledged the privileged status of whiteness when they associated lighter skin with rank or beauty. African Americans even had specific language that highlighted the link between status, economic standing, and skin color. When a black person called someone "yellow wasted," they described, "mulattos or light-skinned African Americans who failed to use their skin color to their advantage to gain social and economic success."[14] Music and films of the interwar era often used skin color to signal attractiveness or desire. "Black women evil," sang bluesman Texas Alexander. "Gonna get me a yellow woman, see what she will do." In some areas, the word *black* carried a negative connotation. "Black was an insult," said Berry. "Black meant the same as a nigger." To insult one another, she recalled, she and friends would taunt one another by saying, "You old black so-and-so" as children. "We used to call each other black when we'd get mad. . . . 'You old black dog.'"[15]

Statements from contemporary black women, however, indicated that not all believed that dark skin was less attractive than skin that appeared closer to white. Sixth Ward native Naomi Polk praised her family's dark skin, which she credited to being "African to the bone" on her mother's side. In her handwritten memoirs, she voiced delight at her "beautiful deep chocolate brown skin." Blues singer and Houston native Sippie Wallace asserted, "I'm so glad I'm brown-skin . . . chocolate to the bone."[16] These Houstonians showed pride in their dark skin even as popular films and newspapers of the time tended to focus on lighter women as symbols of black female beauty.

Celebrations of dark skin could be lost, though, in a society where corporations sold skin lighteners, products designed to whiten dark skin. Altering skin color and hair texture was lucrative business in the 1920s and 1930s, so companies profited handsomely from products that marketed light skin as the standard of beauty. The *Informer* was full of advertisements for skin lighteners. The company that manufactured the skin-lightening tonic Ko-Verra promised to make "the darkest skin look light tan, while those with tan skin look like dark white people." One advertisement quoted salon owner Mrs. Elnora Gresham, who claimed, "Since I have been using Ko-Verra many of the white ladies who come to my beauty shop say they would hardly know I am a Colored lady."[17]

New Negro activists and writers decried skin-color consciousness as a pockmark on black society. At a time when "race pride" became synonymous with activism, divisions over skin color perplexed race leaders of the era. Locally and nationally, activists urged black people to abandon the skin-color hierarchy. Writer Zora Neale Hurston criticized the tendency to promote people with lighter skin, calling it black America's "dirty little secret." Hurston's novels from the 1930s frequently highlighted ways that skin color informed status and desire. In *Their Eyes Were Watching God*, the light-skinned protagonist, Janie Starks, is often seen as an object of desire and derision because of her skin color, as is John Pearson of Hurston's 1934 novel, *Jonah's Gourd Vine*.[18] Meanwhile, Cyril V. Briggs, founder of the African Blood Brotherhood, proclaimed that black people should "[k]ill the caste idea. Stop dividing the race into light and dark."[19] Skin color could be divisive among people of African descent at a time when scholars, writers, and activists pushed for solidarity in order to fight Jim Crow.

Debates over skin color among people of African descent illuminate racial practices that developed within intraracial spaces. Black Americans noted the range of shades and hues that could be found within the broad category of Negro, and they often used racialized language to describe this physical diversity. Some alleged that variations in skin color produced different levels of stigma and privilege within black communities. These hierarchies were rooted in the existence of a Jim Crow society that placed white over black by constantly defaming blackness and privileging whiteness, and they informed relations between people who were legally members of the same race.

Conversations about skin color in the interwar era were not limited to black communities. People of Mexican descent had varying amounts of European, Indian, and/or African ancestry, which produced differences in skin color, and physical appearance could affect their ability to access the privileges of white status. Ethnic Mexicans with darker skin could be marked as nonwhite—and, therefore, subject to segregation—more easily than their lighter peers. A. D. Salazar, a business owner in Magnolia Park, discovered this while driving through Texas. During a stop for food in the town of Gonzalez in the late 1920s, an Anglo woman served Salazar, but not his dark-skinned companion. "We don't serve Mexicans. We'll serve you but not him," she told him. Salazar countered that both he and his friend were Mexican, but the darker man received service only when Salazar asked, "Listen, do you take Mexican money?"[20] Whatever legal claims to white-ness ethnic Mexicans possessed, segregation was often a matter of local practice—and sometimes depended upon the shade of one's skin—rather than official classification.

Texas Mexicans recognized that people with light skin could avoid some of the discrimination their darker peers faced. As historian Neil Foley notes, "Some light-skinned middle-class Mexican Americans had always been able to gain admittance to, if not outright acceptance in, Anglo society."[21] Born to a Tejano family that had migrated to Houston, Carmen Cortés knew that her white skin and light hair color helped her land a job at the Solo-Serve store. "They couldn't tell that I was a Mexican until I said my name," she said of Anglo business owners she encountered.[22] Cortés's features perhaps helped her land a job at city hall. A coalition of business owners and activists worked to find an ethnic Mexican woman who could successfully apply for a clerical position downtown. A group of Mexican American activists, including members of the League of United Latin American Citizens (LULAC), held a series meetings regarding the lack of Mexican American women working at city hall, and they decided to find a candidate who could be hired. On September 1, 1941, Cortés became the first ethnic Mexican woman to work in city hall.[23] The woman with light brown hair and eyes was less prone to attracting negative attention from those Anglo Houstonians who may have harbored anti-Mexican sentiment, so Cortés's physical appearance likely aided her selection.

Organizations founded by ethnic Mexicans in the late 1920s and early 1930s tackled the topic of skin color over the next decade as they negotiated Mexicans' place in the racial hierarchy. One of the city's first organizations for women of Mexican descent, El Club Femenino Chapultepec, grew from the Young Women's Christian Association. The YWCA was a segregated organization; black and white women attended meetings at two different branches. When they began joining in the late 1920s, Mexican American women entered the white branch. Eva Perez, an employee at the chamber of commerce, talked to the YWCA about creating a club for Latinas after seeing that no social organizations for ethnic Mexican women existed in city. The Anglo women initially balked at the idea of letting ethnic Mexicans use the facilities, and they cited religion as the primary reason for their hesitation. They wondered if Catholics fit into the organization's structure, although, as one ethnic Mexican woman asserted, "Catholics are the original Christians." A group of northern-born administrators took the issue to the board, however, and allowed the Catholics to join. The ethnic Mexican women created a subgroup within the white branch that they called El Club Femenino Chapultepec in the early 1930s.[24] (See figure 6.)

The women of El Club Femenino Chapultepec always insisted that they never meant to cause any trouble when they gathered to write a letter about

FIGURE 6. El Club Femenino Chapultepec at Sam Houston Park. Melesio Gómez Family Collection, Houston Metropolitan Research Center, Houston Public Library.

their status as ethnic Mexican people living in Houston, but in 1936 they created a scandal that rocked the regional offices of the YWCA and revealed the tenuous place of people of Mexican descent in Houston. During one of their weekly meetings at the YWCA, they decided to air their grievances about life in Houston. Estela Gómez, the secretary, took notes. Over the next six months, the women continued to meet and talk, and these conversations resulted in a letter that listed their concerns. "We wrote the letter down so we ourselves knew what we had to face in our community and what we had to do to improve the situation," Gómez said. "We wanted to do something for ourselves and our families." The result was a ten-point manifesto that became known as the "Letter from Chapultepec." The letter discussed ethnic slurs and cultural issues like negative portrayals of Mexican people in popular films.

The tenth point of the manifesto related directly to ethnic Mexicans and the question of color. People of Mexican descent, they wrote, "are called 'brown people,' 'greasers,' et cetera and of course want to be called white."[25]

Chapultepec's final issue spoke to how skin color could complicate ethnic Mexicans' place in Houston. The law categorized them as white, but the people coming into the city from Mexico and other parts of Texas often had multiracial ancestry that was reflected in the wide array of skin colors found in ethnic Mexican communities. The term *brown people* marked them as a nonwhite group, which could hurt their claims to whiteness in a place that considered anyone with African roots "colored."

Chapultepec was not the only ethnic Mexican organization to stress whiteness in the 1930s; the League of United Latin American Citizens, founded in Corpus Christi, Texas, in 1929, also made racial categorization part of its political project. LULAC is often deemed an "assimilationist" organization by modern scholars, and its members tended to assert a white racial identity. The designation *Latin American* in its name further allowed them to link themselves to whiteness, since *Mexican* was a racial designation in places like South Texas.[26] In an article from 1932, Tomás A. Garza described Anglo Americans and Latin Americans as "two GREAT PEOPLE, both descended from the White Race."[27] Likewise, in an article titled "Are Texas-Mexicans Americans," another LULAC writer asserted that "the Latin-Americans (Mexicans) who first braved and tamed the Texas wilderness" were "the first white race to inhabit this vast empire of ours."[28] By using a historical argument, LULAC members demonstrated that they considered themselves as a white ethnic group.

Ethnic Mexican organizations in the 1930s frequently mentioned Indian ancestry, which they did not see as a detriment to their ability to claim racial whiteness. LULAC members often discussed their Indian heritage with pride. Frequent contributor Rodolfo A. de la Garza wrote an article for *LULAC News* in 1932 in which he asserted that people of Mexican descent shared "the blood of cultured Aztecs and fierce Apaches, the reddest blood in the world." At the same time, he told fellow Mexican Americans that "in your veins races the hot blood of adventurous Castilian noblemen, the whitest blood in the world." A month later, de la Garza wrote another article, called "Our School Children," which argued that Mexican American children should not be segregated into separate schools in the Rio Grande Valley because of Indian ancestry. "Regardless of the amount of Indian blood in our children," he wrote, "the law has proclaimed them white!"[29] For de la Garza, indigenous heritage did not damage claims to legal whiteness.

Being marked as nonwhite could translate into being defined as "colored," especially in places that relied on a white/black dichotomy for racial classification. Federal and local agencies attempted to group ethnic Mexicans into the same category as African Americans during the Depression. In 1936, the U.S. Census Bureau instructed employers to categorize ethnic Mexicans as "colored" on birth and death records. LULAC lobbied the federal government, which eventually reversed the decision. When one LULAC member detailed how the organization found out about these attempts to mark ethnic Mexicans as nonwhite, he joked that they had found "'the nigger in the woodpile.'"[30] One year later, a white tax collector in Wharton County revealed that he'd been instructed by the White Man Union—a local political organization—to count Mexican Americans as colored. The White Man Union also forbade Mexican Americans to vote or participate in nominating candidates for county offices. LULAC investigated the situation and argued that it was illegal to use "Mexican" to distinguish a race of people. "It is generally conceded that the word 'race' on poll tax receipts is put there to distinguish the black (or colored) and white races," wrote a LULAC member in the *LULAC News*. The writer also noted that the governor of Texas, James Allred, when he was the state attorney general, had "rendered a decision to the effect that all persons of Mexican or Spanish extraction are recognized by law as belonging to the white race."[31] "Mexican," they argued, was not a racial category, but rather a group that could exist within the spectrum of whiteness.

White status signified more than the psychological benefit of racial superiority in a caste society. Whiteness meant access to more political and material benefits. White Texans could vote. White Texans were not lynched or executed in electric chairs at the same rate as black Texans. White children attended better-funded schools than black children, since Negro schools received between 5 and 17 percent of the total funds earmarked for school improvements in the city. White students enjoyed swimming pools, Bunsen burners, and typewriters not available in black schools.[32] When ethnic Mexicans in Houston and eastern Texas asserted that they were white, then, these declarations were efforts to avoid the same stigma that black Americans faced. They observed that black people occupied the bottom rung of society, and they were not eager to join them. People of Mexican descent living in eastern Texas, therefore, had to negotiate racial blackness.

LULAC constantly stressed that "colored" and "Mexican" constituted two different racial groups, and they worked to ensure that the law did not conflate the two. "[T]o be associated with blacks or any other dark race was considered 'an insult,'" writes political scientist Benjamin Márquez.[33]

Assertions of whiteness constituted both a political strategy to avoid legal segregation and a desire to distinguish themselves from a group that was legally restricted from accessing the same rights as white people. To avoid segregation, Mexican Americans had to prove that they were white and not colored; therefore, racial categorization as "white" was a fundamental part of their activism. LULAC activists argued that, as Americans of Mexican descent, they were still racially white.

In Houston, then, claims to whiteness rested on proximity to blackness, which made skin color a delicate topic. Brown-skinned ethnic Mexicans faced difficulties entering white spaces, since Anglos associated dark skin with "colored" status. This range of skin colors present in both ethnic Mexican and black communities often complicated race and hierarchy in Jim Crow Houston.

PASSING AND GROUP SOLIDARITY

Houstonians living in black and ethnic Mexican communities of the interwar era discussed a public phenomenon associated with race and space—the act of passing. When people "passed," they allowed others to believe they were members of another racial or ethnic group in order to avoid discrimination. Passing could occur on different levels. For people of African descent, passing allowed them to circumvent the black/white color line when they entered the racialized spaces created by segregation laws. For ethnic Mexicans, passing enabled them to evade local practices that marked people of Mexican descent as inferior to Anglos. As Houston diversified, a person's ability to pass could be based on visual and sonic markers of race and ethnicity.

Since the legal establishment of Jim Crow at the turn of the century, racially ambiguous Houstonians had economic incentive for crossing the color line. For example, after a 1908 city council ordinance Jim Crow-ed the vice district called the Reservation, economic concerns likely encouraged a prostitute named Thelma Denton to break segregation laws. Denton ran a house of prostitution populated with white and black women, and she ignored the 1908 law that forced sex workers of different races to operate in separate houses. The justice of the peace and an army of constables raided the Reservation in 1909, arrested Denton and twenty-five other black women, and charged them with vagrancy because they refused to move into segregated residences. The twenty-six women sued for their right to integrate and lost. Using census data from 1910, one historian has remarked that the Reservation had been thoroughly segregated after the raid. Yet when census taker E. G. Norton met Denton at her residence that year, he noted that she was white, as were the other occupants of the house. Only a year before, though, she had been listed as "colored" in a city directory. Apparently Denton found a way to earn more money. Rather than submit to Jim Crow and earn less money, Denton passed for white.[34]

Racial passing in black society was largely an urban phenomenon in the Jim Crow era, and linked to narratives of migration from rural to urban areas. Rural locales had fewer social spaces where races met, and people tended to know one another's family histories. But when racially ambiguous people migrated from areas where their family had lived for generations, they had the opportunity to create new narratives for themselves.[35] Houstonians in the interwar era noted the presence of racially ambiguous people who could access "white only" spaces. Writers for the *Informer* drew attention to the phenomenon when the newspaper began circulating after World War I. Cimbee issued a typically tongue-in-cheek commentary on passing that also incriminated beauty-business entrepreneurs who profited from the sale of skin lighteners. In 1924 Cimbee claimed to have burned his face while using Madame Nobia Franklin's skin bleach. A French ocean liner had come through the ship channel, and since only white people were allowed to visit, Cimbee used Franklin's cream to become white enough to see the spectacle.[36]

Creoles of color from rural southwestern Louisiana noted the existence of racially exclusive urban spaces, but some could choose whether or not to reveal their African ancestry when they ventured outside of Frenchtown. Inez Prejean learned to negotiate seating on public transportation in Houston as a young woman. The Prejean family identified as a mixture of races; however, Jim Crow laws in Houston divided the city's institutions and public spaces along a black/white binary. After moving to the Bayou City in 1927, Inez's mother told her children to always sit in the rear, since they were black by law. One day Prejean boarded a streetcar and made her way to an empty seat in the rear, as her mother had instructed her to do. Seeing the fair-skinned, dark-haired young woman in the "colored" section, the white conductor instructed Prejean to move forward. When he realized that the passenger spoke French-accented English, he explained that white people sat in the front. The Prejean family lived in Frenchtown in Fifth Ward, where she attended a "colored" school in the neighborhood; however, Inez realized that she could navigate the city's segregated interracial spaces outside of Fifth

Ward most easily as a white woman. From that day forward, she sat in the front section with white people. Reflecting on Prejean's tenuous place in Jim Crow Houston, an African American teacher in Fifth Ward told her she was "too black to be white and too white to be black" in a city that segregated residents along that very racial dichotomy.[37]

Racially ambiguous Houstonians could also exploit the fact that whiteness had become more difficult to determine using visual cues. The multiethnic reality that existed within Houston's black/white binary allowed some people to more easily transgress the racial line created by Jim Crow. By law, the category of "white" did not include just Anglos, but also ethnic Mexicans and European immigrant groups like Jews and Italians. Since all of these diverse groups had legal claims to whiteness, it was increasingly difficult to determine what "white" looked like. An olive-toned Italian who attended a white public school could be darker than a black student who enrolled at a segregated school for colored children. That visual instability gave racially ambiguous people an opportunity to pass for a member of another group. Creoles of color like Prejean possibly had an easier time entering white spaces in Houston because of the presence of groups who were legally white, but darker than Anglos. After all, if an Italian American, a light-skinned black Texan, a Creole of color, and an ethnic Mexican boarded a bus in Fifth Ward, could a bus driver distinguish between who should sit in the front and who should occupy the rear, based solely on visual cues? The Anglos charged with making these decisions in public spaces tried to avoid falsely accusing a white person of being black. In the 1930s, one person told an interviewer that Anglo southerners "are pretty careful before they call a person a Negro." The same individual also acknowledged that the people who enforced Jim Crow laws especially gave people from other nations the benefit of the doubt. "I look somewhat like a foreigner," he said, "so I can get by without a great deal of trouble."[38] The growth of migrant populations who had legal access to white space made it easier for racially ambiguous people of African descent to transgress the color line.

Some black Americans used ethnic Mexicans' legal claims to whiteness to their benefit. Langston Hughes, who emerged as a top figure in the Harlem Renaissance literati in the 1920s, knew that Mexicans' white legal status, and his own light skin, could allow him to shirk segregation in Texas in the early twentieth century. Hughes was raised in Kansas, but his father left the family and moved to Mexico to escape racism. As a child, young Langston took the train from the Midwest to Mexico City to visit his father, and the route took him through Texas. During one of his first trips with his mother and grand-mother, in around 1906, the black family could not purchase hot food from the dining car when they were hungry because of racial restrictions. When returning home from a summer in Mexico City as a teenager, however, Hughes found a way to access white accommodations. Hughes recalled, "[T]he only way I could purchase sleeping car space after I crossed the border into Texas was by pretending to be Mexican." The young man ignored the Jim Crow signs and asked for a berth by speaking Spanish. He "also ate in the diner all the way across Texas by pretending not to speak English."[39]

In the cases of Inez Prejean and Langston Hughes, their ability to pass was based on sonic, as well as physical, characteristics. Anglo Americans marked race through sound as well as skin color. Some observers claimed, for example, that they could discern distinctive qualities associated with sonic blackness in the timbre of classically trained Marian Anderson's voice when she performed opera.[40] Race was not just visual in Jim Crow America; it was sonic. Racial ambiguity, then, could arise from the way a person spoke. Prejean's French-accented English may not have seemed "Negro" to Houston bus drivers who had little experience with Creoles of color from southwestern Louisiana. When Hughes passed for ethnic Mexican, he played on the fact that some Spanish speakers could enter spaces legally reserved for white people in parts of Texas. For example, El Club Chapultepec organized within the white YWCA, and ethnic Mexican children attended white schools. Although administrators separated them from Anglo students, they were not barred from entering those schools. Hughes's ability to pass for Mexican did not entirely rest on his light skin and wavy hair, but also depended upon his success at speaking Spanish (or at least pretending to not know English).

While light-skinned black Americans may have used ethnic Mexicans' legal white status for their own benefit, some ethnic Mexicans passed as members of other ethnic groups. Migrants from rural Texas and immigrants from Mexico realized that a hierarchy existed between the groups recognized as white, and that some non-Anglo white people may have faced less dis-crimination in the 1930s. The authors of the 1936 "Letter from Chapultepec" voiced concerns that anti-Mexican prejudice made some disavow Mexican roots and pass for a different ethnicity: "Mexicans in [a] desire to get ahead have at times denied their nationality by calling themselves French, Italian, and Spanish," they wrote in the letter. Some felt that they would receive bet-ter treatment if Anglo Houstonians believed they belonged to a European ethnic group. Mexican-born Catalina Gómez Sandoval recalled that her light-skinned brother, Paul, had an easier time in school than she did. The Sandoval family claimed Scottish and Spanish ancestry; her paternal grandmother was a redhead, her mother had reddish-blond hair, and the rest of the family was "very white." Their classmates thought Paul was Jewish, so he faced less taunting at his multiethnic school. (His darker sister told everyone she was an Aztec princess who knew the location of Montezuma's treasure).[41] Jews and Italians certainly faced forms of discrimination, but in the 1920s, when anti-Mexican backlash intensified and politicians pushed for deportation, Sandoval thought her brother's Jewish appearance gave him advantages at the white school.

In order to avoid the stigma associated with Mexican heritage, some ethnic Mexicans preferred to socialize exclusively with Anglos and avoid Spanish-speaking Houstonians. Estela Gómez thought a fellow student resisted forming relationships with other people of Mexican descent because of the stigma of Mexican ancestry in Texas. In the late 1920s, the only other Mexican American girl at Sam Houston High besides Gómez socialized only with Anglo students and dated only Anglo boys. "She just separated herself from any contact with any Spanish-speaking person," Gómez recalled.[42] Spanish-speaking youth faced exclusion from other students within white public schools, so her classmate perhaps felt that she could best avoid discrimination by distancing herself culturally and socially from a recent immigrant like Gómez.

As the accounts from ethnic Mexican migrants and the articles from the *Informer* indicate, Mexican Americans and African Americans often focused on women when discussing the phenomenon of passing. People from both groups discussed women who passed on Main Street in downtown Houston to gain access to certain businesses, for example. Janie Gonzales alleged that only certain ethnic Mexicans could find employment on Main: "One Mexican girl [worked] on Main Street. One. And she was married to an Anglo. And she didn't want to be a Mexican." A 1929 edition of the "Passing Parade," a weekly gossip column in the *Informer,* warned, "If certain Houston women, of light or fair complexion, don't stop 'high-hatting' members of their race and stop trying to pass on Main, the Parader is going to talk out in public! Selah!"[43] The comments from black and ethnic Mexican Houstonians emphasize the exclusive nature of the Main Street shopping district. For black readers of the *Informer,* gendered comments about passing intersect with the publishers' activist goals. Stores were sites of conflict between black female shoppers and white employees in the Jim Crow era. C. F. Richardson had lobbied for a black department store throughout the 1920s and asked readers to patronize black stores so black women would not face insult; his peers fought segregation and degradation through autonomy in their own communities and institutions. New Negroes demanded respect as black people, but African Americans who passed seemed to disrupt that activist project. Racially ambiguous women could avoid public degradation and gain access to white space by allowing people to believe they were white, but that act of individual advancement did not contribute to community activism that would aid all women of African descent who traversed the city's segregated spaces.

New Negroes and ethnic Mexicans frequently linked women's decision to pass with an abandonment of their race and community. For descendants of enslaved southerners, this tendency may be linked to the history of sexual exploitation of women of African descent by white men, and the subsequent creation of multihued families led by those black women. Anglo-American laws in places like colonial Virginia established that a child's race followed its mother in the 1600s. Generations of black women raised their mixed-race children in black communities, took them to black churches, and enrolled them in black schools. If a light-skinned woman left that black community for white circles, the children she bore also lost the communal ties that led a spectrum of light and dark people in the United States to identify as Negroes. Women of African descent who could potentially bear and rear children that did not identify as black became the focus of fictional narratives about passing. The central question of Oscar Micheaux's *Veiled Aristocrats* is whether Rena Walden will continue living as a white woman in South Carolina or marry her black boyfriend and return to the black race. Likewise, the 1930s version of *Showboat, Imitation of Life* from 1934, and *Pinky* from 1949 also focus on light-skinned women who pass for white against the wishes of darker family members, and in each film, racially ambiguous women of color engage in relationships with white men. *Pinky* further depicts the main character's decision to pass for white as a disgrace to her race. Aunt Dicey, played by Academy Award nominee Ethel Waters, tells Pinky that she has denied herself "like Peter denied the good Lord Jesus."[44]

New Negro activists of the interwar era discussed passing as evidence of a lack of racial solidarity. *Informer* contributors characterized passing as one way that black people "are continually pulling apart and working untiringly, insidiously and incessantly against each other." According to one article, three to four hundred thousand "light-colored Negroes" passed for white in every section of the United States. The newspaper also acknowledged the local version of that story, which may have alluded to Frenchtown: "Then, aside from this large number who are really 'passing for white' and getting by with it, a large colony who seem to think that they are white—who will not speak to members of their own race in public places and who paint and powder their faces to such extremes that they look like Mardi Gras celebrators or Hallowe'en pranksters."[45] The allegation that some light-skinned people did not acknowledge African Americans in public may have resonated with people in Fifth Ward. Indeed, some Creoles' ability to transgress racial borders caused problems with the black friends they made. The act of passing weakened community ties for Mary Rose Berry and her lighter neighbors. After watching her classmates sit at the front of the bus in the white section, Berry did not feel friendly: "When we'd get off the bus downtown, then they'd want to start talking with me. And I would just keep walking."[46]

Anger over passing also stemmed from New Negroes' project to uplift black heritage. Being a descendant of slaves gave most black people in the United States a collective racial subjectivity, which was central to African American political strategy since the antebellum abolitionist movement. But people who passed for white complicated those notions of solidarity and group struggle. African Americans of the interwar era responded to white supremacy by stressing their pride in black heritage in Africa and the United States. They emphasized the accomplishments of former slaves in the most dire conditions. Black Houston leaders veered toward cultural, economic, and political autonomy and stressed Negro pride. Two of the most prominent *Informer* writers, editor Clifton F. Richardson and Simeon B. Williams, discussed black achievement in music and culture. Articles spotlighted black self-government across the world, from the elected government officials in the African nation of Liberia to the Mississippi town of Mound Bayou, a place "founded by a Negro, developed by Negroes and governed by Negroes."[47] New Negroes' interest in a broader, multilingual, transnational black world epitomized the worldview that had been shaped by the experiences of migration and urban community building in communities made up of diverse people of African descent. Even the names of popular music venues in interwar Houston, like the Ethiopian Café and Club Ebony, emphasized an international, diasporic sense of black pride. Activists stressed unity between the diverse people living in their neighborhoods. The leisure activities and cultural celebrations and social/political groups formed by migrants were efforts to build community; therefore, New Negroes considered conflict over skin color and passing to be disruptive to those projects.

The political and poetic assertions of New Negroes—from Clifton Richardson and Langston Hughes to Cuban-born poet Nicolas Guillen—emphasized group struggle and solidarity despite differences in skin color, language, or national origin. An awareness of the African diaspora permeated the racial rhetoric of New Negroes in these diversifying urban spaces. As different groups of people with African ancestry made contact with rural migrants from the South in U.S. cities, some members made attempts to include one another in their racial appeals. When Langston Hughes wrote poems like "Brothers," he emphasized kinship across national boundaries.

Hughes and other writers of the era stressed the mutual struggles faced by people of African descent.[48] Similarly, Spanish-speaking New Yorkers from the Caribbean made ties with black southern migrants based on ancestry and the similar forms of discrimination they faced as African-descended people. One Cuban publication referred to New York transplant Nicolas Guillen as "El Mulato Guillen," a description that referred to his mixed racial background. Guillen stressed that mixed heritage in the poem "La canción del bongó," which alluded to a *mulata de africano y espanol.*" These references indicated his racial hybridity as a person with Spanish and African ancestry, yet Guillen formed a close association with black Americans, who he felt shared a diasporic connection.[49] At the same time, curator Arthur Schomburg, an Afro–Puerto Rican who moved to Harlem, collected items for the New York Public Library that pertained to people of African descent from around the world. Over the course of the 1930s, he served on the education committee of the Ethiopian World Federation, received visitors from Haiti, spoke at the eighth anniversary banquet of the Yoruba Lit and Debating Club in Harlem, and took a trip to Cuba earlier that decade to procure materials pertaining to black history on the island nation. Other members of his community, which had previously served as headquarters of Marcus Garvey's Universal Negro Improvement Association, considered the race problem—or race pride—to be an issue that didn't end at the U.S. border. In 1936, an African Methodist Episcopal church in Harlem hosted a Sunday-afternoon discussion of "the Africans and the Latin American and South American Negroes and their contribution to civilization." By referring to people living on other continents as "Negroes," the New Yorkers defined racial blackness in transnational terms. They hailed from different parts of the world, but African ancestry linked them racially.

The African nation of Ethiopia, which had successfully trounced Italy's colonialist ambitions in the Second Italo-Abyssinian War of 1935–36, figured prominently in New Negroes' construction of a transnational blackness. The Universal Ethiopian Students Association met at New York's Abyssinian Baptist Church to discuss the topic "African vs the Imperialist Powers" in October 1935, just one month after the conflict between Ethiopia and Italy erupted in warfare; and two years later, Harlemites held a fund-raiser for Ethiopian war refugees.[50] In an era when people of African descent worked to convey pride in African-descended people, then, racial passing seemed to confirm the privileged, superior status of whiteness. When the *Informer* remarked about the "large colony who seem to think that they are white," the comment suggests that these particular Houstonians were threatening the diasporic sense of group cohesion that New Negroes stressed.

But the act of passing exposes the multiple racial subjectivities that could exist among the diverse people legally categorized as "black." Indeed, some people with African ancestry disagreed with New Negroes' construction of racial blackness. Louis Fremont Baldwin, a mixed-race Californian and self-proclaimed "Exponent of Yogi Philosophy," created a stir by wondering in 1932 whether "there exists to any substantial number among the so-called Negroes, an actual Negro." When his peers, including a Jewish rabbi, accused Baldwin of "denying his race," he responded, "I deny being a Negro myself." Baldwin believed that sexual and cultural mixing with other groups, including Europeans, had eliminated the black race and created new groups in its place. According to Baldwin, "miscegenation and the adoption of customs and habits, dress, language, religion and all else alien to him as a Negro, has completely de-Negroized him."[51] Blackness was not an essentialized idea for Baldwin; he chose to stress hybridity rather than believing that anyone with any amount of African ancestry was a Negro. His assertions point to the different definitions of racial blackness that circulated in the United States.

From the perspective of racially ambiguous people with African ancestry who did not identify as Negro, passing could be transgressive—a way to circumvent the "one-drop rule." Some people with African ancestry argued that passing, as well as the popularity of skin lighteners, did not indicate a desire to be white, but rather signified their desire for better economic opportunity. Segregation forced them to choose when in public spaces, so they chose white because of the associated privileges. The Reverend W. P. Stanley, a black man, argued that the act of passing and the use of cosmetic products to lighten skin and straighten hair should even be applauded because they pointed to black economic aspirations. Stanley noted that "these practices of bleaching one's skin, straightening one's hair and 'passing for white' are praiseworthy efforts to improve one's appearance and to secure pecuniary benefits for one's family."[52] For Stanley, passing was largely an economic attempt to gain the material benefits that the white power structure withheld through the enforcement of racial categories.

Some racially ambiguous people did not regard passing as a rejection of black roots or of racial solidarity, but instead saw it as a defiance against a system that shored up white supremacy by denying mixed racial subjectivities. Creoles' ambivalence toward passing demonstrates their distinct racial subjectivity. What some African Americans perceived as a denial of black ancestry was, for others, a rejection of a black/white racial binary and an assertion of their racial hybridity. As historian Grace Elizabeth Hale argues, passing was "the ultimate resistance to the racial polarities whites set at the center of modern American life."[53] By ignoring the "one-drop rule," racially ambiguous people with African ancestry defied Jim Crow and exposed the socially constructed nature of race. The Creoles of color who migrated from Louisiana identified as a combination of races; however, Jim Crow laws did not acknowledge hybrid racial identities. Since they did not consider themselves members of the black race, they did not consider the act of occupying white space as a denial of racial membership.

These conflicting opinions over passing highlight the fact that "Negro" did not have one static definition, even in an era when Jim Crow laws determined racial status. The migration of diverse people of African descent into urban spaces meant that people who had different definitions of blackness made contact. New Negroes posited a transnational definition of blackness that included everyone with African ancestry. But while activists like C. F. Richardson saw passing as evidence of a lack of racial solidarity, racially ambiguous people may have viewed the act as transgressive. Creoles of color considered themselves a separate group; for them, blackness was not just a matter of African ancestry. Their distinct racial subjectivities informed the way people from different places defined themselves.

Creoles of color who passed did not necessarily do so on a full-time basis. The Creoles who lived in Frenchtown, for example, ultimately did not choose to live their entire lives as white people. Passing was not always a permanent condition, then. A Creole worker might allow her employer to think she was white; but at the end of the day, she returned to Frenchtown because of kinship and social ties. The fact that some members of the same family varied in skin color undoubtedly influenced some people's decision to live near a black community and send their children to black schools rather than trying to mix permanently into white society. The Prejean family, for example, contained some members who were frequently mistaken for white and others who had darker complexions. When a brown-skinned cousin accompanied the Prejean children downtown, people assumed that she was the black maid. "They would ask her if she was babysitting," Inez Prejean said. If some of the Prejeans had decided to continuously pass for white, their decision would have affected familial relations with their darker kin.[54] Discontinuous passing likely appealed to racially ambiguous people who did not want to permanently lose ties to their families and communities. Living in Frenchtown allowed for the maintenance of kinship networks; Frenchtown provided a place where Creoles of color could speak French, practice Catholicism, and live near people with a similar racial subjectivity.

By contrast, continuous passing, the act of permanently identifying as white, resulted in a form of social death.[55] Louisiana Creoles of color had worked to create their own communities; they tended to marry one another, and they maintained cultural and social practices that fostered their group subjectivity. Permanently passing for white would require them to sever ties with Creole communities and culture. Instead, Creoles of color built institutions in the community of Frenchtown to preserve what they had brought from Louisiana. The people who "looked white" but lived in Frenchtown chose ties with other Creoles of color over passing on a permanent basis. Likewise, the ethnic Mexicans who chose to live in Segundo Barrio or Magnolia Park, even when they could "pass" as Italians, made a similar decision.

Since they lived near black Houstonians, and often sent their children to black public schools, Creoles of color who engaged in discontinuous passing in public spaces risked public exposure by African Americans who knew them. Cimbee acknowledged that risk in a typically part-humorous, part-scathing take on people of African descent who crossed the color line. To people who passed on public streets, Cimbee warned that others might expose them as nonwhite: "[Y]u is runnin' er grate big ris' 'cauze awl de black fokes ain't lak me, whut ef dey meets yu w'en yu is passin' fer w'ite an' try ter play lack yu doan see 'em, dey'll walk rite up an make yu no 'em, an dat mought be er' li'l 'barrassin'."[56] Racially ambiguous people who lived near black Houstonians may have had less success with discontinuous passing because black Texans recognized them from places like Fifth Ward. Although Cimbee only joked about exposing racially ambiguous people as black, this situation did occur in some real situations. Victorien Prejean won a job reserved for a white man at the ship channel at the onset of World War II;

however, black workers spotted him one day on the job and alerted management that he was nonwhite. His supervisor promptly fired him.[57] It is also possible that Prejean did not lie about his race, but rather that his supervisor assumed he was white when they met. A person's ability to "pass" involved physical appearance and language, but also behavior and deportment in segregated public space. Anglo Texans expected black men to conduct themselves in a deferential way by stepping aside on sidewalks or removing their hats in the presence of white people. So, when a racially ambiguous person made eye contact with a white person or strode boldly through downtown, he may not have been suspected as a Negro. As a Creole of color, Victorien Prejean may not have carried himself in the way that white Texans expected from black men.

Their spatial practices illustrate Creoles' different levels of racial identification. Prejean lived in Frenchtown with other people who shared his racial subjectivity as a Creole of color. Yet this community of Louisianians sat near an older black neighborhood, so the spaces he occupied shaped his racial experience in Houston. Living in close proximity to black people in Fifth Ward marked Prejean as nonwhite even more so than his African ancestry. Although his skin, hair, and demeanor possibly convinced a white employer that Prejean was not African American, the black men who recognized him considered him a Negro because they likely saw him in Fifth Ward. People from both sides of the Sabine River met at work, made contact in local institutions, and sometimes lived next door to one another. In 1930, Yancy Strawder, a twenty-six-year-old black Texan who moved to Houston from San Jacinto County to work for the Southern Pacific Railroad, bought a home on Josephine Street next door to Clay and Eva Chevalier, who came from a plantation-owning Creole of color family in St. Landry Parish, Louisiana.[58] At work, men like Strawder worked with Creoles who had been recruited by the railroad. And in the public schools Crawford Elementary and Wheatley High, Creole and black Texan children took classes together. Creoles often operated within black spaces; therefore, black Houstonians saw them daily, and they often formed friendships. Mary Rose Berry's observations on city buses show that she had ties to the Creoles of color she met at school. Those spatial relationships help explain why black Houstonians often considered passing as an act of betrayal.

At the same time, some ethnic Mexicans portrayed Houstonians who passed for another ethnicity, or who associated only with Anglos, as traitors who disowned their Mexican heritage and shunned other people of Mexican descent. Janie (Gonzales) Tijerina felt that some Mexicans would come to the country and then turn their backs on other ethnic Mexicans. She had helped some immigrants get apartments and a foothold in their new country, but she felt that "once they [get] a little money, and have a home, intermarriage with Anglo people, things like that, they forget about the things that you did for them, you know."[59] Immigrants' denial of Mexican ancestry in favor of better treatment in an Anglo world seemed to suggest that Mexican heritage was worth hiding.

For Tijerina and the women of Chapultepec, ethnic Mexicans who passed for a member of another group, or associated only with Anglos, threatened their community-building efforts. They founded organizations that pushed to end discrimination, created new neighborhoods that had not existed in 1900, and established churches that included members from both sides of the Rio Grande. These acts distinguished them from other migrant groups who claimed racial whiteness in the city. At one point in Houston history, people of German descent outnumbered ethnic Mexicans. But by 1940, Germans did not maintain German-specific institutions that marked particular parts of the city as "German space." In other words, Germans did not maintain distinctive neighborhoods for the preservation of language, culture, or religion. But ethnic Mexicans did. In the process of building neighborhoods, churches, and social/political organizations, they established ethnic Mexicans as an identifiable group in Houston.

Like Creoles of color, then, ethnic Mexicans enacted multiple layers of group identification. But while the Louisianians asserted that they were a separate race, people of Mexican descent emphasized racial and ethnic memberships. They consistently asserted that they were racially white, but they simultaneously advanced a Mexican ethnic affiliation. Ethnic Mexicans created a sense of community based on Mexican ancestry and shared experience in a new place. The anger that some felt about passing shows that they had developed a group subjectivity that would inform their appeals for equality.

Their labor-organizing work at the ship channel in the 1930s offers one example of how ethnic Mexicans in Houston fostered group solidarity. When they accepted jobs at the docks—the place responsible for the city's postwar economic ascendance and subsequent population boom—ethnic Mexicans entered a historically contested space. The Great Depression exacerbated tension between workers from different backgrounds. Black men won the majority of the longshoring jobs, which angered white workers. A committee organized in 1936 reported that white longshoremen obtained only 30 percent of the work in Houston and 15 percent in Galveston. One white man complained that he had to make do with membership in a Banana and Green Fruit Handler's Local rather than longshoring. Fruit handling paid less than longshoring work, and white men bristled at the thought that they "had to carry bananas on their backs to make a living" while black men earned higher wages.[60] In 1939, the Houston City Council issued a resolution that encouraged ship owners and stevedores to give half of the work in the port to white men.[61] Violence intensified the dangerous atmosphere of the docks in the 1930s. Workers toiled under the guard of machine guns that had been mounted on the docks to keep order during a 1931 strike.[62] Two years later, a union leader named Ralph Landgrebe whipped a black man, and when word of the attack reached the superintendent of one of the lines employing the man, the superintendent shot Landgrebe, leaving the union leader with a permanent limp.[63] Longshoremen witnessed virtual warfare at the ship channel in that decade because of strikes and racial tension.

The increasing presence of ethnic Mexican workers further complicated the already volatile balance of race, space, and labor at the Houston ship channel and other Texas port cities like Galveston, Texas City, and Port Arthur. As early as 1915, longshoremen in Texas City complained of competition from Mexican workers, arguing that they were not "American citizens, nor fit subject to become such."[64] Racialized notions about bodies and labor could also have affected ethnic Mexicans' ability to gain a foothold as longshoremen. Some Anglos doubted that men of Mexican descent had the physical prowess to perform the job. For example, one Anglo writer argued in the 1930s that ethnic Mexicans were better suited for cotton picking because that job "requires nimble fingers rather than physical strength, in which he cannot compete with the white man or the Negro."[65] Longshoring was physically demanding work. It required men to lift extremely heavy loads under the blazing hot Houston sun. In a society where some people assumed that people of Mexican descent were physically smaller than Anglos or African Americans, stereotypes about bodies and physical prowess could dictate the type of labor a person could obtain.

Fear of ethnic Mexican dockworkers acting as scabs during a Depression-era strike, however, eventually convinced some Anglo men to incorporate them into their local. Labor competition at the docks in Houston and Galveston drove a wedge between black and Anglo men, but led to awkward attempts to include the growing number of ethnic Mexican workers. Some Anglos, like fruit handler Tom Hency, decided to unionize with men of

Mexican descent. Hency belonged to the ILA's Banana and Green Fruit Handler's Local, organized in 1934. He asserted that "the Mexican was a whole lot more decent man than the Negro."[66] Part of his animosity toward African American workers stemmed from black men's numerical dominance in longshoring. Thinking his Anglo/Mexican coalition could compete with black men, Hency considered his local his last chance to salvage a job for himself during the Great Depression: "If we let this union fall through our jobs will go to the Negroes."[67]

The Houston ILA also began to incorporate ethnic Mexicans in 1934 by establishing a branch for them. The resulting Local 1581 consisted of ethnic Mexican compress men, warehouse men, and cotton-yard workers—all jobs that paid less than deep-sea and coastwise longshoring jobs, which usually went to black men.[68] The local was not part of the "mainstream" ILA that was numerically dominated by black longshoremen. The ILA mandated that when a local received a job too large to be filled by its membership, the local had to turn the extra work to other union men; however, black and Anglo men in Houston locals often chose to hire nonunion labor rather than give the work to ethnic Mexican workers.[69] In local practice at the ship channel, their legal status did not give ethnic Mexican men advantages over the black men, who enjoyed a statistical majority.

Black workers may have been reluctant to accept ethnic Mexican workers as longshoremen because they feared labor competition. When he visited the city in 1930, scholar Lorenzo Greene spoke with black Houstonians who told him that the ethnic Mexicans claimed the jobs that once went to African Americans. He asserted that the "the only labor which Negroes have a real hold on here is loading and unloading ships."[70] Longshoring was one of few occupations that still provided steady employment to black men during the Great Depression, which may have decreased African Americans' incentive to organize with Mexican American men at the ship channel. Labor competition also drove some black Houstonians to support the forced deportation of ethnic Mexican people from the United States. In 1929, the *Informer* carried a headline that read "Deport Mexicans in Large Numbers Says Labor Agent." The full story focused on Houstonian C. W. Rice, president of the Texas Negro Business and Laboring Men's Association and editor of the *Negro Labor News,* and his efforts to secure work for black laborers on farms and in industries where Mexican deportation had left some jobs available.[71] In total, about two thousand ethnic Mexicans experienced deportation from Houston during the Great Depression.[72]

The persistent denial of work at the docks soon caused ethnic Mexican laborers in Local 1581 to organize as a group. In 1939, members drafted a letter to the district convention asking them for assistance in this matter. The writers referred to themselves as "Latin Americans," a choice that one historian has called an effort to "emphasize their whiteness" and citizenship status while dissociating themselves from the Mexican immigrants portrayed so negatively during the era. These efforts, though, failed to produce any labor equity for Mexican Americans at the ship channel. Mexican workers lacked the numbers or the history of union activism that kept African American longshoremen secure. Anglo men were more concerned with maintaining their own supremacy than ensuring fairness for ethnic Mexicans.[73] Regardless of national origin, ethnic Mexicans showed solidarity when denied access to work by Anglos and African Americans. The efforts of Local 1581 illustrate how ethnic Mexicans established group solidarity in the 1930s. The organization stressed their racial whiteness, but also affirmed their shared Latin American heritage. Furthermore, their shared status in a discriminatory climate influenced them to band together to fight against the bias they experienced. Their subjectivity was shaped by ancestry, the color line, and local racial practices.

The women of El Club Femenino Chapultepec articulated a similar construction of racial and ethnic subjectivity. They viewed their Mexican heritage as a marker of ethnicity, but they still saw themselves as white when it came to the color line. When Estela Gómez first moved to the city, she knew no English and felt like an outcast in the Anglo-majority schools she attended. Her isolation led her to seek ways to build community with other Latinas, which is why she joined Chapultepec. "The community in Houston was small," said Gómez. The YWCA offered specialty clubs, and a group of Anglo women in the business department tried to recruit Mexican American members. They declined, however. "We did not join them because we wanted our own," Gómez stressed, "because we don't even know each other." The women could have organized with Anglo women, but they chose to meet by themselves in order to build community among themselves. They also decided to conduct official business in Spanish, which excluded English-speaking women in the YWCA. At the time, the ethnic Mexican population of Houston was scattered across town, and the first members of the club represented at least several different neighborhoods and two nations. Members lived in Magnolia Park, Segundo Barrio, Fifth Ward, and the Washington Avenue area of Sixth Ward. About half of the members of

Chapultepec had been born in Texas, and the other half had come from Mexico with their parents.[74] The club gave them a forum and a way to forge bonds based on Mexican ancestry and their experiences in Houston.

Ethnic Mexican groups also built community in the 1930s using cultural production. While New Negroes made racial solidarity and diaspora a key aspect of their art, ethnic Mexican organizations like El Club Femenino Chapultepec used cultural performances like dances and pageants to stress the importance of Mexican culture and forge community among Spanish-speaking people who lived in communities spread across the city and who hailed from different nations. For them, white did not mean Anglo; there was room within the spectrum of racial whiteness for Mexican culture. Chapultepec emphasized Mexican heritage instead of anglicization. The name the group chose for themselves and the functions they supported reflected their desire to be linked to Mexico. "They wanted something typically Mexican," recalled Carmen Cortés. *Chapultepec,* a Nahuatl word, refers to a hill outside of Mexico City and the site of a battle in 1847 during the Mexican-American War. "We decided on 'Chapultepec' because we were Mexican American and we wanted to keep our culture, not lose it," asserted Estela Gómez.[75] In addition to political appeals, the women organized cultural festivals, like hosting suppers and parties with Mexican food and celebrating events associated with Mexican history. With the YWCA's backing, they sponsored parties on Mexican holidays.[76] Chapultepec was the first organization in Houston to host Cinco de Mayo and 16 de Septiembre celebrations in 1932. They made friends with other women in the YWCA, and they even invited Anglo members to their banquets. Mexican cultural events and the use of Spanish allowed ethnic Mexican women to carve out a portion of the YWCA for themselves.

Chapultepec's Cinco de Mayo and 16 de Septiembre celebrations in 1932 were performances of citizenship that reflect some gradual change in Anglo depictions of Mexican culture. Held in City Auditorium, these holiday celebrations displayed Mexican heritage in a way that Anglos could see and consume.[77] Anglo journalists covered both events in local newspapers, and their comments showed a marked difference from depictions of Mexican cultural practice than had appeared a decade earlier. While the *Post* wrote disparaging accounts of Mexican Catholics in 1922, Anglo coverage of the festivities a decade later focused on positive aspects of Mexican culture. One journalist wrote a historical description of the meaning behind Cinco de Mayo, explaining the significance to an audience with little to no knowledge of Mexican holidays: "In Houston's 'Little Mexico' dark eyes flashed and men walked proudly Thursday as they recalled the battle of Puebla."[78] The article noted a physical characteristic that Anglos mistakenly assumed all ethnic Mexicans shared—dark eyes—but by covering the event, the journalist showed more acceptance of Mexican culture in Houston. The spatial movement of the celebration out of Mexican-owned venues in Segundo Barrio signaled the event's movement into Anglo consciousness. Chapultepec's celebrations of Mexican heritage also showed Anglos that Mexican Americans would not abandon the Mexican cultural practices they brought with them to Houston.

The women of Chapultepec sought to establish a place for Mexican culture within the broadening spectrum of racial whiteness. Historian Matthew Frye Jacobson argues that between passage of the 1924 Johnson-Reed Act and World War II, Italian, Greek, and Jewish Americans succeeded in claiming white racial identity. According to Jacobson, the "culture-based notion of 'ethnicity'" replaced the older idea that they represented racially distinctive groups. As more people in the United States came to view Italians, Greeks, and Jews as white, these groups defined their differences by culture, and therefore ethnicity, rather than biology. By asserting racial whiteness, while holding on to a Mexican ethnic identity constituted through cultural practice, El Club Femenino Chapultepec attempted to follow a similar path. They argued that they were ethnically Mexican but racially white.[79]

Chapultepec's insistence upon speaking Spanish at meetings and celebrating Mexican holidays distinguished them from LULAC, whose members argued that they should exclusively speak English and celebrate U.S. holidays instead of Mexican ones.[80] In a 1932 article in the *LULAC News* called "The Glory of American Citizenship," a writer argued, "American citizens of the United States should cease to observe the holidays of Mexico and join heartily in observing the holidays of the United States."[81] Filiberto Tijerina, who changed his name to Felix after moving from Mexico to Houston and marrying Janie Gonzales of Sandyfork, served as president of Houston's LULAC, and he later led the national organization after World War II. Tijerina insisted that his children speak English and did not allow them to speak Spanish in their home. At the restaurant he and Janie operated on Main Street, the Tijerinas catered to an Anglo clientele in the area known for its "white only" businesses. His restaurant was not exclusively a community-building space for ethnic Mexicans, but instead served as part of a larger effort to introduce Anglos to Mexican food as a way of smoothing relations between the groups.[82]

Tijerina used positive depictions of Mexican culture to appeal to Anglos who had used cultural difference as the basis for discrimination in the 1920s. Mildly seasoned dishes would introduce Anglos to Mexican food, while being served by Mexican people in a clean facility could improve their image in Anglo minds.[83] (At the time, few local Anglos had eaten Mexican food. The culinary staples found in Segundo Barrio households would have baffled most Houston natives. A newspaper article from the 1930s, for example, described tortillas as "cornmeal frapjacks" to an audience that had little familiarity with the food.[84]) Improving relationships with Anglos was a goal of an organization that Tijerina joined in 1933, a men's organization called Club Cultural Recreativo México Bello. Organized in 1924, México Bello was "strictly a recreational club" launched by local business owners like A. D. Salazar and men who worked for the Southern Pacific Railroad. Members chose "Patria-Raza-Idioma" (homeland, race, language) as their motto, and declared that their intent was to "*hacer un México chiquito en el extranjero*" (create a little Mexico abroad). The *Houston Chronicle* reported in May 1933 that "the primary purpose [was] the promotion of a better understanding between Mexicans and Americans."[85] Because Houstonians and people across the Southwest watched the growth of the ethnic Mexican population with apprehension, activists like Tijerina worked to show native-born white people that ethnic Mexicans could be contributing citizens to the United States. For Tijerina, Anglo acceptance was powerful. After all, Anglo cultural domination was an intrinsic part of the version of white supremacy found in the western South. Since 1836 the language and legal traditions brought west by Anglo Americans had largely dominated the political structure of Jim Crow Texas.

Chapultepec, on the other hand, represented another mode of acculturating to Houston—one that resisted conforming to Anglo standards. By remaining separate, Estela Gómez and other members of El Club Femenino Chapultepec could organize around issues that specifically pertained to the ethnic Mexican population in Houston. Their interests in local affairs transformed Chapultepec from a social club into a political club, which brought suspicion from the federal government. After writing their manifesto in 1936, the women of Chapultepec initially received the support of the Anglo leaders in the YWCA. Their sponsor, Olive Lewis, felt proud of their work and even signed the letter herself. When the letter found its way to the regional office of the YWCA in Macon, Georgia, however, some white administrators felt the letter was inappropriate for a social club. Estela Gómez recalled that administrators said they "shouldn't be complaining about anything of that sort" because "our business was just recreation and activities for recreation."[86] More problems arose when the African American branch of the YWCA discovered the letter and used it for their own purposes. "They heard about our [i.e., ethnic Mexicans'] problems and they said, 'We have some problems, too,'" said Estela Gómez of members of the black branch that contacted her. "'You did a great thing writing all of those things down.'" The African American women asked club officers Cortés and Gómez if they could publish the letter in their organization's magazine, the *Occasional Papers* ("a quarterly publication for Negro [YWCA] branches"), and they agreed.[87]

The Anglo leaders of the national YWCA bristled at the attention. The ethnic Mexican women's stance against segregationist practices showed that they would not blend into the mainstream. Olive Lewis lost her job after the YWCA learned of the letter. Gómez's worst fears were confirmed in late 1937, when federal agents began shadowing her. Two men from the FBI visited her at her family's restaurant on Washington Avenue. "They asked a lot of questions," Gómez recalled. "'Do you believe in God?' 'What schools did you go to?' 'Who are your friends?' 'What organizations do you belong to?' I was kind of scared." She realized that the FBI had questioned her neighbors when someone asked her if she was a Communist. "We were just wondering," the neighbor reported, "because somebody wanted to know. They came in and asked me." Gómez saw FBI agents parked across the street from the restaurant from 1937 until 1941. The men always treated her respectfully, but they asked "scary questions." Since she would not obtain U.S. citizenship until 1945, their interrogation may have been especially frightening for an immigrant woman unsure of her status in the United States.[88]

The work of Estela Gómez and El Club Femenino Chapultepec in the 1930s and early 1940s further illustrates how notions of race in the interwar era were influenced by the legal color line, a plethora of cultural and spatial experiences, and understanding of ancestral heritage. People of Mexican descent joined the same branch of the YWCA as Anglo women in Houston because they were white according to the black/white color line, but their experiences with local discrimination in Houston led them to use that organization as a platform to fight against those slights. Chapultepec also acknowledged ethnic differences between themselves and Anglos when they decided to meet together as a group without Anglo women, speak Spanish at meetings, and host Mexican-themed festivities. Gómez was part of a cohort that strove to connect Houston's diverse ethnic Mexican population through cultural celebrations that linked them to a shared Mexican heritage, while they simultaneously pushed to be legally counted as white. For them, racial whiteness was broad enough to include ethnic Mexicans.

The conversations surrounding passing, skin color, and group solidarity further reveal the multitude of racial constructions that circulated in a migration city during the interwar era. Both ethnic Mexicans and New Negroes fostered solidarity based on transnational notions of group membership. For ethnic Mexicans, this entailed building community among people of Mexican descent who hailed from either side of the Rio Grande. When light-skinned ethnic Mexicans dissolved ties to other Spanish-speaking people, though, some viewed the act as a betrayal that threatened those community-building efforts. "Passing" was, therefore, a central concern for the people working actively to build an ethnic Mexican presence in Houston. For New Negroes, the push for solidarity necessitated counting all people of African descent—irrespective of language, hue, national origin, or how much European ancestry one claimed—as members of the black race who should unite to defeat Jim Crow, colonialism, and versions of white supremacy that existed across the globe. Yet people with African ancestry who passed for white constructed racial blackness in different terms. Some saw the act as a way to advance themselves economically or to temporarily attain additional privileges of whiteness. Others considered passing a rejection of the black/white binary that did not acknowledge their mixed racial subjectivity. These contrasting views highlight the myriad notions of subjectivity, the multitude of ethnic and racial heritages, and the evolving racial practices that informed a person's place in a city where diverse groups made contact.

PART THREE

FIVE

"All America Dances to It"

GILBERT JACQUET AND MILTON LARKIN were born less than three hundred miles away from one another, but when the two men decided to start playing music together in Houston, they represented different worlds. Jacquet was a Catholic, French-speaking Afro-Creole man who had moved to the city from Broussard, Louisiana, to work for the Southern Pacific Railroad in the 1920s. When he wasn't building train engines, he worked as a musician. A bassist and violinist, Jacquet formed and led a band made up of fellow railroad workers, and he played with other musicians after work and on weekends. One of his frequent collaborators was trumpeter and trombonist Milton Larkin. Born in Navasota, Texas, in 1910, Larkin had moved to Houston as a boy with his mother after his father died. He and Jacquet formed a musical partnership sometime in the late 1920s or early 1930s. "I played with him at these beer stands," Larkin recalled. "They'd have us on a platform."[1] The sounds produced by these migrants were both old and new, a product of rural heritage and urban adaptation. Larkin and members of the Jacquet family would especially play a pivotal role in the cultivation of an increasingly diverse jazz scene in Houston that grew from beer stands to high school band rooms to middle-class ballrooms during the Great Depression.

From the mid-1930s through World War II, the form of jazz known as big band swing dominated airwaves across the United States, and in urban Texas, this style attracted black, ethnic Mexican, Creole, and Anglo fans.[2] Some of the first explorations of the form in Houston emerged from public high schools where children from English- and French-speaking families learned to read music, accessed instruments, and created their own interpretation of big band music. Saxophonists from these schools helped develop the style of playing called "Texas tenor." The young musicians ventured out of their schools to play for adult audiences that often included Anglo fans, and they eventually took the sound across the nation. Ethnic Mexicans showed a new appreciation for the sounds produced by people of African descent they heard on the radio. Urban middle-class Tejanos fashioned a Spanish-language version of big band swing called *orquesta,* which was influenced by mainstream jazz and the musical heritages of Mexico and South Texas.

Musical practices that led to the creation of Texas tenor jazz and Mexican American orquesta both reified and rejected the racial binary created by the Jim Crow regime. Legal segregation in public schools kept ethnic Mexicans apart from the "colored" population while bringing Creoles of color into daily contact with black Texans. Through their musical practices in schools, the latter two groups forged cultural, social, and economic ties. At the same time, though, Creoles of color still maintained that they were a distinct group. Notions of racial difference and hierarchy circulated among those who created a shared culture in shared spaces. Local schools illustrate another version of the two public faces of race: the segregation caused by the color line, but the persistence of racial subjectivities that differentiate between people who are legally black. The cultivation of jazz in Houston, then, shows how segregation, subjectivity, and cultural practices in shared urban spaces produced complicated notions of race and community in the decade before World War II.

BUS STOPS, BAND ROOMS, AND BALLROOMS

When Illinois Jacquet walked into the music room of Wheatley High for the first time in the early '30s, he was already a musician and performer. His first experiences came from dancing at house parties and church bazaars at St. Nicholas and Our Mother of Mercy with his three brothers. He had also taught himself to play drums by using his hands to copy the rhythmic patterns of his feet: "What I was doing on my feet," Jacquet recalled, "I would start doing it with my hands." Like most of his classmates, Jacquet didn't know how to read music before he enrolled at Wheatley. But after joining the school band during his first year as a student, Jacquet acquired the instrument that he would use to earn a living for the rest of his working life—a saxophone. Over the next few years the music directors at Wheatley taught him to read music and helped shape the teenager into a wage-earning musician.[3]

Wheatley was one of three local high schools for black students in Houston in the 1930s. Until the mid-1920s, Booker T. Washington High School in Fourth Ward had served the entire city. But the children of migrants packed the halls and classrooms after World War I, so the school board announced the construction of two new secondary schools. Jack Yates High, named for the former slave and pastor from Virginia who helped settle Freedman's Town, served Third Ward students beginning in 1925. Phillis Wheatley High School opened two years later, in 1927, in Fifth Ward.[4]

Although these schools were part of a segregated public school district governed by a white school board, black administrators oversaw daily operations and made decisions on everyday affairs, including the types of classes, clubs, and organizations the schools would offer. Teachers educated at historically black colleges taught courses in Latin and physiology and sponsored clubs with subjects of interest to young people. Yates students organized a Negro History Club in 1938, for example, "to show the contribution of the Negro to the political, social and economic life of the United States and the world."[5] Teachers were esteemed leaders in black communities, and the schools they led became sources of local pride. E. O. Smith served as the first principal of Wheatley while he also acted as president of the local branch of the NAACP in the 1930s. Although his conservative approach to fighting segregation had rankled some NAACP members after World War I, Smith was a hero in the hearts and minds of the local black Houstonians who respectfully called him "the Professor." During the Depression era, the *Informer* dedicated entire pages to high school news with columns called "The Wheatleyite" and "The Washingtonian," so events that transpired within school corridors also reached the streets of Houston. The three high schools symbolized the black community growth that New Negroes had championed since the end of the war.

Music programs developed at Wheatley and Yates soon after the schools opened. Wheatley organized the first band, with college-educated Professor Russell McDavid and his brother, Percy, in charge. Yates soon followed suit. Music-program instructors taught their students to read music—a new skill for the majority of the youth who joined the program. (See figure 7.) Students like Lester Williams and Illinois Jacquet, who hailed from rural East Texas and Louisiana, respectively, learned to shape the musical experiences their families brought from the country into a new way of playing. Before moving to Houston, Williams practiced what he called "ear-training" in tiny Groveton, Texas, where he was born in 1920. Williams and his family had

FIGURE 7. Ms. Sadberry's music class at Douglass Elementary, a segregated school for "colored" children. Elizabeth Montgomery Collection. The African American Library at the Gregory School, Houston Public Library.

scratched out a living as sharecroppers who worked on "thirds," meaning they kept one-third of the crop they grew each year. While in the country, Williams sang in a church choir that performed a cappella arrangements because the congregation could not afford a piano or organ. "We had no instruments at all," he remembered. Williams's musical experiences transformed when he moved to the city and acquired formal education: "Fortunately for me, my mother moved us from the country here to Houston, Texas, in 1927. I had training in [the] Houston public school system here." He attended Crawford Elementary and then Wheatley, where he joined the speech team, learned Latin, played football, and sang as a vocalist in the band.[6]

Students like Williams combined the oral traditions of their families with information learned from high school instructors—like how to play specific instruments and write musical compositions. While Illinois Jacquet always remained adamant that jazz music was a form of music "play[ed] from your heart," he also acknowledged the importance of learning to read music at

FIGURE 8. Illinois Jacquet (foreground) and a fellow musician,
ca. 1947. William P. Gottlieb / Ira and Leonore S. Gershwin Fund
Collection, Music Division, Library of Congress.

school. (See figure 8.) With formal instruction, "you can learn how to cultivate that. Now you can write it out, what you learned, and make a score out
of it."[7] Music gave the students a common interest and emphasized musical
forms beloved by their generation—specifically, jazz and blues.

The music produced by the young Houstonians at Wheatley and Yates
took on qualities that distinguished it from the sounds their parents would
have favored in the countryside. Jazz played by students in high school band
rooms incorporated more instruments and, therefore, produced a louder
sound than Texas country blues, la-la, or the small combos created by people
like Milton Larkin and Gilbert Jacquet in the late 1920s. The schools
launched their own versions of the big bands that dominated jazz between
the mid-1930s and the end of World War II. "We had a good eighteen- to
twenty-piece high school orchestra," remembered Williams. The students

had access to a wider range of instruments in their orchestras, so they added sounds not previously used in East Texas and southwestern Louisiana to their repertoire. Students could play saxophones (which replaced clarinets in jazz bands in the 1930s), trumpets, guitars, bass, piano, and percussion. "And we really played jazz music," remembered Sonny Boy Franklin, who learned guitar at Yates. Students recalled playing popular songs of the era, by artists like Louis Armstrong and Duke Ellington.[8]

High school musicians learned to adapt sonically to urban space. Urbanization brought increased access to a broader range of instruments, while the realities of living in a city influenced the sounds students made with those instruments. When Jacquet blew into his saxophone at a football game, he needed to be heard in the bleachers. While marching in parades, he had to compete with a cacophony of urban noise—the lurch of city buses; cars with honking horns and screeching brakes; or outdoor salespeople peddling issues of the *Informer*.[9] Fourteen-year-old Fifth Ward native Arnett Cobb learned this lesson when he joined the band at Wheatley in 1932 as a violinist. He learned, during rehearsal, that his instrument of choice was not suitable for an urban marching band.

"Son, I can't hear you," Professor McDavid told Cobb one day as the band practiced.

"I can't hear me, either," Cobb replied.

McDavid decided to give the young musician a saxophone instead. When not in school, Cobb practiced religiously, to the annoyance of his neighbors in Fifth Ward. As a compromise, Cobb found a prairie near his home. There, he blew his horn as loudly as possible, practicing techniques that would allow him to be heard in an urban community and amid the sounds of his boisterous marching band.[10] The music played by students like Arnett Cobb mirrored their experiences living in Houston and their generation's turn toward different instruments and styles in the 1930s.

Through the school band and other activities at Wheatley, Texas-born youth like Cobb and Afro-Creoles like Jacquet became acquainted and, in many cases, formed friendships. Houston had schools for two races—black and white—so Creoles of color attended schools for Negro children, while ethnic Mexicans went to white schools. The Creole youth who did not enroll in the parochial schools at St. Nicholas or Our Mother of Mercy attended Wheatley in Fifth Ward, since it was the closest high school to Frenchtown. The children of French- and English-speaking families created social bonds. By the time Hortense Dugar, a Catholic student whose family had roots in

Louisiana, graduated from Wheatley in 1933, people from both groups were an integral part of her academic and social life. Students with French and English last names took part in school activities. Dugar acted in the school play alongside a classmate named Opal Devereaux and took classes with young men named Charles Broussard and Frank Dominguez, the latter of whom also played saxophone in the band.[11] In the late 1930s, Inez Prejean and her sisters danced with the Wheatley drill team. As Creoles of color who took part in the local practices at their schools, they felt less ostracized than they had when they arrived in the 1920s. They learned to speak English, which helped them acclimate to their new hometown. Creole participation in these local activities signaled their entrance into the institutions of black Fifth Ward. Music facilitated that process.

The budding sense of competition between the high schools in Third Ward and Fifth Ward helped these students forge ties to their local communities. When Yates and Wheatley opened, a rivalry quickly developed between the students and the people living in the surrounding neighborhoods. Yates had once served students from both Third Ward and Fifth Ward, but the school's population divided when Wheatley opened in 1927. Wheatley became Fifth Ward's high school for the black population, while Third Ward students remained at Yates. The localization of the schools in these two communities of color fostered an intense sense of loyalty, with the first signs of neighborhood rivalry developing in football matches. Football games drew crowds from across the city and nearby rural communities, and received coverage from the local press. As Third Ward native Sonny Boy Franklin asserted, the rivalry between Yates and Wheatley encompassed "everybody and everything."[12]

By the mid-1930s, the neighborhood rivalry between the students at Wheatley and Yates had extended to music. School bands became the focal point of halftime entertainment at football games and community events. Crowds cheered and danced along to songs played by both bands, so Yates and Wheatley competed to win the audience's approval. "We used to sit out at the football games," said Sonny Boy Franklin. "We'd sit out there and compete for who had the better orchestra." Franklin asserted that students "were given chances to excel" by trying to best the other band. His Wheatley rival Arnett Cobb remembered that he and his bandmates were constantly "hustling and practicing to be the best" and that the competition gave them "something to shoot for." Their bands' musical skills remained a source of tremendous pride for alumni. At sixty-eight years old, Jacquet still boasted about his school's superiority. "They had the best band at Phillis Wheatley," he proclaimed in 1990. Cobb added, "We had quite a few good musicians to come out of both schools with that contest."[13]

Competition between the two schools ran deeper than pigskin and jazz; cultural and economic differences exacerbated the friendly rivalry between the people living in the different wards. Third Ward was home to two universities and a more affluent black population than other parts of the city. Bordered by the University of Houston on its east end, the neighborhood also became the site of Texas State College for Negroes in the 1940s. Some of the most prosperous black residents of the Bayou City called Third Ward home. Dr. Benjamin Covington, the most successful black physician in the city, lived on Dowling Street, the main thoroughfare, while C. F. Richardson edited the *Informer* from the newspaper's headquarters one block away. Aspiring beauticians attended school at a branch of the Franklin Beauty School on Dowling; owners Abbie and James Jemison, who assumed control of the lucrative Franklin beauty business after the death of Nobia Franklin in 1936, lived nearby on Live Oak Street. African Americans living in Fifth Ward considered Third Ward to be more upscale than their neighborhood. Wheatley alum Barbara Berry recalled that Third Ward was more affluent, with "more nice restaurants" than her own community. For Berry, Third Ward "just had their own little thing that was so different from Fifth Ward."[14] Some black residents of the neighborhood were certainly poor, but Third Ward had enough well-to-do African Americans and black enterprises to give it the reputation of being Houston's most elite black community by World War II.

The Creole of color community in Fifth Ward distinguished that area from other parts of Houston. When Yates and Wheatley students saw one another at football games, they may have noticed differences in skin color. Some Creole students based their perceived superiority over Yates on their European features. When asked to comment on the rivalry between Wheatley and Yates, Illinois Jacquet remarked that Wheatley "had the better-looking girls. . . . They were light just like white girls."[15] Not everyone at Wheatley had light skin, but the growing concentration of Creoles of color in Fifth Ward meant that skin color was part of the discourse on beauty and race even among schoolchildren.

Attending school together during the Jim Crow era did not, therefore, erase notions of difference between Creoles of color and black Texans that were often based not only on phenotype but also on racial subjectivity. These students' experiences at Wheatley illustrate how, even within segregated "colored" spaces, multiple layers of racial practice shaped Fifth Ward institutions. Barbara and Mary Rose Berry recalled that in the 1930s and 1940s, their Creole classmates joined school activities and formed friendships with Texans like themselves. Both, however, characterized Fifth Ward schools as black *and* French. So, while Creoles of color who sent their children to segregated public schools seemed to observe the black/white color line at the legal level, local notions of race that circulated within these schools acknowledged two different groups.

Through their public performance of jazz, young people of color from diverse backgrounds staked claims to local space. These practices allowed them to forge a connection to the parts of the city where their parents had migrated a decade earlier. In Fifth Ward, youth from Texas and Louisiana became the public face of Wheatley when they marched and played together. Both groups came to represent the school and surrounding community. They shaped the area into a space that was home to two different groups of African-descended people. Parades that led them out of their neighborhoods in the wards also held interracial significance for the young people living in an era of violently enforced white supremacy. These events took youth of color out of their familiar neighborhoods and into a segregated city with a history of public racial violence. But when they paraded through the streets, young musicians and dancers took the cultural expressions they cultivated in segregated institutions and made them part of the soundscape of the larger Jim Crow city. "Parades thus offered disfranchised Negroes a chance to assertively move their culture through the city's public spaces," writes scholar Thomas Brothers, "the very spaces where African Americans were expected to confirm social inferiority by sitting in the rear of trolley cars and by stepping aside on sidewalks to allow whites to pass."[16] Students from "colored" high schools marched through the same streets where black Houstonians and white police officers had shot and killed one another a decade earlier. The high-stepping, horn-blowing youth marked these spaces of violence with the positive sights and sounds they brought from their schools.

Parading through the city or winning a battle-of-the-bands competition was not only a sign of superior musicianship; the activities boosted the youths' sense of self in the segregated city. Wheatley and Yates symbolized black autonomy in an era of legally enforced white supremacy, and African American teachers and administrators in their schools could shield black youth from the shame of feeling inferior in a segregated city. Jacquet became so involved with his school band at Wheatley in the 1930s that he claimed not to have noticed the city's racial hierarchy outside of Fifth Ward. "I didn't even know that there was segregation in Houston until I would leave school or something and go downtown and I'd see the signs. . . . We didn't realize that was really happening because we had such a great band."[17] When the football team or band won a battle, entire communities could celebrate the triumph of the school at a public competition. Students acquired a fierce sense of pride in their accomplishments and in local schools where college-educated teachers instructed them. The communities' pride in the marching bands inspired activism from adult administrators who saw evidence of black degradation in the Jim Crow society.

Ten years after both schools opened, the rivalry and its popularity encouraged black administrators to advocate on behalf of their staff and students. Coaches used economic leverage to push for higher salaries from the school district. Both football teams boasted perfect records during the 1937 season and were prepared to face off in a championship game. Knowing that white coaches received pay while black teachers earned no extra money for coaching—and that football games between the rival schools brought considerable revenue to the city—Yates coach Bill Holland saw an opportunity for activism. "The board knew that every Black fan would be at that Wheatley–Yates game . . . and didn't want to miss out on all of that money that the game would bring," Holland recalled. "So, I told them that Yates was not going to play Wheatley in anybody's championship game if all of the Black coaches didn't start getting paid for coaching." His plan worked. The next year, coaches at all three black high schools earned money for working with sports teams. Holland also helped end the "Black Band in the Back" practice in parades. In the Jim Crow era, African American bands marched behind the animals and cars. But Holland's band at Yates refused to march for an Armistice Day parade in protest. A year later his band marched in the main line with white schools.[18] In this way, high school bands influenced not only black community life, but, potentially, the racial politics of the city.

Bill Holland came of age during the New Negro era, and music was more than a form of entertainment for that generation. Activists of the interwar era frequently linked the innovative new sounds flowing from urban communities to a cultural rebirth for people of African descent. The *Informer* placed items on music and culture alongside politics—a tendency that may have been related to the editor's personal interest in music. Writers praised black musicians for establishing distinct forms of music that captivated people across the world. "Ragtime and jazz came from the Negro," asserted one *Informer* contributor, "and now all America dances to it."[19]

Richardson and the *Informer* staff believed that their cultural achievements could help defeat white supremacy. Using his flair for blending self-promotion with antiracist activism, Richardson announced that his own choir, the Coleridge-Taylor Choral Club, was "truly doing a missionary work in the field of better race relations" by exposing white southern audiences to black musicians.[20] As the *Informer* noted, jazz electrified audiences across the nation after the Great War. The movement of rural migrants to urban centers spread black vernacular song and dance into new corners of the United States and beyond. In an article circulated by the Associated Negro Press, one writer credited the musical prowess of the late jazz innovator James Reese Europe of the Harlem Hell Fighters with helping defeat Germany:

> "[P]resto! the German hordes melted into thin nothingness before the terrific dissonances of Jim Europe's 'Jazz' onslaughts and there was nothing left for William II to do but take to the woods. . . . [T]hough Jim Europe is dead his spirit goes marching on, threatening to smash the bone-head lines of 'white supremacy' and reduce that famed and valorous band of dyspeptics to the absolute innocuous desuetude."[21]

Their music was political as well as cultural for these writers. The international popularity of music performed by black artists was a source of pleasure and racial uplift.

The widespread popularity of jazz led to economic opportunity for students in high school music programs. Local theaters and ballrooms hired young performers from Wheatley and Yates in the 1930s. Wheatley's glee club played matinees for children at theaters like the Lincoln and the Majestic, the latter of which was owned by a black family. The entire Wheatley orchestra had a recurring gig at the popular Ethiopian Café on Saturday nights. Wearing matching white blazers, dark trousers, and bow ties, they performed for adult crowds and earned between four and five dollars a show. Remembering those days, Lester Williams recalled that the club "would be just packed. In that time we learned to do all kinds of music."[22] Williams earned the nickname "the Boy with the Golden Voice" even before he graduated. These performances turned the students into paid musicians who gained increasing popularity with adult audiences.

Milton Larkin was twenty-six years old when he decided to capitalize on the size of these paying audiences and the abundance of stage-savvy students from local schools. In 1936 he formed an orchestra, modeled after the big bands of the Swing Era that employed over a dozen musicians. Larkin had played with and against various members of the two school bands at local competitions, so he knew what talent lay within the walls of Yates and Wheatley. "It was a local bunch of everybody right here," recalled guitar player Sonny Boy Franklin. "It was the band that was organized out of Yates and Wheatley bands." Other students joined the outfit, which included members from Texas and Louisiana. Larkin had played around Houston with Gilbert Jacquet, so selecting the musician's sons was a logical choice for the bandleader. Illinois Jacquet, the youngest member of the outfit, was only fifteen years old when he joined. Larkin also hired other high-school-trained saxophonists between 1936 and 1941—Wheatleyites Arnett Cobb and Frank Dominguez, as well as Yates's Eddie "Cleanhead" Vinson and "Wild" Bill Moore. An array of performers rounded out the group at different times before World War II: writer-arranger Cedric Haywood, trumpeters Clifford Mitchell and Lonnie Moore, bassist Lawrence Cato, saxophonist and singer I. H. Smalley, and drummer Don Mills. Additionally, four vocalists sang in quartet style. "The band began to sound like it was a Duke Ellington band or something like that," said Jacquet. "We were really proud of this band." Altogether, Larkin added, "[w]e had a very good show."[23]

The sounds they produced bore the imprint of their high school training. Talents cultivated by high school music teachers aided Milton Larkin and His Orchestra, like the ability to write compositions. "I do what you call a header," said Larkin. "I can't write. I have in my head the arrangement that I want, and I give it to the writer." Though Larkin did not write the songs he conceptualized, he could call on a host of young talent trained at Wheatley and Yates to write the arrangements he created. "Wild" Bill Moore notated some of the music Larkin played. The ability to read music became a valued job skill for students from Yates and Wheatley.[24]

Larkin enabled a generation of young performers to earn a living for themselves during the Great Depression. The Eldorado Ballroom in Third Ward was one of the first places to hire Milton Larkin and His Orchestra to play at events. Known as the "Home of the Happy People," the Eldorado was located on the corner of Elgin and Dowling across the street from Emancipation Park, near one of the oldest and busiest areas in black Houston. (See figure 9.) I. H. Smalley led the house band at the Eldorado seven nights a week for eight years. "It was out of sight," he remembered decades later. "The Eldorado was a ballroom. Nothing went on there but dancing."[25] His band

FIGURE 9. The Eldorado Ballroom in Third Ward. Milton Larkin Collection, Houston Metropolitan Research Center, Houston Public Library.

also broadcast live on the radio from there, which attracted a wider following across town. Milton Larkin soon reached Smalley's status when the Harlem Grill hired him and his orchestra as its house band. Black entrepreneur Don Robey opened the Harlem Grill on West Dallas Street in Fourth Ward's San Felipe district in the 1930s. The nightly gigs gave the young musicians steady income. Larkin's orchestra performed six nights a week at the Harlem Grill while most members were still in high school. Patrons paid thirty to forty cents to enter the venue, and the orchestra kept 60 percent of the profits from each show. Since they regularly played to packed houses of dancers, they earned decent wages for their work. Four dollars a gig "was good money" for a young black man in Texas, as Arnett Cobb recalled. According to the saxophone player, pork sausage cost four cents a pound and bread cost three cents, so "I could fry a pan sausage myself and take two pieces of bread and put a couple of sausage and fill myself up."[26] Cobb was raised by his mother and maternal grandfather after his father died of tuberculosis when he was six years old, so regular shows allowed him to ease his working mother's financial burden. He took satisfaction in his financial independence and his ability to help his mother support the family. A longshoreman working at the ship channel during the Depression typically earned between seventeen and twenty-four dollars per week, so after a week's worth of shows, the young musicians could potentially earn wages that were comparable to or higher than what adult men at the docks made.[27]

Cobb's pride in his wages and self-sufficiency reflected the New Negro generation's emphasis on economic autonomy. He came of age in a city where activists campaigned for the establishment of black communities and institutions where African Americans could conduct their daily business without coming into contact with white people. Those goals had supported appeals for the safety of black women and the maintenance of black space. The existence of venues in the wards also allowed the New Negroes to take part in an economy that lay outside of white control.[28] Furthermore, wages from urban labor distanced that generation from their enslaved ancestors and their parents and grandparents who had toiled as sharecroppers. A number of the young musicians came from musical families or communities in the rural South, but Houston-trained musicians were often the first in their families to earn a living playing music. They profited from the fact that they lived in cities with enough wage-earning black people to support a music scene in their neighborhoods.

Those Depression-era supporters were, most often, groups of middle-class Houstonians with enough money to pay for entertainment on weeknights. Prestigious black social clubs and, in some cases, trade organizations booked local ballrooms for parties. The Harlem Grill and the Eldorado Ballroom frequently hosted these groups. On Saturday and Sunday nights the Harlem Grill and the Eldorado opened to anyone, but during the week, local organizations reserved the entire venue. House-band leader Smalley remembered, "[E]ach night was a different club."[29] Orchestras provided the entertainment for those weeknight fetes. The Neapolitan Social Club booked Milton Larkin and His Orchestra, which played for their "pre-Halloween" party at the Harlem Grill in 1938. Nobia A. Franklin's Association of Beauty Culturists also hired them, for a ball held after their annual convention.[30] The cost of paying an orchestra with a dozen members prohibited working-class communities from hiring swing bands, so when Larkin's band played these events, the audience was typically affluent. Whereas working-class Houstonians often hosted house parties with home jukeboxes or cheaply hired musicians (like accordion players in Frenchtown), the Harlem Grill and the Eldorado offered an upscale atmosphere for social clubs and trade organizations who could afford to rent a ballroom and orchestra for an entire evening. Hoping to capture the air of excitement generated by the famous black neighborhood in New York City, Robey filled the Harlem Grill with fine food and orchestral music. As a reporter who visited the venue in 1936 noted, "Every conceivable avenue of pleasure was rampant."[31] Houstonians regarded the Harlem Grill, the "'Rado" (as locals called the Eldorado ballroom), and, later, Club Ebony as high-class establishments.[32] "Club Ebony, the Eldorado—both of them were white-table-cloth kind of places," remembered blues guitarist Joe Hughes, a musician who did not frequent those

FIGURE 10. Milton Larkin and His Orchestra, ca. 1937. *Left to right, standing,* Lonnie Moore, Eddie Vinson, Arnett Cobb, George Lane, Clifford Mitchell, and Lawrence Cato; *seated,* Lester Patterson, Cedric Haywood, Willie Lott Thompkins, Milton Larkin, Charles Gordon, H.S. Sloan, and Frank Dominguez. Milton Larkin Collection, Houston Metropolitan Research Center, Houston Public Library.

establishments. "A guy'd come and take your hat and coat and that shit."[33] By World War II, then, Milton Larkin and His Orchestra helped provide the soundtrack for middle-class entertainment in Houston.

The rise of swank ballrooms and middle-class patronage lent jazz an aura of respectability during the big band era. Whereas Gilbert Jacquet and Milton Larkin had performed at beer stands after work in the late 1920s, Larkin and the younger Illinois Jacquet dressed in formal attire while performing for middle-class audiences in upscale venues a decade later. The change in space and the patronage of bourgeois Houstonians shows jazz's elevation to "respectable" music. The Eldorado was one of the first establishments that hired Milton Larkin and His Orchestra, and since they regularly played for social clubs, the young musicians worked to look the part of middle-class entertainers. Larkin mandated that the men in his band wear suits, and he copied styles he saw musicians from New York wearing in magazines.[34] Their slicked-back hair and matching suits were a signature of the swing years. (See figure 10.) The visual aesthetic Larkin cultivated showed an alternate version of black southern manhood that countered stereotypes found in the popular media. In 1936, the year Larkin started his orchestra, white folklorists John and Alan Lomax were busy creating a hardened, rural image for Huddie "Leadbelly" Ledbetter, whom they had discovered while Ledbetter was serving another sentence after his stint at Central State Prison Farm. After helping secure his release from the penitentiary, the Lomax family dressed the former inmate in overalls and had him sings songs like "Pick a Bale of Cotton," thus introducing the performer to white audiences as a country laborer with a rough past.[35] Meanwhile, Swing Era jazz musicians and other performers in Houston wore suits, so they did not look like they had recently performed any type of labor that made them sweat. Their personal style allowed them to project an urbane image of well-dressed, wage-earning black men.

Adorned in matching suits, young Houston musicians from French- and English-speaking families shared a cultural expression created in local high schools, and they played in venues that also reflected that local diversity. The Eldorado Ballroom especially reflected the growing association between black Texans and Creoles of color in 1930s Houston. The owners, Clarence and Anna Dupree, represented both groups. Anna (Johnson) Dupree was a black woman born in the town of Carthage in 1891, where she and her family picked cotton. She later moved to Galveston and met a Louisiana migrant named Clarence Dupree. A native of Plaquemine Parish, Dupree spoke French and claimed mixed-race ancestry. The two married and eventually settled in Houston. After founding a beauty salon and investing in several other black-owned businesses, the Duprees opened the Eldorado in Third Ward in the mid-1930s.[36] Their union symbolized the increasing level of contact between French-speaking Louisianians and English-speaking Texans.

Houstonians who identified as Negro and Creole also clamored to get inside the venue. As a teenager in the 1940s, Mary Rose Berry told her strict parents that she was going to the movies, but rather than visiting Lyons Avenue in her own neighborhood, she rode the bus from Fifth Ward to Third Ward to dance with friends on nights when the ballroom was open to anyone: "Third Ward was just about where everybody wanted to go all the time because it was a lot places out there . . . like the Eldorado Ballroom." Inez Prejean also took the bus to Third Ward from her home in Frenchtown to attend dances at the popular club. "They used to have big orchestras come in there," she remembered. "And we would swing out—oh, we had fun!"[37] By the late 1930s, the Eldorado developed into another site of contact for people from Texas and Louisiana.

The involvement of Creoles of color in this music scene gave them an increasingly complicated relationship to black Houstonians. On the one hand, the Louisianians asserted a racial difference between themselves and

African Americans from Texas. On the other hand, their participation in the jazz scene—from high schools to ballrooms—made them an integral part of black Houston's social and economic infrastructure. Louisianians of color participated as musicians, club owners, and visitors. Black Texans and Afro-Creoles formed musical associations with one another in school and at local ballrooms. Their collaborations provided the basis for a new musical culture in their city. Music became the foundation of a community that formed around a shared cultural expression and an identification with a particular locale. Their sense of belonging to this community did not obliterate racial differences in the interwar era, but students from diverse backgrounds did come to share a common goal. Furthermore, these culture products helped sustain local neighborhood businesses owned and supported by Texans and Louisianians. From the 1930s onward, the sounds that emerged from these establishments would always involve people with roots in francophone southwestern Louisiana and anglophone eastern Texas.

ANGLOS, ETHNIC MEXICANS, AND JAZZ

As Milton Larkin and His Orchestra's popularity soared in the mid-1930s and early 1940s, their sound attracted some Anglo Texan fans. A few even ventured into nightclubs in Third Ward and Fourth Ward to hear the music. Ed Gerlach, a white tenor saxophone player, became a fan during his orchestra's peak before World War II. Gerlach was born in 1920 to an affluent family in the East Texas town of Livingston, located just seventy-five miles from Houston. His first exposure to music in the city came from his grandmother, who drove him to Houston for saxophone lessons. Although his music teacher wanted him to master "Flight of the Bumblebee," Gerlach felt more inclined to play jazz songs by Cab Calloway's band. He had discovered blues and jazz at a secondhand store in Livingston that sold records for a penny apiece. During his explorations, Gerlach found records by Count Basie, Billie Holiday, and Jelly Roll Morton. But the sounds of Calloway especially drew his attention. "I like the way he sang 'Minnie the Moocher' and 'St. James Infirmary,'" said Gerlach. "And there was a guy named Chu Berry who was one of the great jazz tenor players of all time, and I loved his sound. It was just something there, and I tried to copy that sound."[38]

Houston jazz reached Gerlach as Milton Larkin's popularity spread beyond the city. Gerlach heard the band for the first time while majoring in music at Sam Houston State University, an all-white school in Huntsville, just north of Houston. Milton Larkin and His Orchestra played a concert at a black community center in the college town, and Gerlach attended the show with friends. The concert transformed the young man into a dedicated fan and a student of their sound. "Ed swears I'm the cause of him playing," Larkin later stated. At the time, Gerlach worked as director of the university stage band, which played at school dances. He turned to the Houston band for inspiration. In 1938 or 1939, he paid guitarist Bill Davis from Larkin's orchestra to write arrangements for the white musicians at Sam Houston State. Davis earned seven dollars and fifty cents apiece for arranging seven songs for Gerlach.[39] Although university students danced to music played by white band members, the music itself was influenced by sounds cultivated in segregated institutions in Houston.

His love of jazz prompted Gerlach to break the social-spatial divide of a Jim Crow society. He decided to visit Houston's black-owned nightclubs in person. When the United States joined World War II in 1941, Gerlach enlisted in the air force and was sent to Ellington Field, near Houston. He formed a band called Ed Gerlach and the Houstonians, and the group often drifted into the city. The sounds of jazz drew them into clubs in the wards. At the Eldorado, Gerlach and a friend were conscious of their status as outsiders. "We two were the only white people that were allowed in the ballroom," remembered Gerlach. He began to seek out band members for individual lessons, even calling certain musicians at home. Arnett Cobb especially inspired him: "[I]f Arnett picked up a horn, I tried to be there and listen."[40]

Interracial exposure meant that people of African descent influenced Anglo explorations of jazz. Like Ed Gerlach and the Houstonians, other Anglo Texans ventured into black neighborhoods to hear music. Born in 1905, Bob Wills came of age in Lakeview, Texas, where he frolicked with black playmates and heard their parents singing in the cotton fields. According to his daughter, Wills "once rode 50 miles on horseback" to attend a Bessie Smith concert. As an adult performing in Fort Worth, he incorporated blues songs made popular by black artists into his act. Bob Wills and His Texas Playboys helped create the genre known as "western swing," which fused the musical traditions of country, blues, and jazz. "He had a lot of respect for the musicians and music of his black friends," said his daughter, Rosetta.[41] Recordings by Bob Wills showed the influence of blues, as well as European traditions, like yodeling. In "T for Texas," for example, Wills uses the AAB format commonly found in African American blues.[42]

Anglos had an easier time entering black clubs than vice versa; because of Jim Crow, African Americans were barred from "white only" establishments. The sight of white people at a black-majority establishment was not entirely rare, though. For some white Americans who visited black neighborhoods to gain a taste of the music and culture, the act represented an intentional, but temporary, step down the social ladder. Some called it "slumming."[43] Gerlach was an affluent white man whose family represented the traditional vestiges of eastern Texas wealth. The clan made its money in business, oil, and cotton. Yet Gerlach preferred to spend his time in establishments occupied by the people at the bottom of the hierarchy. He consciously left white spaces because of his attraction to music played in the black sections of the wards.

Segregationists often protested jazz's popularity among white youth like Bob Wills and Ed Gerlach. Jazz music and dance ranked high on Billie Mayfield's list of racial atrocities during the Klan heyday of the 1920s. The "hip wiggling, flat footed pelvic massage, known as the jazz dance," according to Mayfield, was a prime cause of white female ruination. "It is a specie of social license that borders on mental depravity." A 1921 article screamed, "STOP THE BEASTIAL JAZZ DANCE!"[44] In a tongue-in-cheek article from the Associated Negro Press at the end of World War I, a black writer confirmed that jazz might not be the best thing for white people. According to the writer, Europeans experienced an unpleasant physiological reaction to this new music played by black soldiers, and that response had won the war in France. "'Jazz' is a hellofathing," asserted the writer, "that paralyzes the circulation of the blood and thus produces a situation of psychosis fatal to the maintenance of that exalted poise which has characterized the historical course of the white race."[45]

Adverse nervous reactions aside, white audiences listened to black music, and they often had little problem watching performances by a group of people they considered inferior—though most insisted on maintaining the spatial and temporal separation mandated by Jim Crow. "There was a time when black musicians used to do most of the entertaining," remembered Lester Williams, who sometimes sang for white audiences on Friday nights and black audiences on Saturdays. When Sammy Price traveled with the Theatre Owners Booking Association (TOBA) in the 1920s, he performed for a "white only" audience during "Midnight Rambles" on the weekend and for African Americans on other nights. So, even when they did enjoy African American music, most white southerners still enforced the spatial boundaries of Jim Crow. "Music wasn't nothing but segregated," summarized musician Sonny Boy Franklin. When they played at the Texas State Hotel, black musicians had to enter through the backdoor and could not walk through the lobby.[46]

Segregationists also tried to enforce racial difference by segregating music according to a black/white color line. Attempts to segregate music in the Jim Crow South became part of the region's political discourse in the 1920s and 1930s and influenced the creation of country music as a separate genre. Industrialization and demographic change endangered what some white Americans called "traditional" values, and this motivated the trend toward sonic segregation. To downplay the effects of urbanization and the musical influence of people who were not Anglo-Saxon Protestants, scholars, folklore collectors, and other people with an investment in white supremacy began to tout the virtues of musical forms they deemed "Anglo Saxon"—ballads brought from Europe, fiddlers, and string bands.[47] (The fact that the banjos used by these string bands had been brought from Africa by slaves seems to have escaped their attention.)

By the 1930s, record companies like OKeh and Victor were marketing "carefully shaped images of rusticity," like bearded fiddlers garbed in overalls, to white Americans who were increasingly uneasy about the social and economic transformations of the interwar era. Radio stations appealed to this audience by creating shows they called "barn dances." The first radio barn dance was broadcast from a Fort Worth station, WBAP, in 1923, but the tradition soon spread from Texas to the Southeast. In 1925, Nashville radio station WSM debuted what would become the most popular barn dance, a show that eventually became known as the Grand Ole Opry. These barn dances largely focused on white musicians, which created the illusion of racial difference, even in the face of obvious cultural crossover.[48]

Two phenomena complicated segregationists' work: the growth of technology such as recorded music and radio, and the increased mobility of black musicians. Lester Williams, for example, learned to sing by imitating sounds he heard at church and on the family's old crank record player. He enjoyed musicians as diverse as Blind Lemon Jefferson, Bing Crosby, Louis Armstrong, and the Italian opera singer Enrico Caruso. Because they could not see the musicians, some listeners did not know the race of the performers they heard. I. H. Smalley thought Duke Ellington was a white man—an "ofay stud" as he put it—when he first heard him over the airwaves as a boy in Houston: "I had no way of knowing, just hearing him on the radio."[49] Music from across the country or even the world could reach these listeners in southeastern Texas. Through radio and records, music permeated racialized spaces.

These sounds could also be heard in a growing number of ethnic Mexican households. Music of the Swing Era attracted a diverse audience that increasingly included people of Mexican descent. Big band appealed to the young generation of Mexican Americans in places like urban Texas and California. In Los Angeles, Mexican American and African American youth played in swing bands together by the 1940s.[50] But the spatial practices and racial politics of Jim Crow in Houston gave those groups a different level of contact. Black and ethnic Mexican Houstonians had little opportunity to collaborate before World War II because of legal segregation. Yet ethnic Mexicans' love of jazz reflected their growing engagement with culture products by African Americans. In Houston, Lawrence and Mary Helen Villaseñor filled their home with music by black and white artists like Count Basie, Duke Ellington, Tony Bennett, Frankie Laine, and Frank Sinatra.[51]

Fueled by a love of swing, Mexican Americans across the nation experimented with the music themselves. In Texas, the popularity of swing influenced the development of a genre called *orquesta*. Filled with "brassy trumpets and lambent saxophones," orquesta especially appealed to middle-class and wealthy audiences living in urban areas in the mid-1930s through World War II.[52] The size of these outfits made them expensive to hire, so they usually performed in ballrooms frequented by affluent Tejanos, which made them similar to the big bands found at the Eldorado Ballroom and the Harlem Grill. A typical band consisted of eight to twelve musicians who played contrabass saxophone, violin, guitar, and mandolin. The bands were similar to contemporary big bands in size, showing the influence of modern jazz on ethnic Mexican musical expression.

Orquesta signaled a shift away from ranchera music, a form associated with Mexico and rural life. Houston-born Lydia Mendoza dominated ranchera for over a decade. Mendoza transitioned from a local singer who performed at Our Lady of Guadalupe, at the Azteca in Segundo Barrio, and at the marketplace plaza in San Antonio when she signed with the Blue Bird record label in 1934. Her Spanish-language recordings reached audiences from Texas to California. Fans knew her as "La Alondra de la Frontera" (the Meadowlark of the Border), a name given to her by a radio announcer. Although she performed songs she learned from her Mexican mother, Mendoza also wrote some twenty-five to thirty of the songs she recorded. She brought a woman's perspective to a genre that had focused on cowboys and other male figures.

Songs like "Ojos Tristes" and "Mal Hombre" discussed heartbreak from a woman's point of view, tackling issues such as abusive men.[53]

Mendoza's popularity waned by the 1940s, however, as musicians transitioned to orquesta. Los Rancheros ("The Ranch People" or "The Country Folk"), from Magnolia Park, was one of the first orquesta bands in Texas. Los Rancheros formed under the leadership of Mónico García, who had worked as a bandleader in an earlier outfit called the Bacon Orchestra. Los Rancheros personified Mexican American urbanization, even though their name referred to rural life. Whereas Lydia Mendoza had dressed in a style popular in Mexico, Los Rancheros dressed in suits, which reflected the style of the Swing Era. Their outfits were similar to those adopted by members of the Wheatley jazz band and Milton Larkin's orchestra—matching white jackets, black bow ties, and dark pants.[54]

Orquesta musicians adopted instruments found in most swing bands. When Frank and Ventura Alonzo first formed a band in 1938, members played instruments associated with Mexican music in the Borderlands—an accordion, *bajo sexto* (a twelve-string instrument used primarily in conjunto), and contrabass. They called themselves "Alonzo y Sus Rancheros" and played songs favored by rural audiences.[55] They gradually transitioned to the more citified orquesta by changing their instrumentation and name. "I'm gonna get a saxophone," Ventura asserted sometime in the 1940s. The band added two trumpets and three saxophones. She and her husband also dropped the rural-sounding "Rancheros" from their name and switched to "Alonzo y Su Orquesta."[56] As a woman who sang lead in the band, Ventura was an anomaly; most Mexican American orquestas featured male singers.[57] They looked and sounded like a new band, one that performed for an audience that had adapted to urban life.

With instrumentation found in popular big bands of the era, and Spanish lyrics, orquesta linked the musicians and their audience to both Mexico and the United States. It was the preferred music for the group known as the "Mexican American Generation," people who acknowledged Mexican heritage but stressed their loyalty to the United States.[58] The people who played and danced to orquesta claimed racial whiteness, and their Spanish-language big band music expressed a uniquely Mexican American subjectivity. They spoke two languages and lobbied for citizenship rights as white people. LULAC was the generation's most vocal political expression, and orquesta was its musical equivalent. This music, according to scholar Manuel Peña, symbolized a "push toward assimilation." The Mexican American Generation's struggle for acceptance by the Anglo majority "was accompanied by a corresponding effort by members of the generation to loosen their ties to traditional Mexican culture and to put some social distance between themselves and the poorer, less acculturated common workers—especially the immigrants." Mocking the aspirations of their more upwardly mobile peers, less affluent ethnic Mexicans in South Texas called orquesta "*música jaitona*," or high-toned music.[59]

While orquesta flourished in Mexican American communities, people of African descent had little to no knowledge of the music played by Los Rancheros or Alonzo y Su Orquesta. Black Houstonians had few direct musical interactions with ethnic Mexicans before the 1960s. The Alonzos recalled playing primarily for other people of Mexican descent in the interwar era. They occasionally performed for Anglos, but they never played for black audiences. Linguistic differences obviously played some role in the division; the language barrier would have made Spanish-language orquesta lyrics a mystery to most African Americans in Texas.

Even as some ethnic Mexicans enjoyed the sounds of jazz played by black musicians on the radio, they tended to perform their music in separate spaces. In Houston, then, people of African descent did not play with ethnic Mexicans in the 1930s and 1940s, and spatial segregation was a function of the color line. The cultural chasm between blacks and ethnic Mexicans in Houston occurred because African Americans and Mexican Americans did not tend to share space in the Bayou City in the 1930s and 1940s. Although members of both groups lived in the wards, Jim Crow segregated them into different institutions. They did not attend the same schools, eat at the same restaurants, or sit in the same sections of movie theaters or buses. For entertainment, Spanish speakers attended performances held in Mexican American–owned spaces, such as the Mexican restaurant operated by Melesio Gómez and his family on Washington Avenue in Sixth Ward. The restaurant was a new element in urban life for many Mexican-born people in Houston because "Mexican families were not used to going out to eat," as Estela Gómez claimed. Her family kept the restaurant in operation twenty-four hours a day, so young people often went there after dances sponsored by local organizations like México Bello. Music was important to Melesio, a musician who had played with a band from the Southern Pacific Railroad and who also performed in the church band at Our Lady of Guadalupe. He hired Los Rancheros to play at the restaurant. With the familiar food and music creating an appealing ambience, the restaurant emerged as "a center for the Mexican people" by World War II. Although the Gómez family hired a black woman to work in the kitchen of the restaurant, African Americans did not eat there as customers, or dance to music played by Los Rancheros.[60]

Nevertheless, ethnic Mexican musicians did influence the sounds of the music cultivated by people of African descent in other parts of the western South, even if segregation gave them little to no physical contact in Houston. Louisianians and Texans have historically lived along a musical borderlands region, a place marked by what scholar Gaye Theresa Johnson calls an "interchange of cultural knowledges." French-, Spanish-, and English-speaking musicians traded instruments and traditions in the region. Huddie Ledbetter learned to play a *bajo sexto* after encountering ethnic Mexican performers during his travels through Texas with his collaborator Blind Lemon Jefferson. He also purchased his famous twelve-string guitar from a Mexican vendor. Jazz musicians in New Orleans also learned from Mexican teachers in the early twentieth century. Described as "a genius from Mexico," musician Louis "Papa" Tio taught Jelly Roll Morton, a Creole of color, to play clarinet. The jazz that left New Orleans in the 1910s and 1920s already bore the imprint of these relationships.[61]

The interplay between different groups involved with jazz shows that polyculturality can exist even in the face of racial division. People of African descent, including both descendants of enslaved Africans and Creoles of color, pioneered the sounds of jazz in U.S. cities; however, a host of other groups inspired one another. While Houstonians of African and Mexican descent did not play jazz or orquesta together, popular music of the era reflected an ongoing musical dialogue that involved ethnic Mexicans, descendants of slaves, Creoles of color, and Anglos. Modern technology brought the sounds of diverse populations into homes across the nation, and appealed to youth, who did not always know the race of the artists they heard. Listening to the same music did not erase racial divisions, but physical separation in the interwar era also did not prevent different groups from influencing one another culturally. The color line separated people, but music would not be so easily confined.

TEXAS TENORS

The blend of people and cultures that marked Houston's big band era influenced the rest of the nation during World War II. Big bands of the Swing Era tended to travel, which spread local sounds to new people in distant places. Milton Larkin and His Orchestra began touring in 1937. They charted a path similar to that of other territory bands—outfits that toured venues of a particular region. Larkin at first struggled to recruit band members old enough to travel outside of Texas. He frequently had to substitute other musicians for the high school students who were too young to go on tour. When students did embark on these interstate journeys, Larkin took special pains to accommodate their worried families. He didn't allow drinking, and when they returned from touring, he would deposit the high school students on their families' doorsteps first. "I didn't have any trouble with the kids," Larkin said. "But they were all young."[62]

Although they did not garner the same acclaim as the nationally renowned bands that played in Chicago, Los Angeles, or New York, territory bands left an indelible influence on jazz in the '30s and '40s. Territory bands did not tend to record (indeed, Larkin's orchestra never entered a studio together during their pre–World War II heyday). Instead, they gained a following by traveling from city to city, stopping to perform in small towns and rural areas if those places had venues available. Bands like Larkin's played in a variety of settings. If segregation ordinances restricted their access to theaters or ballrooms, then territory bands might play at small cafés or even local high schools. By playing in varied settings, these bands took unfamiliar sounds to new places. Larkin's band helped spread the sounds of Houston ballrooms outside of Texas by crisscrossing the South, Southwest, and West Coast. They traveled to Louisiana, Kentucky, Missouri, and California. In the process, they helped circulate styles between the urban and rural areas, exposing themselves and their audiences to a wide array of sounds.

Milton Larkin and His Orchestra's days as a territory band ended with an invitation to one of the premier nightclubs in the nation, Chicago's Rhumboogie. Playing one thousand miles north meant moving beyond their typical musical territory and into one of the most popular venues in the nation, a place frequented by top acts of the Swing Era. According to Larkin, Joe Louis liked his sound, so the boxer pulled strings to get them invited to the popular nightclub. During those first nights in the midwestern metropolis, the young band from the Bayou City had a strong case of the jitters. The shows were "rough" at first, Larkin said, "because we had never played big shows like this. This was competition to the Cotton Club." To their surprise, the crowd went wild for what they called "the Swinging Band from Texas." The Houston orchestra drew acclaim by battling other bands at the

Rhumboogie. According to Larkin, "one band would play an hour and the next band would play an hour, and then people would applaud what they thought." Although they were young, musicians trained at Yates and Wheatley had experience with battle-of-the-bands competitions from their days playing at football games in Houston. In Chicago they tested their mettle against famous acts like the Jimmie Lunceford Orchestra, one of the top big bands of that generation. After they won a series of battles, the Rhumboogie invited Larkin and the band to play for two weeks, but that stint turned into nine months. Larkin was mystified by their success so far from home. "I did not realize that we were that good," he said decades later. [63]

Winning battles of the band at the Rhumboogie brought acclaim from a broader audience, and, when coupled with the higher wages they earned in Chicago, the attention and money convinced the young musicians to leave Larkin's orchestra after returning to Houston. Money earned at local venues like the Harlem Grill and Eldorado Ballroom could not compete with the wages promised in major cities with larger populations. In 1939, Illinois Jacquet was one of the first to depart, citing higher wages as a key reason for leaving Texas. He used a railroad pass obtained by his father, who worked for the Southern Pacific, and traveled west to Los Angeles. The reputation they earned during their stint at the Rhumboogie attracted popular bandleaders who recruited members of Larkin's orchestra. "All the bands were after the guys I had," Larkin remembered. Lionel Hampton quickly hired Jacquet. Hampton, a former member of the interracial Benny Goodman Orchestra, pioneered the use of the vibraphone in jazz compositions. He made seventeen-year-old Jacquet his lead tenor saxophonist. Meanwhile, Yates student Eddie "Cleanhead" Vinson began touring with Chester Boone's Territory Band before he graduated from high school, but he left Houston in 1940 to play with Cootie Williams. Just a few years after Arnett Cobb graduated from Wheatley in 1935, he joined Count Basie's orchestra. In 1942, he replaced Jacquet in Hampton's orchestra when Jacquet left to tour with Cab Calloway. Other local musicians found work in popular bands. L. F. Simon played with Louis Jordan, and trombonist Willie "Lott" Tomkins toured with Jimmie Lunceford. "It looked like my band was the starter," said Larkin. "They'd come down and just pick them up." As Sonny Boy Franklin asserted in 1975, "[I]f you check back through the leading musicians that are in New York... you'll find out that they're originally from either a Yates or Wheatley band.... Most of these guys that I'm talking about learned C-D-E-F-G-A-B-C in public high schools."[64] By joining nationally recognized orchestras in major U.S. cities, they further disseminated the sounds cultivated in high school band rooms and ballrooms in Houston's wards to a broader audience.

The Houston musicians who toured with Milton Larkin and His Orchestra became linked to an identifiable new sound that listeners associated with the Lone Star State. Larkin favored a robust sound that accentuated the saxophones. The energetic style of horn blowing that Houston musicians took from their high schools to Milton's jazz orchestras came to be known as the "Texas tenor" sound, a method of playing saxophone that became a staple of rhythm and blues in the 1940s and 1950s. Texas tenor saxophonists made their horns honk in their lower register and squeak on high notes, and the style originated through Larkin's preference for battles between saxophonists. Most of the orchestra's performances included onstage battles between Jacquet and Cobb on the tenor saxophone. "That's what led to honking," Larkin asserted. "It's in the phrasing, the repetition, of notes, squealing." Cobb described Texas tenor as a "hard-driving" style. "It's a bigger sound," he said of the music first performed on football fields and parades.[65] Jacquet made the first popular Texas tenor recording as a member of Lionel Hampton's band. In 1942, the orchestra recorded a new version of "Flying Home," a song originally composed and recorded during Hampton's stint with the Benny Goodman Sextet. Hampton's solo on the vibraphone opens the song, but "Flying Home" builds to a climactic conclusion with Jacquet on the tenor saxophone. The nineteen-year-old Creole's solo electrified audiences, who clamored for the sound. After Jacquet left the band, subsequent saxophonists also played the solo, including his old classmate Arnett Cobb. Due to the popularity of "Flying Home" and the Texas tenor sound, saxophone solos remained an integral part of rhythm and blues music after World War II.

The style that Jacquet and other Houstonians popularized illustrates how the sounds that migrants brought from the rural countryside continued to influence urban music. Music played by Wheatley and Yates alumni frequently featured the blues formats favored by black musicians in Texas, even as it featured jazz instrumentation. "Any time there's a Texas band, blues and jazz fit together," asserted Larkin. This incorporation of jazz and blues can be heard on recordings made by Arnett Cobb's orchestra in 1947 in New York, when Larkin joined him as a vocalist. The song "Flower Garden Blues," for example, uses instruments commonly found in jazz orchestras—tenor saxophone, trumpet, trombone, piano, bass, and drums—to play blues in AAB format.

Flower garden baby, what makes your garden grow?
Yes, flower garden baby, what makes your garden grow?
You've got some real fine stems; I love your petunias so.[66]

Former Yates and Wheatley students from that era would continue to fuse blues and jazz as adults living outside of the city. Considered a jazz saxophonist, Eddie "Cleanhead" Vinson released albums with titles like *Jamming the Blues*. Meanwhile, vocalist Lester Williams typically sang twelve-bar blues in AAB format while accompanied by a full orchestra during his career as a solo performer in the 1950s. Illinois Jacquet demonstrated the influence of the blues on his music with albums like *The Blues! That's Me*. Musicians like Cobb, Jacquet, Vinson, and Moore made the saxophones they learned to play at Yates and Wheatley moan and wail like blues singers from the countryside. They punctuated their solos with blasts of honks and high-pitched squeaks that came to characterize the blues-saturated sound. As writer Frank John Hadley asserts, "Texas tenor saxophonists, according to jazz mythos, have the blues stamped on their souls."[67]

For Creoles of color like Jacquet who helped establish the Texas tenor tradition, their love of blues shows a musical engagement with black East Texans that formed the basis of Houston's jazz scene. The sound grew out of daily contact in shared spaces. Bandleader Milton Larkin played with two generations of the Jacquet family in the '20s and '30s, and other territory bands in the western South often contained members from Louisiana and Texas. Arnett Cobb played tenor saxophone in a band formed by a man from Martinsville, Louisiana, before he joined Milton Larkin and His Orchestra. They toured as far as Biloxi, Mississippi, in the summer of 1933 with a band of assorted players from both the Pelican and Lone Star states.[68] As a member of Larkin's band, Cobb played with people like Jacquet and Frank Dominguez. In high schools and ballrooms where students with roots in East Texas and Louisiana interacted, they created a shared musical culture—even if they could not speak the same language when they first met.

The musical relationship between these diverse artists with roots in Texas and Louisiana produced complicated racial practices that both reproduced and rejected legal definitions of blackness. Because of the black/white color line created by Jim Crow laws, Creoles of color and black Texans met in segregated institutions. Music especially brought Creoles of color into increasingly close contact with black Houston in the '30s. Through their mutual cultivation of jazz, the groups established cultural, social, and economic connections. As jazz spread into nightclubs in black neighborhoods like Third Ward and Fourth Ward, Creoles of color became active participants in a black infrastructure that had buttressed the New Negro agenda for racial autonomy. Battle-of-the-bands competitions, local parades, and the proliferation of ballrooms gave the children of migrants an attachment to their local community that helped the local economy of those neighborhoods during the Great Depression. For Creoles of color, though, these activities in shared social spaces did not obliterate racial difference. Many insisted upon maintaining their liminal subjectivity as mixed-race people. Even as Creoles of color benefited from a history of activism in Houston that led to a proliferation of black schools and a local consumer economy, many still rejected the idea that they were Negroes. These cultural and economic activities became the foundation for the creation of a community that was both black and Creole by World War II, even if outsiders viewed all of them as members of the same race.

Musical practices also helped shape ethnic Mexican communities, and their engagements with jazz depict the development of a burgeoning and complex Mexican American subjectivity in the 1930s and 1940s. People of Mexican descent asserted a cultural distinctiveness from Anglos even as they claimed racial whiteness. Those who listened to and played orquesta music rejected the notion that their language and music made them inferior to the Anglo majority, and the cultivation of a distinctive style showed that most would not assimilate into the cultural norms dictated by Anglos. Through cultural production, they attempted to complicate and expand how whiteness looked and sounded. Yet the music of people of African descent also played a role in the development of that subjectivity. Music associated with racial blackness seeped into Mexican American homes via the radio, which in turn differentiated U.S.-born ethnic Mexican youth from their parents. Modern Mexican Americans were increasingly polycultural. They could likely speak two languages, they could dance the foxtrot, and they may have listened to Ventura and Frank Alonzo at a bar and Duke Ellington at home on the radio. Mexican Americans and Creoles of color increasingly showed a sonic engagement with African Americans that provided a foundation for intercultural interactions between these groups after World War II.

SIX

"Blaxicans" and Black Creoles

ARTIE VILLASEÑOR WAS A STUDENT at McReynolds Middle School on the east side of Houston when the school desegregated in 1963. Until then, Mexican Americans and Anglos filled the hallways and classrooms of the segregated school. The "pachucos," as Villaseñor described his friends, didn't form strong bonds with the other group, though. Since the 1920s, Mexican American students had faced discrimination in "white" schools, where administrators labored to keep them socially separate from Anglos. According to Villaseñor, the situation changed when black students arrived at McReynolds in the 1960s, years after the Supreme Court declared segregated schools unconstitutional in the *Brown v. Board of Education* decision of 1954. "All of a sudden we got unified when we found out that the 'black death' was gonna move into our junior high school," Villaseñor jokingly recalled years later. Even in the face of old rivalries, Mexican American and Anglo classmates found they knew one another better than the black youth who now walked the school hallways. They forged a common bond through mutual distrust of the incoming black students.

But black Houstonians would not remain a mystery to Villaseñor. By the end of his teen years, he played in bands with black musicians and performed for black audiences. He had learned to play saxophone as a member of the marching band at McReynolds, and like generations of Houstonians, he parlayed those skills into a professional career while still in his teens. Multiple influences affected his musical repertoire. His parents loved big band swing from the 1930s and '40s. He came of age in the era of rock 'n' roll and rhythm and blues, but he also heard the conjunto and orquesta popular with Texas Mexicans. Villaseñor played in a band made up of Mexican American youth called the Comets, and he later played guitar with a band called the T.S.U.

Toronadoes, named for the historically black university in Third Ward. The only Mexican American musician in the band, Villaseñor played guitar with the Toronadoes for two years. His black bandmates nicknamed him "the Blaxican."[1]

Villaseñor was a key member of a thriving rhythm and blues scene in Houston that involved black Texans, Mexican Americans, and Creoles of color after World War II. Mexican Americans had enjoyed music played by black people since the Swing Era, but that love of jazz had not translated into increased contact between the groups before the war. Postwar rhythm and blues changed that as Houstonians from different racial and ethnic backgrounds shared space while cultivating musical interests. For black Texans and Creoles of color who did have a history of spatial contact, a French-style rhythm and blues showed a blending of "Creole" and "black" that made Creoles' previous assertions of racial difference less apparent. Some of the most popular music emanating from Houston nightclubs and recording studios blended the blues, jazz, la-la, and/or Tejano musical traditions. A diverse cadre of savvy entrepreneurs facilitated the national dissemination of hybrid musical forms like zydeco and Mexican American explorations of soul. Musicians like the Starlights, Rocky Gil and the Bishops, the Comets, Sunny and the Sunliners, Clifton Chenier, Lightnin' Hopkins, Freddy Fender, and the Sir Douglas Quintet made the Bayou City the cultural crossroads of the western South—a place where a multitude of musicians with roots in Mexico, South Texas, East Texas, and southwestern Louisiana recorded popular music in three languages.

Hybrid forms of rhythm and blues highlight postwar transformations in racial subjectivity, and show how music became a foundation for dialogue between groups. After its emergence from black communities in the late 1940s, rhythm and blues music became a multiracial conversation during a time when Mexican American and African American political expressions rarely overlapped. Texas was home to two civil rights movements—one black, one Mexican American—with two different goals. But while politics often divided the groups, cultural expressions increasingly drew them together. The spatial and linguistic divides that separated previous generations gradually diminished. In the 1960s, the notion of "soul" also appealed to Mexican Americans and Creoles of color from Houston, and this cultural affinity indicated a significant racial shift for both groups. Creole and ethnic Mexican youth reconsidered their relationship to blackness and whiteness and, in the process, articulated new racial subjectivities that contrasted sharply with the views of their parents' generation. They organized a racial politics of self-identification and self-determination that Black Power, the Chicano movement, and soul music inspired and embodied. These unique expressions of rhythm and blues and soul illustrate how the culture and politics of the long civil rights movement affected expressions of race in a society facing the legal demise of Jim Crow.

ONE CITY, TWO MOVEMENTS

By the 1940s, both federal and state laws defined ethnic Mexicans as white, or they avoided counting them as "colored" or "negro." But people of Mexican descent did not always have the full benefits of whiteness, since local practice often differed from legal status. As Thomas A. Guglielmo writes, "[A]lthough few Mexicans and Mexican Americans encountered the full power and force of discrimination and prejudice—the legalized and more pervasive forms of disfranchisement, segregation, exclusion, and violence that blacks experienced—still fewer enjoyed the full power and privileges of whiteness."[2] From the treatment of ethnic Mexican children who attended white schools to the withholding of labor from Mexican American workers at the ship channel, people of Mexican descent in Houston understood that being classified as white did not mean that they would be treated the same as Anglos. By World War II, Texas Mexicans had mounted a civil rights movement to ensure that their legal white status translated into full equality.

Tejano music shifted during the war era to incorporate themes related to their burgeoning freedom struggle in Texas. While singers still performed old tunes like "El corrido de Gregorio Cortez," songwriters composed few hero corridos after the 1920s. Instead, a tradition called the "victim corrido" emerged. The new lyrics reflected changes in Mexican American society and politics that began with mass migration and the development of political organizations like LULAC, and continued with activism during World War II. Victim corridos detailed segregationist practices that targeted Mexican Americans, and they supported organized resistance. One of the most famous examples of the era, "Discriminación a un mártir," describes the death of a Mexican American soldier, Private Félix Longoria of Three Rivers, who went to the Philippines to fight in 1944. Longoria died by gunfire while overseas, but the military did not send his body back to the United States with the bodies of other deceased soldiers. Instead, he was buried temporarily in the Philippines, and not exhumed for shipment until 1949. After Longoria's body finally reached Texas, the Anglo-owned Rice Funeral Home refused to accept him for burial. His widow, Beatrice, asked a prominent physician, Dr. Héctor García, for help. "Dr. Hector," as he is still known in Corpus Christi, served as president of the fledgling American G.I. Forum, founded by veterans in that city one year earlier, in 1948. García wrote to Senator Lyndon B. Johnson, who immediately had Longoria's remains flown to D.C. to be buried at Arlington National Cemetery with full military honors. Written in the same year as the American G.I. Forum's victory, "Discriminación a un mártir" was essentially a civil rights anthem for South Texas Mexicans:

En Filipinas murió
este valiente soldado;
pero nunca imaginó
que iba a ser discriminado . . .

Johnson siendo senador
por el estado de Texas
se le ablando el corazón
al escuchar nuestras quejas.

Y pidió a la capital
los restos de este soldado;
y en el panteón nacional
Félix quedó sepultado.

He died in the Philippines,
this valiant soldier;
but he never imagined
that he would be a victim of discrimination…

Johnson, being the senator
for the state of Texas,
felt his heart soften
upon listening to our complaints.

He asked that the soldier's remains
be brought to the capital;
and in the national cemetery
Felix was buried.[3]

Both African Americans and ethnic Mexicans wanted to avoid Jim Crow, but they launched two separate civil rights movements that did not typically involve one another at the political level. While the Houston NAACP mounted legal campaigns against Jim Crow and disfranchisement, Mexican Americans fought to ensure that they would be classified as racially white. Organizations like LULAC and the American G.I. Forum argued that since Mexican Americans were white by law, they should have access to all of the privileges extended to people marked as Caucasian. For example, when two Mexican American activists, M. C. Gonzales of LULAC and Alonso S. Perales of the League of Loyal Americans, persuaded a state representative from San Antonio to introduce a "Racial Equality Bill" in the statehouse on April 14, 1941, the bill called for equal accommodations for "[a]ll persons of the Caucasian Race within the jurisdiction of the State." House Bill 909 had not requested any changes to laws that segregated white from black.[4]

African Americans had a different goal—to tear down Jim Crow permanently. Black Texans could not, therefore, link themselves to what historian Neil Foley has called "a civil rights strategy based on the premise that Mexican Americans were Caucasians, and whose goal it was to end de facto segregation of Mexicans—not de jure segregation of blacks."[5] During the World War II era, black Houstonians had employed old networks, and a renewed commitment from national organizations, to spearhead a civil rights movement in the Bayou City that influenced the national freedom struggle. Houston activists made the local NAACP one of the most successful local branches after winning two high-profile cases with the help of the national office. Newspaper editor C. F. Richardson became president of the branch in 1937 and remained in that position until his death from nephritis two years later. In 1940, under the leadership of black Baptist preacher Albert A. Lucas, the branch attended the annual conference of state branches in Corpus Christi, where they devised a plan with national leaders to end the state's "white only" primary. Thurgood Marshall attended the meeting, and he left with the impression that "this Texas group will really go down in history and they are not afraid to fight for their rights."[6] The Houston branch earned its first major victory with the *Smith v. Allwright* decision. Activists found their case through a lawsuit filed by a local dentist named Lonnie Smith in the summer of 1940. With Marshall acting as his attorney, Smith sued after a county clerk refused to provide an absentee ballot that would allow him to vote in a Democratic primary election. The Supreme Court ruled in Smith's favor in April 1944 when it declared that primary elections must be open to voters of all races—a decision effectively ending the Democratic Party's all-white primary. *Smith v. Allwright* provided further evidence that black activists could successfully convince the federal government to act on their behalf. After the decision, Executive Secretary Lula B. White convinced over five thousand African Americans to join the local NAACP.[7]

These campaigns show a divergence in the Mexican American and African American movements. Both groups faced segregation, but racial exclusion did not always affect them in the same ways. For example, when the NAACP's national office once again partnered with the Houston branch in 1950 to push for the integration of the University of Texas law school, which barred black students from admittance, over one hundred Mexican American students attended the Austin institution. A number of students of Mexican descent were enrolled in the law school. Black Houstonian Heman Sweatt sued after the university refused to admit him in the late 1940s. Marshall represented the plaintiff, and in 1950, the Supreme Court ruled that Sweatt could attend the law school. The decision, known as *Sweatt v. Painter,* desegregated the largest university in the state of Texas.[8]

The most prominent Mexican American activist in Houston, Felix Tijerina, staunchly opposed black activists' participation in nonviolent direct action campaigns in the 1960s. Instigated by students from TSU, the sit-in movement reached Houston in 1960 one month after four students at North Carolina A&T in Greensboro gained national attention for refusing to leave a segregated lunch counter at Woolworth's. Houston's mayor, Lewis Wesley Cutrer, responded by forming an interracial group made up of three dozen business owners called the Citizens' Relations Committee, which included eleven African Americans and LULAC national president Felix Tijerina. The Mexican-born entrepreneur and activist was a likely candidate for the mayor's interracial committee. By 1960, he was a far cry from the penniless young man who had migrated to Houston during the Mexican Revolution. While he and Janie Gonzales Tijerina operated their popular restaurant, he made forays into politics. He served as national president of LULAC for four consecutive terms, from 1956 to 1960. As president, Tijerina extended LULAC into the Midwest, and locally, he established the "Little School of 400"—an educational project that taught Spanish-speaking children four hundred essential English vocabulary words to prepare them for school in Houston.[9] But the LULAC president did not advocate for black civil rights causes. Tijerina refused to allow black Houstonians to enter his "white only" restaurant. During the sit-in movement, Tijerina further dissociated himself from the cause of black civil rights. He firmly believed that demonstrations would lead to "more harm than good." Furthermore, he suggested that the

sit-ins would damage the black community by irritating white business owners, who would no longer hire black workers. "The Negro must remember
that his best friend has been the white man of good will," he wrote in a letter
to the interracial committee. Although he asserted that he also belonged to
"a minority group," he showed no tolerance for what he considered "pressure"
and "threats" from black Houstonians staging sit-ins.[10]

Tijerina faced some criticism among other Mexican American leaders
over his tactics and his method of working with Anglos. A Republican, he
drew criticism from attorney John Herrera, a Democrat, who called Tijerina
"a White Man's Mexican." Tijerina did show some reluctance to anger the
Anglo majority. His concerns led him to distance himself and LULAC from
black activism. As one historian notes, "Tijerina was never happy with the
NAACP and shunned any alliance with the black community for fear of a
possible white backlash."[11] Tijerina's actions shed light on the limited possibilities for political alliances between African Americans and ethnic
Mexicans during the sit-in movement. The local campaign spearheaded by
students succeeded, even without the support of more conservative members
of the committee. By September, black Houstonians could sit at lunch
counters in five dozen local businesses.

But at the very moment that some influential LULAC leaders disdained
cooperation with African American civil rights organizations, and Felix
Tijerina refused to allow black customers into his restaurant, the music
emerging from Houston revealed a closer connection between black and
Mexican American communities than Tijerina would have liked. Rhythm
and blues emerged as a cultural site of contact between the groups. Houston's
rhythm and blues scene involved Mexican Americans and Creoles of color,
who blended sounds from older forms like orquesta and la-la into a genre that
was first established by black artists.

MULTILINGUAL RHYTHM AND BLUES

The rhythm and blues scene in Houston developed after World War II, during a period of economic prosperity. The oil industry made towns from Lake
Charles to Houston a prime destination for a new generation of migrants. In
1950, the Bayou City was home to nearly six hundred thousand people. By
1960, Houston was the seventh-largest city in the nation, with a population
of 938,219.[12] When young people like Fifth Ward native Amos Milburn

returned home after the war, they found a thriving oil city. A musician, Milburn incorporated the new economic climate into the songs he wrote. He recalled an era when cash and liquor flowed freely: "There was a time when there was a lot of money around, and people were really boozin' it up heavy ... and so that's what I was getting—whiskey tunes." His 1954 song "One Scotch, One Bourbon, One Beer" became a hit because of that very atmosphere.[13] In that climate of postwar prosperity, English-speaking black Houstonians cultivated rhythm and blues music, but the local scene quickly spawned hybrid forms created by Creoles of color and Mexican Americans.

As a genre, rhythm and blues was an outgrowth of blues-oriented jazz music and jazz-flavored blues that bands like Milton Larkin and His Orchestra helped create in the 1930s. Jerry Wexler, a Jewish New Yorker who spent much of his youth taking in jazz at Harlem clubs, christened the genre with its new name while he worked as a reporter for *Billboard* magazine. Record companies had used the term *race records* to refer to music made by black artists since the Jazz Age, but the term seemed out-of-date more than two decades later. Wexler suggested to an editor at *Billboard* that they rename the category "rhythm and blues," and the name stuck. What made rhythm and blues an identifiable new sound was the focus on electric guitars, saxophones, and pianos. Electric guitars soared in popularity as more African Americans migrated to cities. From Houston to Chicago, Los Angeles to New York, artists who transitioned from rural to urban frequently plugged in their instruments to produce a louder sound that could be heard over the din in the cities they now called home. Rhythm and blues was thus a music born of urbanization.[14]

The first locally and nationally recognized rhythm and blues artists from Houston emerged from Fifth Ward, which became an early center for the music after the war. Two black-owned clubs especially attracted attention to the neighborhood on the north side of Houston. A wealthy black Houstonian named Louis Dickerson opened Club Matinee on Lyons Avenue. Known as "the Cotton Club of the South," Club Matinee became a meeting spot for musicians, regardless of the time of day. After a gig, the talent retreated next door to Dickerson's other business, the Crystal Hotel, and continued playing and/or networking. The club owner's success garnered national attention; *Ebony* magazine praised Dickerson in an article titled "Negro Millionaires in Texas."[15] His businesses helped make the surrounding neighborhood a focal point in the arena of black entertainment and entrepreneurship in the 1950s.

Another Fifth Ward club, called the Bronze Peacock, also offered customers an upscale flavor, with an added element of danger. Don Robey, the black entrepreneur who had also founded the Harlem Grill in Fourth Ward in the 1930s, opened the Bronze Peacock on February 18, 1946, at the corner of Erastus and Wylie streets. The establishment was one of the swankest nightclubs in the city. Inside, shake dancers and orchestras entertained visitors, who assembled at tables covered with crisp white tablecloths and feasted on fine cuisine. The club did not sell alcohol, so customers purchased setups for the bottles they brought. Like the Eldorado Ballroom and Robey's Harlem Grill, the Bronze Peacock frequently hosted social clubs with middle-class members. "Different companies and social clubs had parties there," remembered an employee. The Peacock's owner brought an aura of urban menace to the swank club. Robey, born in Houston in 1903, had acquired decades of experience in the nightclub industry by the time he opened the Fifth Ward establishment, and he had earned a reputation for ruthlessness. Reportedly quick-tempered, Robey carried a gun and maintained a staff of bodyguards—perhaps because his club allowed illegal practices. Robey, a sporting man, offered separate rooms for games like cards and dice, where patrons could gamble illegally.[16]

The Bronze Peacock transgressed the color line; the club was also an integrated space in a legally segregated city. "The Bronze Peacock attracted a mixed audience, black and white," recalled one business associate.[17] Whereas a few white patrons had visited the Eldorado before the war, the Peacock drew crowds of white people who traveled to the north side nightly. Perhaps because of the illicit activity, the establishment sat on the outskirts of the city. Drummer Earl Palmer recalled, "At night you could look out the Peacock and see lights from another part of town."[18] The people who observed that view could, then, partake in a number of illegal pursuits—from gambling to carousing with a mixed crowd in a Jim Crow society.

Robey also drew customers to his Fifth Ward nightclub by featuring some of the most popular performers of the rhythm and blues era. The Peacock quickly became a requisite stop on the "Chitlin' Circuit"—the nationwide network of clubs and ballrooms that booked African American performers. The club's owner soon created Peacock Records, which enabled him to manage the talent he signed. He launched the label in 1949 in order to record Clarence "Gatemouth" Brown, a Louisiana-born, Texas-reared artist signed to Aladdin Records. He initially worked as Brown's manager, but when he grew tired of Aladdin's timetable for Brown's releases, Robey decided to record the musician himself. After purchasing Memphis-based Duke Records in 1952, the Houston entrepreneur acquired even more musicians, like singer Bobby Bland. He later founded the Songbird and Backbeat labels, and branched out into gospel music. Groups like the Mighty Clouds of Joy, the Dixie Hummingbirds, and the Sensational Nightingales signed on with Robey.

Robey was infamously shrewd; he succeeding in making money from these musicians at every stage of their career. He owned the Lion Publishing Company, and he created the Buffalo Booking Agency to promote Peacock artists. Buffalo also represented artists who were not signed to Duke-Peacock, such as B. B. King and Albert Collins. His business partner Evelyn Johnson managed the agency. Born in Louisiana and raised in Fifth Ward, Johnson was Robey's second-in-command. She oversaw day-to-day operations and helped Robey figure out how the record business worked. Describing her role at Peacock, Johnson recalled, "I was mother, confessor, lawyer, doctor, sister, financier, mother superior, the whole nine yards. What they needed they asked for, and what they asked for they got."[19] Johnson likely added a more personable touch to an enterprise owned by one of the most notoriously shady figures in the black world of show business in the 1950s.

In those early years of rhythm and blues in postwar Houston, the music was largely associated with English-speaking black artists. (Greek American Johnny Otis, who had a contract with Peacock in the 1950s, is a notable exception.) Together Robey and Johnson developed an impressive roster of black talent from Texas and beyond. Robey reportedly did not like "down-home" country blues; instead, he favored the urban-flavored rhythm and blues that typically featured a full band.[20] Marie Adams recorded Peacock's first hit, "I'm Gonna Play the Honky Tonks," in 1952. Robey signed Alabama-born Willie Mae "Big Mama" Thornton in 1951 after hearing her sing in Houston, and "Hound Dog" became the first of her songs to chart. (See figure 11.) Johnny Ace, born John Marshall Alexander, Jr., brought considerable attention to the label before he died playing Russian roulette in late 1954. With talent like Willie Mae Thornton, Johnny Ace, and Bobby "Blue" Bland signed to his label, Don Robey made Houston a center for the production of rhythm and blues.

As rumors about the swank club circulated across Houston and beyond, law-enforcement agencies conducted frequent gambling raids on the Peacock. Johnson maintained that the heightened attention had more to do with the presence of white people than any concerns about illegal gaming. According

FIGURE 11. Andrew Steptoe with Duke-Peacock artist Willie Mae "Big Mama" Thornton. Author's personal collection.

to Johnson, "when just the regular white people in general started coming, well, then that didn't land too well." Police officers stood at the doors of the nightclub, turning away prospective customers. Rather than lose money on the venture, Robey eventually closed the Bronze Peacock after eight years, in the fall of 1953, and focused on recording the acts signed to his label.[21]

The style that Robey and Johnson helped cultivate in the Bayou City after World War II came to dominate the local music scene, and rhythm and blues artists eclipsed the jazz musicians who had been so prominent before the war. The sounds of Peacock artists became so popular that jazz artists like pianist Joe Sample found fewer and fewer Houston venues willing to book them. Born in Fifth Ward in 1939 to a Creole of color family from Louisiana, Joseph Leslie Sample showed an early interest in music, and began taking piano lessons at age five. Like Arnett Cobb and Illinois Jacquet in the 1930s, he formed a jazz band with classmates while attending Wheatley High School. Sample rooted the band's sound in his Creole neighborhood: "The music that was inside us came from our community, from what we heard in the Fifth Ward, what we heard at our little Creole church."[22] After graduation, Sample studied piano at Texas Southern University, which supported jazz after the war. The Third Ward campus had been home to a big band and jazz ensembles since around 1949. The students, like their prewar predecessors, left Houston to take positions in the nation's top orchestras. Duke Ellington recruited one ensemble member, trumpeter Barrie Lee Hall, Jr., to conduct his orchestra. (Anita Moore, another alumnus of the TSU Jazz Ensemble, would later perform with Ellington for sixteen years.)[23] Sample and five other musicians from Fifth Ward—Wilton Felder, Stix Hooper, Wayne Henderson, Henry "La" Wilson, and Hubert Laws—called themselves the Modern Jazz Sextet.[24] The act left TSU in 1958 before Sample graduated, though, and headed to Los Angeles; they cited the lack of a jazz scene in rhythm-and-blues-rich Houston as a primary reason for relocating. "It was always that rhythm and blues was king, and jazz was secondary," Sample recalled. "I remember everybody telling me that I was crazy, and I should think about getting a real job and staying out of music, period." Although jazz musicians could earn a living in Houston in the 1930s and 1940s, after the war, they could not maintain that popularity.[25]

When the artists on the Duke-Peacock label recorded in Houston, Robey took them to a facility called Gold Star Studios, an unassuming recording studio near Third Ward, in southeast Houston. Bill Quinn, an Irish American man from Boston, opened Gold Star in 1941. Quinn soon created his own label, also called Gold Star, which focused on recording what he dubbed "hillbilly" music, blues artists, and French songs played by Louisiana natives. In the following decades, Gold Star remained an important site for the production of diverse musical styles. The Houston location was key. With its proximity to Louisiana, East Texas, and South Texas, Gold Star was accessible to artists from across the western South.

Gold Star was located in a Jim Crow city, but Quinn did not seem to have an investment in a space-based racial hierarchy. The white Bostonian was known for a more liberal attitude on race. "Being an outsider to the region," note music writers Roger Wood and Andy Bradley, "he perhaps lacked the generally ingrained social prejudices of most middle-aged white men in the South at the time."[26] Quinn's ambivalence toward Jim Crow eased racial tension at Gold Star. Inside the studio, black men like Don Robey could occupy positions of authority and leadership. Because Robey employed other black people at his label, those executives garnered considerable clout at white-owned Gold Star. Black executives from Duke-Peacock participated in making and marketing the music recorded, produced, and mixed at the studio. Robey and his staff commanded a type of respect in a white-run business that defied notions of black inferiority.[27]

Gold Star and Duke-Peacock Records brought a new side of the music industry into Houston after World War II. Nightclubs in the wards had long attracted musicians, but the city lacked a solid presence in the recording industry. Gold Star, Duke-Peacock, and smaller companies like Freedom Records changed the scene. Now, for the first time, local artists could record their music in Houston. Rhythm and blues was not just vital to the local economy; the scene helped spread music recorded in Houston to the rest of the country. Increasingly, the sounds recorded at Gold Star reflected the diverse nature of music and race in the city.

In either 1949 or 1950, bluesman Sam "Lightnin'" Hopkins entered a recording booth at Gold Star and recorded a song that offered a glimpse of the new form of music that was emerging from spaces where Creoles of color and black Texans made contact. His label released a tune with the title "Zolo Go." At the beginning of the song, Hopkins proclaims he's going to "*zologo* a little while for you folks" because "young and old likes that." He then, while using an organ to reproduce the sound of an accordion, describes going to a dance. The song was unlike any previous recording made by Hopkins. After about a decade playing the street corners and blues joints in the wards,

Hopkins had transitioned into a recording artist when he signed a contract with Aladdin Records in around 1946. Since he loathed travel, Hopkins preferred to record in the Third Ward studio rather than make the trek to California. He first recorded at Gold Star in 1947, and within a year he had cut over forty songs.[28] During the session that produced "Zolo Go," Lightnin' attempted to reproduce the sounds of Frenchtown and the growth of a rhythm and blues sound that blended southwestern Louisiana with southeastern Texas.

By World War II, musicians living in Frenchtown knew that they could gain a following in Houston by blending traditional Creole tunes with Texas blues. Because they worked, lived, and played with black Houstonians, musicians from Louisiana did not stick exclusively to la-la. Instead, Creoles of color began to experiment with the blues, which attracted black Texans. After Anderson Moss migrated to the city in 1928, he played English-language blues songs like "Stormy Weather" and "Driftin' Blues." Although he performed a different type of music than the kinds his parents probably favored, Moss retained some Creole flavor. Rather than switching to guitar or piano, the instruments favored by East Texas blues players, Moss played his blues with an accordion.[29] The new style suited Fifth Ward—an area where people were familiar with the sounds of la-la and blues, French and English, Creole and East Texan. At house parties, he played music that appealed to both groups.

La-la music, and the language in which lyrics were performed, had been reshaped and remolded after decades of contact between black Texans and Louisianans of color by World War II. Living and going to school in Houston meant that the language of Bayou City Creoles contained increasing numbers of English words. Texas-born children may have teased Inez Prejean and Illinois Jacquet when they spoke French patois at Crawford Elementary in the 1920s, but by the time they were adults, both spoke fluent English. It wasn't uncommon for Creoles to anglicize their names. Marius Chevalier was born in St. Martin Parish, Louisiana, in 1880, but when he died in Houston in the winter of 1974, he went by "Morris." Renaud Landry, born in St. Landry Parish in 1907, later spelled his name "Raynard" as an adult living on Delia Street in Frenchtown.[30] Older Creoles of color were bilingual, but their Houston-born children may not have spoken French at all.

As people like Chevalier and Landry adapted to an English-speaking world, musicians of the post–World War II era began to sonically fuse rhythm and blues with la-la. Singers still used the phrase *les haricots sont pas salés*, the most popular in la-la tradition, in their songs, but they now used the words to signify the blend of genres played in Frenchtown. Musicians added instruments associated with rhythm and blues, like drums and, sometimes, electric guitars. When they described the local form of music that used these instruments, as well as accordions and washboards, people called the music "*les haricots*," or "the beans." Since young Houston-born Creoles did not typically read French (and they certainly did not pronounce the words the same way their parents had in southwestern Louisiana), they spelled and spoke the words differently. Specifically, Houstonians began to spell *les haricots* with a "z" for the "s" in *les*. The people of Frenchtown had not yet settled on a way to spell the name of the music they enjoyed, though. In front of the small nightclubs scattered across the community, signs advertised a music called *zarico, zodico, zordico,* or *zologo.* These were attempts to anglicize French words that had been shared in Louisiana prior to the Creole exodus to Houston and the establishment of Frenchtown. Houstonians, whether Texas or Louisiana born, used the word as a verb or a noun to refer to the style of music and dance that mixed English and French lyrics with Creole instrumentation and rhythm and blues. In Frenchtown, you could dance to *zologo* music, but you could also *zologo* all night long.

Lightnin' Hopkins's "Zolo Go" captures a sonic snapshot of postwar Fifth Ward. When historian and folklorist Robert Burton "Mack" McCormick visited Houston in 1950, black Houstonians told him about Frenchtown and urged him to sample the unique music coming out of that neighborhood. McCormick traveled to the Bayou City during a journey to the Gulf Coast to record blues and folk-music traditions. While scouring the Fifth Ward enclave for interesting music, McCormick first met a "Frenchman" named Dudley Alexander from New Iberia, Louisiana, who sang the blues song "Baby, Please Don't Go" for him. Alexander's knowledge of this popular tune hardly surprised McCormick; however, the collector noticed that the musician took considerable liberties with the song. Not only did he accompany himself with an accordion; he sang the lyrics in a mixture of English and French. As McCormick continued to roam Fifth Ward, he noticed the cultural outgrowth of intermingling between Creoles of color and East Texans everywhere he turned. McCormick asked about the name of the music and dance they performed, but he could not quite understand the words he heard. So he followed local people to their parties and snapped pictures of signs that read "zarico" and "zologo." McCormick then realized that these words were all derived from the French *les haricots*. Even more intriguing to McCormick was that the dance that accompanied this music mimicked the action of snapping beans.[31]

McCormick decided that the music he heard in Frenchtown belonged to its own genre; it was neither rhythm and blues nor la-la. He created a new spelling for the name of the music and dance: "zydeco."[32] The spelling, and the sound that the words describe, reflect cultural fusion that resulted from migration out of southwestern Louisiana and into Houston. The music collector saw rural folk traditions in the process of becoming citified—musical modernity in action. When they moved to Houston, Louisianans had modified the movement of the agricultural practice of bean harvesting into a dance performed in urban spaces. The music had also been adapted to incorporate English lyrics and the rhythm and blues style that emanated from Fifth Ward after World War II. McCormick eventually released a double album that contained some of the music he discovered in Houston. The recordings brought zydeco—a new genre created in Frenchtown—out of the Bayou City and into national conversations about music.

The popularity of zydeco inspired entrepreneurship from Louisiana migrants in Fifth Ward. What had been the domain of Friday-night house parties evolved into a business that fortified the local consumer economy. Owned by a woman named Doris McClendon, the Continental Ballroom featured accordionist Lonnie Mitchell six nights a week. McClendon was born in Louisiana in 1936 and moved to Fifth Ward in 1947. Her grandfather had opened a small nightclub when she was still in her teens. In 1951, the Continental opened its doors, and it soon acquired a reputation as "Houston's premier Creole nightspot." McClendon's contemporary Curley Cormier, a "soft-spoken gentleman fond of three-piece suits," first made a name for himself in Frenchtown by hosting rollicking house parties. Cormier capitalized on his reputation when he opened a zydeco club called Alfred's Place in 1962. Located on Crane Street, Alfred's Place was essentially a shotgun shack converted into a juke joint.[33] The Continental and Alfred's Place lacked the swank atmosphere of the Peacock and Club Matinee, but they offered a glimpse into an emerging local scene that captured a national audience in the 1960s.

Alfred's Place looked small and humble from the outside, but Cormier's club became the launching pad for the man who would become known as the "King of Zydeco." Born in Opelousas in 1925, Clifton Chenier began playing a blues-infused version of la-la in Gulf Coast oil towns. In 1947 he moved to Lake Charles, and then a bit farther west, to Port Arthur, Texas, where he and his brother Cleveland worked at the Gulf Oil refinery. The migrant experience changed the way they played music, and the spaces in which they worked and played literally affected the music they played. In "icehouses"— small shacks, located near refineries, that workers used for entertainment— Clifton used an amplifier so that his accordion could be heard over the din of a rowdy audience. Cleveland played a rubboard, a refashioned washboard that he built using leftover tin he found at the refinery. The brothers moved to Houston in 1958. When Alfred's Place opened, Cormier gave Chenier a standing gig that lasted for five years. With just two pieces—an accordion and rubboard—Chenier played the blues. The abundance of new nightclubs and dance halls that played this new music made Fifth Ward a local "tourist attraction" by the 1950s.[34]

In a merging of cultural practices in shared spaces, black Texan and Creole musical styles converged in ways that had not occurred during the Swing Era. The groups had shared stages since the mid-1930s, when musicians from Louisiana and Texas performed together in high schools and professional orchestras. In the case of the jazz music played at the Harlem Grill or the Eldorado Ballroom, though, the music did not sonically merge traditions from two different places. Instead, the young people created their own "Texas tenor" version of the jazz played popularly on the radio. The music of the Swing Era gave the children of migrants a shared expression that became the basis for a community that had become culturally black Texan and Creole. Zydeco, on the other hand, indicated a different social process. Whereas Texas tenor was a local expression of a national music craze, zydeco actually sounded like a fusion of southwestern Louisiana and East Texas. This postwar style indicated the emergence of a blended culture. Frenchtown was not defined by geopolitical boundaries; rather, cultural practices like zydeco defined the community, shaped its contours, and made it an identifiable place. The sonic hybridity of the music alludes to the cultural and ethnic hybridity that emerged from spaces where Creoles and Texans met. By the time zydeco developed, Frenchtown was not a separate entity from Fifth Ward. Instead, the blended culture came to define the north-side community as a whole.

Texans and Louisianans often shared the stage, producing a sound that fluidly combined traditions and became profitable in a community made up of migrants from different states. Chenier began playing with Lightnin' Hopkins, who had already shown an interest in Creole music, and the men formed a tight partnership that appealed to people from both men's regions. The Continental Ballroom featured both the English-speaking guitar player from Texas and the French-speaking accordion player from Louisiana on the same stage, where they battled one another for crowd approval.[35] Competition facilitated the development of the style. Houston blues, Texas tenor jazz, and zydeco all emerged from a society that valued musical contests and friendly rivalry. By competing onstage, musicians forged a sonic connection between people who felt they had little in common when they first met.

That fusion became part of the recorded-music industry in the early 1960s. Mack McCormick returned to Houston to make field recordings of zydeco with Chris Strachwitz of Arhoolie Records, and Hopkins invited them come to Frenchtown to hear Chenier. Strachwitz recalled that Hopkins took him "to this little beer joint in Houston in an area they call Frenchtown." Chenier was onstage playing a set. "[H]ere was this black man with a huge accordion on his chest and playing the most unbelievable low-down blues I'd ever heard in my life—and singing it in this bizarre French patois!"[36] The first recordings of zydeco took place during sessions at Gold Star. Quinn also had early success with a recording by Cajun performer Harry Choates, whose "Jole Blon" became known as the "Cajun national anthem," so he was likely eager to experiment with other artists from Louisiana.[37] When Arhoolie Records decided to produce Clifton Chenier's first album, they paid for the Louisiana native to record at Gold Star. In 1965, Chenier made his first recordings of the music that blended styles from either side of the Sabine River. Gold Star not only served the artists from Don Robey's various labels, but also became a site for the recording of French/English hybrid sounds.

The blending of sounds represented a growing kinship between groups that had once considered themselves separate. Over time, Hopkins and Chenier formed a musical bond that became familial. When Hopkins introduced Chenier to his contacts in the music industry, he referred to the accordion player from Louisiana as his "cousin." For Lightnin' Hopkins, calling Chenier his cousin was both diasporic and real. Through marriage, Houstonians from both states literally created familial ties. Hopkins married Chenier's cousin from Louisiana. Such unions were not uncommon after World War II. Musician Ashton Savoy "shacked up" with Fifth Ward native Katie Webster, a pianist. Hopkins and Chenier, as well as Savoy and Webster, forged bonds through shared musical interests as well. Savoy met Webster, who played boogie-woogie piano, at a show in Port Arthur.[38] Meanwhile, Hopkins and Chenier also forged a musical form of kinship by playing together, and their years of playing together left an imprint on their recordings. Hopkins's song "Good Morning Little School Girl" and Chenier's "Me and My Chauffeur Blues" have the same melody, for example. The main difference between the tunes is instrumentation. Hopkins plays the melody with his guitar, while Chenier uses an accordion.

Zydeco became part of a broader consumer marketplace because of the city's emerging recording industry and its rhythm and blues music scene. When Milton Larkin and His Orchestra reigned in the 1930s, the city did not have an infrastructure for recording the music that originated in the wards. This changed after World War II in response to Houston's thriving rhythm and blues scene. Zydeco spread from Houston to become a national phenomenon because of this musical world. By fusing their musical traditions with rhythm and blues, Creole music reached large numbers of African American and Anglo audiences for the first time. La-la was not typically included in contemporary discussions of black music because sonic aspects of the genre did not fit dominant perceptions of "blackness-as-performance" shared by most Americans. "No genre has played a more prominent role in racial identity politics in the United States than the blues," writes scholar Christopher Waterman. The blues was "continually invoked as a baseline or core of black experience."[39] But the French lyrics and instrumentation found in la-la were unique to southwestern Louisiana and Afro-Creole culture. It was not a musical culture shared by most other people of African descent in the United States. Zydeco performers, on the other hand, often used the twelve-bar AAB format that fans of blues and rhythm and blues recognized. Furthermore, they sang in English, or a combination of English and French. The music retained the two dominant sonic markers of la-la: accordions and rubboards; nevertheless, the use of English, blues structure, and rhythm and blues instrumentation meant that these were songs that could be marketed as music by black people. For example, Clarence Garlow's hit song from 1950, "Bon Ton Roula," plays on the Creole French expression "Let the good times roll"; however, Garlow sings most of the lyrics in English. The Arhoolie executive gave Chenier's first song, "Louisiana Blues," an English title to make it accessible to deejays across the nation. The change in language made zydeco more marketable. Titles like "All Night Long," "Think It Over," and "Come Go Along with Me Second" could appeal to English speakers.[40] By fusing with Texas blues and rhythm and blues—two genres with established markets—Creole musicians found a broader, more national audience. Through zydeco, black and white Americans outside of the Gulf Coast discovered Creole music. In the process, they experienced some of the diversity found among the people labeled "black" in the United States.

Zydeco is a genre born out of migration, with lyrics that often allude to the experiences of people who have left home or are longing for home. Chenier frequently sang from the perspective of a man away from home. Titles like "Coming Home Tomorrow," "I'm Coming Home," and "I Believe I'll Go Back Home" tell the story of a man torn between two locations—one rural, one urban—and the sonic qualities of those songs indicate the relationship between those places. Lightnin' Hopkins's most blatant incorporation of Afro-Creole music style was "Zolo Go," but he also made songs that incorporated the experiences of Creoles. In "L.A. Blues," East Texas–born Hopkins sings from the perspective of a Louisiana migrant living in Houston.[41]

The marketing of zydeco, however, downplayed the influence of Texas music and the experience of migration on Chenier's music by spatially rooting him in the place he left. Strachwitz titled his first album *Louisiana Blues*. He did not sell the new genre through an association with Houston or Frenchtown. Yet for Mack McCormick, the man who first used the word *zydeco,* the name referred to music from Fifth Ward. Over the years, McCormick began to resent efforts by the state of Louisiana to apply *zydeco* to music that developed east of the Sabine River. He created the modern spelling of *zydeco* in Frenchtown, and he intended the name to refer to that place. "When I'm talking about zydeco," he wrote, "I'm talking about the music of Frenchtown ... and the people who usurped that ... were the Louisiana tourist commissions.... Louisiana's very big on tourists, so when they put out a map that says rice country, zydeco country, jazz country, and they send three million copies of the map, it's over."[42]

Creole musicians in Louisiana born in the 1920s and 1930s also distinguish between the rural music they came of age hearing and playing and the urban zydeco that emerged from Houston after World War II. Canray Fontenot once said that he did not remember the name *zydeco* being used to describe Creole music in Louisiana. "Now they're talking about zydeco music. They never had that. I never known that."[43] As historian Roger Wood asserts, "[T]hough the seminal black Creole dance music la-la surely originated [in Louisiana], modern electric zydeco is arguably the product of a syncretism that was first triggered in Texas, especially in the Bayou City."[44] The roots of the genre were conceived in Louisiana, but zydeco was born in Houston.

The zydeco scene also helped Fifth Ward natives maintain ties to their old neighborhood after they moved away. The music emerged at the same time that the government razed entire sections of the wards to construct highways. In the 1950s, Highway 59 and Interstate 10 cut through Second Ward and Fifth Ward. The construction of these freeways contributed to the gradual depopulation of the wards. The Berry family had to move from their home on Whitty Street when that thoroughfare became the access road for Highway 59. Mary Rose Berry moved to Clinton Park, a black postwar neighborhood established in 1950 near the ship channel. Clinton Park had an elementary school, a park with a swimming pool, and ranch homes with picture windows. Creoles from Frenchtown moved into a nearby community called Pleasantville.[45] Fifth Ward's growing reputation for violence also contributed to the out-migration. Visiting the area meant traveling to a part of the city increasingly linked to vice and violence in the local imagination. Weldon "Juke Boy" Bonner, who played the blues in Fifth Ward during this era, once referred to the intersection of Lyons Avenue and Jensen Drive as "Blood Alley." In a song ominously called "Stay Off Lyons Avenue," Bonner warned listeners that they'd be "living on luck and a prayer" if they visited the neighborhood.[46] Locals started calling the area "Pearl Harbor" sometime after World War II because of the high number of young men who died there.[47] At some point, Fifth Ward also acquired the nickname "the Bloody Nickel." Even as residents moved to other parts of Houston, the churches and nightclubs drew them back to Fifth Ward for festivals and other cultural events. As the home of zydeco, Frenchtown remained a center of culture after members of the community moved to new parts of the city.

Zydeco highlights a fusion of Creole and black Texan culture and society. When the groups made contact in the 1920s, they had cultivated different forms of music—blues and la-la—that illustrated their linguistic, cultural, and racial distinctions. Yet the divide between Frenchtown and the rest of black Fifth Ward lessened over time. By the 1950s, they shared a common language and a form of music that drew from both traditions.

The emergence of a zydeco music scene in Houston contributed to a surge in polycultural rhythm and blues that emerged in the late 1950s and early 1960s and increasingly included Texas Mexicans. Record companies capitalized on the growing multilingual urban communities that had appeared in the United States over the last three decades. Talent scouts scoured the nation for youthful talent that could play the dance-based, blues-inflected music to other young people, but they did so with the knowledge that, in certain parts of the country, those youth had come of age in homes where English was not the primary language spoken. Waves of migration since

World War I had produced a generation of Mexican Americans who could sing the folk songs of their ancestors as well as the hits they heard on the radio and saw performed on *The Ed Sullivan Show.*

Like the fusion that resulted in zydeco, Spanish-language forays into rhythm and blues often grew from contact between different groups with distinct musical traditions. The Texas version of the music that came to be known as "brown-eyed soul" emerged at around the same time as zydeco.[48] A band from San Antonio called Sunny and the Sunglows first brought Mexican American rhythm and blues into black nightclubs in Houston. Two high schoolers, Ildefonso Fraga "Sunny" Ozuna and Rudy Guerra, formed the band in 1957. The students came of age listening to rhythm and blues, conjunto, and urban orquesta acts. Ozuna recalled that they especially followed the Isidro Lopez Orquesta out of Corpus Christi and the Alfonso Ramos Orquesta from San Antonio. At the same time, the students were part of a generation of musicians in that city who drew inspiration from the doo-wop and rhythm and blues of cities like New Orleans and Houston. Fats Domino was one of Ozuna's favorite musicians. Popular San Antonio radio station KUKA responded by catering to a range of tastes. Deejays played rhythm and blues and conjunto.[49]

Mexican Americans' interest in black American musical traditions inspired them to create a unique musical fusion known as the "West Side Sound," named for a historically Mexican American community in San Antonio. Ozuna described the sound as "a little conjunto with doo-wop" with an additional sprinkling of "Texas flavor."[50] One of the architects of the West Side Sound, Abe "Abie" Epstein, who produced over nine hundred songs, typically released the music as double-sided 45 rpm records. Epstein's success stemmed largely from his ability to corral sounds he heard on the streets of West San Antonio. The result was an urban, distinctly Tejano interpretation of rhythm and blues. "It was black, brown and white like no one else mixed up at the time," notes journalist Joe Nick Patoski.[51]

The heavy infusion of Texas blues, and the fact that Tejanos often played in the state's segregated black nightclubs, also distinguished their sound from the rhythm and blues produced by Mexican Americans in places like Los Angeles. "The Southern influence was greater," argues music collector and historian Ruben Molina, "and it seemed easier for kids to be able to get into the clubs and bars that were part of the Chitlin' Circuit." In San Antonio, the black Eastwood Country Club on the east side of the city drew prestigious black talent, as well as Mexican American youth who loved rhythm and blues.

A local black musician named Spot Barnett began to recruit Tejanos into his act. "All of us Chicanos from the Westside spent our time on the Eastside, because it was the black part of town, and everyone wanted to be in Spot Barnett's band," recalled a drummer named Ernie Durawa, who later played with the band called the Texas Tornados. "He was the king of the Eastside, one of our mentors. That's where the groove was, the soul, and that's what we wanted."[52] In the competitive music scene, Mexican American artists learned that they had to appeal to black audiences. "When you walk into an all-black club with eight black musicians and you're the only Chicano, then someone asks, 'Where's the singer?' and the band points at you, you better be able to sell that music," contended a musician known as Little Roger Gonzalez.[53]

Sonically, the music created by young Tejanos melded traditions of older Mexican American styles like orquesta with the music pouring out of black communities after World War II. Artists like Little Jr. Jesse & the Teardrops, Billy Sol, and Danny & the Tejanos emphasized harmonies, organ riffs, and horn sections. The prevalence of brass horns especially steeped the West Side Sound in the orquesta tradition. In most cases, the horns establish the melody of Tejano rhythm and blues songs, which was a common practice in orquesta compositions. But while Mexican American big bands typically had between ten and twelve musicians, rhythm and blues acts played with fewer instruments. "We came up with something that was more like a combo," remembered Sunny Ozuna. "We were just kids out of high school, and we weren't equipped to do that, so we had a tenor sax, alto sax, and a trumpet doing a 1–3–5 harmony. That was as far as the horn section went."[54] Bands from Texas also combined the horns with other instruments popular in the 1960s, like the Hammond organ, which increasingly replaced the accordions found in conjunto songs. Manny Guerra of the Sunglows first used an accordion in his arrangements before deciding that the instrument was "too country." In their arrangements, organs played the same role as the accordions on their parents' records.[55]

The Sunglows were among the first artists to break a spatial divide that had long separated African Americans and Mexican Americans in Houston. They joined the Chitlin' Circuit, which led them to the Bayou City for their first gig, and they played for Tejano audiences at Mexican American venues. They found inspiration for their first band name while on the road. "Our very first little job was in Houston," recalled Ozuna. "I think we got $100 for it. We were on our way to Houston, and we saw a sign on the side of the road that said, 'Sunglow Feed Company.'" They first recorded songs on their own label, Sunglows, before landing a record deal. A Houston-based record producer, Huey Meaux, produced a song by Sunny and the Sunglows, called "Talk to Me," for his Tear Drop label in 1962. The song, which was a remake of a record by black singer Little Willie John, became a national hit. The San Antonio natives appeared on *American Bandstand,* the first Tejanos to do so since Freddy Fender's heyday in the 1950s. "Talk to Me" remained on the Top 40 charts for fourteen weeks in late 1962 and early 1963, and eventually went gold.[56]

A key figure at the increasingly multiethnic/multiracial scene at Gold Star, Huey Purvis Meaux made Mexican American artists who could play rhythm and blues and Spanish-language music part of Houston's soundscape. Huey Meaux was a white southerner; however, his keen awareness of the marketability of music from other ethnic and racial groups perhaps overrode a need to abide by the rules of Jim Crow. Meaux hailed from southern Louisiana, where he came of age hearing music from people of African descent. Born in 1929 to a French-speaking Cajun family who worked as sharecroppers in the fields of Kaplan, he grew up hearing his father play the accordion in their shotgun house. Sharecropping families, whether black, Cajun, or Creole of color, often worked—and played—near one another, so the Meaux family heard a mixture of musical traditions. "Back in them days, my dad worked for the man—picked cotton, hoed, grew rice, shucked it, and harvested it," he once told a reporter. "We had four shotgun houses, two black families, two white families. Music was a release." When Meaux was twelve years old, his family crossed the Sabine River to Winnie, Texas, where they continued working the rice fields.[57] Huey worked as a deejay at radio stations before moving into music production. He first recorded artists who fused the traditions heard in Louisiana and Texas. In 1959, he made his first foray into producing when he recorded a song by a Cajun oil-refinery worker, Jivin' Gene Bourgeois, called "Breaking Up Is Hard to Do," at the KPAC Studios in Port Arthur. The rock 'n' roll song performed by a Cajun in Texas spawned the genre called "swamp pop." His first hit was with a white man, but his next songs included "You'll Lose a Good Thing," by a black woman named Barbara Lynn. Following the success of those records, Meaux created Tear Drop Records and Crazy Cajun Enterprises, which he moved to Conroe, a town just north of Houston. He continued to use Gold Star to record the talent he signed to Tear Drop. By signing artists from Louisiana and different parts of Texas to Gold Star, Meaux profited from the diverse musical heritage of the region. As one writer described it, Meaux recorded

"Gulf Coast music that crossed borders: between Texas and Louisiana and Texas and Mexico, between black and white and brown."[58]

The Sunglows lasted about four and a half years, and in that time they influenced the Houston development of other Mexican American rhythm and blues acts. Under Meaux's management, Ozuna created a new band in 1966. (His old friend and bandmate Rudy Guerra went on to form a band called Latin Breed). Ozuna added three Latinos from Houston—the Villanueva brothers, who called themselves "The Rocking Vs"—and the new group became known as Sunny and the Sunliners. Meaux, raised in francophone Louisiana, encouraged the Sunliners to draw on their bilingual heritage. "Since we were all bilingual—we were all Spanish boys—he [Meaux] figured, 'We ought to try some new ideas,'" Ozuna recalled. The result was a Spanish rhythm and blues song, "Cariño nuevo."[59] Gold Star, which Meaux eventually bought and renamed Sugar Hill, officially became a site for artists who performed in English, French, and Spanish.

Meaux rooted his success in the racial geography of the western South. Houston and the surrounding area was a demographic mix of diverse groups, and Meaux drew on their musical traditions. "The reason why I had so many hits," he said, "was that around this part of the country, you've got a different kind of people every hundred miles—Czech, Mexican, Cajun, black."[60] He searched for talent locally in Houston, but also ventured into his home state of Louisiana, East Texas, and San Antonio. Meaux's business strategy emphasized a sonic marriage of regional music traditions with Top 40 styles. In 1965, for example, the Cajun producer found a way to blend the popular sound of the British Invasion with traditions of the western South. Songs by groups like the Beatles and the Byrds reminded Meaux of the sounds of the region. "[I]t dawned on me that they were playing the Lake Charles two-step that me and my daddy used to play in Cajun country," he recalled. Meaux wanted to capitalize on the popularity of British groups, but he included Tejanos and Anglos. He called San Antonio native Doug Sahm and asked him to record a song with him. "I said, 'Bring your guitar and come over, Doug. I'm drunk, but I've got that beat.'" Meaux fashioned Sahm and his band, which consisted of Mexican American and Anglo youth, into a group called the Sir Douglas Quintet. He then brought the act to Gold Star in 1965 to record "She's about a Mover," a song that drew on a range of sonic traditions. The vocals riff on Ray Charles's performance in "That's What I Say," while using a traditional AAB blues structure. Meanwhile, the song's backbeat blends Cajun and conjunto style, with an organist imitating an accordion (much like Lightnin' Hopkins had done a decade earlier with "Zolo Go," or like Sunny and the Sunliners). The result was a fusion of southwestern Louisiana, East Texas, and South Texas that merged in a Houston recording studio.[61]

The rhythm and blues produced and recorded in Houston emphasizes cultural hybridity. The artists who played the styles performed that hybridity through musical remakes. Clifton Chenier offered accordion-based versions of popular rock 'n' roll and rhythm and blues songs. His "Eh, petite fille" is a French version of Floyd Dixon's "Oooh Little Girl." Chenier's instrumental zydeco track called "Rock Awhile" reinterprets Houstonian Goree Carter's "Let's Rock Awhile," a track often cited as the first rock 'n' roll song. Whereas Carter's song emphasizes guitar solo, Chenier's stresses the accordion.[62] Musicians like Chenier added their first languages, and, in some cases, new instruments, to songs popularized on the U.S. Top 40 charts. Pop music in the United States was no longer an English conversation, nor was it primarily the domain of Anglos and African Americans.

The close affiliation between Creoles of color and black Texas natives, and the closing of spatial gaps between ethnic Mexican and black Houstonians, occurred more readily during the political climate of the 1960s. These hybrid forms of rhythm and blues did not emerge from a vacuum; the music increasingly reflected political change and facilitated new patterns of social relations. The civil rights movement also legally changed the status of black southerners, which affected how other groups perceived racial blackness by the mid-1960s. Furthermore, movements like Black Power and Brown Pride inspired some Mexican Americans and Creoles of color to explore their racial subjectivities, which changed the way these different groups identified themselves and how they related to black Texans.

SOUL AND RACIAL SUBJECTIVITY

Tejanos' appetite for rhythm and blues and rock 'n' roll reflects the cultural changes taking place within Mexican American communities. The difference, in some cases, was generational. By the 1950s, Mexican Americans had developed solid roots in the Bayou City. Historian Roberto Treviño argues that the population "was a bicultural community more so than a 'little Mexico.'" In 1950, only 9 percent of ethnic Mexicans in Houston had been born in Mexico. Even when the number of Mexican Americans in the city grew to seventy-five thousand in 1960, only 13 percent were foreign born. At the time, 938,219 people lived in Houston, which ranked as the seventh-largest city in the nation that year. Latinos made up just under 8 percent of the city's total population.[63]

Mexican American youth who came of age in the 1960s had more spatial and cultural contact with African Americans, especially after they began attending the same schools for the first time. The *Brown* decision and the slow march toward school desegregation coincided with the international popularity of rock 'n' roll and rhythm and blues, music that grew from the same southern soil. The popularity of the music contributed to white conservative backlash over integration. Members of the White Citizens Council, a coalition of influential white southerners who used economic pressure to oppose desegregation, campaigned to eliminate rock 'n' roll and rhythm and blues from jukeboxes in the South. The New Orleans Citizens Council distributed handbills that accused musicians of "undermining the morals of our white youth in America." Sounding much like Klansman Billie Mayfield in the 1920s, a chairman of the Citizens Council announced: "We've set up a twenty-man committee to do away with this vulgar, animalistic, nigger rock 'n' roll bop."[64] Segregationists' fears over interracial contact involved space and sound. If the integration of schools brought black and white youth into the same spaces, then their love of the same music connected them sonically. In the minds of the Citizens Council, both threatened white supremacy.

In Houston, desegregation brought Mexican Americans and black Texans into shared public schools for the first time in Houston history. For Houstonians of Mexican descent, school integration was not a major issue during the civil rights years. Instead, Mexican Americans emphasized the importance of "equitable and quality instruction in the schools."[65] They learned, though, that the issue did affect their communities as the racial composition of Houston schools began to transform during the '60s. In 1970, a U.S. federal district judge in Houston ordered that students would attend schools closest to their homes. Called the "equidistant zoning plan," the order was designed to speed the integration process. Ethnic Mexican parents soon realized, however, that the plan would first integrate Mexican American –majority elementary and middle schools and black institutions. Since the judge identified Mexican Americans as white, his plan sent them into black schools, while sending African Americans into the ten elementary and middle schools where Mexican Americans formed the majority. Activists mobilized to counter the decision. At this point, though, the Mexican American protesters contended that they were not white, but rather, *brown*. As a brown racial minority, they argued, they should not be included in plans to integrate white with black.[66] Nevertheless, growing numbers of Mexican American and African American students enrolled at the same schools. Some Mexican Americans attended schools that blackened after integration. An alumnus of San Jacinto High, Rey Romero, estimated that his school was around 70 percent black in the early 1970s.[67]

Their protest shows that Mexican Americans resisted sending their children to school with black students, but their stance also reflects a different racial identification among the ethnic Mexican population. Activists who came of age in the mid-1960s embraced a new racial subjectivity that conceptualized ethnic Mexican people as brown instead of white. The younger generation of activists called themselves "Chicanos," and they distanced themselves from LULAC and organizations that had stressed whiteness as a civil rights strategy. The Chicano movement grew out of youthful dissatisfaction with the assimilationist desires of Mexican American activists of the 1940s and 1950s. As historian Guadalupe San Miguel writes, "[T]he majority believed that the political methods of moderation and the cultural identity of the Mexican American Generation were ineffective and no longer viable."[68] The Chicano movement signified not only a new political stance, but also a new idea about racial group membership. While LULAC historically made claims to whiteness, Chicano activists showed pride in being descendants of indigenous groups that had thrived in the Americas before the arrival of Europeans. The younger generation did not share older activists' investment in whiteness or their desire for "good will" with Anglos. Musician Steve Salas recalled an emboldened political stance: "Because now it wasn't like we had to hide and try and slide through or, you know, or fall through the cracks. We don't have to say 'excuse me, I'm sorry' anymore."[69] Chicano activists stressed cultural links to indigenous history through art, music, and dance. Groups like the Mexican American Youth Organization (MAYO), United Mexican American Students, and Movimiento Estudiantil Chicana/o de Aztlán (MEChA) embraced a Chicana/o racial subjectivity and asserted an indigenous heritage tied to Aztlán, the place of origin for the Aztec people.[70] Chicanos' pride in brown skin and an indigenous past was more important than white status.

The Chicano movement developed at the moment when black activists provided a powerful political and cultural language for rejecting white supremacy. Five years after the sit-in movement, black youth increasingly felt discouraged with direct-action demonstrations. One reason was the steady perpetuation of white supremacist violence. When white gunmen shot activist James Meredith, the first black student to enroll at the University of Mississippi, during a "March against Fear" in 1965, Student Nonviolent Coordinating Committee (SNCC) chairman Stokely Carmichael declared an end to integrationist strategies. That year, Carmichael first used the phrase "Black Power." According to Carmichael, Black Power would "destroy everything that Western civilization had taught" African Americans by rejecting white norms and standards. His new agenda focused on black empowerment through self-sufficiency and race pride instead of desegregation. A visit from Carmichael in 1967 helped fuel student discontent at TSU in Houston. Students protested in April of that year when school administrators refused to allow Carmichael to speak on campus. Around one hundred students boycotted classes for several days. (Carmichael eventually spoke at the University of Houston, a white-majority institution located just blocks away from TSU.)[71]

Unlike the World War II generation of Mexican American activists, young Chicanos related to the spirit of rebellion crafted by black activists in the 1960s. For young ethnic Mexicans, the Mexican American civil rights movement, with its emphasis on whiteness, may not have held the same liberatory possibilities as the black struggle. "Black victories not only made the Mexican American movement appear stagnant," writes historian Brian Behnken, "they also destroyed Jim Crow and eliminated some of the potential benefits granted by whiteness."[72] Tony Valdez, a news reporter who was part of the East Los Angeles Chicano music scene in the '60s, drew inspiration from the black freedom struggle: "You've got Martin Luther King marching in the South. You've got black pride developing. We're looking at that stuff, and we're seeing that just as our African American brothers can think about roots and going back to Africa, maybe it's important for us to discover the roots that we never paid any attention to because our parents wanted us to become Americans. So you suddenly see the onset of Mexican and Brown Pride."[73] The political and cultural transformations wrought by the radical movements of the mid-1960s appealed to young Chicanos more than the Mexican American Generation's focus on whiteness.

During the era of Black Power and Brown Pride, activists became more aware of the similarities between their struggles. In some cases, they joined forces. Ovide Duncantell, a member of People's Party II, a precursor to the Black Panther Party in Houston, noticed commonalities between the black and Chicano movements: "We saw each other's poverty and we realized that we were all in the same boat." For Duncantell, the solidarity occurred because Chicanos did not embrace whiteness like previous generations of Mexican American activists had. Chicanos, according to Duncantell, realized there "wasn't any virtue in being white if you couldn't be white."[74] Some activists from both groups considered one another when mounting their opposition to white supremacy. Houstonian Carlos Calbillo described his activism as a struggle mounted by African Americans and ethnic Mexicans: "The Chicano movement of the 1960s and 1970s was essentially a grassroots community insurrection and rebellion against a stifling racism and oppression that strangled the Latino and Black communities of Houston and Texas in that time, and a determination to fight and defeat it." Calbillo's work in the Chicano movement began with an act of solidarity with African Americans. As a student in April 1968, he participated in a march from Third Ward to downtown to protest the assassination of Martin Luther King, Jr., in Memphis earlier that month: "[A]lthough there were the obligatory African American and white ministers, priests, a rabbi or two in attendance, I became curious to see if I could find any Latinos in the large crowd. To my surprise, I found only one, other than me." That person was Leonel J. Castillo, a Mexican American man who eventually became city comptroller. His position made Castillo the first Latino elected to citywide office in Houston. (Castillo later became the first Latino to serve as commissioner of the Immigration and Naturalization Service during President Carter's administration.) Through Castillo, Calbillo connected with other Mexican American activists. Soon, he was involved with voter-registration efforts and a member of MAYO, the Mexican American Youth Organization. Members of MAYO formed an alliance with the Black Panther Party, as well as Students for a Democratic Society. "This society we perceived as intolerably oppressive, and it definitely seemed to us 'enlightened' youth to be designed to keep brown and black people down. So we took up 'arms' against it, much to the horror of our parents and other 'gente decente,' such as LULAC and their ilk."[75] Black Power and the Chicano Movement represented a new direction for racial activism and coalitions that involved black and brown youth.

The music of the era brought black and Chicano youth into a cultural dialogue. As sit-ins, boycotts, and marches transformed Jim Crow America, black artists brought the transformative spirit of the movement into a new brand of rhythm and blues music, a style they called *soul*. Whereas 1950s R&B was steeped in the blues, soul musicians turned toward gospel. Singers adapted the "melisma, call and response, and screaming of vocals" of black church choirs, bringing the ecstasy and transformative power of gospel into the rhythm and blues of the 1960s.[76] Soul music captured the spirit of the civil rights era. It pulsated with the energy that fueled the activists who faced down police dogs, tear gas, and angry white mobs. Soul music provided the soundtrack for the generation that stared fearlessly into the dark heart of Jim Crow and transformed society. "Once it emerged from the underground," writes Peter Guralnick in *Sweet Soul Music,* "it accompanied the Civil Rights Movement almost step by step, its success directly reflecting the giant strides that integration was making, its popularity almost a mirror image of the social changes that were taking place."[77]

As a cultural embodiment of the freedom struggle, soul by its very notion celebrated racial blackness. Gospel-flavored anthems conveyed a sense of racial pride. Soul was, as historian William Van Deburg asserts, "a type of primal spiritual energy and passionate joy available only to members of a subculture." The idea also inspired new modes of self-expression and physical movement. "Executed with great flair and rhythmic perfection, these rituals of nonverbal communication served as kinesic counterpoints to the rigid, purportedly robotlike mannerisms of 'uptight' whites. Whatever their specific attire or method of greeting, sixties soulsters assumed a compelling, no-holds-barred swaggering pose as they bop-bop-de-bopped down the road to empowerment."[78] Soul lauded black culture and promoted a rejection of white norms.

That generational shift toward soul applied to Creoles of color along the Gulf Coast who felt inspired by the political transformation and cultural ascendance of blackness in the late 1960s. Because of the long civil rights movement, the legal status of blackness changed. After Lyndon B. Johnson signed the 1964 Civil Rights Act, followed by the Voting Rights Act a year later, African Americans legally claimed the same rights as white people. Culturally, the 1960s brought a heightened focus on the positive aspects of black life. Discrimination certainly persisted after 1965, but the label "black" signified more than stigmatized racial status. Celebrations of soul food, African heritage, naturally kinky hair, and assertions that "black is beautiful" became part of the cultural and political lexicon. Proximity to whiteness may not indicate improved status to the generation that came of age at the height of Black Power and Brown Pride. As Chicano youth rebelled against the Mexican American generation's assertions of whiteness, Creoles of color also explored their relationship to racial blackness. According to historian

Arnold Hirsch, "The enhanced racial consciousness of the civil rights and post–civil rights eras, moreover, robbed [Creoles of color] of their main claim to privilege and transformed their mixed origins into a liability."[79] Creoles continued to celebrate their cultural heritage, with zydeco festivals and crawfish boils, but they increasingly celebrated their black ancestry during the period of Black Power.

Two Frenchtown jazz musicians—pianist Joe Sample and Texas tenor Illinois Jacquet—illustrate the influence of soul and Black Power on Creole racial subjectivity. Sample incorporated the style of black youth into his personal appearance. He released his first solo album, *Fancy Dance,* in 1969, at the height of Black Power. A promotional picture from the era shows Sample sporting an Afro and wearing a colorfully hued, loose-fitting shirt that resembles the popular dashikis that some African Americans had incorporated into their wardrobes. In the same year that Joe Sample donned Afrocentric hair and clothing, Texas tenor Illinois Jacquet explicitly applied the notion of soul to his music by releasing an album called *The Soul Explosion.* The title song, as well as most of the tracks, incorporate elements of other popular soul records of the era, especially the promiscuous use of the Hammond organ.[80] Through sound and sartorial choices, Sample and Jacquet linked themselves to soul, and therefore racial blackness.

By embracing soul and Black Power, artists like Jacquet and Sample distinguished themselves from earlier generations of Creoles of color who saw themselves as a separate race. For them, black and Creole of color were not separate racial categories. The label "black Creole" became an appropriate marker of Creole subjectivity for those who identified with soul and Black Power. That term acknowledged their roots in southern Louisiana, while marking them as part of the black race. By the end of the 1960s, "Creole" had become a cultural designation for many Creoles of color, signifying a rich heritage that existed within a broader spectrum of racial blackness.

The Mexican Americans and Creoles of color who embraced soul offer a similar story in terms of how 1960s freedom struggles affected racial subjectivity. In Houston, both groups historically distinguished themselves from black Texans. They had associated blackness with segregation, disenfranchisement, and racial violence during the era of Jim Crow. By the time Carmichael uttered the words "Black Power," though, youth associated black activism with opposition to white supremacy. Creoles and a growing number of Latinos, then, embraced the concept of soul to further distance themselves from whiteness. As scholar John Márquez asserts, "[T]he region has also witnessed Latinos resisting white hegemony by appropriating Blackness, a development that can be traced to the unique influence of Black political culture and the demographic realities that have shaped Houston."[81] Their engagement with soul mirrored the political turn from whiteness to stressing a Chicano racial subjectivity during the 1960s political movement. Soul became part of an interethnic discourse, a language of protest that signified the development of racialized subjectivities that opposed assimilation into whiteness. As the soundtrack to social and political change from coast to coast, soul music stressed themes of liberation alongside expressions of ethnic and racial pride. In the context of the late 1960s, during the apex of several different freedom struggles, soul was a racialized statement linked to culture and politics.

The sounds of soul spread across Houston from a studio on the corner of Almeda and Wichita streets in Third Ward, where a local deejay would later help connect African American and Mexican American musicians. KCOH deejay Skipper Lee Frazier was easily one of the most recognizable and popular black men in the city in the 1960s. Born in Jasper County in East Texas, Frazier moved to Houston after serving in the Korean War. While still employed as a mail carrier in the mid-1950s, he decided to enroll in Houston's first school for black broadcasters. After graduation, he won a spot as host of two shows on local station KYOK. Known as "Hip Skipper," Frazier hosted a gospel program on Sunday mornings and a jazz program after dark. In 1959, he left KYOK to join the staff of the black-owned station KCOH. Now called "Skipper Lee" while on-air, he began his show by playing the spiritual "Steal Away." As the religious song played, Frazier would intone, "So, here I am, Houston. Here I am, Houston. I've brought a mountain of soul to Houston."[82] Over the next few years, Frazier played a crucial role in the development of the local soul scene, one that increasingly included African Americans and Mexican Americans.

As a deejay, Frazier had access to some of the most innovative local bands in Houston, and in the mid-1960s he launched his own record label, Ovide Records. Like Don Robey, Frazier insisted on handling every aspect of his acts' careers. He managed the bands he discovered, he booked gigs for them, and he produced their records. One of his first discoveries was a band made up of students from Texas Southern called the T.S.U. Toronadoes. Named for their school and their favorite car, the Toronadoes served as the house band for Ovide. Another act, Archie Bell and the Drells, was composed of local singers and dancers. The lead singer, Bell, grew up in Fifth Ward and attended Wheatley High School. Frazier promoted the bands heavily, and they played at popular nightclubs in the city.

Ovide, along with Huey Meaux's Teardrop Records, helped establish a stronger Mexican American soul music scene in Houston. After his success with Sunny and the Sunliners, Meaux searched for Mexican American acts locally in Houston. He signed two bands—Rocky Gil and the Bishops, and the Starlights—in 1965. As part of Meaux's Tear Drop records, both acts released music that was Houston's answer to San Antonio's West Side Sound. The band typically had a full rhythm section and guitar player, as well as a horn section consisting of two saxophones, a trumpet, and a trombone. Like Milton Larkin in the 1930s, Gil led a band full of teenagers, including high schoolers Albert Calderon, Bobby Severson, and Rey Romero. Along with Little Joe and the Embers and the Starlights, Rocky Gil and the Bishops made Mexican Americans a vital part of Houston's rhythm and blues scene. As a teenage member of the Bishops, Albert Calderon had a love of soul music that originated with the politicized songs by James Brown. After hearing a soul song by Brown on the radio, "all I wanted to do was play it," Calderon asserted. Brown became known as the "Godfather of Soul" by incorporating the uplifting messages of church-based gospel music, the hard truths of blues, and the danceability of rhythm and blues. Rocky Gil and the Bishops incorporated Brown's work into their repertoire. Songs like "I Don't Want Nobody to Give Me Nothing (Open Up the Door, I'll Get It Myself)" mirrored the politics of Black Power. "Don't give me integration; give me true communication," Brown demanded.[83] Written and recorded in 1968, the track "Say It Loud (I'm Black and I'm Proud)" reached anthem status. Brown, as well as a host of performers like Aretha Franklin and Curtis Mayfield, rose to fame during an era of racial transformation, and Mexican American bands who played for black audiences learned their songs.

Skipper Lee Frazier forged ties between brown and black youth by hiring Mexican American acts to contribute to tracks by Ovide artists. Sunny and the Sunliners, who worked as session musicians for Meaux at Tear Drop, also worked as the backing band for Archie Bell and the Drells. Since the Drells did not play their own instruments, Frazier often had the Toronadoes or the Sunliners accompany them. The Sunliners and the Drells took their act on the road, performing together throughout Texas and Louisiana. Frazier also recorded the two bands together in San Antonio. Sunny and the Sunliners backed Archie Bell and the Drells on their first records, like the political "Soldiers Prayer 1967."[84] Between the 1920s and World War II, ethnic Mexicans and black residents of Houston were historically divided by space, language, and politics. But soul music presented new opportunities for collaborations between these groups in the 1960s.

Two types of Houston soul acts included Mexican Americans: some were interracial, while others were made up entirely of ethnic Mexicans. Both iterations tended to perform in both black and Mexican American venues. In some acts, black and ethnic Mexican musicians played together. The Toronadoes, for example, were a black-majority band that incorporated Mexican American members like Artie Villaseñor. The band performed at church bazaars at Our Lady of Guadalupe in Segundo Barrio, a place that had hosted Lydia Mendoza singing Spanish-language ballads thirty years earlier, as well as black clubs on the Chitlin' Circuit. Meanwhile, the members of the Sunliners, the Starlights, and Rocky Gil and the Bishops were all Mexican American youth who performed at black dance clubs, as well as Mexican American venues like the Pan-America Ballroom on the north side of the city. By the 1960s, a new generation of musicians moved more easily between black and ethnic Mexican spaces.

These bands did not, however, play the same tunes for black and ethnic Mexican audiences. Whereas they exclusively performed soul music for African Americans, bands like Rocky Gil and the Bishops played a variety of styles for Mexican American youth, who enjoyed English- and Spanish-language music. Tejano youth tended to listen to diverse styles, including orquesta, rock 'n' roll, and rhythm and blues, so these acts developed a vast repertoire. A young man named Bobby Severson, who played with a host of bands, including Rocky Gil and the Bishops, came of age in Magnolia Park and illustrates how Mexican Americans often developed wide-ranging musical tastes. Severson's family exposed him to religious music and orquesta during his childhood. His grandfather had played bass in an orquesta band, but after an audience member killed him onstage, the family shifted away from professional music. But Severson returned to the profession as a teenager by playing trumpet at his church, and then joining several bands as a young man. He and his bandmates shared an affinity not only for James Brown, but also for British Invasion bands like the Beatles. When Mexican American musicians like Severson took the stage, they knew how to play a wide range of music to satisfy an audience that was familiar with multiple styles in two different languages. Known as the premier nightspot for Latinos, the Pan-America Ballroom acknowledged this musical diversity by inviting musicians from different backgrounds who played in diverse styles. Albert Calderon remembered Fats Domino performing at the ballroom at the height of his popularity, and Calderon played the popular venue as a member of the Bishops. "If you played the Pan-America Ballroom, you were big-time," he asserted.[85] Bands that appeared before Mexican American audiences at places like the Pan American had to please crowds whose cultural background included music performed by Texas Mexicans, African Americans, and Anglos. Shaped by family, radio, and lived experience in Houston, their tastes reflect Mexican American youth's polyculturality. They increasingly identified with indigenous Mexican roots, but their subjectivities were also influenced by their experiences in Houston and increasing contact with black Texans.

Severson's early career as a Houston musician points to another type of Mexican American soul act; he joined a band made up of Mexican American youth who played exclusively for black audiences. They called themselves the Spades. Since they catered to black listeners, they eliminated music with Spanish lyrics. Skipper Lee Frazier promoted the Spades to black audiences, and they performed regularly in African American clubs.[86] Their willingness to play in black-majority venues reflected a change in black and ethnic Mexican relations in the Bayou City. The spatial divide that historically separated local African Americans and Mexican Americans decreased. The soul scene launched a new era of rhythm and blues in Houston, one marked by the participation of people who identified as black and brown.

The names these bands gave themselves may have increased their earning potential in black communities. Band names like Sunny and the Sunliners, the Embers, and the Starlights did not indicate an ethnic heritage. The name chosen by the Spades possibly reminded listeners of a term associated with blackness. And although Gil is a Spanish surname, the Anglicized pronunciation ("Gill") may not have indicated Latin American heritage to English speakers unfamiliar with Spanish. When Skipper Lee played Mexican American bands on KCOH, most listeners likely never suspected that the artists they heard were not black. Any black Houstonians who felt dubious about listening to Mexican American bands would not learn the ethnic makeup up of the band until the musicians appeared onstage at a concert.

If black fans listened carefully, though, they would have heard the unmistakable sounds of Texas Mexican music in the soul songs played on Houston radio. Mexican Americans left a sonic imprint on the local soul scene. Tejano music inspired a crucial element of the Drells' biggest hit, "Tighten Up," from 1968. The song originated as an instrumental dance track by the T.S.U.

Toronadoes. It became their theme song, the one guaranteed to pack the dance floor at gigs. Seeing the popularity of the song, Frazier brought singer Archie Bell into the studio to ad-lib a few lyrics for the track. According to Frazier, the idea behind the words was "basically 'tighten up' on everything and make it mellow."

For the key ingredient of "Tighten Up," Frazier drew inspiration from Mexican American horn-playing techniques. The arrangement spotlights a horn section that plays in the style of orquesta bands. "We made it mellow with the horns," Frazier explained, "which sounded more like the bright, crisp horns you hear in many Mexican bands." He released the song on Ovide, though he marketed the track as an Archie Bell and the Drells release rather than one by the Toronadoes. Huey Meaux heard "Tighten Up" and approached Frazier about taking the Drells to Atlantic Records. After gaining the approval of executive producers like Jerry Wexler, the track went on to become one of the most successful soul releases of the year, though most listeners probably did not suspect that the song incorporated elements of urban Texas Mexican music, or that it was composed by the Toronadoes.[87] "Tighten Up," the most popular soul song to emerge from Houston in the 1960s, then, bore the sonic imprint of a developing cultural relationship between Mexican Americans and African Americans.

Black Houstonians did not listen to orquesta in the 1940s, but their children danced to soul music played by—and influenced by—Mexican Americans twenty years later. Skipper Lee Frazier continued his support of Tejano soul by playing songs by Rocky Gil and the Bishops on his radio show on KCOH. Since the station catered to black listeners, they gained black fans. The audience received them enthusiastically. One of their songs reached the top ten on the station's weekly countdown.[88] With the support of Meaux at Tear Drop and Frazier at Ovide, young musicians like the Toronadoes, the Drells, the Sunliners, and the Bishops helped strengthen the musical connection between Tejanos and black Texans.

Musicians in different regions of the country developed particular ways of playing soul, and Houston's emphasized the racial and cultural terrain shaped by Mexican Americans and African Americans.[89] Records like Rocky Gil and the Bishops' 1968 song "Soul Party" incorporated sonic elements of black music traditions to create a message of unity. "Soul Party" contains a breakdown that spotlights the different instruments used in the song, much like the soul records "Memphis Soul Stew" and Archie Bell and the Drells' "Tighten Up." The Houston musicians highlight the rhythm instruments first, and the bassist has the first solo, which may be an effort to ground the song in African American musical sensibilities that emphasize rhythm. Gil then boasts, "We've got a rhythm that's out of sight, so come on horns, we're gonna groove all night." Similarly, "Boot Leg," an instrumental track by the Starlights, was mainly built around call and response between the horn section and a Hammond organ.[90] The orquesta-style horns and rhythm section offer a musical interplay between black and brown.

Tejano soul music especially bridged communities through dance. Latino and African American musicians fashioned dancers into "momentary communities," which strengthened the link between black and ethnic Mexican music lovers. Historian Juan Flores notes, "Popular Latin bands thus found themselves creating a musical common ground by introducing the trappings of Black American culture into their performances and thus getting the Black audiences involved and onto the dance floor."[91] Songs like Little Joe and the Embers' "Soul Finger" and Little Joe and the Latinaires' "Soul Pride" were dance tunes that would have appealed to African Americans and Latinos. Rocky Gil and the Bishops make the connection between dance and community explicit by literally inviting everyone to join their "Soul Party": "We're going to have a party," the singer announces. "Everybody's invited to the action. . . . Come on over and dance the night away." The lyrics stress that this party has no racial or ethnic boundaries. "Everybody get together and come together," Gil sings. As news coverage of the war in Vietnam and the assassination of Robert Kennedy and Martin Luther King, Jr., showed a nation torn apart by violence at home and abroad, Gil's band issued a message of inclusion.[92] Just twenty years earlier, Mexican Americans and African Americans in Houston had not included one another in their burgeoning civil rights movements; however, by the late 1960s, black and Latino musical practices offered the first signs of connection between two groups that would increasingly share social space, and eventually make up the majority of Houston's population. Differences between the groups did not evaporate overnight, but musical practices facilitated some of the first social connections between black and brown Houstonians.

Postwar Houston emerged as the geographic center of a polycultural music scene in the western South, one that highlights ongoing racial and spatial transformations. Creole and Mexican American engagement with soul points to the new racial subjectivities that emerged as a result of radical movements of the 1960s. While some Creoles reconsidered their relationship to racial blackness, young Mexican Americans rethought their relationship to racial whiteness. The civil rights era was not only a watershed moment for the defeat of legal forms of segregation, then; people also emerged from the 1960s with new ways of defining themselves racially. At the local level, zydeco, as well as soul music played by Mexican Americans, grew from interethnic, interracial contact with black people. The proliferation of zydeco signaled that Frenchtown was not a separate entity in Fifth Ward. And, when Mexican Americans played instruments in a band backed by African Americans, or performed onstage for an African American audience, they eliminated a spatial divide that had long separated the groups. Rhythm and blues and soul music played a crucial role in the development of significant social processes that demonstrate how notions of race continually shifted in the twentieth-century United States.

Conclusion

RACE IN THE MODERN CITY

THE CONTROVERSY OVER THE SINGER'S skin color first began in 2008. That year, the September issue of most fashion magazines in the United States contained advertisements for the cosmetics company L'Oréal Paris that featured the entertainer Beyoncé. The print ad and accompanying television commercials were part of L'Oréal's campaign for its hair-coloring product Féria. At the time, Beyoncé already had one of the most recognizable faces in show business. The problem for fans and critics alike was that the face that appeared in the L'Oréal ads was significantly lighter than the caramel-colored shade they first saw a decade earlier, when she was a teenage member of Destiny's Child. With her naturally dark-brown hair transformed into long, honey-colored tresses, Beyoncé seemed to be a very blond, considerably lighter version of herself.

Backlash commenced immediately. Newspapers and blogs ran before-and-after photographs that showed Beyoncé's alleged physical transformation. In a report by the *New York Post,* Eric Deggans, chairman of the media-monitoring committee of the National Association of Black Journalists, remarked that her "skin is lighter than the way I'm used to seeing her." Furthermore, Deggans warned, "[a]dvertisers and magazines need to be careful about this, even if it's just a production process."[1] Even the foreign press commented on the issue. "It appears that L'Oréal has caused not just her hair but her skin to change colour as well," wrote Dan Glaister, a reporter for the *Guardian.* The public outcry prompted L'Oréal to issue a statement that denied any skin bleaching. "It is categorically untrue," said a spokesperson, "that L'Oréal Paris altered Ms. Knowles' features or skin tone in the campaign for Féria hair color."[2]

Beyoncé continued to model for L'Oréal over the next few years, and later ads spotlighted her racial heritage. In 2012, she became one of several famous women to endorse L'Oréal's "Find Your True Match" cosmetics, a line of products the company claims will blend with any woman's complexion, regardless of her ethnic heritage. A range of celebrities from diverse backgrounds posed as spokespersons for the campaign, including Jennifer Lopez and Zoe Saldana. The print and television advertisements featuring Beyoncé focused on the star's racial hybridity. "There's a story behind my skin," she says in a voice-over. "It's a mosaic of all the faces before it." Meanwhile, the words "African American, Native American and French" fade onto the screen.

The suggestion that Beyoncé's face is a "mosaic" of African, American Indian, and European refers to her African American father, Matthew Knowles, as well as the Creole background she inherited from her mother, Celestine (Tina) Knowles. The name Beyoncé is derived from her mother's maiden name, Beyincé, a French surname. Her maternal grandparents, Lumis Beyincé and his wife, born Agnes Dereon, both hailed from francophone southern Louisiana. In 1920, nine-year-old Lumis lived in Iberia Parish, while eleven-year-old Agnes lived with her family in Vermilion. Agnes's parents, Eugene and Adelia Dereon, were descendants of *gens de couleur libre* from francophone southern Louisiana.[3]

Beyoncé often confounds modern notions of racial blackness by stressing her Creole heritage while simultaneously linking herself to African American people and culture.[4] As an actress, Beyoncé has portrayed iconic African American characters. In *Austin Powers: Goldmember,* she donned an Afro wig for the role of Foxxy Cleopatra, a character who spoofed 1970s blaxploitation heroines played by actresses like Pam Grier. In 2006, she appeared in *Dreamgirls* as Deena Jones, a role written specifically for an African American actress. Two years later, she portrayed soul singer Etta James in the film *Cadillac Records.* Her marriage to Shawn Carter, the Brooklyn-born rapper known as Jay Z, further links her to black culture and black communities. But as one of the most popular singers of the early 2000s, Beyoncé also stresses her diverse heritage to an international audience. One particular song from that era describes her racial hybridity. In "Creole," Beyoncé suggests that, like gumbo, she represents a fusion.

Beyoncé's assertions that she is Creole have confused and angered some black consumers. These modern controversies surrounding Beyoncé relate to much older conversations surrounding Creoles. Some modern critics allege that Beyoncé's claims to Native American and French ancestry in the L'Oréal ad demonstrate a desire to deny her blackness. "She does everything in her image to make it look like she is 'exotic,' instead of embracing she is a black girl from HOUSTON, TEXAS!" asserts a writer for the website Destiny's Rehab. "Her father and mother are black. Tina comes from a family with creole decent [*sic*], which is still BLACK."[5]

For some Creoles of color living in the post–civil rights United States, "black" and "Creole" are not mutually exclusive categories. They argue that Beyoncé's Creole subjectivity represents one part of a broader category of racial blackness. A website dedicated to Creole culture argues that Beyoncé "is a bonafied CREOLE." The anonymous writer asserts, "Because her Father is African American does not dissolve the Creole Ancestry she possesses. Many Creoles have African American Mix.... You must remember that Prior to 1920 Creoles were defined as a separate ethnic group." The writer suggests that Creoles married into African American families for purposes of self-preservation. "Now with the infusion of the One drop rule which literally strip[p]ed Creoles of their separate identity, many of Us Creoles became closer to the African Community to insure Our survival. Although many of Our Creole People have intermixed with the African American Population We have never forgotten Our roots nor Heritage."[6] For the writer, blackness is an integral part of Creole subjectivity; mixing with African Americans did not eliminate Creoles, but rather, allowed them to survive and thrive.

Beyoncé and a host of modern Houstonians exemplify the polycultural nature of race in modern U.S. cities. Notions of race constantly shift. As this book has argued, our understandings of race have been shaped not only by legal and political maneuvers, but also by social and cultural transformations, and a host of local negotiations that can produce multiple layers of identification. For Beyoncé, that includes a Creole of color subjectivity from her maternal family who migrated to Houston, and the experience of coming of age in black Third Ward in the 1980s. Yet Beyoncé's notions of being a Creole likely differ from the subjectivities shared by her Creole of color ancestors living during the era of Jim Crow. Racial subjectivities that emerged from the Black Power era have shaped the way some modern Americans identify as black and Creole simultaneously. Beyoncé's public persona illustrates how the meanings associated with "Creole" have been affected by migration, urban community building, and sociocultural changes in the twentieth century.

Beyoncé's musical choices also reflect a childhood spent in a city with a growing Latino population. Like Selena, the late Tejano-music singer, Beyoncé heard a range of sounds in southeastern Texas. Born in Lake Jackson in Brazoria County, Selena first loved disco singers like Donna Summer before her father convinced her to sing in Spanish. Even as she climbed to the top of the Tejano charts, Selena continued to dance between Spanish and English, Tejano and rhythm and blues. She performed a disco medley in front of the largest crowd ever assembled at the Houston Livestock Show and Rodeo in 1995. When she died later that year, Selena had recently completed work on an English-language album that included pop and R&B songs. The young Tejana's legacy left a mark on Beyoncé. "I've always loved the way Spanish sounds with music and with melodies. It's just so beautiful and so passionate," Beyoncé told *Latina* magazine in 2006. "I also grew up in Texas and I remember listening to Selena all the time," she said. In a nod toward her Mexican American fans, and the profitability of Spanish-language music, Beyoncé released a Spanish-language EP called *Irreemplazable* that contained a *norteño* remix of her hit song "Irreplaceable." With its prominent accordion, the song sounded like the type of music Selena helped popularize in the 1990s.[7]

Beyoncé's desire for "crossover appeal" with Latinos shows an acknowledgment of the demographics of her hometown and native state. The Houston that she knew as a child in the 1980s and 1990s was a city transformed by migration from Latin America, and Spanish altered the soundscape. By the turn of the twenty-first century, Houston had "the largest total Black and Brown population in a southern urban area." In 2000, 742,207 Latinos and 461,584 African Americans made up 63 percent of Houston.[8] The ever-growing Latino population has contributed to her popularity and the music Beyoncé creates, and she has benefited tremendously from Latino consumption of her music.

The growth of the Latino population in Houston first began to outpace that of the black population in the 1970s, when economic depression in Mexico occurred at the same time as an oil boom that changed Houston's fortunes. The price of oil rose from an average of $12.64 to $21.59 a barrel in 1979, and approached forty dollars by the early 1980s.[9] As a result, the economy of the Houston metropolitan area was inextricably linked to "black gold." Eighty-two percent of Houston's economy relied on the energy business by 1982.[10] Oil prices eventually plummeted to around twenty dollars a barrel, but during those previous years of prosperity, Houston's population surged. The overall number of people living in the city grew by 46 percent as people flocked to the Bayou City in pursuit of jobs. A new surge in Mexican immigration began in the mid-1970s during the oil boom as Mexico experienced a period of economic upheaval. In 1980, the U.S. Census Bureau counted 116,084 Latinos, mostly from Mexico, in Houston. Forty percent of those immigrants had moved to Houston in the previous five years. For the first time in Houston history, the number of Latinos equaled the number of African Americans.[11]

Spanish-speaking newcomers to modern Houston tended to settle in African American neighborhoods. Since the 1970s, then, black people have been among the first people that Latin American immigrants encountered when they entered Houston. The new pattern of settlement is a departure from the Jim Crow era. Whereas the participants in the first major wave of ethnic Mexican migration into Houston attended Anglo-majority schools and had to assert racial whiteness in order to maintain that place in society, the removal of segregation laws in the 1960s, and the spread of immigrants into black neighborhoods, have meant consistent, daily contact with African Americans. The movement of Latinos into African American communities "created substantial overlap of social spaces" that increased the amount of contact between the groups. African Americans and Latin American immigrants attended the same schools, visited the same parks, and shopped at the same malls.[12]

The proximity of black and ethnic Mexican Houstonians has produced tension and cooperation. A schoolyard fight between African American and Mexican American freshmen resulted in one student slitting another's throat with a box cutter in 2010. But as scholar John Márquez points out, although instances of violence between black and brown Houstonians receive the most news coverage, these reports obscure coalitions and cooperation between the groups.[13] In some instances, black Houstonians have responded positively to the changing demographics. John Branch, who spent most of his fifty years in Independence Heights, decided to take Spanish courses as more and more of his neighborhood filled with Latinos. Independence Heights, the site of the first black town in Texas, was home to just as many Latinos as African Americans in the early twenty-first century. "We have the history of being the first black city," Branch said, "but we're not going to discriminate."[14]

The wards could more accurately be described as "black-brown" at the turn of the twenty-first century. In Third Ward and Fifth Ward, schools that once facilitated the growth of black culture housed growing numbers of students with Spanish surnames. Of the 1,067 students who attended Wheatley High in Fifth Ward in 2010, around 62 percent were African American, while just over 38 percent were Latino.[15] At Texas Southern University in

Third Ward the enrollment of students who do not identify as black grew by 64 percent in twenty years. Noticing Houston's changing demographics, President John Rudley began "aggressively recruiting Latino high school students."[16] The historically black university's law school was 48 percent African American, 20 percent Latino, and 20 percent white in 2012.[17]

The decline of African American populations in old Houston neighborhoods, together with the subsequent growth of Latino residents, is partly due to black suburbanization. At the turn of the twenty-first century, black Houstonians increasingly left the city and relocated to suburbs that emerged in the old Sugar Bowl. African Americans from those rural plantation counties had historically moved to the Bayou City, but the next century saw a reverse trend. Urban sprawl in the metropolitan area transformed Sugar Bowl towns into Houston suburbs, with huge schools and malls that often catered to black transplants from the city. Thousands of black Houstonians moved to the suburbs of Missouri City, in Fort Bend County, and Pearland, in Brazoria County, in the early 2000s. Only 2,006 black people lived in Pearland in 2000, for example, but 14,962 resided there in 2010.[18]

As the Latino population climbed, Houston's hip-hop scene morphed into a fusion of Latino and African American by the turn of the twenty-first century. Rap music in Houston first emerged from black communities in the 1980s.[19] The more recent emergence of Latino rappers led to a sonic and visual synthesis of cultures. Chingo Bling, a child of immigrants, exemplifies how Latinos merge black and brown. The rapper incorporates diverse aspects of Houston's racial and cultural composition into his music. His songs regularly reference the immigration experience; he titled one album "They Can't Deport Us All." On the cover of the CD, an Anglo sheriff chases the rapper as he jumps over a barbed-wire fence. He asserts in one song, "We're in your country now and there's a lot of us. So watch out, 'cause now we're rappin', *hijo su.*"[20]

Like Simeon Williams's trickster figure from 1920s-era columns in the *Informer,* "Chingo Bling" is a character created by Pedro Herrera III, who uses cultural expression to offer satirical, political observations about life in Texas. But unlike Cimbee, Chingo Bling portrays Latino/African American fusion. Whereas Cimbee spoke in black East Texas dialect, Herrera's raps incorporate hip-hop and Spanish slang. Even as he explicitly makes use of Mexican culture (like tongue-in-cheek references to his rooster, Cleto, or the tamales he sells from the trunk of his car), Chingo Bling merges those cultural signifiers with references to styles and products popularized by black Houstonians. On the aforementioned CD cover, he carries a glass full of "purple drank," a codeine-infused concoction primarily consisting of prescription cough medicine. Countless African American rappers from the Bayou City made the drug, which is also called "sizzurp" or "lean," part of Houston's hip-hop culture. Furthermore, Chingo Bling releases "chopped and screwed" versions of his music, a style created by a black Houstonian known as DJ Screw, who died from a codeine overdose in 2000.

To some Latinos outside of Houston, this fusion between black and brown is problematic. At the same time that Beyoncé worked to gain a Latino following, Mexican Americans in Houston faced criticism for their ties to their black peers. Chingo Bling has encountered resistance from rappers in Los Angeles who think he is a "sellout" because of his close relationship to African Americans. "They're like, 'Those Texans think they're black.' . . . They call us brother-lovers." Other rappers recall hearing more derogatory terms, like *naco*. According to Andres Garcia-Lopez, who opened a recording studio called Broadway Studios with the young Latino rapper H-Town Slim, the word means "nigger taco." Garcia-Lopez heard the slur from Mexican-Americans in the Rio Grande Valley after he decided to play some hip-hop on a boom box during a visit.[21] While Latino and African American cultures often blend in Houston, that fusion is not always celebrated.

H-Town Slim linked the musical fusion to neighborhoods where the groups share space. He contrasted the local scene to Los Angeles, which he depicts as more racially divided: "Out there East L.A. is *puro mexicano*. But here, if you go over to the north side, like by Elysian and Hardy, where is the line between the black and Mexican neighborhoods? We share our cultures." Chingo Bling considers the racial animosity between African Americans and Latinos as the primary reason for separation on the West Coast. While "the strife is real bad" in California, he asserts that "in Texas we just blend better."[22]

A music video made by Beyoncé in 2013 for the song "No Angel" further confirms the close cultural and spatial ties forged by people of African and Mexican descent. In the clip, a series of images depicts Houston's first black neighborhood, the place known as Freedman's Town, and the San Felipe district at different times since 1865. A young black man proudly displays the words "4th Ward" shaved into his hair. Cars bearing the name of the neighborhood and the words "Dirty South" slowly crawl through city streets. Beyoncé herself struts and poses on the front steps of an ancient-looking shotgun house that closely resembles the ones still found in parts of Fourth Ward and Third Ward. In one shot, a group of Latinos display a sign that reads, "Dat Mexican Holding." By using a phrase taken from African

American vernacular, the Mexican Americans featured in the video use sound to link themselves to black culture. The very language used by the Latinos reinforces the spatial and cultural relationship.[23]

Like Beyoncé, these young Latinos demonstrate a polycultural notion of race shaped by multiple heritages and experiences. Ethnic Mexican migrants before World War II balked when Houstonians referred to them as "brown people," but modern Mexican Americans like Chingo Bling assert a brown racial subjectivity inspired by the Chicano movement. Chingo Bling's subjectivity as a person of Mexican descent is also derived, in part, from his immigrant parents, who raised him in the Bayou City, and from constant attacks on the Latin American migrant population in border states. Yet spatial contact with black Texans has also affected his articulations of race and culture. Chingo Bling and others draw criticism from people who see "black" and "Mexican" as static categories. A multitude of heritages and local experiences with race produce racial subjectivities that continue to transform.

Generations of Houstonians, their neighborhoods, and their cultural expressions illustrate some of the ways that migration has affected the multiple meanings of race in twentieth-century cities. Legal segregation certainly influenced Houstonians' place, but so have migrants' own distinct racial subjectivities, spatial negotiations at the local level, and meanings assigned to cultural practice. Modern African Americans, Creoles of color, and Latinos in Houston express racial subjectivities and articulations of community that have been shaped by an eighty-year history of migration and settlement. Spatial contact between Creoles and East Texans helped them build community in the 1930s, and Latinos joined these institutions beginning in the 1960s. During that decade, radical movements also helped foster the development of new racial subjectivities. Unlike previous generations of migrants, the young people who referred to themselves as Chicano tended to reject whiteness as a political claim. Meanwhile, some Creoles of color felt inspired by the long civil rights movement to claim blackness as a racial subjectivity while still asserting Creole cultural pride. These groups' use of soul music reflected changes in racial subjectivity and strengthened ties with black Houstonians. A generation later, entertainers like Beyoncé and Chingo Bling perform music that bears the indelible imprint of life in a city where these groups share neighborhoods and influence one another's cultural expressions.

This book has focused on culture because expressions like music can reveal hidden histories of race and community formation. Disfranchised Tejanos played corridos that depicted an Anglo/Mexican binary and illustrated ethnic Mexicans' position as a racial group in South Texas. By 1945, orquesta was the music of middle-class, urban Mexican Americans who identified as members of the white race and Mexican ethnicity. Yet the people who played Tejano soul and hip-hop after 1965 had rejected whiteness as a racial subjectivity. For Afro-Creoles, the differences between the la-la first heard in Frenchtown in the late 1920s and the blues played by black Texans reinforced differences between the groups. Through jazz, though, Afro-Creole and Texan youth forged cultural ties in shared institutions in the 1930s and 1940s. By the 1960s, changes in music reflected the development of new racial identifications. Each musical style illuminates a particular moment in its group's racial re-formation. In the 2000s, the cultural products by performers like Beyoncé and Chingo Bling illustrate how these histories have led to polycultural articulations of race that show how multiple heritages, experiences with migration, and spatial contact between diverse communities have shaped modern racial subjectivities.

Other international and interstate migrations continue to change the demographics of Houston. The percentage of Asians in the Houston metropolitan area has steadily risen since the 1990s, growing from 3.4 percent in 1990 to 6.5 percent in 2010. Furthermore, Houston is currently home to the largest community of Nigerian expatriates in the United States. Nigerians make up an estimated 2 percent of the city's total population. Louisianians still move to Houston, contributing to a trend that began with the influx of Creoles of color in the 1920s. In 2005, thousands of evacuees from New Orleans arrived in Houston in the aftermath of Hurricane Katrina. Some reports estimate that between 150,000 and 250,000 residents of New Orleans relocated to Houston in the aftermath of the storm.[24]

The woman born Mary Rose Berry watched Houston transform since her childhood. She lived in various Houston neighborhoods where groups of migrants made contact. Born to a young woman from southwestern Louisiana in 1929 and raised by black migrants from East Texas and Shreveport, Berry spent her childhood in Fifth Ward, attended school with children from Frenchtown, and experienced controversies over skin color and "passing" with her friends. Her cultural life was also influenced by contact with Creoles of color. She converted to Catholicism as a teenager and graduated from the parochial school at Our Mother of Mercy. She slipped away to the Eldorado Ballroom in the 1940s to hear big bands made up of black Texans and Creoles of color. The sights and sounds of her life involved a

FIGURE 12. Mary Rose (Berry) Strawder with several of her neighbors' children, Monterrey, Mexico, 2004. Photo courtesy of Mary Rose (Berry) Strawder.

fusion of Texans and Louisianians. When one of her children married a Creole man, Mary danced to zydeco music at the wedding reception. And when she remarried in the mid-1980s, she wed a migrant from New Orleans.

As an octogenarian, she lives in a neighborhood, new to her, that has been shaped most dramatically by the migration of people from Latin America. Like others who came of age during the era of Jim Crow, she began discussing a black/brown racial dynamic in the late twentieth century. The movement of younger black Houstonians to the suburbs, and the influx of Latino families into African American communities, have meant that older black Houstonians tend to live near younger Latino families. None of Mary Rose's grandchildren lived in Houston by 2000; many resided in Missouri City, in Fort Bend County. Meanwhile, she lived ten miles east of her childhood home in Fifth Ward, in a neighborhood populated by young Latino families and retired African Americans. On her street, the people over the age of fifty tended to be African American, while their neighbors were young families from Latin America.

Ethnic Mexicans directly influenced the life of Mary Rose in her eighth decade as a Houstonian. As she learned more about her Spanish-speaking neighbors, she began to incorporate the tamales and homemade tortillas produced by local women into her own family's meals. She formed an especially close relationship with her neighbors, a Mexican-born couple raising three children in the city. Mary Rose celebrated holidays and birthdays with the younger Peña family. She eventually took a trip across the border to Monterrey with them to experience Mexican culture firsthand. (See figure 12.) Although Mary Rose could not communicate in Spanish, and her new friends spoke very little English, they formed a tight bond that both considered familial. And on her diversifying street on the eastern edge of Houston, the children of Mexican migrants call Mary Rose "Grandma."[25]

ACKNOWLEDGMENTS

When I was an undergraduate student majoring in Radio-Television-Film at the University of Texas at Austin, my film professor, Rachel Tsangari, armed her students with 16-mm cameras and told us each to produce a "visual poem." I spent days pondering the assignment before inspiration struck. I decided to go home. I drove to Houston that weekend and took my camera to Clinton Park, the neighborhood where I was born and where my father and his siblings were raised. The resulting film represented my first foray into nonfiction storytelling, but the project also sparked my interest in the rich history of Houston neighborhoods. Although I certainly did not go to graduate school with the intention of writing about Houston, I wound up there again, continuing a journey I began my junior year in Austin. Writing *Houston Bound* has allowed me to stay connected to my hometown, even as I made new homes in different parts of the country.

Several people and agencies made themselves a vital part of the making of this book. Thanks to Niels Hooper, my editor at the University of California Press, for taking an interest in this project. I also appreciate the hard work and dedication of the UC Press staff, including former assistant editor Kim Hogeland, Pamela J. Polk, and Dore Brown, who steered the book through the various stages of production. I would also like to thank Carl Walesa for copyediting the final draft and Anne Canright for proofreading. Additionally, Victoria Wolcott and an anonymous reviewer from the University of California Press offered thoughtful reader reports that helped me fine-tune the book before publication.

Research funding for this book came from an array of sources: a Ford Foundation Diversity Dissertation Fellowship, a Woodrow Wilson Career Enhancement Fellowship for Junior Faculty, a research travel award from the

Department of History at the University of Wisconsin–Madison, and a Royalty Research Fund Scholars Program Award from the University of Washington. I thank my Wilson mentor, Tera Hunter, for her early input. As the Summerlee Fellow for the Study of Texas History in 2012–13, I spent a year at the Clements Center for Southwest Studies at Southern Methodist University. Grace Elizabeth Hale and Kevin Mumford traveled to Dallas to participate in my manuscript workshop in November 2012, and both provided critical feedback that helped me land a book contract. I am grateful to the Clements Center's Andrew Graybill, Sherry Smith, Ruth Ann Elmore, and Andrea Boardman for providing constant support and encouragement. I would also like to thank Neil Foley and John Chávez for welcoming me to the larger community of historians at SMU. Last but not least, fellows Paul Conrad, Darren Dochuk, Ruben Flores, and Paula Lupkin provided valuable manuscript feedback and camaraderie during my year in Dallas.

I began this project as a graduate student at the University of Wisconsin–Madison. My dissertation committee, which included Stephen Kantrowitz, Nan Enstad, and Christina Greene, raised questions that I still pondered years later when crafting this book. I am especially grateful to committee members Susan Lee Johnson and Camille Guérin-Gonzales, whose passion for history and social justice continues to inspire me. Susan encouraged me to pursue this project when I first took her western history seminar during my first semester in the Department of History, and has continued to support this project since I left Madison. Even now, reading her beautiful prose pushes me to work harder at my craft.

I'd like to thank my wonderful crew of friends in Madison, people who read drafts, listened to presentations, and provided laughs when I needed them most. Matt Blanton, Mark Goldberg, Kori Graves, Brenna Greer, Michel Hogue, Adam Malka, Leah Mirakhor, Stacey Smith, Maia Surdam, Zoë Van Orsdol, Ryan Quintana, and Stephanie Westcott filled me with warmth on the coldest days in Madison. A special shout-out goes to the members of Blixie for great times on- and offstage.

While in Madison, I had the opportunity to participate in several communities of scholars that shaped the way I think about race and culture. Conversations held over pizza and beer during our monthly Friday Night Music Club meetings affected how I thought about culture and race. Thank you, Craig Werner, for assembling the group and pushing me to consider new ways of thinking about music. I also appreciate Alexander Shasko's willingness to share his mind-numbingly extensive music collection when he hosted our gatherings. Special thanks go to Dave Gilbert, who continues to exchange writing with me years after we left Madison. His smart critiques of my chapters made all the difference in the last year before publication. I also appreciate Story Matkin-Rawn and Heather Stur, formerly known as the "Angelic Brewery Writer's Collective." Each week, we met and swapped pages from our works-in-progress. Both women kept me on track with their willingness to write under the toughest circumstances. I raise a pint of Wisconsin's finest to you, Story and Heather.

I moved to Tucson to take a position in the Department of History at the University of Arizona in 2014, and I am grateful to have received the support of my new colleagues as I completed this book. Katherine Morrissey showed enthusiasm for this project even before I arrived. Department head Kevin Gosner provided support while I finished writing. Prior to my move to the Southwest, scholarly communities at the University of Washington in Seattle helped me convert my dissertation into a book. Words cannot express how much I appreciate the mentorship and friendship of Stephanie Smallwood. Stephanie has provided feedback on drafts, written letters of recommendation, and offered moral support when I needed it most. Thanks for helping me navigate the world of academia as an assistant professor. Stephanie Camp also read chapter drafts as part of our writing group, and helped welcome me to Seattle. I will forever miss her brilliance and kindness. I would also like to thank Moon-Ho Jung for offering feedback on the manuscript in its final stages, and Quintard Taylor for attending my talks, inviting me to participate in roundtables, and showing enthusiasm for my research. Colleagues Sonnet Retman and Michelle Habell-Pallan never failed to answer my questions and put me at ease. Thank you, Sonnet, for pushing me to apply for fellowships and for supporting those applications. I also appreciate the encouragement and camaraderie of colleagues Rick Bonus, Gail Nomura, Carolyn Pinedo-Turnovsky, LaShawnDa Pittman, and Steve Sumida in the Department of American Ethnic Studies. Women Investigating Race, Ethnicity, and Difference (WIRED)—the beautiful brainchild of Ralina Joseph, Janine Jones, and Habiba Ibrahim—provided me with a wonderful community of scholars and friends during my time at UW.

During my last few years in Seattle, guitar lessons with musician Danny Francoeur gave me a richer understanding of musical performance. As my instructor, he taught me to play rhythm and blues, country, reggae, and rock 'n' roll. He also gave me the courage to try my first blues solos. In the process of teaching me chord progressions, blues scales, and fingering techniques, Danny also made me a better student. Thanks for sharing your gifts with me.

Several extraordinary Houstonians shared personal stories that appear in these pages. In 2006, artist Denise Labrie introduced me to her mother, Inez (Prejean) Calegon, who allowed me to record her account of her family's journey from Scott, Louisiana, to Frenchtown. The words and images of the Prejean family gave this project life at an early stage of its development. Albert Calderon, Jr., not only responded to my e-mail inquiry, he also introduced me to three of his old friends: Rey Romero, Bobby Severson, and Artie Villaseñor. I will never forget the bright Saturday afternoon we spent together. I am especially indebted to my grandmother, Mary Strawder, and my second cousin, Barbara Johnson, for bringing old Fifth Ward to life through their personal accounts. Thanks for sharing your stories and photos, and for teaching me more about a crucial part of Houston's history.

Several people helped me procure the images that appear in *Houston Bound*. I must thank cartographer William Nelson for creating the maps. I would also like to recognize the staffs at the African American Library at the Gregory School, the Houston Metropolitan Research Center, and all of the libraries I visited over the years. Timothy J. Ronk, at the Houston Public Library, and Allison Zaragoza, of the Gregory School, helped me locate and purchase most of the images in this book. I also must thank Oscar and Ana Peña for sharing their family pictures.

I could not have written this book without the constant support of my family, old and new. Since I started this project, I've gained new kinfolk by marrying into the Dotson family of Georgia. I've also enjoyed reconnecting with my maternal family, the Franklins, and discovering dozens of aunts, uncles, cousins, brothers, and sisters. Additionally, writing this book has allowed me to gain a deeper understanding of my paternal family's experiences in eastern Texas and the South. I thank my father, Andrew Steptoe, and my extended family—Leaneice Strawder Brown, Fredrick Brown, Delores Ingram, Bobby Ingram, William Strawder, Cheryl Strawder, Reginald Steptoe, Djan Ingram, Desirée Strawder, Darian Strawder, and Loren Brown—for their encouragement over the years.

I am especially indebted to my partner, Jerome Dotson, Jr., for years of support and love. Thank you for listening to my ideas, asking tough questions, reading drafts, chauffeuring me through Houston neighborhoods while I snapped pictures, and for making sure I ate several meals a day during the final stages of this project. (I look forward to doing the same for you over the next few years.) Most of all, thank you for sharing your life with me. This book is dedicated to you.

NOTES

INTRODUCTION

1. Mary Rose learned the truth about her birth only in 1960, after Leanna had passed away in a hospital in Tacoma, Washington, where she spent her last years. Elizabeth's real surname remains unknown. Mary (Berry) Strawder, interview with the author, January 3, 2006, Houston; Barbara (Berry) Johnson, interview with the author, Houston, January 2, 2006.

2. *1920 United States Federal Census,* Houston, Harris County, Texas; Howard Beeth and Cary D. Wintz, eds., *Black Dixie: Afro-Texan History and Culture in Houston* (College Station: Texas A&M University Press, 1992), 89; Bernadette Pruitt, "For the Advancement of the Race: The Great Migrations to Houston, Texas, 1914–1941," *Journal of Urban History* 31, no. 4 (May 2005): 436.

3. Works that examine Creoles of color in rural Louisiana and the city of New Orleans include Gary B. Mills, *The Forgotten People: Cane River's Creoles of Color* (Baton Rouge: Louisiana State University Press, 1977); Arnold R. Hirsch, *Creole New Orleans: Race and Americanization* (Baton Rouge: Louisiana State University Press, 1992); Carl A. Brasseaux, Keith P. Fontenot, and Claude F. Oubre, *Creoles of Color in the Bayou Country* (Jackson: University Press of Mississippi, 1994); Arthé A. Anthony, "'Lost Boundaries': Racial Passing and Poverty in Segregated New Orleans," *Louisiana History* 36, no. 3 (1995): 291–312; George Cable, *The Creoles of Louisiana* (New Orleans: Pelican Publishing, 2000); Sybil Klein, ed., *Creole: The History and Legacy of Louisiana's Free People of Color* (Baton Rouge: Louisiana State University Press, 2000); Thomas Brothers, *Louis Armstrong's New Orleans* (New York: W. W. Norton and Company, 2006); and Mary Gehman, *The Free People of Color of New Orleans: An Introduction* (Donaldsonville, LA: Margaret Media, 2009). See also Blair L. M. Kelley's discussion of New Orleans in *Right to Ride: Streetcar Boycotts and African American Citizenship in the Era of Plessy v. Ferguson* (Chapel Hill: University of North Carolina Press, 2010).

4. For more on Afro-diasporic communities in the twentieth century, see Frank Andre Guridy, *Forging Diaspora: Afro-Cubans and African Americans in*

a World of Empire and Jim Crow (Chapel Hill: University of North Carolina Press, 2010).

5. Arnoldo De León, *Ethnicity in the Sunbelt: A History of Mexican Americans in Houston* (Houston: Mexican American Studies Program, University of Houston, 1989), 6–8.

6. U.S. Census Bureau, "No. HS-7. Population of the Largest 75 Cities: 1900 to 2000," in *Statistical Abstract of the United States: 2003*, www.census.gov/statab/hist /HS-07.pdf.

7. As historian Grace Elizabeth Hale asserts, white southerners imposed "an absolute division that dissolved any range of racially mixed subjectivities." Grace Elizabeth Hale, *Making Whiteness: The Culture of Segregation in the South, 1890– 1940* (New York: Vintage Books, 1998), 8.

8. The people described in this book often disagreed on how to label different groups; however, I hope to avoid some confusion by defining the terms I use. *Creole of color* refers to Louisianians with some African ancestry. Their ancestors were free before the Civil War. Since Creoles of color and descendants of slaves have African ancestry, I use *people of African descent* to simultaneously refer to both groups. *Anglo* describes English-speaking white Americans. *Ethnic Mexican* refers to all people of Mexican descent. I often use *Mexican American* to identify ethnic Mexicans born in the United States and naturalized citizens, and *Tejano* to specifically describe Texas-born people of Mexican descent. *Mexican immigrant* indicates a person who relocated to the United States from Mexico.

9. Robin D. G. Kelley, "Polycultural Me," *Colorlines,* September–October 1999, http://www.utne.com/politics/the-people-in-me.aspx. Kelley asserts that the term *polycultural* better depicts the hybridity and fluidity of race than *multicultural,* which threatens to reify racial categories by implying that "cultures are fixed, discrete entities that exist side by side."

10. A few historians have analyzed migrant groups in the South before World War I; their works include Nancy Hewitt, *Southern Discomfort: Women's Activism in Tampa, Florida, 1880s–1920s* (Urbana: University of Illinois Press, 2001); and Moon-Ho Jung, *Coolies and Cane: Race, Labor, and Sugar in the Age of Emancipation* (Baltimore: Johns Hopkins University Press, 2006). Other historians have focused specifically on black migrations within the South; see Luther Adams, *Way Up North in Louisville: African American Migration in the Urban South, 1930–1970* (Chapel Hill: University of North Carolina Press, 2010); Earl Lewis, *In Their Own Interests: Race, Class, and Power in Twentieth-Century Norfolk, Virginia* (Berkeley: University of California Press, 1991); and Bernadette Pruitt, *The Other Great Migration: The Movement of Rural African Americans to Houston, 1900–1941* (College Station: Texas A&M University Press, 2013). For studies of migrants in the Midwest and Northeast and on the West Coast, see Davarian L. Baldwin, *Chicago's New Negroes: Modernity, the Great Migration, and Black Urban Life* (Chapel Hill: University of North Carolina Press, 2007); Juan R. García, *Mexicans in the Midwest, 1900–1932* (Tucson: University of Arizona Press, 2004); James N. Gregory, *American Exodus: The Dust Bowl Migration and Okie Culture in California (*New York:

Oxford University Press, 1991); James N. Gregory, *The Southern Diaspora: How the Great Migrations of Black and White Southerners Transformed America* (Chapel Hill: University of North Carolina Press, 2007); James Grossman, *Land of Hope: Chicago, Black Southerners, and the Great Migration* (Chicago: University of Chicago Press, 1991); Camille Guérin-Gonzales, *Mexican Workers and American Dreams: Immigration, Repatriation, and California Farm Labor, 1900–1939* (New Brunswick, NJ: Rutgers University Press), 1994; Michael Innis-Jiménez, *Steel Barrio: The Great Mexican Migration to South Chicago, 1915–1940* (New York: NYU Press, 2013); Huping Ling, *Chinese Chicago: Race, Transnational Migration, and Community since 1870* (Stanford, CA: Stanford University Press, 2012); Khalil Gibran Muhammad, *The Condemnation of Blackness: Race, Crime, and the Making of Modern Urban America* (Cambridge, MA: Harvard University Press, 2011); Lara Putnam, *Radical Moves: Caribbean Migrants and the Politics of Race in the Jazz Age* (Chapel Hill: University of North Carolina Press, 2013); George J. Sánchez, *Becoming Mexican American: Ethnicity, Culture, and Identity in Chicano Los Angeles, 1900–1945* (New York: Oxford University Press, 1993); Quintard Taylor, *The Forging of a Black Community: Seattle's Central District from 1870 through the Civil Rights Era* (Seattle: University of Washington Press, 2001); Joe Trotter, *Black Milwaukee: The Making of an Industrial Proletariat, 1915–45* (Champaign: University of Illinois Press, 1985); Shirley Ann Wilson Moore, *To Place Our Deeds: The African American Community in Richmond, California, 1910–1963* (Berkeley: University of California Press, 2001); Isabel Wilkerson, *The Warmth of Other Suns: The Epic Story of America's Great Migration* (New York: Random House, 2010); and Victoria W. Wolcott, *Remaking Respectability: African American Women in Interwar Detroit* (Chapel Hill: University of North Carolina Press, 2001).

11. I borrow the term *western South* from other scholars who have analyzed the states between the Mississippi River and the Rio Grande. Neil Foley describes central Texas as the western South in his depiction of ethnic Mexicans, Anglos, and African Americans during the Jim Crow era; see Neil Foley, *The White Scourge: Mexicans, Blacks, and Poor Whites in Texas Cotton Culture* (Berkeley: University of California Press, 1997). James Gregory also uses the designation to describe regions of the "Dust Bowl," including Texas, Oklahoma, and Missouri; see Gregory, *American Exodus.*

12. Historians who analyzed multiracial Texas in the twentieth century include Foley, *The White Scourge;* Michael Phillips, *White Metropolis: Race, Ethnicity, and Religion in Dallas, 1841–2001* (Austin: University of Texas Press, 2006); Neil Foley, *Quest for Equality: The Failed Promise of Black–Brown Solidarity* (Cambridge, MA: Harvard University Press, 2010); Brian D. Behnken, *Fighting Their Own Battles: Mexican Americans, African Americans, and the Struggle for Civil Rights in Texas* (Chapel Hill: University of North Carolina Press, 2011); and Jason McDonald, *Racial Dynamics in Early Twentieth-Century Austin, Texas* (Lanham, MD: Lexington Books, 2012).

13. Michael Omi and Howard Winant pioneered use of the term *race formation,* which they define as "the process by which social, economic and political forces

determine the content and importance of racial categories, and by which they are in turn shaped by racial meanings"; see Michael Omi and Howard Winant, eds., *Racial Formations in the United States,* 2nd ed. (New York: Routledge, 1994), 12. Tomás Almaguer builds on the work of Omi and Winant with his study of race formation in California in the second half of the nineteenth century. Almaguer examines ethnic Mexicans, American Indians, and Asians in California's racial hierarchy; see Tomás Almaguer, *Racial Fault Lines: The Historical Origins of White Supremacy* (1994; reprint, Berkeley: University of California Press, 2008).

14. On European immigrants and whiteness, see David R. Roediger, *The Wages of Whiteness: Race and the Making of the American Working Class* (1991; reprint, New York: Verso Books, 2007); Matthew Frye Jacobson, *Whiteness of a Different Color: European Immigrants and the Alchemy of Race* (Cambridge, MA: Harvard University Press, 1998); Thomas A. Guglielmo, *White on Arrival: Italians, Race, Color, and Power in Chicago, 1890–1945* (New York: Oxford University Press, 2003); and D. Roediger, *Working toward Whiteness: How America's Immigrants Became White; The Strange Journey from Ellis Island to the Suburbs* (New York: Basic Books, 2006). On Mexican Americans and whiteness, see Ariela Gross, "'The Caucasian Cloak': Mexican Americans and the Politics of Whiteness in the Twentieth-Century Southwest," *Georgetown Law Journal* 95, no. 337 (2007): 338–92; and Thomas A. Guglielmo, "Fighting for Caucasian Rights: Mexicans, Mexican Americans, and the Transnational Struggle for Civil Rights in World War II Texas," *Journal of American History,* March 2006, 1212–37. Ian Haney-López discusses multiple groups, such as Mexican Americans and Japanese Americans, in *White by Law: The Legal Construction of Race* (New York: New York University Press, 1996).

15. Roediger, *Working toward Whiteness,* 8. Guglielmo also distinguishes between what he calls "color" and "race" in *White on Arrival.* Scholars who have analyzed race formation through the lens of law and politics include Ian Haney-López and Ariela Gross in *What Blood Won't Tell: A History of Race on Trial in America* (Cambridge, MA: Harvard University Press, 2008). Natalia Molina primarily uses law and policy to examine the meanings of Mexican American citizenship in relation to other racial groups' citizenship rights; see *How Race Is Made in America: Immigration, Citizenship, and the Historical Power of Racial Scripts* (Berkeley: University of California Press, 2014). On postwar multiracial politics in California, see Mark Brilliant, *The Color of America Has Changed: How Racial Diversity Shaped Civil Rights Reform in California, 1941–1978* (New York: Oxford University Press, 2010); and Scott Kurashige, *The Shifting Grounds of Race: Black and Japanese Americans in the Making of Multiethnic Los Angeles* (Princeton, NJ: Princeton University Press, 2010).

16. Nan Enstad, *Ladies of Labor, Girls of Adventure: Working Women, Popular Culture, and Labor Politics at the Turn of the Twentieth Century* (New York: Columbia University Press, 1999), 13.

17. The writing of several different geographers and historians has influenced my understanding of space and society. In *The Production of Space,* Henri Lefebvre demonstrates that social practice produces space, and space produces social practice; together they create "social space"; see Henri Lefebvre, *The Production of Space*

(Boston: Blackwell Publishers, 1991). Edward Soja builds upon Lefebvre's work by analyzing different types of spaces in human life. *Firstspace,* or perceived space, is the material aspect of spatiality—our "built environment." *Secondspace* is the symbolic or interpretational aspect of space. Soja asserts that Firstspace and Secondspace then create "Thirdspace," which is our lived experience. See Edward W. Soja, *Thirdspace: Journeys to Los Angeles and Other Real-and-Imagined Places* (Malden, MA: Blackwell Publishers, 1996), 75. Historian Robert O. Self adds to this conversation by describing three dimensions of space: "space as property, space as social imagination, and space as political scale"; see Robert O. Self, *American Babylon: Race and the Struggle for Postwar Oakland* (Princeton, NJ: Princeton University Press, 2003), 17.

18. Patricia Pando, "Two Worlds a Mile Apart: A Brief History of the Fourth Ward," *Houston History* 8, no. 2 (2011): 38; P. Pando, "In the Nickel, Houston's Fifth Ward," *Houston History* 8, no. 3 (2011): 33.

19. Lisa Gray, "Bayous for Dummies," *Houston Chronicle,* October 17, 2010.

20. Self, *American Babylon,* 18–19, 343.

21. Stephanie M. H. Camp, *Closer to Freedom: Enslaved Women and Everyday Resistance in the Plantation South* (Chapel Hill: University of North Carolina Press, 2004), 12–13.

22. On the emergence of segregation and the racial order of the New South, see C. Vann Woodward, *The Strange Career of Jim Crow* (1955; reprint, New York: Oxford University Press, 2002). See also Howard Rabinowitz, "From Exclusion to Segregation: Southern Race Relations, 1865–1890," *Journal of American History* 63 (September 1976): 325–50. Other historians have emphasized the significance of public space on the production of racial hierarchy in the post–Civil War South. See Jane Dailey, *Before Jim Crow: The Politics of Race in Postemancipation Virginia* (Chapel Hill: University of North Carolina Press, 2000); Edward Ayers, "The Promise of the New South," in *When Did Southern Segregation Begin?* ed. John David Smith (Boston: Bedford/St. Martin's, 2002); and Kelley, *Right to Ride.* On the segregation of commercial spaces for business and leisure, see Hale, *Making Whiteness;* and Victoria W. Wolcott, *Race, Riots, and Roller Coasters: The Struggle over Segregated Recreation in America* (Philadelphia: University of Pennsylvania Press, 2012).

23. Joel Williamson, "The Separation of the Races," in *When Did Southern Segregation Begin?* ed. John David Smith (Boston: Bedford/St. Martin's, 2002), 63.

24. George Lipsitz, "The Racialization of Space and the Spatialization of Race: Theorizing the Hidden Architecture of Landscape," *Landscape Journal* 26, no. 1 (January 1, 2007): 12.

25. Gaye Theresa Johnson, *Spaces of Conflict, Sounds of Solidarity: Music, Race, and Spatial Entitlement in Los Angeles* (Berkeley: University of California Press, 2013), 63.

26. Thomas J. Sugrue, *The Origins of the Urban Crisis: Race and Inequality in Postwar Detroit* (1996; reprint, Princeton, NJ: Princeton University Press, 2005), 229. See also Self, *American Babylon,* 19; N. Molina, *How Race Is Made,* 8.

27. As Earl Lewis shows in his work on black residents of Norfolk, Virginia, in the twentieth century, disenfranchised communities have historically turned

segregation into "congregation," which allowed them to produce their own understandings of space and advance cultural expressions and institutions that solidified group ties; see Lewis, *In Their Own Interests,* 90–92. Historian Gaye Theresa Johnson incorporates Lewis's ideas about congregation into her work on Mexican Americans and African Americans in twentieth-century Los Angeles. Johnson advances the idea of "spatial entitlement"—a concept that refers to the ways in which marginalized communities create "new collectivities" based on their use of space, technology, and creative pursuits; see Johnson, *Spaces of Conflict.*

28. Innis-Jiménez, *Steel Barrio,* 10.

29. George Lipsitz, *Footsteps in the Dark: The Hidden Histories of Popular Music* (Minneapolis: University of Minnesota Press, 2007), xv.

30. Susan J. Smith, "Beyond Geography's Visible Worlds: A Cultural Politics of Music," *Progress in Human Geography* 21, no. 4 (1997): 510.

31. As scholar Lisa Lowe argues, "[b]ecause culture is the contemporary repository of memory, of history, it is through culture, rather than government, that alternative forms of subjectivity, collectivity, and public life are imagined"; see Lisa Lowe, *Immigrant Acts: On Asian American Cultural Politics* (Durham, NC: Duke University Press, 1996), 22.

32. Gross, "'Caucasian Cloak,'" 342.

33. Tera Hunter, *To 'Joy My Freedom: Black Women's Lives and Labors after the Civil War* (Cambridge, MA: Harvard University Press, 1997), 162.

34. Ronald Radano, *Lying Up a Nation: Race and Black Music* (Chicago: University of Chicago Press, 2003), 73.

35. See the discussion of race and sound in Nina Sun Eidsheim, "Marian Anderson and 'Sonic Blackness' in American Opera," *American Quarterly* 63, no. 3 (September 2011): 641–71. On music and the color line, see Karl Hagstrom Miller, *Segregating Sound: Inventing Folk and Pop Music in the Age of Jim Crow* (Durham, NC: Duke University Press, 2010).

36. On cultural expressions, identity, and subjectivity, see George Sánchez on the popularity of swing music in Los Angeles Mexican American communities in *Becoming Mexican American,* 171–87; Nan Enstad on women's labor and consumerism in *Ladies of Labor, Girls of Adventure;* Tera Hunter on black women, music, and dance in *To 'Joy My Freedom;* Anthony Macías on music and dance in Los Angeles in *Mexican American Mojo: Popular Music, Dance, and Urban Culture in Los Angeles, 1935–1968* (Durham: Duke University Press, 2008); and Luis Alvarez's work on zoot suits in *The Power of the Zoot: Youth Culture and Resistance during World War II* (Berkeley: University of California Press, 2009).

37. Radano, *Lying Up a Nation,* 62.

38. Davarian Baldwin focuses on how New Negroes in Chicago created a "mass consumer marketplace to challenge the dehumanizing effects of capitalism and etch out a world of leisure that could cater to their labor demands." He roots this phenomenon in the Great Migration and the formation of communities in the urban North. I build on Baldwin's argument to demonstrate how these economic activities provided the basis for Houstonians' fight against Jim Crow. See Baldwin, *Chicago's*

New Negroes, 7; See also David Levering Lewis, *When Harlem Was in Vogue* (New York: Penguin Books, 1997).

39. While historian Bernadette Pruitt does examine New Negroes in Houston, she analyzes political movements, the development of a black consumer economy, and cultural expressions as separate phenomena. This book shows the connections between these activities, and their relationship to the fight against Jim Crow. Pruitt, *The Other Great Migration.*

40. Ariela Gross uses the term *racially ambiguous* to describe people with multiple or contested racial identities that do not conform to the black/white binary. See Gross, *What Blood Won't Tell.*

41. On the influence of Latinos on rhythm and blues and soul in the United States, see Ruben Molina, *Chicano Soul: Recordings & History of an American Culture* (La Puente, CA: Mictlan Publishing, 2007); Juan Flores, *From Bomba to Hip Hop: Puerto Rican Culture and Latino Identity* (New York: Columbia University Press, 2000); Juan Flores, "Boogaloo and Latin Soul," in *The Afro-Latin@ Reader: History and Culture in the United States,* edited by Miriam Jiménez Román and Juan Flores (Durham, NC: Duke University Press, 2010), 199–206; and Macías, *Mexican American Mojo.*

42. This characterization of African American and Mexican American civil rights can be found in Behnken, *Fighting Their Own Battles;* Guglielmo, "Fighting for Caucasian Rights"; and Foley, *Quest for Equality.*

1. THE BAYOU CITY IN BLACK AND WHITE

1. The title of the song "Midnight Special" alludes to the train that ran between Houston and San Antonio on Route 90. This train would pass through Sugar Land at approximately midnight each night, shining a light over the prison. In this song, and in the minds of Sugar Land inmates, the train symbolizes freedom. Leadbelly, *Complete Recorded Works Volume 1: 1939–1947,* Document Records 5226, 1995, compact disc; Charles K. Wolfe, *The Life and Legend of Leadbelly* (New York: Harper Collins Publishers, 1992), 79–84; Alan Govenar, *Texas Blues: The Rise of a Contemporary Sound* (College Station: Texas A&M University Press, 2008), 92–93.

2. Scholar George Lipsitz argues that forms of music that originate in specific places "never completely lose the concerns and cultural qualities that give them determinate shape in their places of origin. Through music we learn about place and about displacement." George Lipsitz, *Dangerous Crossroads: Popular Music, Postmodernism and the Poetics of Place* (London and New York: Verso, 1994), 3–4.

3. Matthew Mancini, *One Dies, Get Another: Convict Leasing in the American South* (Columbia: University of South Carolina Press, 1996), 175–76.

4. Alain Locke, "Enter the New Negro," *Survey Graphic,* March 1925.

5. Randolph B. Campbell, *An Empire for Slavery: The Peculiar Institution in Texas, 1821–1865.* (Baton Rouge: Louisiana State University Press, 1989), 58.

6. Campbell, *Empire for Slavery*, 2; Alwyn Barr, *Black Texans: A History of African Americans in Texas, 1528–1995* (Norman: University of Oklahoma Press, 1996), 15–17.

7. Writers' Program of the Work Projects Administration, *Houston: A History and Guide* (Houston: Anson Jones Press, 1942), xi; Beth Ann Shelton, Nestor P. Rodriguez, Joe R. Feagin, Robert D. Bullard, and Robert D. Thomas, *Houston: Growth and Decline in a Sunbelt Boomtown* (Philadelphia: Temple University Press, 1989), 71.

8. Frederick Law Olmsted, *A Journey through Texas: or, A Saddle-Trip on the Southwestern Frontier* (1857; reprint, Austin: University of Texas Press, 1978), 361–63.

9. For a discussion of the creation of a plantation regime in colonial North America, see Ira Berlin, *Generations of Captivity: A History of African-American Slaves* (Cambridge, MA: Harvard University Press, 2003), 51–96. See also Clyde Woods, *Development Arrested: The Blues and Plantation Power in the Mississippi Delta* (London and New York: Verso, 1998).

10. *1860 United States Federal Census.*

11. On slaves' formation of new kinship networks and communities during the internal slave trade, see Berlin, *Generations of Captivity*, 190–93. For more on slave community politics and culture, see Steven Hahn, *A Nation under Our Feet: Black Political Struggles in the Rural South from Slavery to the Great Migration* (Cambridge, MA: Harvard University Press, 2003); and Radano, *Lying Up a Nation*. On hush harbors, see Albert J. Raboteau, *Slave Religion: The "Invisible Institution" in the Antebellum South* (1978; reprint, New York: Oxford University Press, 2004), 215–19.

12. Archeologist Kenneth Brown has uncovered significant evidence of enslaved cultural practices in Texas Sugar Bowl counties. In this context, the bakongo cosmogram is a symbol that marks the point where a person stands to make an oath to God. The symbol has been linked to Kongo ritual, and has been found across the African diaspora, including parts of the U.S. South and eastern Texas. Kenneth L. Brown, "Material Culture and Community Structure: The Slave and Tenant Community at Levi Jordan's Plantation, 1848–1892," in *Working toward Freedom: Slave Society and Domestic Economy in the American South,* edited by Larry E. Hudson, Jr. (Rochester, NY: University of Rochester Press, 1994), 95–118. Musicologist Eileen Southern describes the ring shout as a "religious dance ceremony of African origin"; see Eileen Southern, *The Music of Black Americans: A History* (1971; reprint, New York: W. W. Norton, 1997), 88.

13. On Juneteenth, see Elizabeth Hayes Turner, "Juneteenth Emancipation and Memory," in Elizabeth Hayes Turner and Gregg Cantrell, eds., *Lone Star Pasts: Memory and History in Texas* (College Station: Texas A&M University Press, 2006), 143–75.

14. On freedpeople's labor in Texas, see Barr, *Black Texans,* 52–60. For discussions of labor contracts during Reconstruction, see Eric Foner, *Reconstruction: America's Unfinished Revolution* (New York: Harper & Row, 1988), 60, 102–9; and Hahn, *A Nation under Our Feet,* 147–56.

15. Howard Beeth and Cary D. Wintz, eds., *Black Dixie: Afro-Texan History and Culture in Houston* (College Station: Texas A&M University Press, 1992), 20. Enough freedpeople made the move from country to city after the Civil War that the black populations of the ten largest cities of the former Confederacy doubled between 1860 and 1870. Foner, *Reconstruction*, 81. See also Hunter, *To 'Joy My Freedom*.

16. Beeth and Wintz, *Black Dixie*, 21–22.

17. Writers' Program, *Houston: A History and Guide*, 81–82.

18. David G. McComb, *Houston, a History* (Austin: University of Texas Press, 1981), 38; Shelton et al., *Houston: Growth and Decline*, 71.

19. *1870 United States Federal Census*, Houston, Harris County, Texas, Fourth Ward section, p. 20. William H. Parsons was born in New Jersey, but his family moved to Alabama when he was a boy. He married a woman from Georgia, attended Emory University, and eventually served in the Mexican War under Zachary Taylor. During the Civil War, Parsons joined the Confederacy. After a failed attempt at starting a colony in Honduras when the war ended, Parsons and his family moved to Houston. He soon served in the Senate of the Twelfth Legislature from District Fourteen. Although he was a former Confederate, Parsons sided with Radical Republicans and urged other Texans to support "the party which conquered us." President Ulysses S. Grant appointed Parsons U.S. centennial commissioner in 1871, so he moved to New York that year. Patsy McDonald Spaw, *The Texas Senate: Civil War to the Eve of Reform, 1861–1889* (College Station: Texas A&M University Press), 106–7.

20. Beeth and Wintz, *Black Dixie*, 90–98.

21. Berlin uses the phrase "Second Middle Passage" in *Generations of Captivity*. See his discussion of the "Migration Generations," 159–244.

22. Rev. Jack Yates Family and Antioch Baptist Church Collection, Houston Metropolitan Research Center (HMRC), Houston Public Library (HPL), MSS 281, box 1, folder 1; Beeth and Wintz, *Black Dixie*, 25; *1870 United States Federal Census*, Houston, Harris County, Texas, Fourth Ward, p. 51.

23. *1870 United States Federal Census*, Atlanta County, Georgia, and Houston, Harris County, Texas.

24. Pruitt, "Advancement of the Race," 441. As Earl Lewis notes, African Americans in southern cities "tended to scatter across the urban landscape;" see Lewis, *In Their Own Interests*, 67.

25. Pando, "In the Nickel," 34.

26. Thelma Scott Bryant, interview by Patricia Smith Prather, August 3, 2007, Houston, Texas, Houston Oral History Project, Mayor Bill White Collection, HPL; Arnett Cobb quote taken from the liner notes of the compact disc *Arnett Blows for 1300*, Delmark DD-471, 1994.

27. Beeth and Wintz, *Black Dixie*, 88, 211. By barring black voters from participating in primary elections, Texas and southern states established a "white primary."

28. Beeth and Wintz, *Black Dixie*, 88; Thomas C. Mackey, "Thelma Denton and Associates: Houston's Red Light Reservation and a Question of Jim Crow," *Houston*

Review 14, no. 3 (1992): 139–52; *Charter of the City of Houston and General Ordinances, 1910* (Houston: Coyle and Co., 1910), 124–27; City Council Meeting Minutes, Houston, Texas, March 30, 1908, book P, 290–94, Texas and Local History Room, HMRC, HPL.

29. Description of Juneteenth at Emancipation Park taken from Naomi Polk Collection, HMRC, MSS 270, box 1, folder 1; Milton Larkin, interview by Louis Marchiafava and Charles Stephenson, January 5, 1988, HMRC, Milton Larkin Collection, MSS 252.

30. Beeth and Wintz, *Black Dixie,* 90–98; Cheryl Knott Malone, "Autonomy and Accommodation: Houston's Colored Carnegie Library, 1907–1922," *Libraries and Cultures* 34, no. 2 (Spring 1999): 95–112.

31. *Houston Post,* January 17, 1915; Independence Heights Collection, HMRC, RG M4, box 1; *1920 United States Federal Census,* Independence Heights, Harris County, Texas. Independence Heights lasted for thirteen years as a town. In its last four years of existence, the town entered into a receivership agreement with Houston. Residents paid taxes to the city in exchange for improvements. Some residents complained that the city did not honor its end of the agreement, and others opined that these improvements would be made if the community actually became part of Houston again. As a result, townspeople voted for dissolution in November 1928, and Houston annexed Independence Heights that year.

32. Testimony of Lee Sparks, Records of the Citizens Committee of Houston, Texas, 1917, South Texas College of Law, page 238.

33. Martha Gruening, "Houston: An N.A.A.C.P. Investigation," *Crisis* 15 (November 1917): 14; Robert V. Haynes, *A Night of Violence: The Houston Riot of 1917* (Baton Rouge: Louisiana State University Press, 1977), 93.

34. For more on Buffalo Soldiers in Texas, see Garna L. Christian, *Black Soldiers in Jim Crow Texas, 1899–1917* (College Station: Texas A&M University Press, 1995).

35. *Crisis* 14 (October 1917).

36. *Houston Press,* August 1, 1917; August 17, 1917; *Houston Chronicle,* August 20, 1917; *Houston Press,* August 30, 1917.

37. Gruening, "Houston," 15–16; Sparks, Citizens Committee, 486.

38. Gruening, "Houston," 15.

39. Sparks, Citizens Committee, 240–41, 486–89.

40. Gruening, "Houston," 15.

41. Testimony of Kneeland S. Snow, *U.S. v. Nesbit et al.* (Records of the Judge Advocate General, U.S. War Department, Record Group 153), 64; testimony of Captain Haig Shekerjian, *U.S. v. Nesbit et al.,* 132.

42. Testimony of Abe Blumberg, *U.S. v. Nesbit et al.,* 587.

43. Estimates of the number of soldiers who participated vary, but range between eighty-five and one hundred. For more on the riot, see Edgar A. Schuler, "The Houston Race Riot, 1917," *Journal of Negro History* 29, no. 3 (July 1944); Haynes, *Night of Violence;* Calvin C. Smith, "The Houston Riot of 1917, Revisited," *Houston History* 13, no. 2 (1991); Christian, *Black Soldiers in Jim Crow Texas;* Tyina Steptoe, "'If You Ever Go to Houston, You Better Walk Right': The Houston Riot of 1917," M.A.

thesis, University of Wisconsin–Madison, 2002; Adriane Lentz-Smith, *Freedom Struggles: African Americans and World War I* (Cambridge, MA: Harvard University Press, 2011).

44. *Houston Post,* August 27, 1917; *Houston Chronicle,* August 27, 1917.

45. Haynes, *Night of Violence,* 203–4.

46. Beeth and Wintz, *Black Dixie,* 89; Karen Benjamin, "Progressivism Meets Jim Crow: Segregation, School Reform, and Urban Development in the Interwar South," Ph.D. diss., University of Wisconsin–Madison, 2007, 24.

47. Bruce Andre Beauboeuf, "War and Change: Houston's Economic Ascendancy during World War I," *Houston Review* 14, no. 2 (1992): 90, 101.

48. See Pete R. Daniel, *Breaking the Land: The Transformation of Cotton, Tobacco, and Rice Cultures since 1880* (Urbana: University of Illinois Press, 1986).

49. Wendell Phillips Terrell, "A Short History of the Negro Longshoreman," Houston College for Negroes, Department of History, located in the Labor Movement in Texas Collection, Barker Center for American History, University of Texas at Austin, box 2E304 Black Longshoremen, folder 4. Longshoremen were central to urban labor and black community growth in other port cities in the South. On longshoremen in New Orleans, see Eric Arneson, *Waterfront Workers of New Orleans: Race, Class, and Politics, 1863–1923* (New York: Oxford University Press, 1991). On Richmond, Virginia, see Lewis, *In Their Own Interests,* 49–58.

50. The description of the music of black dockworkers is from Writers' Program, *Houston: A History and Guide,* 6.

51. Pruitt, "Advancement of the Race," 457.

52. Haynes, *Night of Violence,* 28.

53. *1920 Federal Census,* Justice Precinct 3, Wharton, Texas, p. 12B, Enumeration District 165; *1930 Federal Census,* Precinct 3, Wharton, Texas, p. 29B, Enumeration District 7; Johnson, interview, January 2, 2006; Strawder, interview, January 3, 2006.

54. *1880 United States Federal Census,* Precinct 2, Newton, Texas, p. 547C, Enumeration District 55; *1900 United States Federal Census,* Navasota Ward 4, Grimes County, Texas, p. 2A, Enumeration District 21; *1910 United States Federal Census,* Navasota Ward 4, Grimes, Texas, p. 6B, Enumeration District 0033; Larkin, interview, January 5, 1988.

55. E. O. Smith to Walter White, May 22, 1918, National Association for the Advancement of Colored People branch files, Houston (hereafter cited as NAACP branch files, Houston); Assistant Secretary Walter White to E. O. Smith, June 3, 1918, NAACP branch files, Houston.

56. Henry L. Mims to John Shillady, July 5, 1918, NAACP branch files, Houston.

57. *1920 United States Federal Census,* Houston Ward 4, Harris, Texas, p. 7A, Enumeration District 70; See also Pruitt, *The Other Great Migration.*

58. Patricia Prather and Bob Lee, *The Texas Trailblazers,* ser. 2, no. 23 (Houston: Texas Trailblazer Preservation Association, 1997).

59. Henry L. Mims to John Shillady, July 5, 1918, NAACP branch files, Houston.

60. E. O. Smith to Walter White, June 10, 1918, NAACP branch files, Houston; C. F. Richardson to John Shillady, June 17, 1918, NAACP branch files, Houston; Pruitt, *Other Great Migration,* 156–58.

61. R. A. Hill, "Introduction—Racial and Radical: Cyril V. Briggs, The Crusader Magazine, and the African American Blood Brotherhood, 1918–1922," in *The Crusader,* edited by Cyril V. Briggs, vol. 1 (New York: Garland Press, 1987), xii; William Pickens, "Negro Leadership," *Houston Informer,* March 13, 1920.

62. Story found in the *Houston Informer,* June 28, 1919.

63. *Houston Informer,* July 17, 1920.

64. *Houston Informer,* January 15, 1927.

65. Leon Litwack discusses the use of the word *nigger* in this context in *Been in the Storm So Long: The Aftermath of Slavery* (New York: Vintage Books, 1979), 254–55.

66. On Anglo nostalgia in the South, see Hale, *Making Whiteness,* 51–53.

67. Johnny Walls's story appears in Lorenzo Greene, *Selling Black History for Carter G. Woodson: A Diary, 1930–1933* (Columbia: University of Missouri Press, 1996), 126.

68. C. F. Richardson, "When Is an Old Man Young and a Young Man Old in Business?" *Houston Informer,* February 9, 1929.

69. David M. Chalmers, *Hooded Americanism: The History of the Ku Klux Klan* (Chicago: Quadrangle Paperbacks, 1965), 39–40, 46; Charles C. Alexander, *The Ku Klux Klan in the Southwest* (Lexington: University of Kentucky Press, 1965), 38–39.

70. *Houston Informer,* August 15, 1925; Chalmers, *Hooded Americanism,* 41.

71. Cliff Richardson, Jr., interview, June 9, 1975, HMRC, Oral History Collection 150; Pruitt, *Other Great Migration,* 161.

72. *Houston Post-Dispatch,* May 11, 1928; see also NAACP branch files, Houston.

73. A black reporter for the Associated Negro Press wrote, "Houston, the capital of modern Dixie, must symbolize to the nation on this occasion its policy of white supremacy" (*New York Times,* June 21, 1928); *New York Times,* May 13, 1929 (reprint of an editorial by Louis Isaac Jaffe, *Norfolk Virginian-Pilot,* June 22, 1928); *Houston Informer,* July 21, 1928. On armed self-reliance, see Timothy B. Tyson, *Radio Free Dixie: Robert F. Williams and the Roots of Black Power* (Chapel Hill: University of North Carolina Press, 1999).

74. James M. Sorelle, "'The Darker Side of Heaven': The Black Community in Houston, Texas, 1917–1945," Ph.D. diss., Kent State University, 1980, 74.

75. Richardson, interview, June 9, 1975.

76. Du Bois quoted in Baldwin, *Chicago's New Negroes,* 15.

77. "The New Negro Has No Fear," photograph, Schomburg Center for Research in Black Culture, New York Public Library, Astor, Lenox, and Tilden Foundations.

78. *Houston Informer,* July 16, 1927.

79. Dr. J. B. Covington, quoted in Greene, *Selling Black History,* 130.

80. Hill, "Racial and Radical," xii. On notions of black manhood that circulated during this era, see Martin Summers, *Manliness and Its Discontents: The Black Middle Class and the Transformation of Masculinity, 1900–1930* (Chapel Hill: University of North Carolina Press, 2004).

81. *Houston Informer,* December 1, 1923. The Houston and Harris County branch of the NAACP also remained involved in the Houston riot aftermath, even arguing with the national office that it was a local issue that should be investigated by the local branch; NAACP branch files, Houston.

82. Danielle L. McGuire, "'It Was Like All of Us Had Been Raped': Sexual Violence, Community Mobilization, and the African American Freedom Struggle," *Journal of American History* 91, no. 3 (December 2004): 907; Danielle L. McGuire, *At the Dark End of the Street: Black Women, Rape, and Resistance: A New History of the Civil Rights Movement from Rosa Parks to the Rise of Black Power* (New York: Vintage Books, 2001).

83. *Houston Informer,* June 14, 1919.

84. *1910 United States Federal Census,* Houston, Third Ward, Harris County, Texas Ward 3, Harris, Texas, p. 13B, Enumeration District 97.

85. Christia Adair, interview by Dorothy R. Robinson, April 25, 1977, Houston, TX, Christia Adair Collection, HMRC, MSS 109, box 4, folder 2. On White and Adair's work in the NAACP, see Merline Pitre, *In Struggle against Jim Crow: Lula B. White and the NAACP, 1900–1957* (College Station: Texas A&M University Press, 1999); Pruitt, *Other Great Migration,* 176–77.

86. *Houston Informer,* September 6, 1919.

87. *Houston Informer,* August 9, 1919.

88. See Bertram Wilbur Doyle, *The Etiquette of Race Relations in the South: A Study in Social Control* (New York: Shocken Books, 1971).

89. Lawrence Levine discusses animal and human tricksters in *Black Culture and Black Consciousness: Afro-American Folk Thought from Slavery to Freedom* (Oxford: Oxford University Press, 1977), 102–32. John W. Roberts also examines these figures' relationship to older African tricksters, as well as the folk figures that developed after the Civil War; see John W. Roberts, *From Trickster to Badman: The Black Folk Hero in Slavery and Freedom* (Philadelphia: University of Pennsylvania Press, 1989).

90. Robin D. G. Kelley describes this cultural history as part of "the age-old tradition of black rebellion" in *Race Rebels* (New York: Macmillan, 1994), 109.

91. *Houston Informer,* November 10, 1923; May 25, 1929.

92. *Houston Informer,* March 26, 1927.

93. Woods, *Development Arrested,* 30.

94. Scholar Craig Werner describes and remixes Ellison's notions of the blues impulse; see Craig Werner, *A Change Is Gonna Come: Music, Race & the Soul of America* (Ann Arbor: University of Michigan Press, 2006), 69.

95. Texas Alexander, *Texas Alexander Vol. 1* (1927), Document Records MBCD 2001, 1995.

96. *Houston Informer,* November 3, 1928; September 18, 1926.

97. Quoted in Werner, *A Change Is Gonna Come,* 68.

98. As scholar Christopher A. Waterman asserts, "[T]he process of urbanization itself involved the production of 'the rural' as a category. Culture products that reminded migrants of the rural life they left behind gave them 'a reminiscence of

their rural past combined with a sense of being above it.'" Christopher Waterman, "Race Music: Bo Chatmon, 'Corrine Corrina,' and the Excluded Middle," in *Music and the Racial Imagination,* ed. Ronald Radano and Philip V. Bohlman (Chicago: University of Chicago Press, 2000), 180.

99. On the significance of black space in the Jim Crow South, see Lewis, *In Their Own Interests.*

100. Sammy Price, interview, September 9, 1987, Sammy Price Collection, HMRC, OH 453; Writers' Program, *Houston: A History and Guide,* 106.

101. On the closing of red-light districts, see Kevin Mumford, *Interzones: Black/White Sex Districts in Chicago and New York in the Early Twentieth Century* (New York: Columbia University Press, 1997), 19–35.

102. Cornel West, "Black Strivings in a Twilight Civilization," in *The Cornel West Reader* (New York: Basic Civitas Books, 1999), 102.

103. Roger Wood, *Down in Houston: Bayou City Blues* (Austin: University of Texas Press, 2003), 85; Lightnin' Hopkins, "I First Come into Houston," *The Complete Prestige/Bluesville Recordings,* Prestige/Bluesville 4406, 1991; Alan Govenar, *Lightnin' Hopkins: His Life and Blues* (Chicago: Chicago Review Press, 2010), viii–ix; Govenar, *Texas Blues,* 42.

104. Larkin, interview, January 5, 1988.

105. Price, interview, September 9, 1987.

106. Govenar, *Texas Blues,* 245–46, 260; I. H. Smalley, interview by Louis Marchiafava, February 17, 1976, HMRC, MSS 349, box 1, folder 2; I. H. Smalley, interview by Bud Jackson, August 21, 1979, Houston, HMRC, MSS 349, box 1, folder 2.

107. Wood, *Down in Houston,* 138; Govenar, *Texas Blues,* 245–46.

108. *Houston Informer,* February 7, 1920.

109. Larkin, interview, January 5, 1988. Ironically, Booker T. Washington High eventually formed a band that went on to earn national acclaim.

110. Larkin, interview, January 5, 1988.

111. Thomas Brothers, *Louis Armstrong's New Orleans* (New York: W. W. Norton and Company, 2006), 20.

112. John Nova Lomax, "The Nickel: A Musical History of the Fifth Ward, Part 2," *Houston Press,* February 18, 2009.

113. Lomax, "The Nickel"; Sippie Wallace, "The Man I Love," *Complete Recorded Works, Vol. 2 (1925–1945),* Document Records 5400, 1995; Govenar, *Texas Blues,* 260–61.

114. I. H. Smalley, interview, February 17, 1976, HMRC; I. H. Smalley, interview August 21, 1979, HMRC.

115. Shelton et al., *Houston: Growth and Decline,* 71.

116. Greene, *Selling Black History,* 125–26; Shelton et al., *Houston: Growth and Decline,* 71

117. Paulette Williams Grant, interview by David Goldstein, June 30, 2008, Houston Oral History Project, Mayor Bill White Collection, HPL.

118. Writers' Program, *Houston: A History and Guide,* 172.

119. Greene, *Selling Black History,* 135–36.

120. Paul Kenneth Edwards, *The Southern Urban Negro as a Consumer* (College Park, MD: McGrath Publishing, 1932), 39. In his work on African American lumber workers in the Jim Crow South, historian William P. Jones argues that industrial wages gave black laborers the economic foundation to construct "schools, churches, and other institutional bases of what became southern proletarian societies." William P. Jones, *The Tribe of Black Ulysses: African American Lumber Workers in the Jim Crow South* (Urbana: University of Illinois Press, 2005), 8–9.

121. *Houston Informer*, November 1, 1919.

122. Greene, *Selling Black History*, 127–35.

123. "Population of the 100 Largest Urban Places: 1940," U.S. Census Bureau, June 15, 1998. Modern visitors experience an even heightened sense of urban sprawl. By the end of the twentieth century, Houston was the fourth-largest city in the United States, and had grown to 549 square miles. Approximately thirty-four hundred people occupied each square mile. By comparison, twenty-six thousand urban dwellers resided in each of New York City's 303 square miles; see Roni Sarig, *Third Coast: Outkast, Timbaland, and How Hip-Hop Became a Southern Thing* (Cambridge, MA: Da Capo Press, 2007), 36.

124. Pruitt, "For the Advancement of the Race," 441.

125. *Houston Informer*, May 28, 1921; Laura Rabinovitz, *For the Love of Pleasure: Women, Movies, and Culture in Turn-of-the Century Chicago* (New Brunswick, NJ: Rutgers University Press, 1998), 77.

126. *Houston Informer*, May 28, 1921.

127. Richardson, interview, June 9, 1975.

128. *Colonel Mayfield's Weekly*, December 31, 1921.

129. *Houston Informer*, June 14, 1919.

130. Bryant, interview, August 3, 2007.

131. O'Neta "Pink" Cavitt, interview by Nicolas Castellanos, May 22, 2010, HPL, OH GS 0013; Bryant, interview, August 3, 2007.

132. *Houston Informer*, August 25, 1923; January 7, 1928.

133. Michele Mitchell, *Righteous Propagation: African Americans and the Politics of Racial Destiny after Reconstruction* (Chapel Hill: University of North Carolina Press, 2004), 175. Urbanization and wage labor contributed to the growth of the black middle class; see Summers, *Manliness and Its Discontents*, 6–7.

134. *Houston Informer*, March 12, 1921; March 1, 1924

135. Mitchell, *Righteous Propagation*, 175; Baldwin, *Chicago's New Negroes*, 77–78.

136. Franklin Beauty School Collection, HMRC, RG D 44; *Houston Informer*, January 8, 1921.

137. Tiffany M. Gill, *Beauty Shop Politics: African American Women's Activism in the Beauty Industry* (Urbana: University of Illinois Press, 2010), 2. See also Davarian Baldwin's discussion of Madame C. J. Walker in *Chicago's New Negroes*, 53–90; and Kathy Peiss, *Hope in a Jar: the Making of America's Beauty Culture* (New York: Owl Books, 1999).

138. *Houston Informer*, May 1, 1920.

139. *Houston Informer,* November 28, 1925.

140. Booker T. Washington Annual, 1928, Yates Family and Antioch Baptist Church Collection, box 3, folder 5.

2. OLD WARDS, NEW NEIGHBORS

1. Inez Prejean Calegon, interview by the author, January 27, 2006, Houston, Texas, tape recording.

2. Janie (Gonzales) Tijerina, interview, October 16, 1978, HMRC, OH 234.

3. *1930 United States Federal Census;* Pruitt, "Advancement of the Race," 442; De León, *Ethnicity in the Sunbelt,* 6–8.

4. *New York Times,* April 22, 1927; May 6, 1927; May 14, 1927; July 8, 1927; *Houston Informer,* April 30, 1927; John M. Barry, *Rising Tide: The Great Mississippi Flood of 1927 and How It Changed America* (New York: Simon and Schuster, 2008).

5. Alan Lomax and John A. Lomax, *The Classic Louisiana Recordings: Cajun and Creole Music II, 1934–1937,* Rounder Records 611843, 1999.

6. Michael Tisserand, *Kingdom of Zydeco* (New York: Arcade Publishing, 1998), 77.

7. Illinois Jacquet, interview, June 1, 1990, tape recording, HMRC, MSS 403; *1920 United States Federal Census,* Police Jury Ward 5, Lafayette, Louisiana, p. 10B, Enumeration District 37; 1930 *United States Federal Census,* Houston, Harris County, Texas, p. 21B, Enumeration District 143.

8. Tisserand, *Kingdom of Zydeco,* 76.

9. A map of northeast Houston from 1946 shows that these railroad lines crossed Fifth Ward. Accessed April 9, 2008, through the Perry Castaneda Library at the University of Texas at Austin, http://www.lib.utexas.edu/maps/historical /houston_ne46.jpg.

10. *1930 United States Federal Census.*

11. Wood, *Down in Houston,* 157. Wood quoted these figures from Diana Kleiner, who writes for *The Handbook of Texas Online.*

12. Greene, *Selling Black History,* 136.

13. Of 227 households in that area, 109 contained at least one adult born in Louisiana; *1930 United States Federal Census,* p. 62B, Enumeration District 142. This includes records for districts 142 and 50 in Houston in the 1930 census. Specifically, I counted households on the streets of Whitty, Brackenridge, Gregg, Lelia, Brewster, Josephine, Des Chaumes, Staples, Binghurst, Adelia, and Delia. Although the streets between Collingsworth Street and Jensen Drive formed the core of the fledgling Frenchtown community, Louisianians of color lived throughout the ward. For example, on one stretch of Quitman Street, which lay just south of Frenchtown proper, 56 percent of households contained at least one Louisianian. Large numbers of families from Louisiana also resided on Lyons Avenue, New Orleans Street, and several other streets in Fifth Ward.

14. Gwendolyn Midlo Hall, *Africans in Colonial Louisiana: The Development of Afro-Creole Culture in the Eighteenth Century* (Baton Rouge: Louisiana State University Press, 1995), 267–68, 271.

15. Brasseaux et al., *Creoles of Color,* xii.

16. Lyle Saxon, Edward Dreyer, and Robert Tallant, *Gumbo Ya-Ya: A Collection of Louisiana Folk Tales* (Gretna, LA: Pelican Publishing, 1987), 430; Hall, *Africans in Colonial Louisiana,* 237.

17. *1850 United States Federal Census,* Western District, Lafayette, Louisiana, p. 254A; information regarding the birth and marriage of Louis Gustave Prejean found in the *Family Data Collection—Marriages,* online database (Provo, UT: Generations Network, 2001); the Prejeans were part of a wave of Canadian immigrants to arrive in colonial Louisiana in the late 1700s. After being expelled from Canada in 1755 for not taking an oath of loyalty to the British king, French settlers called Acadians, who lived in present-day Nova Scotia, made their way to Louisiana, where French colonists welcomed them. Denise Labrie details the Prejean family tree in *Houston Frenchtown,* vol. 4 of *The Creole Chronicles* (Natchitoches, LA: Louisiana Creole Heritage Center, Northwestern State University, 2002); Prejean Calegon, interview, January 27, 2006.

18. Mills, *Forgotten People,* 88.

19. Prejean Calegon, interview, January 27, 2006.

20. Kelley, *Right to Ride,* 59.

21. Historian Alecia Long discusses interracial sex and marriage in Louisiana in *The Great Southern Babylon: Sex, Race, and Respectability in New Orleans, 1865–1920* (Baton Rouge: Louisiana State University Press, 2004).

22. *1880 United States Federal Census,* 3rd Ward, Lafayette, Louisiana, p. 467B, Enumeration District 23.

23. See Kelley, *Right to Ride,* 70–76.

24. Keith Weldon Medley, *We as Freemen: Plessy v. Ferguson* (Gretna, LA: Pelican Publishing Company, 2003), 14.

25. Brief for Homer A. Plessy by Albion W. Tourgée, "File Copies of Briefs 1895 (October term, 1895)," reprinted in Otto H. Olsen, ed., *The Thin Disguise: Turning Point in Negro History; Plessy v. Ferguson; a Documentary Presentation, 1864–1896* (New York: Humanities Press, 1967), 81–85.

26. Prejean Calegon, interview, January 27, 2006.

27. *1880 United States Federal Census,* 3rd Ward, Lafayette, Louisiana, p. 467B, Enumeration District 23; Labrie, *Houston Frenchtown;* Prejean Calegon, interview, January 27, 2006.

28. Tisserand, *Kingdom of Zydeco,* 2–3.

29. *1920 United States Federal Census.*

30. Johnson, interview, January 2, 2006.

31. Mr. W. G. Bell, Local 325, 1030 Sherman St., Beaumont, August 4, 1936, Labor Movement in Texas Collection, Center for American History, University of Texas at Austin, folder 5.

32. Meeting, Ship Channel Progressive Committee, Houston, July 2, 1936, Labor Movement in Texas Collection, folder 7.

33. *Houston Informer,* June 13, 1925.

34. Caroline Stanwix, "Mississippi Love," printed in the *Houston Informer,* November 10, 1928.

35. Prejean Calegon, interview, January 27, 2006; Jacquet, interview, June 1, 1990.

36. Barry Shank, "The Political Agency of Musical Beauty," *American Quarterly* 63, no. 3 (September 2011): 832.

37. Tisserand, *Kingdom of Zydeco,* 44–45.

38. Tisserand, *Kingdom of Zydeco,* 4–5.

39. Tisserand, *Kingdom of Zydeco,* 4–5; Alan Lomax's recordings of la-la can be heard on *Cajun and Creole Music, Vol. 2.* See also Barry Jean Ancelet, "Zydeco/Zarico: Beans, Blues and Beyond," *Black Music Research Journal* 8, no. 1 (1988): 33–49.

40. Tisserand, *Kingdom of Zydeco,* 25–26.

41. Prejean Calegon, interview, January 27, 2006.

42. Tisserand, *Kingdom of Zydeco,* 77–78.

43. Writers' Program, *Houston: A History and Guide,* 173.

44. De León, *Ethnicity in the Sunbelt,* 6.

45. Guérin-Gonzales, *Mexican Workers and American Dreams,* 1.

46. See Innis-Jiménez, *Steel Barrio.*

47. *1920 United States Federal Census.*

48. Guadalupe San Miguel, *Brown, Not White: School Integration and the Chicano Movement in Houston* (College Station: Texas A&M University Press, 2001), 5. Over time, Magnolia Park spread westward, while Segundo Barrio spread farther to the east. The communities eventually fused, with locals calling the entire area the "east side."

49. De León, *Ethnicity in the Sunbelt,* 6–8; Shelton et al., *Houston: Growth and Decline,* 10; Beeth and Wintz, *Black Dixie,* 89.

50. De León, *Ethnicity in the Sunbelt,* 6–8.

51. Foley, *Quest for Equality,* 10–11; Foley, *White Scourge,* 61.

52. See Herman L. Bennett, *Africans in Colonial Mexico: Absolutism, Christianity, and Afro-Creole Consciousness, 1570–1640* (Bloomington: Indiana University Press, 2003), 18–27.

53. Foley, *Quest for Equality,* 10–11.

54. Ruben Flores, *Backroads Pragmatists: Mexico's Melting Pot and Civil Rights in the United States* (Philadelphia: University of Pennsylvania Press, 2014). See also Molina, *How Race Is Made,* 63.

55. *1920 United States Federal Census,* Houston, Harris County.

56. Olmsted, *A Journey through Texas,* 454–56.

57. Foley, *White Scourge,* 19.

58. Olmsted, *A Journey through Texas,* 427.

59. Description taken from an interview with Mrs. Felix Morales, February 5, 1979, HMRC, OH 246.

60. David Montejano, *Anglos and Mexicans in the Making of Texas, 1836–1986* (Austin: University of Texas Press, 1987), 4–5, 160–61.

61. Benjamin Johnson, *Revolution in Texas: How a Forgotten Rebellion and Its Bloody Suppression Turned Mexicans into Americans* (New Haven, CT: Yale University Press, 2005); James Sandos, *Rebellion in the Borderlands: Anarchism and the Plan of San Diego, 1904–1923* (Norman: University of Oklahoma Press, 1992).

62. Manuel Peña, *Música Tejana: The Cultural Economy of Artistic Transformation* (College Station: Texas A&M Press, 1999), 20, 38.

63. Peña, *Música Tejana,* 73–74.

64. Américo Paredes, *With His Pistol in His Hand* (Austin: University of Texas Press, 1958), 155; Peña, *Música Tejana,* 75; Johnson, *Revolution in Texas,* 22.

65. Thomas H. Kreneck, *Mexican American Odyssey: Felix Tijerina, Entrepreneur and Civic Leader, 1905–1965* (College Station: Texas A&M University Press, 2001), 31.

66. Carmen Cortés, interview by Tom Kreneck, December 16, 1983, HMRC, OH 313.

67. Ralph and Mary Villagomez, interview, April 16, 1979, HMRC, MSS 367, OH 255.

68. Estela Gómez Reyes, interview by Tom Kreneck, June 15, 1979, OH 261.

69. R. and M. Villagomez, interview, April 16, 1979.

70. R. and M. Villagomez, interview, April 16, 1979. See also Emma Pérez, *The Decolonial Imaginary: Writing Chicanas into History* (Bloomington: Indiana University Press, 1999), 83–84.

71. Kreneck, *Mexican-American Odyssey,* 40.

72. Kreneck, *Mexican-American Odyssey,* 59–60.

73. Frank and Ventura Alonzo, interview, February 18, 1982, HMRC, MSS 202.

74. Peña, *Música Tejana,* 44–46, 92; Manuel Peña, *The Texas-Mexican Conjunto: History of a Working-Class Music* (Austin: University of Texas Press, 1985).

75. Gary Hartman, "The Roots Run Deep: An Overview of Texas Music History," in *The Roots of Texas Music,* ed. Lawrence Clayton and Joe W. Specht (College Station: Texas A&M University Press, 2003), 9; F. and V. Alonzo, interview, February 18, 1982; Rosa Linda Alonzo Saez, "Frank and Ventura Alonzo: Houston Big Band Leaders," April 1982, HMRC, MSS 202, folder 1, box 1.

76. F. and V. Alonzo, interview, February 18, 1982; Lydia Mendoza, interview, October 16, 1978, HMRC, Lydia Mendoza Collection, MSS 123, box 2; Chris Strachwitz with James Nicolopulos, *Lydia Mendoza: A Family Autobiography* (Houston: Arte Público, 1993), 11. See also Yolanda Broyles-Gonzalez, *Lydia Mendoza's Life in Music / La Historia de Lydia Mendoza* (New York: Oxford University Press, 2006).

77. Socorro Sarabia, interview, August 28, 1980, HMRC, OH 245; Alfredo Sarabia, interview, February 16, 1979, HMRC, OH 245; Mrs. Felix Morales, interview, February 5, 1979, HMRC, OH 246.

1. Ralph and Mary Villagomez, interview, April 16, 1979.
2. *Houston Post,* April 17, 1922.
3. Gross, "Caucasian Cloak," 342.
4. *Houston Post,* April 8, 1922. On Anglo efforts to Americanize Mexican immigrants, see Sánchez, *Becoming Mexican American,* 87–107.
5. San Miguel, *Brown, Not White,* 28–30.
6. Catalina Gómez Sandoval, interview by Tom Kreneck and Emma Pérez, February 3, 1989, HMRC, OH 377.
7. Cortés, interview, December 16, 1983.
8. Reyes, interview, February 5, 1988.
9. San Miguel, *Brown, Not White,* 21.
10. San Miguel, *Brown, Not White,* 23.
11. San Miguel, *Brown, Not White,* 26.
12. Elliott Young, "Red Men, Pocahontas, and George Washington: Harmonizing Race Relations in Laredo at the Turn of the Century," *Western Historical Quarterly* 29, no. 1 (Spring 1998): 71.
13. Adair, interview, April 25, 1977, p. 24.
14. For a history of streetcar boycotts at the turn of the twentieth century, see Kelley, *Right to Ride.*
15. Sorelle, "'Darker Side of Heaven,'" 26–29.
16. Testimony of Officer George Patton, Citizens Committee, 278–81; testimony of B. M. Spiegel, Citizens Committee, 6–12; testimony of Ed Stoermer, Citizens Committee; *Houston Chronicle,* August 20, 1917.
17. Gerald Horne, *Black and Brown: African Americans and the Mexican Revolution, 1910–1920* (New York and London: New York University Press, 2005), 87.
18. Horne, *Black and Brown,* 13–32, 87.
19. *Houston Informer,* February 23, 1924.
20. *Houston Informer,* November 1, 1919.
21. W. L. Davis and E. O. Smith, "Why Not?" *Western Star,* May 10, 1918. Reprinted in the papers of the NAACP, Houston branch. The reference to black fidelity echoes Booker T. Washington's "Atlanta Compromise" speech at the Cotton States and International Exposition on September 18, 1895. Washington told the crowd, "As we have proved our loyalty to you in the past, in nursing your children, watching the sick-bed of your mothers and fathers . . . so in the future, in our humble way, we shall stand by you with a devotion that no foreigner can approach, ready to lay down our lives, if need be, in defense of yours, interlacing our industrial, commercial, civil, and religious lives with yours in a way that shall make the interests of both races one." Washington's speech can be found in Quintard Taylor, ed., *From Timbuktu to Katrina: Sources in African-American History,* vol. 1 (Boston: Thomson Wadsworth, 2007), 168–70.
22. E. O. Smith to Walter White, June 10, 1918, NAACP branch files, Houston.

23. *1880 United States Federal Census; 1920 United States Federal Census,* Houston, Harris County, Texas.

24. Cheryl Greenberg, *Troubling the Waters: Black-Jewish Relations in the American Century* (Princeton, NJ: Princeton University Press, 2006), 15, 27.

25. The first Houston synagogue, the Hebrew Congregation Beth Israel, was built in 1859. Later known as Congregation Beth Israel, it was also the first in Texas. Elaine H. Maas, "Jews," in *The Ethnic Groups of Houston,* ed. Fred R. von der Mehden (Houston: Rice University Press, 1984), 142–44.

26. Guglielmo, *White on Arrival,* 59; Jacobson, *Whiteness of a Different Color,* 93.

27. *Houston Informer,* December 11, 1926.

28. Historians of race formation have debated the whiteness of Italians and other immigrant groups in the United States in the first decades of the twentieth century. Thomas Guglielmo distinguishes between color and race, arguing that from the 1880s through 1920s, Italians considered themselves part of an Italian race, and sometimes faced forms of discrimination based on racial distinction. At the same time, he asserts that Italians enjoyed white *color* status in the eyes of the law. According to Guglielmo, Italian immigrants were "largely accepted as white by the widest variety of people and institutions." From the 1930s onward, Italians shifted to a racial identity as white. Guglielmo, *White on Arrival,* 6. David Roediger argues that the social exclusion of immigrants points to the fact that their whiteness was not always guaranteed. He posits that before World War II, immigrants could best be described as "inbetween peoples." They existed between "nonwhiteness and full inclusion as whites." Roediger, *Working toward Whiteness,* 12–13.

29. Prejean Calegon, interview, January 27, 2006.

30. Roberto Treviño, *The Church in the Barrio: Mexican American Ethno-Catholicism in Houston* (Chapel Hill: University of North Carolina Press, 2006), 33.

31. *1920 United States Federal Census,* Houston, Harris County, TX, district 92, sheet 11.

32. *1930 United States Federal Census,* Houston, Harris County, TX. The Aguirre and Bourgeois families appear in census enumeration district 101–50, sheet 64A. The Butcher and Alisi families can be found in the same district on sheet 102A.

33. *1920 United States Federal Census,* Independence Heights, Harris County, Texas, pp. 1A–8A.

34. *Colonel Mayfield's Weekly,* April 28, 1923.

35. Chalmers, *Hooded Americanism,* 41.

36. *Colonel Mayfield's Weekly,* April 1, 1922.

37. *Houston Informer,* November 3, 1923; June 15, 1929.

38. Richardson, interview, June 9, 1975. On the Klan's attitude toward immigrant groups who were not Anglo or Scandinavian, see Alexander, *Ku Klux Klan in the Southwest,* 15–16.

39. *Colonel Mayfield's Weekly,* December 31, 1921.

40. *Houston Informer,* June 7, 1919.

41. *Houston Post,* April 21, 1922, 6.

42. Johnson, interview, January 2, 2006; Mary (Berry) Strawder and Barbara (Berry) Johnson, interview by the author, June 21, 2013, Humble, TX.

43. Johnson, interview, January 2, 2006; Kreneck, *Mexican American Odyssey,* 39.

44. *Houston Informer,* February 2, 1924.

45. *Houston Informer,* October 3, 1925.

46. *Houston Informer,* December 3, 1927.

47. *Houston Post,* June 19, 1922.

48. Kreneck, *Mexican American Odyssey,* 47.

49. Treviño, *Church in the Barrio,* 43.

50. Treviño, *Church in the Barrio,* 23–46.

51. Price, interview, August 7, 1987.

52. Tisserand, *Kingdom of Zydeco,* 14.

53. Jacquet, interview, June 1, 1990; R. and M. Villagomez, interview, April 16, 1979; Reyes, interview, June 15, 1979; Mendoza, interview, October 16, 1978.

54. Strawder, interview, January 3, 2006.

55. Albert J. Raboteau, *A Fire in the Bones: Reflections on African-American Religious History* (Boston: Beacon Press, 1995), 127.

56. Over time, ethnic Mexicans came to form the majority of parishioners at Immaculate Conception. By 2014, the church held services in Spanish and English, and offered Rosaries to Our Lady of Guadalupe. R. and M. Villagomez, interview, April 16, 1979; Kreneck, *Mexican American Odyssey,* 44. The church website for Immaculate Conception shows its current acknowledgment of the large ethnic Mexican population (accessed November 7, 2014, http://immaculateconception-houston.org/).

57. *Colonel Mayfield's Weekly,* March 11, 1922; March 25, 1922.

58. *Colonel Mayfield's Weekly,* February 25, 1922.

59. Timothy B. Tyson, *Radio Free Dixie: Robert F. Williams and the Roots of Black Power* (Chapel Hill: University of North Carolina Press, 1999), 34.

60. Patricia Bernstein, *The First Waco Horror: The Lynching of Jesse Washington and the Rise of the NAACP* (College Station: Texas A&M University Press, 2006); James M. SoRelle, "The 'Waco Horror': The Lynching of Jesse Washington," *Southwestern Historical Quarterly* 86 (April 1983): 517–36. See also Grace Elizabeth Hale's discussion of the lynching of Washington in *Making Whiteness,* 215–26.

61. *Colonel Mayfield's Weekly,* May 26, 1923.

62. Undated *Houston Press* article from 1926, NAACP branch files, Houston; *Houston Informer,* September 18, 1926.

63. The *California Voice* credited the Houston branch with winning a "spectacular fight" and mentioned that the local branch "declared it could and would finance the case itself." Likewise, the *Washington Eagle* told its readers that the Houston Branch of the NAACP refused to accept money from the national office. *California Voice,* October 1, 1926; *Washington Eagle,* October 6, 1926; NAACP branch files, Houston; *Houston Informer,* September 18, 1926.

64. *Houston Informer,* February 19, 1921.

65. *Houston Informer,* November 1, 1919.

66. *1920 United States Federal Census.*

67. Jacquet, interview, June 1, 1990. Other Catholics recalled the presence of white people at mass and other church events. Prejean Calegon, interview, January 27, 2006; Strawder, interview, January 3, 2006.

68. R. and M. Villagomez, interview, April 16, 1979; Kreneck, *Mexican American Odyssey,* 44.

69. R. and M. Villagomez, interview, April 16, 1979.

70. Labrie, *Houston Frenchtown,* 2; Prejean Calegon, interview, January 27, 2006.

71. Writers' Program, *Houston: History and Guide,* 173; Treviño, *Church in the Barrio,* 33. The Basilica of Sainte-Anne-de-Beaupré is a pilgrimage site in Québec.

72. Prejean Calegon, interview, January 27, 2006.

73. John Castillo, interview, December 16, 1985, HMRC, OH 328.

4. "WE WERE TOO WHITE TO BE BLACK AND TOO BLACK TO BE WHITE"

1. Strawder, interview, January 3, 2006.

2. Arthé A. Anthony offers this definition of discontinuous passing; see Anthony, "'Lost Boundaries,'" 307.

3. Haney-López, *White by Law,* 12.

4. Lightnin' Washington, "My Pretty Little Yellow Gal," *Black Texicans: Balladeers & Songsters,* Rounder 611821, 1999.

5. According to legal scholar Ariela Gross, "A community struggling to establish itself might be more likely to allow people to live on the margins of social orders that were still emerging." Gross, *What Blood Won't Tell,* 34.

6. Trudier Harris, "'The Yellow Rose of Texas': A Different Cultural View," *Callaloo* 20, no. 1 (Winter 1997): 8–19.

7. Lucy Lewis and Cinto Lewis, Work Projects Administration, *Slave Narratives: A Folk History of Slavery in the United States from Interviews with Former Slaves,* vol. 16, *Texas Narratives, Part 3.* E-book. http://www.gutenberg.org/files/35380/35380-h/35380-h.html#lucy-lewis.

8. Johnson, interview, January 2, 2006.

9. Donaville Broussard, *Born in Slavery: Slave Narratives from the Federal Writers' Project, 1936–1938,* 151–53; Christia Adair, interview, HMRC, MSS 109, box 4, folder 2, p. 4.

10. Emily Clark, *The Strange History of the American Quadroon: Free Women of Color in the Revolutionary Atlantic World* (Chapel Hill: University of North Carolina Press, 2013), 164–65; Deborah Gray White, *Ar'n't I a Woman: Female Slaves in the Plantation South* (New York: W. W. Norton and Company, 1985), 29, 37.

11. Kia Lilly Caldwell, "'Look at Her Hair': The Body Politics of Black Womanhood in Brazil," *Transforming Anthropology* 11, no. 2 (July 2003): 21.

12. *St. Louis Blues*, DVD, directed by Dudley Murphey (1929; Kino Video, 2001); *Cabin in the Sky*, DVD, directed by Vincent Minnelli (1943; Warner Home Video, 2006).

13. Johnson, interview, January 2, 2006.

14. Sherman E. Pyatt and Alan Johns, *A Dictionary and Catalog of African American Folklife of the South* (Westport, CT: Greenwood Press, 1999), 55.

15. Texas Alexander, "Evil Woman Blues," *Texas Alexander Vol. 1*; Johnson, interview, January 2, 2006.

16. Naomi Polk Collection, HMRC, MSS 270; Sippie Wallace, "I'm So Glad I'm Brownskin," *Sippie Wallace Vol. 1 (1923–1925)*, Document Records 5399, 1995.

17. *Houston Informer*, February 16, 1924.

18. *Zora Neale Hurston: Jump at the Sun*, directed by Sam Pollard (DVD, San Francisco: California Newsreel, 2008); Zora Neale Hurston, *Jonah's Gourd Vine* (1934; reprint, New York: Harper Perennial Modern Classics, 2008); Zora Neale Hurston, *Their Eyes Were Watching God* (1937; reprint, New York: Harper Perennial Classics, 1998).

19. Quoted in William Van Deburg, *Modern Black Nationalism: From Marcus Garvey to Louis Farrakhan* (New York: NYU Press, 1997), 36.

20. A. D. Salazar, interview by Tom Kreneck, July 2, 1981, HMRC, OH 365.

21. Foley, *Quest for Equality*, 18.

22. Carmen Cortés, interview, May 2, 1989, HMRC, OH 313.

23. Cortés, interview, December 16, 1983.

24. Cortés, interview, December 16, 1983; Cortés, interview, May 2, 1989.

25. Estela Gómez Reyes, interviews, June 8, 1979, and June 15, 1979, HMRC, OH 261; Pérez, *The Decolonial Imaginary*, 84–88.

26. See Benjamin Márquez, *LULAC: The Evolution of a Mexican American Political Organization* (Austin: University of Texas Press, 1993); and Foley, *Quest for Equality*, 34.

27. Tomás A. Garza, "LULAC A Future Power," *LULAC News* 1, no. 7 (February 1932).

28. "Are Texas-Mexicans Americans?" *LULAC News* 1, no. 9 (April 1932).

29. Rodolfo A. De La Garza, "Who Are You," *LULAC News* 2, no. 1 (September 1932); Rodolfo A. De La Garza, "Our School Children," *LULAC News* 2, no. 3 (November 1932).

30. B. Márquez, *LULAC*, 32–33; Foley, *White Scourge*, 210.

31. *LULAC News* 4, no. 1 (February 1937); *LULAC News* 4, no. 2 (March 1937).

32. Benjamin, "Progressivism Meets Jim Crow," 36–38.

33. B. Márquez, *LULAC*, 33.

34. Denton's story appears briefly in Thomas C. Mackey, "Thelma Denton and Associates: Houston's Red Light Reservation and a Question of Jim Crow," *Houston Review* 14, no. 3 (1992): 139–52; *Charter of the City of Houston and General Ordinances, 1910* (Houston: Coyle and Co., 1910), 124–27; City Council Meeting Minutes, Houston, March 30, 1908, book P, 290–94, Texas and Local History Room, HPL.

35. Literary and cinematic portrayals of racial passing often focus on people of African descent who have migrated to new places in the 1930s and 1940s. In *Veiled Aristocrats,* filmmaker Oscar Micheaux's 1932 exploration of passing, siblings John and Rena Walden live as white people only after they leave their hometown and move to South Carolina. Likewise, the title character of the film *Pinky,* which premiered seventeen years after *Veiled Aristocrats,* passes for a white woman when she leaves her small southern town to attend school in the North. *Veiled Aristocrats,* DVD, directed by Oscar Micheaux (Phoenix: Grapevine Video, 1932); *Pinky* (1949), DVD, directed by Elia Kazan (Beverly Hills, CA: Twentieth Century-Fox, 2005).

36. *Houston Informer,* March 1, 1924.

37. Prejean Calegon, interview, January 27, 2006.

38. Quote taken from Hale, *Making Whiteness,* 195.

39. Langston Hughes, "Jim Crow Texas," *New York Post,* December 13, 1963.

40. See Eidsheim, "Marian Anderson and 'Sonic Blackness.'"

41. Catalina Gómez Sandoval, interview by Tom Kreneck and Emma Pérez, February 3, 1989, HMRC, OH 377.

42. Reyes, interview, February 5, 1988.

43. Tijerina, interview, October 16, 1978; *Houston Informer,* December 14, 1929.

44. *Veiled Aristocrats,* 1932; *Showboat* (1936), DVD, directed by James Whale, Universal Studios (ClassicLine Brazil, 2003); *Imitation of Life,* directed by John M. Stahl (Universal City, CA: Universal Studios, 1936); *Pinky,* 1949.

45. *Houston Informer,* March 1, 1924; March 1, 1921.

46. Strawder, interview, January 3, 2006.

47. *Houston Informer,* October 30, 1926; July 23, 1927.

48. Langston Hughes, "Brothers," in *Jim Crow's Last Stand* (1943), 15; Langston Hughes, "Negro," transcripts found in Langston Hughes collection (microfilm), Schomburg Center for Research in Black Culture, New York Public Library (NYPL).

49. Both journal articles are located in the Nicolas Guillen Scrapbook (microfilm). See the poems "La canción del bongó" and "Pequeña oda a un negro boxeador cubano," Schomburg Center, NYPL. See also Frank Guridy's discussion of the Afro-diasporic visions of Hughes and Guillen in *Forging Diaspora,* 107–50.

50. Dorothy H. Bayen to Arthur Schomburg, February 22, 1938; L. Hollingsworth Wood to Arthur Schomburg, May 17, 1932; Carlton A. Bertrand to Arthur Schomburg, November 12, 1935; letter (dated April 12, 1933) that discusses Schomburg's trip, which he called "My Trip to Cuba in Quest of Negro Books"; R. G. Bundy to Arthur Schomburg, January 6, 1936 (discusses the Salem A.M.E. church's Negro History Program); Louis Austin, president of the Universal Ethiopian Students Association, to Arthur Schomburg, September 16, 1935; invitation to the "Giftday for the Benefit of the Ethiopian Refugees," June 1937, Arthur A. Schomburg Papers (microfilm), Schomburg Center, NYPL.

51. Louis Fremont Baldwin to Arthur Schomburg, March 23, 1932, Arthur A. Schomburg Papers (microfilm), Schomburg Center, NYPL.

52. Rev. W. P. Stanley, "Ethiopia's Place in the World's History," *Houston Informer*, March 31, 1923.

53. Hale, *Making Whiteness*, 40.

54. Prejean Calegon, interview, January 27, 2006. The account from Mary Rose Berry (Penn) was taken from the same interview.

55. Allyson Hobbs explores the grief and isolation experienced by people of African descent who spent their lives passing for white in *A Chosen Exile: A History of Passing in American Life* (Cambridge, MA: Harvard University Press, 2014).

56. *Houston Informer*, June 13, 1925.

57. Prejean Calegon, interview, January 27, 2006.

58. *1930 United States Federal Census,* Houston, Harris County, Texas, p. 29A, Enumeration District 50; *1920 United States Federal Census,* St. Landry, Louisiana, p. 4B, Enumeration District 87.

59. Tijerina, interview, October 16, 1978.

60. Labor Movement in Texas Collection, International Longshoreman's Association (henceforth ILA), folder 5; Meeting, Local 1350, ILA Galveston (Banana Local), July 17, 1936, Labor Movement in Texas Collection, folder 7.

61. Rebecca Montes, "Working for American Rights: Black, White, and Mexican American Dockworkers during the Great Depression," in *Sunbelt Revolution: The Historical Progression of the Civil Rights Struggle in the Gulf South,* ed. Samuel C. Hyde, Jr. (Gainesville: University Press of Florida, 2003), 115.

62. F. N. Hunter, interview, June 30, 1936, Labor Movement in Texas Collection, folder 7.

63. Ralph Landgrebe, President, White Deep Sea Local, interview, 1273, ILA, June 30, 1936, Labor Movement in Texas Collection, folder 7.

64. *Texas City Times,* 1919, p. 35 (found in the Labor Movement in Texas Collection, folder 5.)

65. Labor Movement in Texas Collection, box 2e304, folder 13.

66. L. M. Balderach and Tome Hency, interview, July 15, 1936, Labor Movement in Texas Collection, folder 7.

67. Labor Movement in Texas Collection, ILA, folder 5; meeting, Local 1350, ILA Galveston (Banana Local), July 17, 1936, Labor Movement in Texas Collection, folder 7.

68. Three classes of longshoremen organized through the ILA. Deep-sea longshoremen handled cargo from foreign ships, while coastwise workers handled cargo from the United States. A third group, warehouse workers, handled freight going between cars and warehouses. Each type of longshoreman earned different pay, with deep-sea longshoremen earning the most and warehouse longshoremen earning the least. A deep-sea longshoreman usually earned at least 80 cents an hour in the 1930s, while a coastwise earned 75 cents an hour, and a warehouse earned 50 cents. Mr. Nelson and Mr. Curtis, Colored Deep Sea Local, 872, Houston, July 1, 1936; Ralph Landgrebe, President, White Deep Sea Local, 1273, ILA, June 30, 1936, Labor Movement in Texas Collection, folder 7.

69. Montes, "Working for American Rights," 122.

70. Greene, *Selling Black History*, 123.

71. *Houston Informer*, August 10, 1929.

72. Treviño, *Church in the Barrio*, 25–26; De León, *Ethnicity in the Sunbelt*, 47.

73. Montes, "Working for American Rights," 122.

74. Reyes, interview, June 8, 1979; Melesio Gómez Family Collection, HMRC, MSS 135, box 1, folder 19.

75. Cortés, interview, December 16, 1983; Reyes, interview, February 5, 1988.

76. The YWCA's sponsorship was significant, since ethnic Mexicans often had trouble renting space. "They thought [that when] Mexican people get together, there was fights, there was a knifing . . . or there was disorder," recalled Estela Gómez Reyes. Reyes, interview, June 8, 1979; Cortés, interview, December 16, 1983.

77. As historian Elliott Young shows in his work on celebrations and pageants in Laredo at the turn of the century, these cultural events played a significant role in establishing ties between Anglos and ethnic Mexicans in Texas. Young, "Red Men, Pocahontas, and George Washington," 48–85.

78. The undated article can be found in a 1930s scrapbook in the Melesio Gómez Family Collection, HMRC, MSS 135, box 1, folder 18.

79. Jacobson, *Whiteness of a Different Color*, 96.

80. See B. Márquez, *LULAC*.

81. *LULAC News* 2, no. 4 (December 1932).

82. Tijerina, interview, October 16, 1978.

83. Kreneck, *Mexican American Odyssey*, 53, 62–63.

84. The description of tortillas is part of an undated article, "Tortilla Code Is Voted in Spanish," found in a scrapbook in the Melesio Gómez Family Collection, HMRC, MSS 135, box 1, folder 18.

85. "Tortilla Code," Melesio Gómez Family Collection; Cortés, interview, December 16, 1983; *Houston Chronicle*, May 1933.

86. Reyes, interview, June 8, 1979.

87. Reyes, interview, June 8, 1979; Gómez Family Collection, box 1, folder 19; and Pérez, *Decolonial Imaginary*, 88–90.

88. Reyes, interview, February 5, 1988.

5. "ALL AMERICA DANCES TO IT"

An earlier version of this chapter was published as "Jazz, Migration, and Community in Interwar Houston," *Journal of the West* 53, no. 3 (Summer 2014): 42–50.

1. Larkin, interview, January 5, 1988; Jacquet, interview, June 1, 1990.

2. On the popularity of swing among diverse Americans, see David W. Stowe, *Swing Changes: Big-Band Jazz in New Deal America* (Cambridge, MA: Harvard University Press, 1996); Lewis A. Erenberg, *Swingin' the Dream: Big Band Jazz and the Rebirth of American Culture* (Chicago: University of Chicago Press, 1998); and Anthony Macías, *Mexican American Mojo: Popular Music, Dance, and Urban Culture in Los Angeles, 1935–1968* (Durham, NC: Duke University Press, 2008).

3. Jacquet, interview, June 1, 1990. By 1930, his older brothers Linton and Jewel both worked professionally as musicians in an orchestra. *1930 United States Federal Census,* Houston, Harris County, Texas, p. 21B, Enumeration District 143.

4. On the creation of the three high schools in the 1920s, see Benjamin, "Progressivism Meets Jim Crow," 30–39.

5. Rev. Jack Yates Family and Antioch Baptist Church Collection, HMRC, MSS 281, box 3, folder 7.

6. Williams, interview, October 25, 1989; Jacquet, interview, June 1, 1990.

7. Jacquet, interview, June 1, 1990.

8. Williams, interview, October 25, 1989; Jacquet, interview, June 1, 1990; Sonny Boy Franklin, interview by Louis Marchiafava, June 17, 1975, HMRC, MSS 350.

9. Historian Joel Dinerstein demonstrates how the sounds of urban life and labor influenced black music and dance during the interwar era in *Swinging the Machine: Modernity, Technology, and African American Culture between the World Wars* (Amherst: University of Massachusetts Press, 2003).

10. Arnett Cobb, interview, February 11, 1988, HMRC, MS 322.

11. Dugar's senior year scrapbook from 1933 can be found in the C. F. Hortense Smith Collection, The African American Library at the Gregory School, Houston Public Library, Houston, MSS 0003, box 1, folder 7.

12. Franklin, interview, June 17, 1975.

13. Franklin, interview, June 17, 1975; Cobb, interview, February 11, 1988; Jacquet, interview, June 1, 1990.

14. Johnson, interview, January 2, 2006.

15. Jacquet, interview, June 1, 1990.

16. Brothers, *Louis Armstrong's New Orleans,* 21.

17. Jacquet, interview, June 1, 1990.

18. Rev. Jack Yates Family and Antioch Baptist Church Collection, HMRC.

19. *Houston Informer,* February 7, 1920.

20. *Houston Informer,* May 4, 1929.

21. "American Jazz Defeats Germans," *Houston Informer,* reprinted from the Associated Negro Press, 1921. For more on the activities of James Reese Europe, see David Gilbert, "Clef Club Inc.: James Reese Europe and New York's Musical Marketplace," *Journal of Popular Music Studies* 24, no. 4 (December 2012): 430–56.

22. Cobb, interview, February 11, 1988; Williams, interview, October 25, 1989.

23. Jacquet, interview, June 1, 1990; Larkin, interview, January 5, 1988.

24. Larkin, interview, January 5, 1988.

25. Smalley, interview, February 17, 1976.

26. Cobb, interview, February 11, 1988.

27. Data on longshoremen's wages were contained in a 1932–33 study pertaining to the standard of living for dockworkers in Houston. Labor Movement in Texas Collection, box 2E305, folder 8.

28. Franklin, interview, June 17, 1975; Cobb, interview, February 11, 1988; Williams, interview, October 25, 1989.

29. Smalley, interview, February 17, 1976.

30. Party invitations found in Helen G. Perry Collection, HMRC, box 1, folder 8; Franklin Beauty School Collection, HMRC, RG D44, box 35, folder 14; Cobb, interview, February 11, 1988.

31. Preston Lauterbach, *The Chitlin' Circuit and the Road to Rock 'n' Roll* (New York: W. W. Norton & Company, 2011), 96.

32. Wood, *Down in Houston,* 75.

33. Wood, *Down in Houston,* 89.

34. Larkin, interview, January 5, 1988.

35. *The March of Time,* a weekly newsreel series in the United States, documented Huddie Ledbetter's performances in 1935 and told the story of how John Lomax first saw him at Angola State Prison in Louisiana. See also Wolfe, *Life and Legend of Leadbelly.*

36. Pruitt, *Other Great Migration,* 277.

37. Strawder, interview, January 3, 2006; Prejean Calegon, interview, January 27, 2006.

38. Ed Gerlach, interview by Louis J. Marchiafava and Charles Stephenson, October 18, 1989, Houston Oral History Project, OH 474; Ed Gerlach Collection, HMRC, MSS 0388;

39. Gerlach, interview, October 18, 1989; Larkin, interview, January 5, 1988.

40. Gerlach, interview, October 18, 1989.

41. Charles R. Townsend, *San Antonio Rose: The Life and Music of Bob Wills* (Urbana: University of Illinois Press, 1976), 4; Denize Springer, "'Ahhhh-HA!': Discovering Bob Wills," *San Francisco State News,* February 23, 2005.

42. Bob Wills, "T for Texas," *Bob Wills and His Texas Playboys 1932–1947,* Frémeaux FA 164, 2002.

43. For more on slumming, see Mumford, *Interzones.*

44. *Colonel Mayfield's Weekly,* December 3, 1921; December 17, 1921.

45. *Houston Informer,* May 21, 1921.

46. Williams, interview, October 25, 1989; Price, interview, August 7, 1987; Franklin, interview, June 17, 1975.

47. David E. Whisnant, *All That Is Native and Fine: The Politics of Culture in an American Region* (1983; reprint, Chapel Hill: University of North Carolina Press, 2009), 183–84. See also Karl Hagstrom Miller, *Segregating Sound: Inventing Folk and Pop Music in the Age of Jim Crow* (Durham, NC: Duke University Press, 2010), 211.

48. Whisnant, *All That Is Native and Fine,* 183. In the early years of WSM, DeFord Bailey was the only black performer the station allowed.

49. Williams, interview, October 25, 1989; Smalley, interview, February 17, 1976.

50. On Los Angeles, see Sánchez, *Becoming Mexican American,* 171–87. Macías discusses interracial swing bands in Los Angeles high schools in *Mexican American Mojo,* 27–32.

51. Albert Calderon, Rey Romero, Bobby Severson, and Artie Villaseñor, interview by the author, June 22, 2013, Houston.

52. Manuel Peña, *The Mexican American Orquesta: Music, Culture, and the Dialectic of Conflict* (Austin: University of Texas Press, 1999), 1.

53. Lydia Mendoza, interview, Lydia Mendoza Collection, HMRC, MSS 123, box 2; Hartman, "Roots Run Deep," 10.

54. Peña, *Mexican American Orquesta*, 127–28.

55. F. and V. Alonzo, interview, February 18, 1982; Rosa Linda Alonzo Saez, "Frank and Ventura Alonzo: Houston Big Band Leaders," April 1982, HMRC, MSS 202, folder 1, box 1.

56. Peña, *Música Tejana*, 131.

57. F. and V. Alonzo, interview, February 18, 1982. On Ventura Alonzo and gender, see Deborah R. Vargas, *Dissonant Divas in Chicana Music: The Limits of La Onda* (Minneapolis: University of Minnesota Press, 2012), 108–41.

58. Sánchez, *Becoming Mexican American*, 186; see also B. Márquez, *LULAC*.

59. Peña, *Mexican American Orquesta*, 25, 2. Meanwhile, working-class rural Tejanos remained committed to conjunto or ranchera. With fewer instruments, conjunto could be played almost anywhere for considerably less money than orquesta. Musicians who played conjunto sometimes added fiddles or bass instruments when available. See Hartman, "Roots Run Deep," 9–10.

60. Estela Gómez Reyes, interview, June 22, 1979, HMRC, OH 261.

61. Gaye Theresa Johnson, "'Sobre Las Olas': A Mexican Genesis in Borderlands Jazz and the Legacy for Ethnic Studies," *Comparative American Studies* 6, no. 3 (September 2008): 227.

62. Larkin, interview, January 5, 1988. On territory bands, see Johnson, "'Sobre Las Olas,'" 229–32.

63. Cobb, interview, February 11, 1988; Larkin, interview, January 5, 1988.

64. Larkin, interview, January 5, 1988; Cobb, interview, February 11, 1988; Franklin, interview, June 17, 1975.

65. Govenar, *Texas Blues*, 258; Jacquet, interview, June 1, 1990; Cobb, interview, February 11, 1988.

66. Wood, *Down in Houston*, 82; Govenar, *Texas Blues*, 258; Arnett Cobb, "Flower Garden Blues," *Arnett Blows for 1300*, Delmark Records DD-471, 1947.

67. Frank John Hadley, *The Grove Press Guide to the Blues on CD* (New York: Grove Press, 1994), 105; Eddie "Cleanhead" Vinson, *Jammin' the Blues*, Black Lion 760188 (originally released in 1974); Illinois Jacquet, *The Blues! That's Me*, Original Jazz Classics 6142, 2000 (originally released in 1969).

68. Cobb, interview, February 11, 1988.

6. "BLAXICANS" AND BLACK CREOLES

1. Calderon et al., interview, June 22, 2013.

2. Guglielmo, "Fighting for Caucasian Rights," 1216.

3. Peña, *Música Latina*, 76–79.

4. Guglielmo, "Fighting for Caucasian Rights," 1219–20.

5. Neil Foley, "Over the Rainbow: *Hernandez v. Texas, Brown v. Board of Education*, and Black v. Brown," *Chicano Latino Law Review* 25 (2005): 139–52.

6. Adair, interview, April 25, 1977; Pitre, *In Struggle against Jim Crow*, 34.

7. Pitre, *In Struggle against Jim Crow*, 43.

8. Foley, *Quest for Equality*, 18; Behnken, *Fighting Their Own Battles*, 21.

9. Kreneck offers a detailed description of Tijerina's work as LULAC president in *Mexican American Odyssey*. See also Behnken, *Fighting Their Own Battles*, 46.

10. F. Kenneth Jensen, "The Houston Sit-In Movement of 1960–61," in *Black Dixie: Afro-Texan History and Culture in Houston*, ed. Howard Beeth and Cary D. Wintz (College Station: Texas A&M Press, 1992), 217; Lynwood Abram, "Texas from 3 Viewpoints," *Houston Chronicle*, September 23, 2001; Kreneck, *Mexican American Odyssey*, 261–62.

11. Kreneck, *Mexican American Odyssey*, 204–5.

12. Beeth and Wintz, *Black Dixie*, 89; U.S. Bureau of the Census, "Population of the 100 Largest Urban Places: 1960," June 15, 1998.

13. Amos Milburn, *The Best of Amos Milburn: Down the Road Apiece*, compact disc, EMI Records E2 27229, 1993; quote taken from the CD notes.

14. Werner, *A Change Is Gonna Come*, 24. After leaving the magazine and joining Ahmet Ertegun's independent label, Atlantic Records, Wexler played a key role in producing records in the newly minted category. See Jerry Wexler and David Ritz, *Rhythm and Blues: A Life in American Music* (New York: St. Martin's Press, 1994); and "Jerry Wexler, a Behind-the-Scenes Force in Black Music, Is Dead at 91," *New York Times*, August 15, 2008.

15. Wood, *Down in Houston*, 159–60; *Ebony*, "Negro Millionaires in Texas," August 1952.

16. Lauterbach, *Chitlin' Circuit*, 113–30; Wood, *Down in Houston*, 188; Alan Govenar, *The Early Years of Rhythm and Blues: Focus on Houston* (Houston: Rice University Press, 1990), 5.

17. Govenar, *Early Years of Rhythm and Blues*, 5.

18. Lauterbach, *Chitlin' Circuit*, 130.

19. Govenar, *Early Years of Rhythm and Blues*, 5–8.

20. Govenar, *Early Years of Rhythm and Blues*, 9–10.

21. Wood, *Down in Houston*, 189.

22. William Michael Smith, "A Brief History of Joe Sample and the Crusaders," *Houston Press*, Friday, March 8, 2013.

23. Steve Jansen and William Michael Smith, "The New Crusaders," *Houston Press*, March 6, 2013. Musician Kirk Whalum and flutist/pianist Bobbi Humphrey also attended TSU.

24. Jansen and Smith, "New Crusaders."

25. Chris Gray, "Houston's Jazz History," *Houston Press*, September 4, 2008. In an effort to help revive the jazz scene in Houston and at Texas Southern, Sample became an artist in residence and leader of the Joe Sample Jazz Orchestra in 2012; see Jansen and Smith, "New Crusaders."

26. Wood, *Down in Houston*, 150; Andy Bradley and Roger Wood, *House of Hits: The Story of Houston's Gold Star/Sugarhill Recording Studios* (Austin: University of Texas Press, 2010), 18.

27. Bradley and Wood, *House of Hits,* 119.

28. Lightnin' Hopkins, "Zolo Go (Zydeco)," *The Gold Star Sessions, Volume I,* Arhoolie CO-330, 1993; Bradley and Wood, *House of Hits,* 23–26; Govenar, *Lightnin' Hopkins,* 43–51.

29. Tisserand, *Kingdom of Zydeco,* 77–78.

30. Morris Chevalier—*1880 United States Federal Census,* 5th Ward, St. Martin, Louisiana, Enumeration District 37, p. 116D; *1930 United States Federal Census,* Houston, Harris, Texas, Enumeration District 49, p. 25A; *Social Security Death Index* (online database). Raynard Landry—*1920 United States Federal Census,* Police Jury Ward 1, St. Landry, Louisiana, Enumeration District 86, p. 16A; *1930 United States Federal Census* Houston, Harris County, Texas, Enumeration District 142, p. 62B; *Texas Death Index, 1903–2000* (online database), accessed via www.ancestry.com.

31. Tisserand, *Kingdom of Zydeco,* 17–19.

32. Tisserand, *Kingdom of Zydeco,* 17–19.

33. Wood, *Down in Houston,* 139–40.

34. Tisserand, *Kingdom of Zydeco,* 17–19.

35. Wood, *Down in Houston,* 139–40.

36. Bradley and Wood, *House of Hits,* 126.

37. Bradley and Wood, *House of Hits,* 21.

38. Wood, *Down in Houston,* 150.

39. Waterman, "Race Music," 177.

40. Clifton Chenier, *Bayou Blues,* Specialty Records 2139, 1989.

41. Lightnin' Hopkins, "L.A. Blues," *The Complete Aladdin Recordings, Disc 1,* Aladdin/EMI E2–96843, 1991.

42. Tisserand, *Kingdom of Zydeco,* 20.

43. Fontenot quoted in Tisserand, *Kingdom of Zydeco,* 27.

44. Wood, *Down in Houston,* 138.

45. Strawder and Johnson, interview, June 21, 2013.

46. Weldon "Juke Boy" Bonner, *Life Gave Me a Dirty Deal,* compact disc (liner notes), Arhoolie CD375, 1992.

47. Wood, *Down in Houston,* 157.

48. In rural Texas, José María de León Hernández, otherwise known as "Little Joe," played rhythm and blues in the 1950s. Born and raised in Temple in 1940, Hernández joined a local band in 1957 called David Coronado and the Latinaires, and he eventually became the lead singer. At around the same time, another young Tejano named Baldemar Garza Huerta also helped to reinterpret rhythm and blues and rock 'n' roll in the 1950s. Huerta was born in San Benito, a small town near the Mexican border, in 1937. In bars and nightclubs scattered across Texas and Louisiana, Huerta developed a stage persona and a musical repertoire that bridged the English-language music heard on the radio and the ballads played by his Mexican-born father and Mexican American mother. His fans acknowledged this blend of cultures by calling him "El Bebop Kid." In around 1957, he officially

changed his name to Freddy Fender, a moniker inspired by his favorite guitar. His early success came from making Spanish versions of rhythm and blues songs. The 1961 album *Interpreta el Rock* features a cover of Ray Charles's "What I Say" called "Vamos a Bailar," as well as a revamped version of Little Richard's "Rip It Up" titled "Bailando el Rock & Roll." He also reimagined the old blues song "See See Rider" as an up-tempo dance song he named "Si Si Rider." Fender's early career was cut short in 1961, however, after he was arrested in Louisiana at the age of twenty-three. Although officers in Baton Rouge officially detained Fender for marijuana possession, some speculated that the real cause of his five-year prison sentence may have been the fact that he was cavorting in Louisiana with a married Anglo woman. Pamela A. Aguilar and Daniel McCabe, directors, "The Chicano Wave," season 1, episode 3, *Latin Music USA,* DVD (PBS 2011); Peña, *Música Latina,* 152–53.

49. Greg Beets, "La Onda Chicano," *Austin Chronicle,* July 21, 2006.

50. Beets, "La Onda Chicano."

51. Hector Saldaña, "Producer of 'Iconic West Side Sound' Dies," accessed October 11, 2012, www.mysanantonio.com/default/article/Producer-of-iconic-West-Side-sound-dies-3481280.php.

52. Ruben Molina and Ernie Durawa quoted in Margaret Moser, "A Browner Shade of Black," *Austin Chronicle,* December 28, 2007.

53. Moser, "A Browner Shade of Black."

54. Beets, "La Onda Chicano."

55. Moser, "A Browner Shade of Black."

56. Moser, "A Browner Shade of Black"; Beets, "La Onda Chicano."

57. Joe Nick Patoski, "Sex, Drugs and Rock & Roll," *Texas Monthly* 24, no. 5 (May 1996): 116–26; Steve McVicker, "Wasted Days, Wasted Lives (Part I)," *Houston Press,* February 22, 1996.

58. McVicker, "Wasted Days, Wasted Lives (Part I)."

59. Ozuna quoted in Peña, *Música Latina,* 157–58.

60. Quoted in Patoski, "Sex, Drugs and Rock & Roll."

61. Meaux quoted in McVicker, "Wasted Days, Wasted Lives (Part I)." See also Bradley and Wood, *House of Hits,* 136–37.

62. Goree Carter was raised at 1310 Bayou Street, near the hub of Fifth Ward at Lyons Avenue and Jensen Drive. He learned to play guitar by watching musicians in his neighborhood at Drewstel Park. Barely out of his teen years, he performed at Club Matinee and Dreamland while recording around sixty songs for local record labels. He cut a tune called "Rock Awhile" in 1947 for the short-lived Freedom Records, which existed only from 1948 to 1952. Although Carter left the music business in 1954, the song left a lasting influence. *New York Times* music critic Robert Palmer cited "Rock Awhile" as the first rock 'n' roll song. "The clarion guitar intro differs hardly at all from some of the intros Chuck Berry would unleash on his own records after 1955," Palmer wrote. "[T]he guitar solo crackles through an overdriven amplifier; and the boogie-based rhythm charges right along. The subject matter, too,

is appropriate—the record announces that it's time to 'rock awhile,' and then proceeds to show how it's done. To my way of thinking, Carter's 'Rock Awhile' is a much more appropriate candidate for 'first rock and roll record' than the more frequently cited 'Rocket '88.'" Robert Palmer, *Rock & Roll: An Unruly History* (New York: Harmony Books, 1995), 19; John Nova Lomax, "Searching for the First Rock Song," *Houston Press,* August 9, 2001.

63. Treviño, *Church in the Barrio,* 36; U.S. Bureau of the Census, "Population of the 100 Largest Urban Places: 1960," June 15, 1998, accessed May 21, 2013, www.census.gov/population/www/documentation/twps0027/tab19.txt.

64. Michael Bertrand, *Race, Rock, and Elvis* (Urbana: University of Illinois Press, 2000), 164.

65. San Miguel, *Brown, Not White,* 75.

66. San Miguel, *Brown, Not White,* 74.

67. Calderon et al., interview, June 22, 2013.

68. San Miguel, *Brown, Not White,* 57.

69. Aguilar and McCabe, "Chicano Wave."

70. On the Chicano Movement, see San Miguel, *Brown, Not White;* Carlos Muñoz, Jr., *Youth, Identity, Power: The Chicano Movement* (New York: Verso Books, 1989); Armando Navarro, *Mexican American Youth Organization: Avant-garde of the Chicano Movement in Texas* (Austin: University of Texas Press, 1995); F. Arturo Rosales, *Chicano! The History of the Mexican American Civil Rights Movement* (Houston: Arte Publico Press, 1997); and Behnken, *Fighting Their Own Battles.*

71. On events at TSU in 1967, see Jensen, "Houston Sit-In Movement"; and Behnken, *Fighting Their Own Battles.*

72. Behnken, *Fighting Their Own Battles,* 10.

73. Valdez quoted in *Latin Music USA,* "The Chicano Wave."

74. Duncantell quoted in Behnken, *Fighting Their Own Battles,* 187.

75. Carlos Calbillo, "The Chicano Movement in Houston and Texas: A Personal Memory," *Houston History* 9, no. 1: 25–26.

76. Robert Pruter, *Chicago Soul* (Urbana: University of Illinois Press, 1991), xiv, 3.

77. Peter Guralnick, *Sweet Soul Music: Rhythm and Blues and the Southern Dream of Freedom* (Boston: Little, Brown and Company, 1999), 2.

78. William L. Van Deburg, *Black Camelot: African-American Culture Heroes in Their Times, 1960–1980* (Chicago: University of Chicago Press, 1997), 71–74.

79. Arnold R. Hirsch, "Fade to Black: Hurricane Katrina and the Disappearance of Creole New Orleans," *Journal of American History* 94 (December 2007): 756.

80. Joe Sample, *Fancy Dance,* Sonet Records 788, 1969; Illinois Jacquet, *The Soul Explosion,* Prestige Records 7629, 1969.

81. John Márquez, "The Browning of Black Politics: Foundational Blackness and New Latino Subjectivities," *Subjectivity* 4 (2011): 57.

82. Skipper Lee Frazier, *The Man Who Brought a Mountain of Soul to Houston: Autobiography of a Disc Jockey* (Bloomington, IN: Trafford Publishing, 2012), 122–24; *Houston Chronicle,* March 9, 1999.

83. James Brown, "I Don't Want Nobody to Give Me Nothing (Open Up the Door, I'll Get It Myself)," *Sex Machine,* Polydor 9004, 1970.

84. Frazier, *Mountain of Soul,* 53.

85. Calderon et al., interview, June 22, 2013.

86. Calderon et al., interview, June 22, 2013.

87. Frazier, *Mountain of Soul,* 63.

88. Calderon et al., interview, June 22, 2013.

89. On diverse soul scenes, see Juan Flores, "Boogaloo and Latin Soul," in *The Afro-Latin@ Reader: History and Culture in the United States,* ed. Miriam Jiménez Román and Juan Flores (Durham, NC: Duke University Press, 2010), 199–206; Guralnick, *Sweet Soul Music;* R. Molina, *Chicano Soul;* Pruter, *Chicago Soul;* and Werner, *A Change Is Gonna Come.*

90. Rocky Gil and the Bishops, "Soul Party," Tear Drop Records 3199, 1968; Brett Koshkin, "When Tejano Found Its Soul Power," *Bayou City Soul,* September 20, 2010, accessed December 10, 2012, http://bayoucitysoul.wordpress.com/2010/09/20/when-tejano-found-its-soul-power/#more-182.

91. Flores, "Boogaloo and Latin Soul," 200–201; Werner, *A Change Is Gonna Come,* 28.

92. Rocky Gil and the Bishops, "Soul Party."

CONCLUSION

1. *New York Post,* August 8, 2008.

2. *Guardian,* August 8, 2008.

3. Eugene and Adelia Dereon were born during the Civil War. They could not read or write, they rented a home, and they were listed as "mulatto" in the census. The Beyincé family was more affluent. In 1920, Marie Beyincé, Lumis's mother, was a forty-eight-year-old widow who could read and write, and she owned her own home. *1920 Federal Census,* Police Jury Ward 2, Vermilion, Louisiana, p. 9A, Enumeration District 104; *1920 Federal Census,* Police Jury Ward 1, Vermilion, Louisiana, p. 26A, Enumeration District 103.

4. See Daphne A. Brooks, "Suga Mama, Politicized," *Nation,* November 30, 2006, http://www.thenation.com/article/suga-mama-politicized.

5. Real FedUp, "WTF Files: Beyonce L'Oreal Ad—Misunderstood or Self Hate?" *Destiny's Rehab: Spilling the Tea on America's Favorite Celebs,* January 18, 2012, http://destinysrehab.com/2012/01/18/wtf-files-beyonce-loreal-ad-misunderstood-or-self-hate/.

6. http://www.frenchcreoles.com, accessed October 29, 2012.

7. On Selena, see Deborah R. Vargas, "Cruzando Frontejas: Remapping Selena's Tejano Music Crossover," in *Chicana Traditions: Continuity and Change,* ed. Norma Cantú and Olga Nájera-Ramírez (Urbana: University of Illinois Press, 2002), 224–36; D. Vargas, *Dissonant Divas in Chicana Music;* and Deborah Paredez, *Selenidad: Selena, Latinos, and the Performance of Memory* (Durham, NC: Duke

University Press, 2009). Beyoncé quoted in Angie Romero, "EXCLUSIVE: Beyoncé Says She's Jealous She Wasn't Born Latina!" *Latina,* February 26, 2008, accessed November 1, 2012, http://www.latina.com/entertainment/music/qa-beyonce.

8. Tatcho Mindiola, Jr., Yolanda Flores Niemann, and Nestor Rodriguez, *Black-Brown Relations and Stereotypes* (Austin: University of Texas Press, 2002), 4. On post–civil rights black communities in Houston, see Robert D. Bullock, *Invisible Houston: The Black Experience in Boom and Bust* (College Station: Texas A&M University Press, 1987).

9. Roger M. Olien, "Oil and Gas Industry," *Handbook of Texas Online,* Texas State Historical Association, accessed January 9, 2013, http://www.tshaonline.org /handbook/online/articles/doogz; *Houston Chronicle,* February 24, 2008.

10. Cathy Booth Thomas, "Topping Out in Houston Again," *Time,* May 28, 2001, p. 60.

11. Mindiola et al., *Black-Brown Relations,* 11–12.

12. Mindiola et al., *Black-Brown Relations,* 13.

13. "Boy Stabbed in School Speaks to FOX 26 News," MyFoxHouston.com, May 26, 2010, accessed September 27, 2012, http://www.myfoxhouston.com /story/18218853/boy-stabbed-in-...1. On African American and Latino coalition building, see J. Márquez, "Browning of Black Politics," 51; and John Márquez, *Black-Brown Solidarity Racial Politics in the New Gulf South* (Austin: University of Texas Press, 2014).

14. *Houston Chronicle,* July 25, 2011.

15. "Wheatley High School," *Texas Tribune,* accessed October 8, 2012, www.texastribune.org/public-ed/explore/houston-isd/wheatley-high-school.

16. *Houston Chronicle,* October 1, 2009.

17. Lydia Lum, "Renowned Trial Attorney Donates Law Library to Texas Southern University," *Diverse Issues in Higher Education,* April 12, 2012.

18. *Houston Chronicle,* July 25, 2011.

19. On the growth of the Houston rap scene, see Maco L. Faniel, *Hip-Hop in Houston: The Origin and the Legacy* (Charleston, SC: History Press, 2013).

20. John Nova Lomax, "Hip-Hop, Tejas—Latinos Take on Rap Music and Make It Their Own," *Houston Press,* December 4, 2003; Chingo Bling, *They Can't Deport Us All,* Asylum Records, 2007; J. Márquez, "Browning of Black Politics."

21. Lomax, "Hip-Hop, Tejas"; Bling, *They Can't Deport Us All*; J. Márquez, "Browning of Black Politics," 62.

22. Lomax, "Hip-Hop, Tejas"; J. Márquez, "Browning of Black Politics," 63.

23. Beyoncé, "No Angel," *Beyoncé,* music video, directed by @LILINTERNET, 2013.

24. The number of Asian Americans in the city began to climb slowly in 1975 after the fall of Saigon, when U.S. troops helped thousands of Vietnamese refugees relocate to the United States. In Houston, over four hundred Vietnamese families moved into Allen Parkway Village, a working-class apartment community in the historically black section of Fourth Ward. Some of the migrants moved next door to black families. Vietnamese residents eventually made up two-thirds of the

population of Allen Parkway Village, and by the end of the twentieth century, Houston had the second-largest Vietnamese population in the United States. Most of the Asian American population is of Vietnamese descent, followed by East Indian and Chinese. As the percentage of Asians and Latinos continues to increase, the percentage of black and Anglo Houstonians falls. Those groups made up 16.8 percent and 39.7 percent of the population in 2010, respectively. Yet, the "black" population continues to diversify. These changes led Rice University to declare in 2012 that Houston had surpassed New York and Los Angeles as the most diverse city in the nation. See Houston Institute for Culture, "The Asian American Experience: Building New Saigon," accessed December 4, 2012, http://www.houstonculture.org/cultures/viet.html. See also Michael O. Emerson, Jenifer Bratter, Junia Howell, and Wilner Jeanty, *Houston Region Grows More Ethnically Diverse, with Small Declines in Segregation: A Joint Report Analyzing Census Data from 1990, 2000, and 2010* (Houston: Kinder Institute for Urban Research & the Hobby Center for the Study of Texas, Rice University, 2012), 4; Greater Houston Partnership Research Department, "Social, Economic and Demographic Characteristics of Metro Houston with Projections to 2040 and 2050," Houston, January 2014. Statistics on the Nigerian population are taken from the City of Houston's "Fiscal Year 2012 Budget," accessed April 1, 2014, http://www.houstontx.gov/budget/12budadopt/I_EO.pdf. Statistics on Katrina evacuees are taken from Thom Patterson, "Katrina Evacuees Shift Houston's Identity," *CNN* August 12, 2011, accessed January 17, 2013, http://www.cnn.com/2011/US/08/12/katrina.houston/index.html.

25. Strawder and Johnson, interview, June 21, 2013.

BIBLIOGRAPHY

MANUSCRIPT SOURCES

Houston, Texas
  The African American Library at the Gregory School
    Willie Blackmon Collection
    Burns Family Collection
    Roscoe Cavitt Collection
    Minne Marjorie Harvey Collection
    Hazel McCullough Collection
    Elizabeth Montgomery Collection
    Patricia Smith Prather Collection
    C.F. Hortense Smith Collection
  Fred Parks Law Library, South Texas College of Law
    Records of the Citizens Committee of Houston, 1917
  Houston Metropolitan Research Center (HMRC)
    Christia Adair Collection
    Frank and Ventura Alonzo Collection
    Arnett Cobb Collection
    Carmen Cortés Collection
    Ethel Ransom Art and Literacy Club Collection
    Franklin Beauty School Inc. Collection
    Sonny Boy Franklin Collection
    Ed Gerlach Collection
    Melesio Gómez Family Papers
    HMRC Oral History Collection (HMRC, OH)
    Houston Oral History Project
    Illinois Jacquet Oral History
    Independence Heights Collection
    Milton Larkin Collection

Lydia Mendoza Collection
Felix Morales Collection
Helen G. Perry Collection
Naomi Polk Collection
Sammy Price Collection
The Reverend Jack Yates Family and Antioch Baptist Church Collection
Cliff Richardson Oral History
C. F. Richardson Papers
Mariano Rosales Ypina Collection
A. D. Salazar Printing Company Collection
I. H. Smalley Collection
Texas Commission on Interracial Cooperation Collection
Texas Methodist and Methodist Episcopal Collection
Felix Tijerina, Sr. Family Collection
Ralph and Mary Villagomez Oral History
Ramón and Delfina Villagomez Family Collection
Lester Williams Collection
Houston Oral History Project, Houston Public Library
Bryant, Thelma Scott, interview by Patricia Smith Prather, August 3, 2007
Cavitt, O'Neta "Pink," interview by Nicolas Castellanos, May 22, 2010
Grant, Paulette Williams, interview by David Goldstein, June 30, 2008
Johnson, Conrad, interview by David Goldstein, December 19, 2007
Prather, Patricia Smith, interview by Vince Lee, October 5, 2010
Young, Hazel Haynesworth, interview by Elma Barrera, October 5, 2007
Schomburg Center for Research in Black Culture, New York Public Library
Nicolas Guillen Scrapbook
Langston Hughes Collection
Arthur A. Schomburg Papers
The University of Texas at Austin
Benson Latin American Collection
League of United Latin American Citizens (LULAC) Archives
The Center for American History
Labor Movement in Texas Collection
Washington, D.C.
Library of Congress
Manuscript Division
National Association for the Advancement of Colored People Papers
Music Division
William P. Gottlieb/Ira and Leonore S. Gershwin Fund Collection
National Archives and Records Administration
Records of the Judge Advocate General, U.S. War Department, Record Group 153

NEWSPAPERS AND PERIODICALS

Austin Chronicle
Bayou City Soul
The California Voice
Colonel Mayfield's Weekly
Crisis: A Record of the Darker Races
The Crusader
Diverse Issues in Higher Education
Ebony
The Guardian
Houston Chronicle
Houston Forward Times
Houston Defender
Houston Informer
Houston Post
Houston Press
Latina
LULAC News
San Francisco State News
New York Post
New York Times
Texas City Times
Texas Monthly
Texas Tribune
The Nation
The Washington Eagle

GOVERNMENT DOCUMENTS

Charter of the City of Houston and General Ordinances, 1910. Houston: Coyle and Co., 1910.
Houston Chamber of Commerce. *Growth of Houston.* Houston: City of Houston Planning Department, 1965.
U.S. Bureau of the Census. *Eighth Census of the United States* (1860)
U.S. Bureau of the Census. *Ninth Census of the United States* (1870)
U.S. Bureau of the Census. *Tenth Census of the United States* (1880)
U.S. Bureau of the Census. *Eleventh Census of the United States* (1890)
U.S. Bureau of the Census. *Twelfth Census of the United States* (1900)
U.S. Bureau of the Census. *Thirteenth Census of the United States* (1910)
U.S. Bureau of the Census. *Fourteenth Census of the United States* (1920)
U.S. Bureau of the Census. *Fifteenth Census of the United States* (1930)

U.S. Bureau of the Census. *Sixteenth Census of the United States* (1940)
U.S. Bureau of the Census. "Population of the 100 Largest Urban Places: 1960," June 15, 1998.

SECONDARY BOOKS, ARTICLES, AND NOVELS

Adams, Luther. *Way Up North in Louisville: African American Migration in the Urban South, 1930–1970.* Chapel Hill: University of North Carolina Press, 2010.
Alexander, Charles C. *The Ku Klux Klan in the Southwest.* Lexington: University of Kentucky Press, 1965.
Almaguer, Tomás. *Racial Fault Lines: The Historical Origins of White Supremacy.* 1994. Reprint, Berkeley: University of California Press, 2008.
Alvarez, Luis. *The Power of the Zoot: Youth Culture and Resistance during World War II.* Berkeley: University of California Press, 2009.
Ancelet, Barry Jean. "Zydeco/Zarico: Beans, Blues and Beyond." *Black Music Research Journal* 8 no 1 (1988): 33–49.
Anthony, Arthé A. "'Lost Boundaries': Racial Passing and Poverty in Segregated New Orleans," *Louisiana History* 36, no. 3 (1995): 291–312.
Arneson, Eric. *Waterfront Workers of New Orleans: Race, Class, and Politics, 1863–1923.* New York: Oxford University Press, 1991.
Baldwin, Davarian L. *Chicago's New Negroes: Modernity, the Great Migration, and Black Urban Life.* Chapel Hill: University of North Carolina Press, 2007.
Barr, Alwyn. *Black Texans: A History of African Americans in Texas, 1528–1995.* Norman: University of Oklahoma Press, 1996.
Barry, John M. *Rising Tide: The Great Mississippi Flood of 1927 and How It Changed America.* New York: Simon and Schuster, 2008.
Beauboeuf, Bruce Andre. "War and Change: Houston's Economic Ascendancy during World War I." *Houston Review* 14 no. 2 (1992): 89–112.
Bederman, Gail. *Manliness and Civilization: A Cultural History of Race and Gender in the United States, 1880–1917.* Chicago: University of Chicago Press, 1995.
Beeth, Howard, and Cary D. Wintz, eds. *Black Dixie: Afro-Texan History and Culture in Houston.* College Station: Texas A&M University Press, 1992.
Behnken, Brian D. *Fighting Their Own Battles: Mexican Americans, African Americans, and the Struggle for Civil Rights in Texas.* Chapel Hill: University of North Carolina Press, 2011.
Benjamin, Karen. "Progressivism Meets Jim Crow: Segregation, School Reform, and Urban Development in the Interwar South." Ph.D. diss., University of Wisconsin–Madison, 2007.
Bennett, Herman L. *Africans in Colonial Mexico: Absolutism, Christianity, and Afro-Creole Consciousness, 1570–1640.* Bloomington: Indiana University Press, 2003.
Berlin, Ira. *Generations of Captivity: A History of African-American Slaves.* Cambridge, MA: Harvard University Press, 2003.

Bernstein, Patricia. *The First Waco Horror: The Lynching of Jesse Washington and the Rise of the NAACP*. College Station: Texas A&M University Press, 2006.

Bertrand, Michael. *Race, Rock, and Elvis*. Champaign-Urbana: University of Illinois Press, 2000.

Blee, Kathleen M. *Women of the Klan*. Berkeley: University of California Press, 1991.

Bradley, Andy, and Roger Wood. *House of Hits: The Story of Houston's Gold Star/Sugarhill Recording Studios*. Austin: University of Texas Press, 2010.

Brasseaux, Carl A., Keith P. Fontenot, and Claude F. Oubre. *Creoles of Color in the Bayou Country*. Jackson: University Press of Mississippi, 1994.

Brilliant, Mark. *The Color of America Has Changed: How Racial Diversity Shaped Civil Rights Reform in California, 1941–1978*. New York: Oxford University Press, 2010.

Brothers, Thomas. *Louis Armstrong's New Orleans*. New York: W. W. Norton and Company, 2006.

Brown, Kenneth L. "Material Culture and Community Structure: The Slave and Tenant Community at Levi Jordan's Plantation, 1848–1892." In *Working toward Freedom: Slave Society and Domestic Economy in the American South*, edited by Larry E. Hudson, Jr., 95–118. Rochester, NY: University of Rochester Press, 1995.

Broyles-Gonzalez, Yolanda. *Lydia Mendoza's Life in Music / La Historia de Lydia Mendoza*. New York: Oxford University Press, 2006.

Bullock Robert D. *Invisible Houston: The Black Experience in Boom and Bust*. College Station: Texas A&M University Press, 1987.

Cable, George. *The Creoles of Louisiana*. New Orleans: Pelican Publishing, 2000.

Calbillo, Carlos. "The Chicano Movement in Houston and Texas: A Personal Memory." *Houston History* 9, no. 1.

Caldwell, Kia Lilly. "'Look at Her Hair': The Body Politics of Black Womanhood in Brazil." *Transforming Anthropology* 11, no. 2 (2004).

Camp, Stephanie M. H. *Closer to Freedom: Enslaved Women and Everyday Resistance in the Plantation South*. Chapel Hill: University of North Carolina Press, 2004.

Campbell, Randolph B. *An Empire for Slavery: The Peculiar Institution in Texas, 1821–1865*. Baton Rouge: Louisiana State University Press, 1989.

Carawan, Guy, and Candie Carawan, eds. *Sing for Freedom: The Story of the Civil Rights Movement through Its Songs*. Montgomery, AL: NewSouth Books, 2008.

Chalmers, David M. *Hooded Americanism: The History of the Ku Klux Klan*. Chicago: Quadrangle Paperbacks, 1965.

Christian, Garna L. *Black Soldiers in Jim Crow Texas, 1899–1917*. College Station: Texas A&M University Press, 1995.

Clark, Emily. *The Strange History of the American Quadroon: Free Women of Color in the Revolutionary Atlantic World*. Chapel Hill: University of North Carolina Press, 2013.

Clayton, Lawrence, and Joe W. Specht, eds. *The Roots of Texas Music*. College Station: Texas A&M University Press, 2003.

Dailey, Jane. *Before Jim Crow: The Politics of Race in Postemancipation Virginia.* Chapel Hill: University of North Carolina Press, 2000.

———. "Deference and Violence in the Postbellum Urban South: Manners and Massacres in Danville, Virginia." *Journal of Southern History* 63, no. 3 (August 1997): 553–91.

Daniel, Pete R. *Breaking the Land: The Transformation of Cotton, Tobacco, and Rice Cultures since 1880.* Urbana: University of Illinois Press, 1986.

De León, Arnoldo. *Ethnicity in the Sunbelt: A History of Mexican Americans in Houston.* Houston: Mexican American Studies Program, University of Houston, 1989.

Dinerstein, Joel. *Swinging the Machine: Modernity, Technology, and African American Culture between the World Wars.* Amherst: University of Massachusetts Press, 2003.

Dinnerstein, Leonard. *The Leo Frank Case.* Athens: University of Georgia Press, 1999.

Doyle, Bertram Wilbur. *The Etiquette of Race Relations in the South: A Study in Social Control.* New York: Shocken Books, 1971.

Du Bois, W. E. B. *The Souls of Black Folk.* New York: Bantam Books, 1989.

Eidsheim, Nina Sun. "Marian Anderson and 'Sonic Blackness' in American Opera." *American Quarterly* 63, no. 3 (September 2011): 641–71.

Emerson, Michael O., Jenifer Bratter, Junia Howell, and Wilner Jeanty. *Houston Region Grows More Ethnically Diverse, with Small Declines in Segregation: A Joint Report Analyzing Census Data from 1990, 2000, and 2010.* Houston: Kinder Institute for Urban Research & the Hobby Center for the Study of Texas, Rice University, 2012.

Enstad, Nan. *Ladies of Labor, Girls of Adventure: Working Women, Popular Culture, and Labor Politics at the Turn of the Twentieth Century.* New York: Columbia University Press, 1999.

Erenberg, Lewis A. *Swingin' the Dream: Big Band Jazz and the Rebirth of American Culture.* Chicago: University of Chicago Press, 1998.

Faniel, Maco L. *Hip-Hop in Houston: The Origin and the Legacy.* Charleston, SC: History Press, 2013.

Flores, Juan. "Boogaloo and Latin Soul." In *The Afro-Latin@ Reader: History and Culture in the United States,* edited by Miriam Jiménez Román and Juan Flores, 199–206. Durham, NC: Duke University Press, 2010.

———. *From Bomba to Hip-Hop: Puerto Rican Culture and Latino Identity.* New York: Columbia University Press, 2000.

Flores, Ruben. *Backroads Pragmatists: Mexico's Melting Pot and Civil Rights in the United States.* Philadelphia: University of Pennsylvania Press, 2014.

Foley, Neil. "Over the Rainbow: *Hernandez v. Texas, Brown v. Board of Education,* and *Black v. Brown.*" *Chicano Latino Law Review* 25 (2005): 139–52.

———. *Quest for Equality: The Failed Promise of Black-Brown Solidarity.* Cambridge, MA: Harvard University Press, 2010.

———. *The White Scourge: Mexicans, Blacks, and Poor Whites in Texas Cotton Culture.* Berkeley: University of California Press, 1999.

Foner, Eric. *Reconstruction: America's Unfinished Revolution.* New York: Harper & Row, 1988.

Frederickson, George M. *The Black Image in the White Mind: The Debate on Afro-American Character and Destiny, 1817–1914.* New York: Harper & Row, 1971.

Freehling, William W. *The Road to Disunion.* Vol. 2, *Secessionists Triumphant, 1854–1861.* New York: Oxford University Press, 2007.

García, Juan R. *Mexicans in the Midwest, 1900–1932.* Tucson: University of Arizona Press, 2004.

Gehman, Mary. *The Free People of Color of New Orleans: An Introduction.* Donaldsonville, LA: Margaret Media, 2009.

Gilbert, David. "Clef Club Inc.: James Reese Europe and New York's Musical Marketplace." *Journal of Popular Music Studies* 24, no. 4 (December 2012): 430–56.

Gill, Tiffany M. *Beauty Shop Politics: African American Women's Activism in the Beauty Industry.* Urbana: University of Illinois Press, 2010.

Goodwyn, Lawrence C. "Populist Dreams and Negro Rights: East Texas as a Case Study." *American Historical Review* 76, no. 5 (December 1971): 1435–56.

Govenar, Alan. *The Early Years of Rhythm and Blues: Focus on Houston.* Houston: Rice University Press, 1990.

———. *Lightnin' Hopkins: His Life and Blues.* Chicago: Chicago Review Press, 2010.

———. *Texas Blues: The Rise of a Contemporary Sound.* College Station: Texas A&M University Press, 2008.

Greenberg, Cheryl. *Troubling the Waters: Black-Jewish Relations in the American Century.* Princeton, NJ: Princeton University Press, 2006.

Gregory, James N. *American Exodus: The Dust Bowl Migration and Okie Culture in California.* New York: Oxford University Press, 1991.

———. *The Southern Diaspora: How the Great Migrations of Black and White Southerners Transformed America.* Chapel Hill: University of North Carolina Press, 2007.

Gross, Ariela J. "'The Caucasian Cloak': Mexican Americans and the Politics of Whiteness in the Twentieth-Century Southwest." *Georgetown Law Journal* 95, no. 337, 338–392.

———. *What Blood Won't Tell: A History of Race on Trial in America.* Cambridge, MA: Harvard University Press, 2008.

Grossman, James. *Land of Hope: Chicago, Black Southerners, and the Great Migration.* Chicago: University of Chicago Press, 1991.

Guérin-Gonzales, Camille. *Mexican Workers and American Dreams: Immigration, Repatriation, and California Farm Labor, 1900–1939.* New Brunswick, NJ: Rutgers University Press, 1994.

Guglielmo, Thomas A. "Fighting for Caucasian Rights: Mexicans, Mexican Americans, and the Transnational Struggle for Civil Rights in World War II Texas." *Journal of American History* 92, no. 4 (March 2006): 1212–37.

———. *White on Arrival: Italians, Race, Color, and Power in Chicago, 1890–1945.* New York: Oxford University Press, 2003.

Guralnick, Peter. *Sweet Soul Music: Rhythm and Blues and the Southern Dream of Freedom*. Boston: Little, Brown and Company, 1999.

Guridy, Frank Andre. *Forging Diaspora: Afro-Cubans and African Americans in a World of Empire and Jim Crow*. Chapel Hill: University of North Carolina Press, 2010.

Hadley, Frank John. *The Grove Press Guide to the Blues on CD*. New York: Grove Press, 1994.

Hahn, Steven. *A Nation under Our Feet: Black Political Struggles in the Rural South from Slavery to the Great Migration*. Cambridge, MA: Harvard University Press, 2003.

Hale, Grace Elizabeth. *Making Whiteness: The Culture of Segregation in the South, 1890–1940*. New York: Vintage Books, 1998.

Hall, Gwendolyn Midlo. *Africans in Colonial Louisiana: The Development of Afro-Creole Culture in the Eighteenth Century*. Baton Rouge: Louisiana State University Press, 1995.

Haney-López, Ian. *White by Law: The Legal Construction of Race*. New York: New York University Press, 1996.

Harris, Trudier. "'The Yellow Rose of Texas': A Different Cultural View." *Callaloo* 20, no. 1 (Winter 1997).

Hartman, Gary. "The Roots Run Deep: An Overview of Texas Music History." In *The Roots of Texas Music*, ed. Lawrence Clayton and Joe W. Specht (College Station: Texas A&M University Press, 2003), 3–36.

Haynes, Robert V. *A Night of Violence: The Houston Riot of 1917*. Baton Rouge: Louisiana State University Press, 1977.

Hewitt, Nancy. *Southern Discomfort: Women's Activism in Tampa, Florida, 1880s–1920s*. Urbana: University of Illinois Press, 2001.

Hill, Robert, ed. *The Crusader*. Vol 1. New York: Garland Press, 1987.

Hirsch, Arnold R. *Creole New Orleans: Race and Americanization*. Baton Rouge: Louisiana State University Press, 1992.

———. "Fade to Black: Hurricane Katrina and the Disappearance of Creole New Orleans." *Journal of American History* 94 (December 2007): 752–61.

Hobbs, Allyson. *A Chosen Exile: A History of Passing in American Life*. Cambridge, MA: Harvard University Press, 2014.

Hodes, Martha. "The Sexualization of Reconstruction Politics: White Women and Black Men in the South after the Civil War." *Journal of the History of Sexuality* 3, no. 3 (1993): 402–17.

———. *White Women, Black Men: Illicit Sex in the Nineteenth-Century South*. New Haven, CT: Yale University Press, 1997.

Hopkins, Natalie. *Go-Go Live: The Musical Life and Death of a Chocolate City*. Durham, NC: Duke University Press, 2012.

Horne, Gerald. *Black and Brown: Black and Brown: African Americans and the Mexican Revolution, 1910–1920*. New York and London: New York University Press, 2005.

Hunter, Tera. *To 'Joy My Freedom: Black Women's Lives and Labors after the Civil War*. Cambridge, MA: Harvard University Press, 1997.

Hurston, Zora Neale. *Jonah's Gourd Vine.* 1934. Reprint, New York: Harper Perennial Modern Classics, 2008.

———. *Their Eyes Were Watching God.* 1937. Reprint, New York: Harper Perennial Classics, 1998.

Innis-Jiménez, Michael. *Steel Barrio: The Great Mexican Migration to South Chicago, 1915–1940.* New York: NYU Press, 2013.

Jacobson, Matthew Frye. *Whiteness of a Different Color: European Immigrants and the Alchemy of Race.* Cambridge, MA: Harvard University Press, 1998.

Jensen, F. Kenneth. "The Houston Sit-In Movement of 1960–61." In *Black Dixie: Afro-Texan History and Culture in Houston,* edited by Howard Beeth and Cary D. Wintz. College Station: Texas A&M Press, 1992.

Johnson, Benjamin. *Revolution in Texas: How a Forgotten Rebellion and Its Bloody Suppression Turned Mexicans into Americans.* New Haven, CT: Yale University Press, 2003.

Johnson, Gaye Theresa. "'Sobre Las Olas': A Mexican Genesis in Borderlands Jazz and the Legacy for Ethnic Studies." *Comparative American Studies* 6, no. 3 (September 2008): 225–40.

———. *Spaces of Conflict, Sounds of Solidarity: Music, Race, and Spatial Entitlement in Los Angeles.* Berkeley: University of California Press, 2013.

Jones, William P. *The Tribe of Black Ulysses: African American Lumber Workers in the Jim Crow South.* Urbana: University of Illinois Press: 2005.

Jung, Moon-Ho. *Coolies and Cane: Race, Labor, and Sugar in the Age of Emancipation.* Baltimore: Johns Hopkins University Press, 2006.

Kelley, Blair L. M. *Right to Ride: Streetcar Boycotts and African American Citizenship in the Era of Plessy v. Ferguson.* Chapel Hill: University of North Carolina Press, 2010.

Kelley, Robin D. G. "Polycultural Me." *Colorlines,* September–October 1999.

———. *Race Rebels.* New York: Macmillan, 1994.

Kienzle, Rich. *Southwest Shuffle: Pioneers of Honky Tonk, Western Swing, and Country Jazz.* New York: Routledge, 2003.

Klein, Sybil, ed. *Creole: The History and Legacy of Louisiana's Free People of Color.* Baton Rouge: Louisiana State University Press 2000.

Kreneck, Thomas H. *Mexican American Odyssey: Felix Tijerina, Entrepreneur and Civic Leader, 1905–1965.* College Station: Texas A&M University Press, 2001.

Kurashige, Scott. *The Shifting Grounds of Race: Black and Japanese Americans in the Making of Multiethnic Los Angeles.* Princeton, NJ: Princeton University Press, 2010.

Labrie, Denise. *Houston Frenchtown.* Vol. 4 of *The Creole Chronicles.* Natchitoches, LA: Louisiana Creole Heritage Center, Northwestern State University, 2002.

Lauterbach, Preston. *The Chitlin' Circuit and the Road to Rock 'n' Roll.* New York: W. W. Norton & Company, 2011.

Lefebvre, Henri. *The Production of Space.* Boston: Blackwell Publishers, 1991.

Lentz-Smith, Adriane. *Freedom Struggles: African Americans and World War I.* Cambridge, MA: Harvard University Press, 2011.

Levine, Lawrence. *Black Culture and Black Consciousness: Afro-American Folk Thought from Slavery to Freedom.* Oxford: Oxford University Press, 1977.

Lewis, David Levering. *When Harlem Was in Vogue.* New York: Penguin Books, 1997.

Lewis, Earl. *In Their Own Interests: Race, Class, and Power in Twentieth-Century Norfolk, Virginia.* Berkeley: University of California Press, 1991.

Ling, Huping. *Chinese Chicago: Race, Transnational Migration, and Community since 1870.* Stanford, CA: Stanford University Press, 2012.

Lipsitz, George. *Dangerous Crossroads: Popular Music, Postmodernism and the Poetics of Place.* London and New York: Verso, 1994.

———. *Footsteps in the Dark: The Hidden Histories of Popular Music.* Minneapolis: University of Minnesota Press, 2007.

———. "The Racialization of Space and the Spatialization of Race: Theorizing the Hidden Architecture of Landscape." *Landscape Journal* 27, no. 1 (January 1, 2007): 10–27.

Litwack, Leon. *Been in the Storm So Long: The Aftermath of Slavery.* New York: Vintage Books, 1979.

Long, Alecia. *The Great Southern Babylon: Sex, Race, and Respectability in New Orleans, 1865–1920.* Baton Rouge: Louisiana State University Press, 2004.

Lowe, Lisa. *Immigrant Acts: On Asian American Cultural Politics.* Durham, NC: Duke University Press, 1996.

Lum, Lydia. "Renowned Trial Attorney Donates Law Library to Texas Southern University." *Diverse Issues in Higher Education,* April 12, 2012.

Macías, Anthony. *Mexican American Mojo: Popular Music, Dance, and Urban Culture in Los Angeles, 1935–1968.* Durham, NC: Duke University Press, 2008.

Mackey, Thomas C. "Thelma Denton and Associates: Houston's Red Light Reservation and a Question of Jim Crow." *Houston Review* 14, no. 3 (1992): 139–52.

MacLean, Nancy. "The Leo Frank Case Reconsidered: Gender and Sexual Politics in the Making of Reactionary Populism." *Journal of American History* 78 (December 1991): 917–48.

Malone, Cheryl Knott. "Autonomy and Accommodation: Houston's Colored Carnegie Library, 1907–1922." *Libraries and Cultures* 34, no. 2 (Spring 1999): 95–112.

Mancini, Matthew. *One Dies, Get Another: Convict Leasing in the American South.* Columbia: University of South Carolina Press, 1996.

Márquez, Benjamin. *LULAC: The Evolution of a Mexican American Political Organization.* Austin: University of Texas Press, 1993.

Márquez, John. *Black-Brown Solidarity; Racial Politics in the New Gulf South.* Austin: University of Texas Press, 2014.

———. "The Browning of Black Politics: Foundational Blackness and New Latino Subjectivities." *Subjectivity* 4 (2011) 47–67.

McComb, David G. *Houston, a History.* Austin: University of Texas, 1981.

McDonald, Jason. *Racial Dynamics in Early Twentieth-Century Austin, Texas.* Lanham, MD: Lexington Books, 2012.

McGuire, Danielle L. *At the Dark End of the Street: Black Women, Rape, and Resistance; A New History of the Civil Rights Movement from Rosa Parks to the Rise of Black Power.* New York: Vintage Books, 2011.

———. "'It Was Like All of Us Had Been Raped': Sexual Violence, Community Mobilization, and the African American Freedom Struggle." *Journal of American History* 91, no. 3 (December 2004): 906–23.

Medley, Keith Weldon. *We as Freemen: Plessy v. Ferguson.* Gretna, LA: Pelican Publishing Company, 2003.

Miller, Karl Hagstrom. *Segregating Sound: Inventing Folk and Pop Music in the Age of Jim Crow.* Durham, NC: Duke University Press, 2010.

Mills, Gary B. *The Forgotten People: Cane River's Creoles of Color.* Baton Rouge: Louisiana State University Press, 1977.

Mindiola, Tatcho, Jr., Yolanda Flores Niemann, and Nestor Rodriguez. *Black-Brown Relations and Stereotypes.* Austin: University of Texas Press, 2002.

Mitchell, Michele. *Righteous Propagation: African Americans and the Politics of Racial Destiny after Reconstruction.* Chapel Hill: University of North Carolina Press, 2004.

Molina, Natalia. *How Race Is Made in America: Immigration, Citizenship, and the Historical Power of Racial Scripts.* Berkeley: University of California Press, 2014.

Molina, Ruben. *Chicano Soul: Recordings & History of an American Culture.* La Puente, CA: Mictlan Publishing, 2007.

Montejano, David. *Anglos and Mexicans in the Making of Texas, 1836–1986.* Austin: University of Texas Press, 1987.

Montes, Rebecca. "Working for American Rights: Black, White, and Mexican American Dockworkers during the Great Depression." In *Sunbelt Revolution: The Historical Progression of the Civil Rights Struggle in the Gulf South,* edited by Samuel C. Hyde, Jr., 102–32. Gainesville: University Press of Florida, 2003.

Muhammad, Khalil Gibran. *The Condemnation of Blackness: Race, Crime, and the Making of Modern Urban America.* Cambridge: Harvard University Press, 2011.

Mumford, Kevin J. *Interzones: Black/White Sex Districts in Chicago and New York in the Early Twentieth Century.* New York: Columbia University Press, 1997.

Muñoz, Carlos, Jr. *Youth, Identity, Power: The Chicano Movement.* New York: Verso Books, 1989.

Navarro, Armando. *Mexican American Youth Organization: Avant-Garde of the Chicano Movement in Texas.* Austin: University of Texas Press, 1995.

Omi, Michael, and Howard Winant, eds. *Racial Formations in the United States.* New York: Routledge, 1994.

Oshinsky, David M. *Worse than Slavery: Parchman Farm and the Ordeal of Jim Crow Justice.* New York: Free Press, 1996.

Palmer, Robert. *Rock & Roll: An Unruly History.* New York: Harmony Books, 1995.

Pando, Patricia. "In the Nickel: Houston's Fifth Ward." *Houston History* 8, no. 3 (2011): 33–37.

———. "Two Worlds a Mile Apart: A Brief History of the Fourth Ward." *Houston History* 8, no. 2 (2011): 38.

Paredes, Américo. *With His Pistol in His Hand.* Austin: University of Texas Press, 1958.

Paredez, Deborah. *Selenidad: Selena, Latinos, and the Performance of Memory.* Durham, NC: Duke University Press, 2009.

Peiss, Kathy. *Hope in a Jar: The Making of America's Beauty Culture.* New York: Owl Books, 1999.

Peña, Manuel. *The Mexican American Orquesta: Music, Culture, and the Dialectic of Conflict.* Austin: University of Texas Press, 1999.

———. *Música Tejana: The Cultural Economy of Artistic Transformation.* College Station: Texas A&M University Press, 1999.

———. *The Texas-Mexican Conjunto: History of a Working-Class Music.* Austin: University of Texas Press, 1985.

Pérez, Emma. *The Decolonial Imaginary: Writing Chicanas into History.* Bloomington: Indiana University Press, 1999.

Phillips, Michael. *White Metropolis: Race, Ethnicity, and Religion in Dallas, 1841–2001.* Austin: University of Texas Press, 2006.

Pitre, Merline. *In Struggle against Jim Crow: Lula B. White and the NAACP, 1900–1957.* College Station: Texas A&M University Press, 1999.

Prather, Patricia, and Bob Lee. *The Texas Trailblazers.* Ser. 2, no. 23. Houston: Texas Trailblazer Preservation Association, 1997.

Pratt, Mary Louise. "Arts of the Contact Zone." In *Ways of Reading,* edited by David Bartholomae and Anthony Petrosky, 582–96. New York: Bedford/St. Martin's, 1999.

Pruitt, Bernadette. "For the Advancement of the Race: The Great Migrations to Houston, Texas, 1914–1941." *Journal of Urban History* 31, no. 4 (May 2005): 435–78.

———. *The Other Great Migration: The Movement of Rural African Americans to Houston, 1900–1941.* College Station: Texas A&M University Press, 2013.

Pruter, Robert. *Chicago Soul.* Urbana: University of Illinois Press, 1991.

Putnam, Lara. *Radical Moves: Caribbean Migrants and the Politics of Race in the Jazz Age.* Chapel Hill: The University of North Carolina Press, 2013.

Pyatt, Sherman E., and Alan Johns. *A Dictionary and Catalog of African American Folklife of the South.* Westport, CT: Greenwood Press, 1999.

Rabinovitz, Laura. *For the Love of Pleasure: Women, Movies, and Culture in Turn-of-the Century Chicago.* New Brunswick, NJ: Rutgers University Press, 1998.

Rabinowitz, Howard. "From Exclusion to Segregation: Southern Race Relations, 1865–1890." *Journal of American History* 63 (September 1976): 325–50.

Raboteau, Albert J. *A Fire in the Bones: Reflections on African-American Religious History.* Boston: Beacon Press, 1995.

———. *Slave Religion: The "Invisible Institution" in the Antebellum South.* 1978. Reprint, New York: Oxford University Press, 2004.

Radano, Ronald. *Lying Up a Nation: Race and Black Music.* Chicago: University of Chicago Press, 2003.

Reed, T. V. *The Art of Protest: Culture and Activism from the Civil Rights Movement to the Streets of Seattle.* Minneapolis: University of Minnesota Press, 2005.

Roberts, John W. *From Trickster to Badman: The Black Folk Hero in Slavery and Freedom*. Philadelphia: University of Pennsylvania Press, 1989.

Roediger, David. *The Wages of Whiteness: Race and the Making of the American Working Class*. 1991. Reprint, New York: Verso Books, 2007.

———. *Working toward Whiteness: How America's Immigrants Became White; The Strange Journey from Ellis Island to the Suburbs*. New York: Basic Books, 2006.

Rosales, F. Arturo. *Chicano! The History of the Mexican American Civil Rights Movement*. Houston: Arte Publico Press, 1997.

Sánchez, George J. *Becoming Mexican American: Ethnicity, Culture, and Identity in Chicano Los Angeles, 1900–1945*. New York: Oxford University Press, 1993.

San Miguel, Guadalupe. *Brown, Not White: School Integration and the Chicano Movement in Houston*. College Station: Texas A&M University Press, 2001.

Sarig, Roni. *Third Coast: Outkast, Timbaland, and How Hip-Hop Became a Southern Thing*. Cambridge, MA: Capo Press, 2007.

Saxon, Lyle, Edward Dreyer, and Robert Tallant. *Gumbo Ya-Ya: A Collection of Louisiana Folk Tales*. Gretna, LA: Pelican Publishing, 1987.

Schuler, Edgar A. "The Houston Race Riot, 1917." *Journal of Negro History* 29, no. 3 (July 1944): 331–33.

Self, Robert O. *American Babylon: Race and the Struggle for Postwar Oakland*. Princeton, NJ: Princeton University Press, 2003.

Shank, Barry. "The Political Agency of Musical Beauty." *American Quarterly* 63, no. 3, (September 2011): 833–55.

Shelton, Beth Anne, Nestor Rodriguez, Joe R. Feagin, Robert D. Bullard, and Robert D. Thomas. *Houston: Growth and Decline in a Sunbelt Boomtown*. Philadelphia: Temple University Press, 1989.

Smith, C. Calvin. "The Houston Riot of 1917, Revisited." *Houston Review* 13, no. 2 (1991): 85–102.

Smith, Susan J. "Beyond Geography's Visible Worlds: A Cultural Politics of Music." *Progress in Human Geography* 21, no. 4 (1997): 502–29.

Soja, Edward W. *Thirdspace: Journeys to Los Angeles and Other Real-and-Imagined Places*. Malden, MA: Blackwell Publishers, 1996.

SoRelle, James M. "'The Darker Side of Heaven': The Black Community in Houston, Texas, 1917–1945." Ph.D. diss., Kent State University, 1980.

———. "The 'Waco Horror': The Lynching of Jesse Washington." *Southwestern Historical Quarterly* 86 (April 1983).

Southern, Eileen. *The Music of Black Americans: A History*. 1971. Reprint, New York: W. W. Norton, 1997.

Spaw, Patsy McDonald. *The Texas Senate: Civil War to the Eve of Reform, 1861–1889*. College Station: Texas A&M University Press, 1999.

Steptoe, Tyina. "'If You Ever Go to Houston, You Better Walk Right': The Houston Riot of 1917." M.A. thesis, University of Wisconsin-Madison, 2002.

Stowe, David W. *Swing Changes: Big-Band Jazz in New Deal America*. Cambridge, MA: Harvard University Press, 1996.

Strachwitz, Chris, with James Nicolopulos. *Lydia Mendoza: A Family Autobiography.* Houston: Arte Público, 1993.

Sugrue, Thomas J. *The Origins of the Urban Crisis: Race and Inequality in Postwar Detroit.* 1996. Reprint, Princeton, NJ: Princeton University Press, 2005.

Summers, Martin. *The Black Middle Class and the Transformation of Masculinity, 1900–1930.* Chapel Hill: University of North Carolina Press, 2004.

Taylor, Quintard. *The Forging of a Black Community: Seattle's Central District from 1870 through the Civil Rights Era.* Seattle: University of Washington Press, 2001.

———, ed. *From Timbuktu to Katrina: Sources in African-American History.* Vol. 1. Boston: Thomson Wadsworth, 2007.

———. *In Search of the Racial Frontier: African Americans in the West, 1528–1990.* New York: W. W. Norton & Company, 1999.

Terrell, Wendell Phillips. "A Short History of the Negro Longshoreman." Thesis, Houston College for Negroes, Department of History.

Tisserand, Michael. *Kingdom of Zydeco.* New York: Arcade Publishing, 1998.

Townsend, Charles R. *San Antonio Rose: The Life and Music of Bob Wills.* Champaign-Urbana: University of Illinois Press, 1976.

Treviño, Roberto R. *The Church in the Barrio: Mexican American Ethno-Catholicism in Houston.* Chapel Hill: University of North Carolina Press, 2006.

Trotter, Joe. *Black Milwaukee: The Making of an Industrial Proletariat, 1915–45.* Champaign: University of Illinois Press, 1985.

Turner, Elizabeth Hayes, W. Fitzhugh Brundage, and Gregg Cantrell, eds. *Lone Star Pasts: Memory and History in Texas.* College Station: Texas A&M University Press, 2006.

Tyson, Timothy B. *Radio Free Dixie: Robert F. Williams and the Roots of Black Power.* Chapel Hill: University of North Carolina Press, 1999.

Van Deburg, William L. *Black Camelot: African-American Culture Heroes in Their Times, 1960–1980.* Chicago: University of Chicago Press, 1997.

———, ed. *Modern Black Nationalism: From Marcus Garvey to Louis Farrakhan.* New York: New York University Press, 1997.

Vargas, Deborah R. "Cruzando Frontejas: Remapping Selena's Tejano Music Crossover." In *Chicana Traditions: Continuity and Change,* edited by Norma Cantú and Olga Nájera-Ramírez, 224–36. Urbana: University of Illinois Press, 2002.

———. *Dissonant Divas in Chicana Music: The Limits of La Onda.* Minneapolis: University of Minnesota Press, 2012.

von der Mehden, Fred R., ed. *The Ethnic Groups of Houston.* Houston: Rice University Press, 1984.

Wald, Gayle. "Soul Vibrations: Black Music and Black Freedom in Sound and Space." *American Quarterly* 63, no. 3 (September 2011).

Waterman, Christopher. "Race Music: Bo Chatmon, 'Corrine Corrina,' and the Excluded Middle." In *Music and the Racial Imagination,* edited by Ronald Radano and Philip V. Bohlman, 167–205. Chicago: University of Chicago Press, 2000.

Watkins-Owens, Irma. *Blood Relations: Caribbean Immigrants and the Harlem Community, 1900–1930.* Bloomington: Indiana University Press, 1996.

Werner, Craig. *A Change Is Gonna Come: Music, Race & the Soul of America.* Ann Arbor: University of Michigan Press, 2006.

West, Cornel. "Black Strivings in a Twilight Civilization." In *The Cornel West Reader.* New York: Basic Civitas Books, 1999.

Wexler, Jerry, and David Ritz. *Rhythm and Blues: A Life in American Music.* New York: St. Martin's Press, 1994.

Whisnant, David E. *All That Is Native and Fine: The Politics of Culture in an American Region.* 1983. Reprint, Chapel Hill: University of North Carolina Press, 2009.

White, Deborah Gray. *Ar'n't I a Woman: Female Slaves in the Plantation South.* New York: W. W. Norton and Company, 1985.

Wilkerson, Isabel. *The Warmth of Other Suns: The Epic Story of America's Great Migration.* New York: Random House, 2010.

Williamson, Joel. "The Separation of the Races." In *When Did Southern Segregation Begin?* edited by John David Smith. Boston: Bedford/St. Martin's, 2002.

Wilson Moore, Shirley Ann. *To Place Our Deeds: The African American Community in Richmond, California, 1910–1963.* Berkeley: University of California Press, 2001.

Wolcott, Victoria W. *Race, Riots, and Roller Coasters: The Struggle over Segregated Recreation in America.* Philadelphia: University of Pennsylvania Press, 2012.

———. *Remaking Respectability: African American Women in Interwar Detroit.* Chapel Hill: University of North Carolina Press, 2001.

Wolfe, Charles K. *The Life and Legend of Leadbelly.* New York: Harper Collins Publishers, 1992.

Wood, Roger. *Down in Houston: Bayou City Blues.* Austin: University of Texas Press, 2003.

Woods, Clyde. *Development Arrested: The Blues and Plantation Power in the Mississippi Delta.* London and New York: Verso, 1998.

Woodward, C. Vann. *The Strange Career of Jim Crow.* 1955. Reprint, New York: Oxford University Press, 2002.

Young, Elliot. "Red Men, Pocahontas, and George Washington: Harmonizing Race Relations in Laredo at the Turn of the Century." *Western Historical Quarterly* 29, no. 1 (Spring 1998): 48–85.

PERSONAL ACCOUNTS AND CONTEMPORARY SOURCES

Born in Slavery: Slave Narratives from the Federal Writers' Project, 1936–1938. http://memory.loc.gov/ammem/snhtml/snhome.html.

Calderon, Albert, Rey Romero, Bobby Severson, and Artie Villaseñor. Interview by the author, June 22, 2013, Houston Digital recording.

Edwards, Paul Kenneth. *The Southern Urban Negro as a Consumer.* College Park, MD: McGrath Publishing, 1932.

Frazier, Skipper Lee. *The Man Who Brought a Mountain of Soul to Houston: Autobiography of a Disc Jockey.* Bloomington, IN: Trafford Publishing, 2012.
Greene, Lorenzo. *Selling Black History for Carter G. Woodson: A Diary, 1930–1933.* Columbia, MO: University of Missouri Press, 1996.
Johnson, Barbara (Berry). Interview by the author, January 2, 2006, Houston. Tape recording.
Johnson, James Weldon. *Along This Way: The Autobiography of James Weldon Johnson.* New York: Viking Press, 1933.
Locke, Alain. "Enter the New Negro." *Survey Graphic,* March 1925.
Lomax, Alan. *The Land Where the Blues Began.* New York: New Press, 1993.
Olmsted. Frederick Law. *A Journey through Texas; or, A Saddle-Trip on the Southwestern Frontier.* 1857. Reprint, Austin: University of Texas Press, 1978.
Olsen, Otto H., ed. *The Thin Disguise: Turning Point in Negro History; Plessy v. Ferguson: A Documentary Presentation, 1864–1896.* New York: Humanities Press, 1967.
Polk's Houston City Directory. Houston: R. L. Polk and Company, 1917.
Prejean Calegon, Inez. Interview by the author, January 27, 2006, Houston. Tape recording.
Slave Narratives: A Folk History of Slavery in the United States from Interviews with Former Slaves: Volume XVI, Texas Narratives, Part 3. Accessed online.
Strawder, Mary (Berry). Interview by the author, January 3, 2006, Houston. Tape recording.
Strawder, Mary (Berry), and Barbara (Berry) Johnson. Interview by the author, June 21, 2013, Humble, TX. Digital audio recording.
Writers' Program of the Work Projects Administration. *Houston: A History and Guide.* Houston: Anson Jones Press, 1942.

SOUND RECORDINGS, ARTWORK, FILM

Aguilar, Pam, and Daniel McCabe, directors. "The Chicano Wave." Season 1, episode 3 of *Latin Music USA.* DVD. PBS, 2011.
Alexander, Texas. *Texas Alexander Vol. 1 (1927).* Document Records, 1995.
Beyoncé. "No Angel." *Beyoncé.* Music Video. Directed by @LILINTERNET. 2013.
Biggers, John. *Shotgun, Third Ward #1.* 1966. Tempera and oil on canvas. 30 × 48 in. Smithsonian Art Museum, Washington, DC.
Bling, Chingo. *They Can't Deport Us All.* Asylum Records, 2007.
Brown, James. "I Don't Want Nobody to Give Me Nothing (Open Up the Door, I'll Get It Myself)." *Sex Machine.* Polydor, 1970.
Chenier, Clifton. *Bayou Blues.* Specialty Records, 1989. CD.
Cobb, Arnett. *Arnett Blows for 1300.* Delmark Records, 1947.
Gil, Rocky, and the Bishops. "Soul Party." *Soul Party/After Party.* Tear Drop Records, 1968.
Hopkins, Lightnin'. *The Complete Aladdin Recordings, Disc 1.* Aladdin/EMI, 1991. CD.

————. *The Gold Star Sessions, Volume I.* Arhoolie, 1993. CD.

Jacquet, Illinois. *The Blues! That's Me.* Original Jazz Classics, 2000. CD.

————. *The Soul Explosion.* Prestige Records, 1969.

Kazan, Elia, director. *Pinky.* DVD. Beverly Hills, CA: Twentieth Century-Fox, 2005.

Leadbelly. *Complete Recorded Works Volume 1: 1939–1947.* Document Records, 1995. CD.

Lomax, Alan, and John A. Lomax. *The Classic Louisiana Recordings: Cajun and Creole Music II, 1934–1937.* Rounder Records, 1999. CD.

Micheaux, Oscar, director. *Veiled Aristocrats.* DVD. Phoenix: Grapevine Video, 1932.

Milburn, Amos. *The Best of Amos Milburn: Down the Road Apiece.* EMI Records, 1993. CD.

Murphey, Dudley, director. *St. Louis Blues.* DVD. Kino Video, 2001.

Murphy, Michael Martin. *Cowboy Songs.* Warner Bros., 1989. CD.

Pollard, Sam. *Zora Neale Hurston: Jump at the Sun.* DVD. San Francisco: California Newsreel, 2008.

Sample, Joe. *Fancy Dance.* Sonet Records, 1969.

Stahl, John M. *Imitation of Life.* Universal City, CA: Universal Studios, 1936.

Vinson, Eddie. "Cleanhead." *Jammin' the Blues.* Black Lion, 1974.

Wallace, Sippie. *Sippie Wallace Vol. 1 (1923–1925).* Document, 1995. CD.

Washington, Lightnin'. "My Pretty Little Yellow Gal." *Black Texicans: Balladeers & Songsters.* Rounder, 1999. CD.

Waters, Ethel. *Cabin in the Sky.* DVD. Directed by Vincent Minnelli. Los Angeles: Warner Home Video, 2006.

Whale, James, director. *Showboat (1936).* DVD. ClassicLine Brazil, 2003.

Wills, Bob. *Bob Wills and His Texas Playboys 1932–1947.* Frémeaux, 2002. CD.

INDEX

The letter f following a page number denotes a figure.

African Americans *(continued)*
183–90, 205–8, 210–13, 216–222, 226–
230, 232–33; and forced labor, 22; generational differences in, 41; immigrating
to Mexico, 99, 133; and Independence
Heights, 30–31, 43, 105, 227, 248n31;
and Italians, 101–5, 107–8; and Jews,
104–7; literacy rate of, 58; as longshoremen, 36, 143–46; and lynchings, 40, 43,
99, 115–16, 130; in *Mississippi Love*
(Stanwix), 74–75; moving to suburbs,
228, 232; and musical cultures, 3, 11, 13,
48–53, 75–76, 155–56, 159–73, 175,
177–78, 181–85, 190–97, 200–210,
213–22, 228–30; and notions of black
inferiority, 142, 196; and passing for
white, 121–22, 131–142, 151; in post-Civil
War era, 27–30; as Protestants, 110, 112;
purchasing power of, 55; and race pride,
31, 67, 125–26, 137–140, 157, 212, 214;
and racial violence, 22–23, 31–34, 83;
resentment of segregation, 97–98;
retirement of, 232; and rhythm and
blues, 4, 15–16, 181, 184–86, 190–99,
245n41; as sharecroppers, 26–27, 36;
and skin color, 121–26, 130–140; and
stereotypes, 73, 124, 169; and transnational blackness, 137–140, 151; in World
War I era, 31–37. *See also* freed people;
New Negroes; slaves/slavery; *entries
beginning with* black
African American tricksters, 46–47, 251n89
African Blood Brotherhood, 126
African descent, people of, 2, 5, 16, 46, 63,
240n8; and antebellum legal status of
ancestors, 68–70, 72; and Beyoncé, 224;
as Catholics, 116–18; and civil rights
movements, 212, 215; and Creoles of
color, 68–70, 72–73, 76, 123–24, 132,
140–42, 215; and ethnic Mexicans,
81–82, 99–100, 126, 128–29, 178; and
group solidarity, 122, 126, 136–39, 151;
and Guillen, Nicolas, 138; and interracial sexual relationships, 68–70, 72–73,
123–24; and musical cultures, 156,
163–64, 172, 177–78, 183, 202, 207; and
passing for white, 122, 131–33, 136,
138–142, 151; and skin color, 123–26,

128–29, 132–33, 136, 138–142; and sub-
Saharan Africa ancestors, 68; and
transnational blackness, 137–140.
See also African Americans
African diaspora, 3, 137–39, 147, 201; Kongo
ritual in, 246n12
African Methodist Episcopal church, 138
Afro hair styles, 215, 224
Afro–Puerto Ricans, 138
agricultural labor, 26–27, 34–36, 79; and
African Americans, 145; and ethnic
Mexicans, 79, 87–88, 145; and lynch-
ings, 115; and la-la music, 76–77, 199
Alabama, 26, 28, 30, 105, 193, 247n19
Aladdin Records, 192, 197
alcoholic drinks, 179, 191–92, 208
Alexander, Alger "Texas," 48–49, 125
Alexander, Dudley, 198
Alexander, John Marshall, Jr.. *See* Ace,
Johnny
Alfred's Place, 199–200
Alisi, Joe, 105
Alisi family, 103, 105
Allen, Augustus and John, 8, 24
Allen Parkway Village, 274n24
Allen's Landing, 8
"All Night Long" (song), 202
Allred, James, 130
Almaguer, Tomás, 241n13
Alonzo, Frank, 16, 87–88, 176–77, 183
Alonzo, Ventura, 16, 88, 176–77, 183
Alonzo y Su Orquesta, 176–77
"Amadie Two Step" (song), 76
American Bandstand, 207
American G.I. Forum, 187–88
Ancient Order of Pilgrims, 38
Anderson, Marian, 134
Anglos, 4–5, 12, 14–15, 240n8; and African
American equality, 94, 97–98, 100,
105–6, 258n21; in antebellum era, 22, 24,
26; architecture of, 80–81; and civil
rights movements, 189–90; and Creoles
of color, 74, 202; and ethnic Mexicans,
63–64, 80, 82–87, 95–98, 104, 106, 108,
126–27, 129, 143–150, 176–77, 183–84,
189–90, 211, 265nn76–77; and immigration laws, 101; and Italians, 101, 103–5,
108; and Jews, 101, 105–8; and linguistic

119; and passing issue, 121, 132, 134; and
religious differences, 112, 117, 260n56;
and Selena, 226
Enstad, Nan, 7
entrepreneurs, urban, 23, 167, 185, 189,
191–93, 199
Epstein, Abe "Abie," 205
equality, racial: and African Americans, 94,
97–98, 100, 105–6, 114–15, 119, 258n21,
260n63; and Catholics, 114–16; and
ethnic Mexicans, 97–98, 104, 143, 186,
188; "social equality," 114–16, 260n63
Ertegun, Ahmet, 269n14
Ethiopia, 138–39; and war refugees, 139
Ethiopian Café, 137, 165
Ethiopian World Federation, 138
Europe, James Reese, 165
European ancestry, 5, 53, 63, 73, 151; and
Beyoncé, 224; and Creoles of color, 123,
162; and ethnic Mexicans, 81, 126; and
musical cultures, 76, 162, 172–74; and
skin color, 123, 125, 162. See also French
ancestors; Spanish descent, people of
European immigrants, 6–7, 100–105, 108,
116, 118, 134. See also Italian immi-
grants/Americans; Jewish immigrants/
Americans
evil spirits, 26

Falcon, Joe, 65
Fancy Dance (album), 215
FBI (Federal Bureau of Investigation), 150
Federal Writers' Project, 123
Felder, Wilton, 195
Fender, Freddy, 185, 207, 270n48
Féria (hair-coloring product), 223
fiddlers, 76–77, 174, 268n59. See also vio-
lins/violinists
Fifteenth Amendment, 27, 70
Fifth Ward, 1, 3–4, 8, 9 map, 80 map, 231–
32; and African Americans, 29, 51, 56,
60–61, 66–67, 73–75, 78, 104–5, 108,
141–42, 160–64, 227; as "the Bloody
Nickel," 204; and Catholics, 112–13,
117–18, 160; construction of public
schools in, 157; and Creoles of color, 60,
63, 65–68, 73–75, 77–78, 90, 120, 132–
33, 141–42, 160–64, 254n13; and ethnic

Mexicans, 61, 108, 113, 146, 227; and
highway construction, 204; and Italians, 103–4, 108; and musical cultures,
160–64, 190–93, 195, 197–201, 203–4,
216, 222, 271n62; and passing for white,
132–33, 136–37, 141–42; railroad lines
crossing, 66, 254n9; violence in, 204;
and Wallace, Sippie, 51. See also Frenchtown; Wheatley High School
Fifth Ward Boys, 11
First Ward, 8, 9 map
Fisk University, 55
floods, 35–36, 62–65, 67–68, 101; Mississippi Flood (1927), 2, 60, 64–65, 68,
74, 78
Flores, Juan, 221
Flores, Ruben, 81
"Flower Garden Blues" (song), 181–82
"Flying Home" (song), 181
Foley, Neil, 82, 127, 188, 241n11
folk culture, black: and "Cimbee's Ramblings," 46–48, 109; and Sugar Land,
21–22; and trickster figures, 46–47, 109,
251n89
folklore: and Creoles of color, 65, 72;
and Lomax family, 65, 123, 169–170,
267n35; and McCormick, Mack, 198,
201; and musical cultures, 169–170, 174,
198, 201, 267n35; and Yellow Rose,
122–23
folk music: and Creoles of color, 65, 198–
99, 203; and ethnic Mexicans, 205; and
Lomax, Alan, 65; and McCormick,
Mack, 198–99, 203; with migration
theme, 65
folk traditions, Mexican, 85
Fontenot, Canray, 77, 203
food, ethnic, 228, 232; and Creoles of color,
224; and ethnic Mexicans, 87, 112,
147–49, 177–78, 265n84; and New
Negroes, 23
football, 158, 160–62, 164, 180–81; championship game in, 164
Fort Bend County (Tex.), 22, 24, 25 map,
32, 228, 232
Fort Worth (Tex.), 58, 172, 174
Four Jacquet Dancing Brothers, 112
Fourth of July festivities, 30

ethnic Mexicans, 82, 189–90, 216, 218, 227; and musical cultures, 163, 172, 183, 210, 218, 222. *See also* multiethnic/ multiracial public

interracial marriages, 70–72; and ethnic Mexicans, 83, 143; legalized in Louisiana, 70–71; and musical cultures, 201; and passing issue, 143

interracial sexual relationships, 30; and anti-Catholicism, 114–16; and Fender, Freddy, 270n48; and motion-picture industry, 105; and musical cultures, 201; as racial history, 68–70, 72, 123; and racial violence, 42, 115–16; and "relations of affection," 70; and sexual exploitation of slave women, 44, 68–70, 72, 124, 136

Irish Americans, 195–96

Irreemplazable (EP), 226

"Irreplaceable" (song), 226

Italian immigrants/Americans, 94, 101–5, 107–10, 148, 259n28; as Catholics, 110, 113, 116–18; and passing issue, 121, 133–35, 141; white racial identity of, 101–4, 148, 259n28

Italy, 138–39

Jack Yates High School. *See* Yates High School

Jacobson, Matthew Frye, 101, 148

Jacquet, Gilbert, 65–66, 75, 118, 155, 159, 166, 169, 180

Jacquet, Illinois, 16; as Catholic, 112, 116; and French patois, 75, 197; as high school musician, 156–164, 159f, 195; as professional musician, 166, 169, 180–82, 215; and soul music, 215

Jacquet, Jewel, 266n3

Jacquet, Linton, 266n3

Jacquet, Marquette, 66, 75, 118

Jacquet family, 65–66, 75, 112, 118, 155, 182, 266n3. *See also* names *of Jacquet family members*

Jaffe, Louis Isaac, 250n73

James, Etta, 224

James Green Grocery and Meat Market, 55

Jamming the Blues (album), 182

Jay Z, 224

jazz, 13, 15, 155–183, 185, 215–16, 231; blues-oriented jazz, 191; jazz bands, 160, 176, 195; jazz dance, 173; "jazz suits," 107; as lowbrow music, 53; and Modern Jazz Sextet, 195; and orquesta, 15, 156, 175–78, 183; and religious differences, 111; and rhythm and blues, 191, 195, 269n25; and territory bands, 179–182; and Texas tenors, 155–56, 181–82, 200–201

Jazz Age, 35, 43, 50–53, 94, 191

Jefferson, Blind Lemon, 174, 178

Jefferson Davis Hospital, 43

Jemison, Abbie, 162

Jemison, James, 162

Jensen Drive, 66–67, 80 map, 204, 254n13, 271n62

"Jesse B. Semple" character, 45

Jette, Mary, 105

Jette, Sterle, 105

Jewish immigrants/Americans, 94, 101, 104–9, 259n25; and anti-Semitism, 105–7; boycotts of, 106–7; and consumer economy, 106–8; legally marked as white, 106–8, 148; and musical cultures, 191; and passing issue, 133, 135, 139

"Jezebel" myth, 124

Jim Crow society, 5–7, 9–10, 12–15, 17, 28–31, 232; and anti-Catholicism, 93, 105–6, 114–19, 127, 147, 261n67; and civil rights movements, 187–88, 212–15; and Creoles of color, 63, 70–72, 89–90, 94, 97, 121, 132–33, 162–63, 225; demise of, 186, 227; double Jim Crow system, 16, 97; and ethnic Mexicans, 63, 82–85, 89–90, 93–100, 103–6, 110, 149, 177, 186–88; and Hughes, Langston, 133–34; and Italians, 94, 101–5; and Jews, 94, 104–5; and linguistic differences, 94–104; and musical cultures, 156, 162–64, 172–75, 177, 182, 192, 196, 207; and New Negroes, 14, 23, 39–40, 44–46, 49, 56, 59, 66, 253n120; and passing issue, 121–22, 131–35, 140, 151; and skin color, 121–22, 126–27, 131–35, 140. *See also* segregation; white supremacy

John (human trickster), 46–47

John, Little Willie, 207

racial blackness, 2, 13–14; and African Americans, 46, 68, 102, 109, 138–39, 209, 214–15; in antebellum era, 26; and Beyoncé, 224–25; and Catholics, 118; and civil rights movement, 209, 214; and Creoles of color, 63–64, 68, 71–73, 76, 78, 140, 185, 214–15, 221; and ethnic Mexicans, 82, 130–31; and musical cultures, 76, 182–83, 214–15; and passing for white, 138–39, 151; transnational blackness, 137–140

racial epithets. *See* slurs

"Racial Equality Bill" (1941), 188

racial hierarchies, 5, 8–9, 12–15; and African Americans, 26, 30, 34, 46, 59, 69, 94, 97–100, 103, 106–7, 126; and anti-Catholicism, 94, 114, 116–19; and Creoles of color, 63, 69, 72; and ethnic Mexicans, 63, 81, 83, 94–100, 108, 127, 134; and Houston Riot (1917), 34; and Italians, 94, 101–4, 108; and Jews, 106–8; and linguistic differences, 94–104; multiethnic/multiracial hierarchies, 104–9; and musical cultures, 156, 164, 196; and passing for white, 121–22, 126; in World War I era, 34

racial histories, 68–72, 74, 129, 136–37

racial hybridity, 71, 82, 121, 138–140; and Beyoncé, 224

racial identities, 2–5, 245n40; and Catholics, 117; and Creoles of color, 70–74, 121, 142; and ethnic Mexicans, 129, 143, 148, 176, 211; and Greeks, 148; and Italians, 148, 259n28; and Jews, 106–8, 148; and musical cultures, 176, 202; and passing issue, 121–22, 129, 136, 142

racial mixing, 2, 4–5, 240n7

racial order. *See* racial hierarchies

racism, 213; and anti-Catholicism, 114; cultural racism, 12, 95; immigrating to Mexico to avoid, 99, 133

Radano, Ronald, 13

Radical Republicans, 27, 247n19

radio, 155–56, 166–67, 174–75, 177–78, 183, 200, 216–17, 219, 270n48; and deejays, 202, 205, 207, 216, 219–220; KCOH radio station, 216, 219–220; KPAC radio station, 207; KUKA radio

station, 205; KYOK radio station, 216; radio barn dances, 174; WBAP radio station, 174; WSM radio station, 174

ragtime, 52, 165

railroads, 62; and Creoles of color, 66, 67f, 68, 73–74, 155, 254n9; and creosote, 80; and ethnic Mexicans, 79–80, 83, 86; Missouri Pacific Railroad, 66, 254n9; and racial violence, 83; Santa Fe Railroad, 52; and segregation, 29, 71, 133–34; and smoking cars, 71; Southern Pacific Railroad, 66, 67f, 68, 73–74, 79, 86, 112, 142, 149, 155, 177, 180, 254n9

Ramos, Alfonso, 205; Alfonso Ramos Orquesta, 205

ranchera music, 88, 175–76, 268n59

Los Rancheros band, 176–78

ranches, 83, 88

rape, 44, 68, 115–16. *See also* violence, racial

rap music/rappers, 11, 224, 228–29

raza blanca, 81

raza indigena, 81

raza mezclada, 81

Real Building and Loan Association, 38

Reconstruction, 6, 28–29, 34, 41, 66, 102, 112

recording industry, 76, 89, 111, 171–72, 181–82; and crank record players, 174; and double-sided 45 rpm records, 205; and gold records, 207; and "race records," 191; recording studios, 16, 179, 185, 195–97, 201, 207–9, 216, 229; record labels, 174–75, 178, 191–93, 194f, 195–97, 201–2, 204, 206–7, 216–17, 220, 269n14, 271n62; as technological advance, 174–75; Top 40 charts, 207–9; and zydeco, 199, 201

"Red Heifer," 123

red-light district. *See* Reservation

religious differences, 2–4, 12, 14–15; in antebellum era, 26, 246n12; and anti-Catholicism, 93, 105–6, 114–19; and atheism, 95; and conversions, 110; and high art, 53; and Jim Crow society, 93–95, 97, 105–6, 109–19, 127; in post-Civil War era, 27; and YWCA, 127. *See also names of religious groups, e.g.,* Catholics

Republicans, 27, 35, 70–71, 190

Reservation, 50, 53, 131–32

restaurants, 30, 57–58, 148–150, 162, 177–79, 189–90

Rhumboogie nightclub (Chicago), 179–180

rhythm and blues, 4, 15–16, 181, 184–86, 190–210, 194f, 222, 245n41, 269n25; and "brown-eyed soul," 205; and Creoles of color, 185, 191, 195–205; and ethnic Mexicans, 191, 204–10, 217, 270n48; hybrid forms of, 185, 191, 209; and jazz, 191, 195, 269n25; and la-la music, 185, 197–99, 202; and Selena, 226; and soul music, 13, 15–16, 185–86, 205, 213–15, 217–19, 245n41; and urban life, 191; and Wexler, Jerry, 191, 269n14; and zydeco, 13, 15–16, 185, 198–205

Rice, C. W., 145

Rice Funeral Home, 187

Rice Hotel, 36–37

Rice Institute, 97

rice markets, 65, 207

Rice University, 274n24

Richard, Little, 270n48

Richardson, C. F. (Clifton Frederick), 37–43, 39f, 47–49; and armed self-reliance, 43; as churchgoer, 38, 40; death of, 38, 188; as editor, 38, 40–43, 47–49, 52, 99, 107, 116, 162, 164–65; and ethnic Mexicans, 65, 99–100; and Jews, 107; and Ku Klux Klan, 42–43, 57; motto of ("Getting 'Em Told"), 40; as musician, 38, 52, 65, 164–65; and passing issue, 135–38, 140; as president of NAACP branch, 188; and relief efforts for flood victims, 65; sued for libel, 40, 47

Richardson, Cliff, Jr., 57

Richardson, Ruby Leola, 37

Richardson family, 42, 63, 107. *See also names of Richardson family members*

ring shouts, 26, 246n12

Rio Grande, 12, 63–64, 81, 86, 88–89, 95, 99, 143, 151

Rio Grande Valley, 14, 63, 82–85, 87, 90, 129, 229

"Rip It Up" (song), 270n48

Roberts, John W., 251n89

Robey, Don, 167–68, 192–93, 195–96, 201, 216

"Rock Awhile" (song), 209, 271n62

"Rocket '88'" (song), 271n62

The Rocking Vs, 208

rock 'n' roll, 184, 207, 209–10, 218, 270n48; first rock 'n' roll song, 209, 271n62

Roediger, David R., 7, 259n28

Romero, Rey, 211, 217

Roosevelt, Franklin D., 78

Rosenfield, Julius, 106

rubboards, 200, 202. *See also* washboards

Rudley, John, 228

rural-to-urban migration, 3, 5; and "Cimbee's Ramblings," 45–48; and musical cultures, 155, 157–59, 165, 191, 199, 203; and New Negroes, 45–49; and passing for white, 132; and police brutality, 31–34; in post-Civil War era, 26–29, 249n15; in World War I era, 31–37; and Yates family, 28

Rusk Elementary School, 85–86, 95, 97

Russian roulette, 193

Sabine River, 2–3, 60, 65, 70, 142, 201, 203, 207

Sahm, Doug, 208–9

Sakowitz department store, 106–7

Salas, Steve, 211

Salazar, A.D., 126, 149

Saldana, Zoe, 224

saloons, 12, 24; and musical cultures, 50, 53; segregation of, 30

Sam Houston High School, 96, 135

Sam Houston Park, 128f

Sam Houston State University, 172

Sample, Joe (Joseph Leslie), 195, 215, 269n25; Joe Sample Jazz Orchestra, 269n25

San Antonio (Tex.), 6, 25 map, 58, 79–80, 89, 114, 175, 188, 205–8, 217, 245n1; Eastside, 205–6; West San Antonio, 205–6; and West Side Sound, 205–6, 217

Sandoval, Catalina Gómez, 96, 134–35

Sandoval, Paul, 135

Sandyfork (Tex.), 60, 148

San Felipe district, 31–34, 37, 53–56, 54f, 103; and Beyoncé, 229; and boycotts of streetcars, 98; and Italians, 109; and musical cultures, 167. *See also* Freedman's Town

trumpets/trumpeters, 51–53, 155, 160, 166,
175–76, 181, 195, 206, 217–18
T.S.U. Toronadoes, 184–85, 216–220
Turnbo-Malone, Annie M., 59
Turpin, Ben, 105
Tyson, Timothy B., 114–15

Union National Bank of Houston, 44
United Brothers of Friendship, 38
United Mexican American Students, 211
Universal Ethiopian Students Association,
139
Universal Negro Improvement Association,
43, 138
University of Houston, 162, 212
University of Mississippi, 212
University of Texas law school, 189
urbanization, 59, 64, 102, 106; and musical
cultures, 51, 160, 174, 176, 191; sonic
markers of urban life, 102, 160, 266n9;
urban spaces, 8, 10–12, 28, 72, 132, 138,
140, 156, 160; and urban sprawl, 228,
253n123

vagrancy, 131–32
Valdez, Tony, 212
"Valse de Opelousas" (song), 76
"Vamos a Bailar" (song), 270n48
Van Deburg, William, 214
vaudeville shows, 89
Veiled Aristocrats (1932 film), 136, 263n35
vernacular traditions: in antebellum era, 21,
23; and "Cimbee's Ramblings," 45–48;
from country, 45–49, 76–77, 165; and
Creoles of color, 76–77; and New
Negroes, 23, 45–49
veterans, 172, 186–88, 190–91, 216
vibraphones, 180–81
vice districts, 50, 53, 131–32
Victor (record company), 174
Vietnamese, 274n24
Vietnam War, 221, 274n24
Villagomez, Mary, 86–87, 93, 110, 117
Villagomez, Ralph, 86–87, 93, 110, 117
Villagomez family, 86–87, 93, 98, 103. See
also names of Villagomez family
members
Villanueva brothers, 208

Villaseñor, Artie, 184–85, 218; as "the
Blaxican," 185
Villaseñor, Lawrence, 175
Villaseñor, Mary Helen, 175
Villistas, 86
Vinegar Hill, 50, 53
Vinson, Eddie "Cleanhead," 166, 180, 182
violence, racial, 14; and abusive men, 175–
76; and African Americans, 39–43, 49,
56, 83, 98, 115–16, 144, 163, 212, 227; and
armed self-reliance, 35, 42–43; and civil
rights movements, 212, 215; and Creoles
of color, 73, 163; and desegregation, 227;
and ethnic Mexicans, 83–85, 175–76,
227; and Houston Riot (1917), 22, 33–34,
43–44, 98; and interracial contact, 106,
163; and Ku Klux Klan, 42–43, 56, 106,
115; and lynchings, 40, 43, 83–84,
115–16; and New Negroes, 39–43, 49,
56; and Plan de San Diego, 83; and
police brutality, 22, 31–34, 38–39, 56, 73,
98; in post-Civil War era, 22–23; in
World War I era, 31–35, 38–40
violins/violinists, 155, 160, 175. See also
fiddlers
Virginia, 26, 28, 46, 157; colonial Virginia,
68, 123, 136
vocalists, 158, 165–66, 175–76, 181–82, 206,
213–14, 216, 270n48. See also names of
vocalists
"La voluntina" (song), 112
voting rights, 27, 29; and African Americans, 29, 34, 40–41, 99–102, 107,
247n27; and Creoles of color, 70; and
disfranchisement, 29, 34, 85, 95, 101–4,
130, 186; and ethnic Mexicans, 85, 95,
99–100, 130, 186; exclusion of black
Texans from voting in primaries, 29,
247n27; and freed people, 70; and
Italians, 101–4; and Jews, 107; and New
Negroes, 40–41, 99–102, 107; and poll
tax, 29; and voter registration efforts, 213
Voting Rights Act (1965), 214

Wallace, Matt, 51
Wallace, Sippie, 16, 51–53, 111, 125; and
brown skin, 125; as "The Texas Nightingale," 53